Puritanism and Revolution

Christopher Hill was educated at St Peter's School, York, and at Balliol College, Oxford, where he received a 'first' in modern history in 1934. That year he was also made a fellow of All Souls College, Oxford. In 1936 he was lecturer in modern history at University College, Cardiff, and two years later tutor in modern history at Balliol. During his war service he had a variety of posts: Field Security Police, Oxfordshire and Buckinghamshire Light Infantry, Intelligence Corps and the Foreign Office. He returned to Oxford in 1945 and from 1958 until 1965 was university lecturer in sixteenth- and seventeenth-century history. He was Ford Lecturer in English History in 1962. From 1965 to 1978 he was Master of Balliol College. After leaving Balliol he became a Professor at the Open University for a time but has now retired. In 1965 he was made D.Litt., Oxon. Dr Hill, a Fellow of the Royal Historical Society and of the British Academy, was a member of the editorial board of *Past and Present* (1952–68), and since 1961 of the Yale University Press edition of the Complete Prose of John Milton. He was made Hon.D.Litt., Hull, in 1966; of Sheffield in 1967; East Anglia in 1968; Glasgow in 1976; Exeter and Wales, 1979; Hon.LLD. Bristol in 1976; D. Univ., York in 1978 and of the Open University in 1982; and Hon. Dr Sorbonne Nouvelle in 1979. He is at present honorary visiting professor at the University of Warwick.

His publications include *The English Revolution* (1940), *Lenin and the Russian Revolution* (1947), *Economic Problems of the Church* (1956), *The Century of Revolution* (1961), *Society and Puritanism in Pre-Revolutionary England* (1964), *Intellectual Origins of the English Revolution* (1965), *Reformation to Industrial Revolution* (1967), *God's Englishman: Oliver Cromwell and the English Revolution* (1970), *Antichrist in 17th Century England* (1971), *The World Turned Upside Down* (1972), *Change and Continuity in 17th Century England* (1974), *Milton and the English Revolution* (1978), which won the Royal Society of Literature Award, *Some Intellectual Consequences of the English Revolution* (1980), *The World of the Muggletonians* (1983), *The Experience of Defeat: Milton and Some Contemporaries* (1984), *Writing and Revolution in 17th Century England* (1985), *Religion and Politics in 17th Century England* (1986), *People and Ideas in 17th Century England* (1986), *A Turbulent, Seditious and Factious People – John Bunyan and his Church* (1988), which won the W. H. Smith Literary Award, *A Nation of Change and Novelty: Radical Politics, Religion and Literature in 17th Century England* (1990) and *The English Bible and the 17th Century Revolution* (1993). He also contributed to *Rebels and their Causes*, a collection of essays to celebrate the seventy-fifth birthday of A. L. Morton. Dr Hill has travelled in Europe generally, in Japan and India and in the USA. He is married, with two children.

CHRISTOPHER HILL

PURITANISM
AND REVOLUTION

Studies in Interpretation of the
English Revolution of the 17th Century

Secker & Warburg
London

First published in Great Britain in 1958
by Martin Secker & Warburg Limited,
an imprint of Reed Consumer Books Limited,
Michelin House, 81 Fulham Road, London SW3 6RB
and Auckland, Melbourne, Singapore and Toronto

A CIP catalogue record for this book
is available from the British Library
ISBN 0 436 20320 0

Typeset by Deltatype Limited, Ellesmere Port, Cheshire
Printed and bound in Great Britain
by Clays Ltd, St Ives plc

For my former pupils,
who taught me most

Contents

Preface

These essays were originally written, independently, on various occasions between 1940 and 1958. Such unity as they have derives from their concern with the interpretation of what used to be called 'The Puritan Revolution'. The title of the book is intended to emphasize a double disability from which I believe English historians suffer in their approach to this revolution. First, few of us have any experience of revolutions. The British tradition since the seventeenth century has been almost entirely gradualist: revolutions are things we learn about from books. Secondly, most of us think that we do know all about Puritanism. But too often we are thinking – whether with conscious hostility or unconscious sympathy – not of Puritanism at all but of later nonconformity. They differ as much as vinegar does from wine. How many nineteenth-century nonconformists, for instance, would have agreed with Milton that a man may be a heretic in the truth? So we have to make a deliberate intellectual effort to open our minds to revolutionaries, and to clear them of erroneous prepossessions about Puritans. When we are dealing with men who were simultaneously Puritans and revolutionaries the task is doubly exacting. 'By God I have leapt over a wall, by God I have run through a troop, and by God I will go through this death, and He will make it easy to me.' The last words of Major-General Harrison are outside the experience of most of us in this country, though they might seem less strange to members of resistance movements during the late war.

The essays here collected have all, I believe, a bearing on the interpretation of the seventeenth-century revolution, of the ideas which helped to produce it and resulted from it, and of the relation between these ideas and economic and political events. Each essay tackles the problem from a different angle, though I believe they are united by a coherent approach. Their diversity may help to emphasize my conviction that the revolution was a complex event, understanding of which is hindered rather than helped by dwelling exclusively on one aspect of it, whether religious or constitutional or economic or biographical. Men make movements and movements make men.

Most of the essays were substantially rewritten and expanded for this volume. Where I quote from seventeenth-century editions I have retained the original spelling and capitalization, but I have occasionally modernized punctuation and use of italics.

Postscript

It comes as rather a shock to reread nearly forty years later what one wrote in the brash exuberance of early middle age. I think I agree with most of what I published in 1958, but I have gone on thinking and writing about Puritanism and Revolution ever since. The chapter headed 'Recent Interpretations of the Civil War' should now more properly read 'Interpretations which were current thirty-six years ago'. An article on 'Parliament and People in 17th Century England', republished in my *People and Ideas in 17th Century England* (1986), did something to update it thirteen years ago, but that is now dated too. Rather than attempt to rewrite these essays, I have given references on p. xi to later writings of mine bearing on the same subject.

But the last thing I would claim for any of these pieces is that they are definitive: they represent starting points from which later ideas developed. One conviction which I have not abandoned is that to look only at debates in Parliament or only at 'the county community' of the gentry is not the way to understand the seventeenth-century revolution. There were quite a lot of other people about who had to do the fighting and pay the taxes.

In quotations from seventeenth-century sources spelling, capitalization and punctuation have been modernized except in titles of books.

November 1994

Some of the questions discussed in this book are further considered in the following of my works:

Chapter One: Recent Interpretations of the Civil War
  The Century of Revolution, 1603–1714 (1961), Chapter 8.
  Intellectual Origins of the English Revolution (1965), Chapters II–V and Appendix.
  God's Englishman: Oliver Cromwell and the English Revolution (1970), Chapters 8–10.
  The World Turned Upside Down: Radical Ideas During the English Revolution (1972), Chapter 8.
  The Experience of Defeat: Milton and Some Contemporaries (1984), Chapter Six, 3, and Chapter Ten, 3.
  Writing and Revolution in 17th Century England (1985), Chapter 6.
  Religion and Politics in 17th Century England (1986), Parts II and III, *passim*, Chapter 15.
  People and Ideas in 17th Century England (1986), Chapters 1–3, 5.
  A Turbulent, Seditious and Factious People: John Bunyan and his Church (1988), Chapters 11–13.
  A Nation of Change and Novelty: Radical Politics, Religion and Literature in 17th Century England (1990), Chapters 2–6, 10–11.

  See also, *passim*, *Society and Puritanism in Pre-Revolutionary England* (1964) and *The English Bible and the 17th Century Revolution* (1993).

Chapter Five: The Agrarian Legislation of the Revolution
  The Century of Revolution (1961), Chapters 3, 9, 13, 17.
  Reformation to Industrial Revolution (1967), Part II, Chapter 8, Part IV, Chapters 3 and 5.

Abbreviations

The following abbreviations have been used in the notes:

C.C.C.	*Calendar of the Committee for Compounding with Delinquents.*
C.J.	*Commons' Journals.*
C.S.P. Col.	*Calendar of State Papers, Colonial.*
C.S.P. Dom.	*Calendar of State Papers, Domestic.*
C.S.P. Venetian.	*Calendar of State Papers, Venetian.*
D.N.B.	*Dictionary of National Biography.*
Econ. H.R.	*Economic History Review.*
E.H.R.	*English Historical Review.*
L.J.	*Lords' Journals.*
H.M.C.	Historical Manuscripts Commission.
Trans. R.H.S.	*Transactions of the Royal Historical Society.*

PART ONE

Movements and Men

ONE

Recent Interpretations
of the Civil War

The adherents of the king were chiefly composed of the nobility and higher gentry, men who, by their wealth and station, had much to lose; and who, in the annihilation of monarchy, and in the anarchy that was likely to follow, foresaw the ruin of their fortunes, and the extinction of their consideration and influence. The middling and inferior gentry, together with the inhabitants of towns; those who entertained a jealousy of the nobles, and of the king, or who, by the changes in the state of society, had lately been raised to independence, became, on the other hand, the great supporters of parliament.

John Millar, *An Historical View of the English Government*, III
(published posthumously, in 1803), p. 295.

I

IN 1913 R. G. Usher wrote: 'The English Revolution of 1640 is as much an enigma today as it was to Charles. It is a riddle which has to be solved. No one has tried to solve it because all assumed it was solved by repeating the Great Remonstrance. Every Englishman born since 1800 has . . . been born into a view of English history.'[1]

Anyone who has studied the pages of the *Economic History Review* recently will agree that the English Revolution is still an enigma, though not now because historians repeat the Grand Remonstrance. One school of thought appears to believe (roughly) that the revolution was caused by the rise of the gentry during the century before 1640. Another school believes (roughly) that it was caused by that section of the gentry which was declining during the same period. The subscriber pays his guinea and takes his choice. The object of this essay is to take

1 R. G. Usher, *The Historical Method of S. R. Gardiner*, p. 156.

stock of the present state of the controversy over the causes of the civil war.

We have to start with Gardiner. His eighteen volumes on the history of England between 1603 and 1656, supplemented by Firth's *Last Years of the Protectorate*, established fifty years ago an interpretation of the civil war as 'the Puritan Revolution', a struggle for religious and constitutional liberty. Gardiner's immense learning and mastery of the then available sources, his narrative gifts and his knack of hitting on the telling quotation – all this has made his authority very difficult to overthrow.

Yet Usher long ago pointed out Gardiner's bewildering eclecticism of method; and the case against Gardiner has been reinforced by much detailed research published since he wrote, especially in the field of economic history. A. P. Newton's *Colonizing Activities of the Early Puritans* showed that Pym and many of the Long Parliament's leaders had important trading connections. J. U. Nef's *Rise of the British Coal Industry*, and other works by Nef himself, Wadsworth and Mann, Ramsay, Dobb, Court and others have established the existence of something like an industrial revolution in the century before 1640. Professor Tawney's *The Agrarian Problem of the Sixteenth Century*, Professor Arkhangelsky's two volumes on *The Agrarian Legislation of the English Revolution* (in Russian) and Mrs. Thirsk's articles[1] have revealed agrarian problems whose depth Gardiner does not seem to have suspected. All these works – and many more could be cited – suggest that far more importance should be given to economic developments in preparing for civil war than Gardiner allowed. Moreover, Professor Tawney's *Religion and the Rise of Capitalism*, popularizing a great deal of German work on that subject, stated a connection between Puritanism and the rise of capitalism which most historians would now accept, even if they differed about which was cause and which effect. It is difficult to go on speaking about 'the Puritan Revolution' *tout court*.

Finally, since the publication of Professor Namier's great works on eighteenth-century politics historians have got into the habit of asking new questions. They have become more interested in the 'connec-

---

1 Mrs. Thirsk has shown that large numbers of royalists regained their confiscated estates even before 1660 ('The Sales of Royalist Land during the Interregnum', *Economic History Review, Second Series*, V, pp. 188–207; 'The Restoration Land Settlement', *Journal of Modern History*, XXVI, pp. 315–28). Space has not permitted a discussion of this very important contribution, which must modify our view of the Restoration.

tions', whether of patronage or economic interest, of historical characters, than in their proclaimed political principles. The 'Namier method' has already been extended forward to analyse nineteenth-century parliaments and back to the fifteenth century. The witenage-mot still awaits Namierization: not so the Long Parliament.

Today, then, the 'Puritan Revolution' is in eclipse, though many of its assumptions still haunt our thinking. The view which explains the civil war as a struggle for liberty is little more acceptable to historians trained to ask 'liberty for whom to do what?' It is a question to which many answers can be given. Liberty for witch-hunters to burn witches, and liberty for wicked capitalists to grind the faces of the poor, have been two of the simpler and least convincing, which I shall not be discussing.

In many ways the reaction against Gardiner has been healthy. 'The Puritan Revolution' was a nineteenth-century invention: there is virtue in going back to explanations current in the seventeenth and eighteenth centuries. Men so diverse in their political outlook as Winstanley, Harrington, Hobbes, Baxter, Clarendon, all explained the civil war in terms of social forces which we are today less likely to dismiss than Gardiner was.[1] We hardly need to be reminded, in this ideological age, that there were more reasons than religious conviction for supporting a 'protestant' foreign policy which expressed itself in war to open up the Spanish empire to English trade; that a greedy citizen of London might object to paying tithes no less than a pious Quaker; we observe remarks like that of the servant giving notice: 'I would have the liberty of my conscience, not to be catechized in the principles of religion',[2] because we now realize that the liberating effects of toleration extended beyond the purely religious sphere.

But many of the reactions against Gardiner have so far been rather negative. To be told that many of those whom we call 'Presbyterians' opposed the establishment of a Presbyterian church in England, and that many of those whom we call 'Independents' were Presbyterian elders,[3] is helpful in so far as it stops us thinking of the two great parties as primarily religious groupings. But that is only half our problem.

1 But Gardiner had his moments of insight. Cf. his excellent analysis of the social function of Scottish Presbyterianism in his *History of the Great Civil War* (1901), I, pp. 226–8.

2 T. Edwards, *Gangraena* (1646), p. 138.

3 J. H. Hexter, 'The Problem of the Presbyterian Independents', *American Historical Review*, XLIV, pp. 29–49.

Gardiner's interpretation of the English Revolution will no longer do: yet no alternative interpretation has yet acquired general acceptance, and none has been put forward, in this country, which can compare with Gardiner's in scope and solidity.[1] It is noteworthy that in the *Oxford* and the *Penguin Histories of England* the volumes dealing with this period are among the least satisfactory in the series. They have not escaped from Gardiner, though they supply the evidence for showing that his (and their) interpretation is no longer convincing.

II

Professor Tawney came nearest to establishing a new orthodoxy, especially in his 'The Rise of the Gentry' and 'Harrington's Interpretation of his Age', both printed in *History and Society: Essays by R. H. Tawney* (ed. J. M. Winter, 1978). Professor Tawney's views are familiar and easily accessible, so I shall not attempt to summarize them: they amount to an adaptation of Harrington's theory that the civil war was fought to redress the balance of property which had been upset by the redistribution of land in the century before 1640. This position seemed to be strengthened by an article by Mr. Stone, 'An Anatomy of the Elizabethan Aristocracy', which suggested that a majority of the peerage was heavily indebted by the end of Elizabeth's reign, and was saved only by subsidies from her successor. Mr. Stone's figures, however, were criticized by Professor Trevor-Roper, and Mr. Stone himself modified some of his original statements, though he did not abandon his general argument.[2]

In 1953 Professor Trevor-Roper produced his own rival interpretation. Criticizing Professor Tawney's use of the concept 'gentry', he argued that the civil war was caused not by the rise but by the decline of a section of the gentry. The really big profits in the century before 1640 were made not by farming but by holding court office, by the practice of the law, or by taking part in industry or trade. The 'mere gentry', those who enjoyed none of these alternative sources of income, inevitably got into financial difficulties.[3] They struggled to get positions at court.

1 The only one known to me is a two-volume collective work published in the U.S.S.R. in 1954 entitled *The English Bourgeois Revolution of the 17th century*, whose 800 large pages interpret the revolution in Marxist terms as 'one of the most important turning-points in English, European, and world history'.

2 *Econ. H.R.*, XVIII, Nos. 1 and 2; *Second Series*, III, No. 3; IV, No. 3.

3 H. R. Trevor-Roper, *The Gentry, 1540–1640 (Econ. H.R. Supplement)*, pp. 24–31.

Essex's revolt in 1601, and Gunpowder Plot in 1605, are to be seen as desperate attempts by the 'outs' to get 'in'.[1] So apparently is the civil war. Professor Trevor-Roper explains that as a gentleman became impoverished, he retired to his estates and set about economic reorganization. For this he needed 'an ideology of economy, of retrenchment'. Such an ideology he found either in Roman Catholicism, or in extreme Puritanism. His adherence to either of these beliefs would complete his isolation from the Court and strengthen the bonds between himself and others of his like who had been through similar experiences. Independency and Roman Catholicism are both creeds of the declining gentry.[2]

A summary so bald cannot do justice to the vigour and cogency with which Professor Trevor-Roper argues his case. He has certainly established the need for more, and more reliable, statistics before we can safely generalize about 'the gentry' in this period. He has performed a useful service in emphasizing the importance of court office as a source of windfall profits for the fortunate few. Nevertheless, on balance, I do not myself feel happy about the thesis as a whole.

Although he criticizes Professor Tawney's use of the category 'the gentry', Professor Trevor-Roper's own use of it is not altogether satisfactory. We must surely start from the fact that 'the gentry' were not an economic class. They were a social and legal class; economically they were divided. The inflationary century before 1640 was a great watershed, in which, in all sections of the community, economic divisions were taking place. Some yeomen were thriving to gentility; others were being submerged. Some peers were accumulating vast estates; others were on the verge of bankruptcy. It is easy to argue that 'the gentry' were either 'rising' or 'declining' if we take samples of the class: for some families were doing the one and others the other. It is not helpful to speak of the legal class as though it were in any sense an economic class. What we need is a far more precise analysis of the way in which the gentry was dividing, as well as a more accurate chronology of the movements, upwards and downwards, of individual families. I suspect that more useful categories than Professor Trevor-Roper's 'court' and 'country' gentry[3] might be those who were becoming mere rentiers, and those who were actively engaged in productive activities,

1 *Ibid.*, pp. 32, 38–42.
2 *Ibid.*, p. 31.
3 *Ibid.*, p. 26.

whether in agriculture, industry, or trade. This latter group would include those very important rising yeomen whom Professor Trevor-Roper barely considers at all; it would also include those gentlemen clothiers or investors in overseas enterprise whom Professor Trevor-Roper indeed mentions but perhaps insufficiently emphasizes.

Secondly, Professor Trevor-Roper seems to me to slide too easily from the concept of 'the mere gentry', 'the lesser gentry', to 'the declining gentry'. But the lesser gentry included those who had successfully risen from the yeomanry. Professor Trevor-Roper's assumption that no profits were made from agriculture is not proven. Indeed it seems to stand in logical contradiction to his own emphasis on the large fortunes made by members of the legal profession. For where did lawyer's profits come from? Most lawyers' clients were litigating about land. Men may have wanted to own land for social as well as economic reasons; but how did landowners pay for their litigation? Some may have ruined themselves by law-suits, may even have been bought out by lawyers who thus brought capital into the countryside; but many gentlemen did finance and win law-suits. Where did the money come from if not from agriculture?

Professor Trevor-Roper accuses Professor Tawney of 'hatred of the English gentry' because he suggests that landowners' profits were made at the expense of the peasantry. Economic power, Professor Trevor-Roper thinks, was gained 'at the expense less of the peasantry than of the Crown'.[1] But money did not grow on trees at Whitehall. The King, like the country gentleman, had to collect it from somebody who had earned it by hard work; one may suspect that peasants ultimately paid the taxes which financed the Court no less than they paid the rents which financed the gentry. Professor Trevor-Roper appears to include lawyers in the same category as courtiers, as opposed to the 'mere' gentry. But when he speaks of the 'court' gentry as a whole (including the lawyers) he tends to equate them with the Royalists in the civil war,[2] whereas at least a large section of the common lawyers are known to have supported Parliament.

Indeed, Professor Trevor-Roper's use of his analysis to explain the civil war is altogether unconvincing. Two main sources are used to illustrate those whom he describes as the declining gentry: *A Royalist's Notebook* (Sir John Oglander's) and the *Calendar of the Committee for*

1 *Ibid.*, p. 25.
2 *Ibid.*, pp. 26–7, 33–4.

Compounding with Delinquents. It is therefore a little odd that he should expect us to accept his equation of the declining gentry with the Independents. On his own evidence we should have expected to find them on the other side. After the criticisms of Professor Trevor-Roper and Mr. Cooper[1] it seems clear that the statistics with which Professor Tawney buttressed his theory prove little more than that land was passing from the crown to the gentry in the century before 1640. But Professor Trevor-Roper has produced no statistics at all. The declining gentry may or may not exist, may or may not be politically significant, may or may not be Independents: but none of this has been established statistically. Professor Trevor-Roper's method is that of sampling and inference. It is consequently harder to disprove than an argument based on statistics. But it should not therefore be regarded as established. Nor does Professor Trevor-Roper convince me that Harrington's theory (that the civil war was caused by the balance of property being upset) was merely 'the cry of the relatively poor mere gentry', 'uttered, regardless of truth, to inspire waverers in a difficult and uncertain struggle'.[2]

Fortunately Mrs. Keeler's recently-published biographical dictionary of *The Long Parliament* enables us to examine the Independent M.P.s in some detail. Over sixty of the M.P.s who sat after Pride's Purge were gentlemen whom it would be difficult to call either lesser or declining. At least nine were lawyers, and as many had been courtiers or royal officials; many more came of lawyers' or courtiers' families. A number of those Independents who were 'mere' gentlemen entered the House as 'recruiters' after 1645, and so cannot be used as evidence for the origins of the civil war. Wales and the western counties, which one would have expected to contain a large proportion of 'mere' gentry, had a considerably *smaller* proportion of M.P.s in the Rump than did the rest of the country.[3] When we look at the leaders of the Independents we encounter men of considerable wealth – Vane, Hesilrige, Mildmay, Pennington, Whitelocke. Henry Marten at first sight would seem to fit Professor Trevor-Roper's conception of a declining gentleman who was an Independent, for all that most of us know about Marten is that he was a republican and heavily in debt. Closer investigation, however,

1 J. Cooper, 'The Counting of Manors', *Econ. H.R.*, *Second Series*, VIII, No. 3.

2 *The Gentry*, pp. 46–50. I state my reasons for being unconvinced on pp. 292–4 below.

3 M. Keeler, *The Long Parliament*, *passim*; D. Brunton and D. H. Pennington, *Members of the Long Parliament*, p. 43.

reveals that he was the exact opposite of Professor Trevor-Roper's declining gentleman who used the civil war to recoup his fortunes; he was rich enough to be a county M.P. in 1640, and incurred his debts by voluntary expenditure on Parliament's behalf during the civil war.[1] Professor Trevor-Roper frequently mentions Oliver Cromwell as an Independent who was also a declining gentleman, and he is a more plausible example than most. But Cromwell would do equally well if one wished to prove that the civil war was fought exclusively over religious issues. The really declining branch of the Cromwell family was that of the extravagant Sir Oliver of Hinchingbrooke – the *Royalist* branch.

Even if we could accept the equation of Independents with declining gentlemen, it would not help us to explain the civil war. For when the war began the men in control at Westminster were not those whom we call Independents, and certainly not declining gentlemen; they were great peers like Warwick, Essex, Manchester (the last named a *court* peer who had bought out the declining *Royalist* Cromwells); Hampden, the richest commoner in England; Pym, government employee and treasurer of a City company; Holles, son of a gentleman rich enough to buy an earldom. When the Five Members escaped from the King's attempt to arrest them in January 1642, they did not flee to the backwoods: they retired to the City of London, where they were warmly welcomed. The civil war might not have been won without the Independents, but they did not start it. Professor Trevor-Roper speaks always of Presbyterians and Royalists as though they were 'on the same side',[2] which is absurd in the years before 1647.

But the point at which Professor Trevor-Roper's analysis seems to me least satisfactory of all is his attitude to religion. For him the economic needs of a declining gentleman might be expressed either by Roman Catholicism or by Independency, and it seems to have been of no significance which of the two he happened to take up. For the declining gentry were behind all the political upheavals of the early seventeenth century – Essex's revolt, Gunpowder Plot, 1642. Even if this thesis fitted the English facts (which it does not), it would still be intolerably provincial. For over a century before 1640 men all over

1 For Marten I am indebted to Professor C. M. Williams's unpublished Oxford D.Phil. thesis. Cf. Robert Wallop, the regicide, son of one of the wealthiest commoners of his day, who in 1649 said that he had lost £50,000 through the war (Keeler, *op. cit.*, pp. 377–8).

2 *Op. cit.*, pp. 33–4, 42–3, 53.

Europe had been suffering, dying, and killing for what they held to be high ideals; from the sixteen-twenties a great war was being waged on the Continent over ideological issues which aroused the intensest excitement in England and created a profound cleavage of opinion about questions of foreign policy. Professor Trevor-Roper asks us to see in all this only a reflection of the financial difficulties of a section of the English gentry. The spiritual wrestlings of a Milton, a Vane, a Roger Williams are nothing but the epiphenomena of economic decline. The idea is difficult to dismiss seriously. Only three brief points may be made. First, if we are to look for causal connections between recusancy and economic decline, it is surely less likely that a gentleman turned Catholic because of poverty than that his poverty was caused by recusancy fines? Secondly, radical Puritanism is specifically associated by contemporaries with the towns, as indeed similar creeds had been all over Europe since Calvin's day. Thirdly, one of the few generalizations we can make about the civil war is that Catholics and Independents were on opposite sides. So if they were both declining gentlemen fighting to get back to the spoils of office, both 'outs' trying to become 'ins', on which side were the 'ins'? Perhaps they were the Clubmen, the only neutralist party?

III

Professor Trevor-Roper has had second thoughts on the Independents, published in a brilliantly argued essay on 'Oliver Cromwell and his Parliaments'.[1] In this 'the Independents' are divided into two sharply contrasted categories. The first is 'the Whigs' – men like Hesilrige, Scot, Bradshaw, Slingsby Bethel. These are in fact those whom most of us regard as the main parliamentary leaders of the Independents, though for Professor Trevor-Roper they have now become 'the republican usurpers'. The second category comprises 'those ordinary Independent gentry whom Cromwell represented', the back-benchers and the officers.[2] This distinction has validity: but what remains now of the thesis that it was the Independents, the declining gentry, 'who made the revolution'? To define the Independents proper in such a way as to exclude the majority in the Rump, and

1 In *Essays Presented to Sir Lewis Namier* (ed. R. Pares and A. J. P. Taylor), pp. 1–48. On p. 28 Professor Trevor-Roper is mistaken in saying that the Instrument of Government preserved the old property qualifications.

2 *Ibid.*, pp. 16, 20, 45–6; cf. Professor Trevor-Roper in *Annales* (1956) p. 493.

simultaneously to attribute the making of the revolution to them, is like saying that the French Revolution was 'made' by those Jacobins who were to support Napoleon after 1802. How many of those now claimed as the real Independents even sat in Parliament before 1645? It surprises Professor Trevor-Roper, but need surprise no one else, that those who sought to create 'an Independent political caucus' for Cromwell in the Parliaments after the expulsion of the Rump 'were not real Independents but, all of them, ex-royalists' – Ashley-Cooper, Wolseley, Broghill.[1] A 'real' Independent is clearly a rare bird. It seems to me that in refining and improving his definition to suit his argument Professor Trevor-Roper has destroyed his own thesis about the causes of the civil war.

Professor Trevor-Roper's forceful analysis seems to me defective in a second respect. He argues that Cromwell, like James I and Laud, was unable to 'manage' Parliament or elections, and suggests that this was due to incompetence, to the back-bencher attitude typical of the Independent small gentry. Professor Trevor-Roper almost conveys the impression that a Cecil or a John Robinson could have established the Protectorate on a secure basis. This assumes that 'Parliamentary management' is an art which can be applied irrespective of political circumstances.[2] The Duke of Newcastle could control Parliaments because, in the words of Sir Lewis Namier, 'the nation was at one in all fundamental matters, and whenever that happy but uninspiring condition was reached, Parliamentary contests lose reality and un-avoidably change into a fierce though bloodless struggle for places'.[3] Burghley, though with more difficulty, could control Parliaments because in the last resort the opposition preferred the existing government to any possible alternative. Under James and Charles, and still more in the sixteen-fifties, the political nation was not 'at one in all fundamental matters'. It was rent by political disagreements which led to civil war. The Parliamentarians were in sufficient agreement for Pym to be able to manage those who remained at Westminster; after the war was won political disagreements re-appeared which led to purges of Parliament and to military dictatorship. The feelings of

1 *Ibid.*, pp. 18, 46–7. Wolseley was born in 1630.
2 *Ibid.*, pp. 12, 45.
3 Namier, *The Structure of Politics at the Accession of George III* (1929), p. 21. It is characteristic of Sir Lewis to make this important point, even though it was not his immediate concern, and of his rasher disciples to ignore it, though it should have been their concern.

Ludlow and Prynne about Oliver Cromwell were different from those of a disappointed office-seeker about the Duke of Newcastle. Even if Oliver had 'studied the necessary rules of the game', his enemies were more interested in bringing about the kingdom of God upon earth than in playing cricket. The Protector failed to come to terms with his first Parliament, and managed to do so with his second, not because Broghill was a better Parliamentary manager than Thurloe, still less because this opportunist ex-Royalist was seeking 'to save the real aims of the revolution',[1] but because in 1656 the government was prepared to surrender to the political programme demanded by the majority in Parliament, whereas in 1654 it had not been. Without a change of policy by the executive, no amount of management could have secured it a majority, even with many M.P.s excluded. At such a price James I could have secured a favourable majority too: Buckingham did in 1624. 'Management' enables good Parliamentarians to obtain collaboration in working for agreed objectives, or in sharing out spoils when objectives are not in dispute; it does not enable the best politicians in the world to square circles.

IV

Another recent work which discusses the line-up in the civil war is that of Messrs. Brunton and Pennington, *Members of the Long Parliament*. This book has been rightly praised by many reviewers, and it contains a wealth of valuable information. If I dwell on what seem to me its less satisfactory aspects it is, first, because I believe some reviewers have claimed too much for it (indeed, more than its authors would); secondly, because I believe harm may be done if it is too easily assumed that its negative conclusions are irrefutable; and thirdly because I believe methodological considerations of some importance for future work on the subject are involved.[2]

The authors analysed the personnel of the Long Parliament, and asked themselves whether this analysis threw light on the causes of the civil war. Their conclusions were entirely negative. Gentlemen, lawyers, and merchants were found among M.P.s on either side. The only significant difference was that the average age of Royalist M.P.s

1 *The Gentry*, pp. 47–8.
2 See a Review of *Members of the Long Parliament* by B. Manning in *Past and Present*, No. 5 (1954) and a discussion between Messrs. Manning and Pennington in *ibid.*, No. 6.

was thirty-six, that of their opponents forty-seven. Therefore, the authors concluded, attempts to explain the civil war in terms of class divisions are unfounded.

This conclusion may be criticized on two grounds. First, I believe the facts have in certain important respects been incorrectly interpreted; secondly, even if the interpretation were correct, the conclusion would not follow.

(1) Even on Messrs. Brunton and Pennington's own analysis, significant differences between the two groups of M.P.s can be seen. Though there were merchants on either side, they were not equally divided. Of the London merchants elected to the House of Commons, the twelve monopolists were expelled; in the civil war they naturally supported the court through which their profits had come. Of the remaining nineteen London merchants, eighteen were Parliamentarians. The one exception, George Lowe, held estates in Wiltshire and was connected by marriage with Edward Hyde.[1] Provincial merchants were more equally divided. But in the Eastern Association merchants were solidly Parliamentarian, and even in the Royalist-occupied areas a small majority among the merchant M.P.s had the courage to declare for Parliament.[2] The authors did not ask how many of the Royalist merchants were royal officials like the customs farmer and Duchy of Lancaster official who were returned for the borough of Lancaster, presumably thanks to Duchy pressure. Nor did they ask how many were members of urban governing oligarchies maintained in their privileged position by the royal charters which the Levellers and Diggers wanted to abolish. The Royalist M.P.s Hooke and Long 'represented actually the merchant oligarchy of Bristol',[3] a city in which Sir Samuel Luke was told in 1643, 'they are all Roundheads . . . except the maior and 2 or 3 aldermen'.[4]

Similarly, to say that the numbers of gentlemen on either side were roughly equal does not get us very far. The authors warn against the dangers of dividing the landed from the mercantile interest, especially in the clothing counties.[5] But should we not attempt to divide *within* the

1 Keeler, *op. cit.*, pp. 257–8.
2 Brunton and Pennington, *op. cit.*, p. 62.
3 Keeler, *op. cit.*, pp. 47, 53.
4 Ed. I. G. Philip, *Journal of Sir Samuel Luke* (Oxfordshire Record Society), p. 218; cf. the similar remarks in John Corbet's *Historical Relation of the Military Government of Gloucester* (1645), in *Bibliotheca Gloucestrensis* (1823), I, p. 14.
5 Brunton and Pennington, *op. cit.*, p. 73.

landed interest? The economic life of most gentlemen in Cumberland or Wales was very different from that of gentlemen in Norfolk or Surrey. Messrs. Brunton and Pennington brush aside altogether too lightly the distinction between the economically-advanced south and east of the country, which was Parliamentarian, and the economically-backward north and west, which was Royalist. Mr. Pennington admits that 'a study of how the estates of landed members were managed might reveal an economic line of cleavage corresponding to the political one'.[1] Until this question has been investigated it is premature to tell us what the answer to it is.

The authors also note that

> 'among county families it is easier to find Parliamentarian than Royalist members who were exploiting local assets and opportunities. More characteristic of the Royalists are the supplementary sources of income that could be picked up through connections at the court and in the capital'.[2]

This contrast between local economic activity (whether in industry or agriculture) and the economic parasitism of the Court would be a profitable field of research for those looking for divisions between M.P.s (and among the gentry as a whole). And were such activities only local? Mrs. Keeler notes some 60 M.P.s known to have been members of trading companies, and there were no doubt many more: most of them seem to have been Parliamentarians.[3] A thorough exploration of all these business activities, central and local, might even help us towards answering Messrs. Brunton and Pennington's rhetorical question: 'What is it that makes one great grandson of a Tudor copyholder or a Tudor judge a progressive bourgeois and another a feudal aristocrat?'[4] We are at least more likely to find the answer here than in even the most exhaustive examination of members' pedigrees. Independency, the authors note, was strong among M.P.s from the clothing counties: it was weakest in the north and west.[5]

Further, to divide members of the House of Commons into two

1 *Past and Present*, No. 6, p. 88. This most important reservation was mentioned in the last dozen lines of *Members of the Long Parliament*.
2 Brunton and Pennington, *op. cit.*, pp. 166–7.
3 Keeler, *op. cit.*, pp. 25, 30; Brunton and Pennington, *op. cit.*, pp. 162–4.
4 *Ibid.*, p. 178.
5 *Ibid.*, pp. 43–4.

parties, labelled 'Royalist' and 'Parliamentarian', and then to treat all members of the two groups as statistically equivalent, is misleading. Side by side with men prepared to sacrifice property to principle, like Henry Marten or Sir Bevil Grenville, our authors perforce list the marginal turncoat on either side who had no principles at all. They were aware of the dangers here, and they may be right in arguing that no other division was possible. But statistics so compiled are of highly dubious value. Mr. Pennington recognizes that 'the crucial problem' is the M.P.s who were firm opponents of Strafford (and, we might add, continued to oppose the Court throughout 1641) and yet fought for the King.[1] Mrs. Keeler's book shows the very large number of M.P.s who no doubt owed their place in the Commons to their opposition to the government and yet ultimately changed sides. Nineteen Cornish M.P.s swung over to the King between the summer of 1642 and the end of 1643.[2]

There might be many reasons for this: fear of the consequences of treason;[3] fear for the safety of one's estates; alarm at social disorder (anti-enclosure riots, refusal of rents, pressure of London citizens on M.P.s, 'mechanick preachers'). John Hotham, for instance, turned traitor to Parliament because, as he told the Earl of Newcastle, 'no man that hath any reasonable share in the commonwealth can desire that either side should be absolute conqueror. . . . It is too great a temptation to courses of violence'. Moreover, he feared that 'the necessitous people of the whole kingdome will presently rise in mighty numbers, and whosoever they pretend for att first, within a while they will sett up for themselves to the utter ruine of all the Nobility and Gentry of the kingdome'. The West Riding, he added, 'affords mighty numbers of them which, I am very confident, you will see necessitated and urged to rise in far greater bodyes than thrice the armies that are already gathered here. My Lord, necessity teaches us to seek a subsistence, and if this unruly rout have once cast the rider, itt will run like wildfire in the Example through all the Counties of England'.[4]

1 *Past and Present*, No. 6, p. 87.
2 R. N. Worth, *Buller Papers*, p. viii.
3 See a discussion of this point between the Oxinden cousins in *The Oxinden Letters, 1607–42* (ed. D. Gardiner), pp. 308–9.
4 A. M. W. Stirling, *The Hothams*, I, pp. 64–5, gives a better text than that in *Portland MSS.* (H.M.C.), I, p. 87. For the way in which Bradford summoned the countryside to fight for Parliament, and so forced Fairfax into action and Hotham into

Another reason for changing sides might be the possession of estates in areas occupied by the royal forces. Something approaching 100 M.P.s who transferred their support to the King after 1642 came from areas controlled by Royalist armies in the early stages of the war. Even an old opponent and victim of the Court like John Dutton, M.P. for Gloucestershire, deserted the parliamentary cause (at the last possible moment) 'for the preservation of his house and estate'.[1] In Herefordshire Robert Kirle gave social reasons for changing sides, rather like those of Hotham, though his enemies said he was more concerned to save his estates from the royal forces: he changed back again as soon as Parliament was clearly winning.[2] Of townsmen M.P.s, Mrs. Keeler tells us, only one quarter were Royalists, some belatedly; and most of these came from the strongly Royalist areas.[3] Less significant numerically, but also worthy of study, are those M.P.s returned from royal nomination boroughs in the areas controlled by Parliament who switched over to the locally winning side. Where accidental personal considerations must necessarily have played so large a part in deciding the course of action of all M.P.s who lacked strong convictions, it is surely rash to draw from their behaviour conclusions about the nature of the division between the two sides who fought the war. The men of principle were no doubt a minority on either side of the House.

(2) As in dealing with Professor Trevor-Roper's views about management of the Commons, so here we are faced with the larger question of the applicability of 'the Namier method' to periods of acute political crisis. The method was originally devised to illuminate English politics at the accession of George III. It would be difficult to find a period in the whole of English history when the political nation was more 'at one in all fundamental matters'. It was therefore legitimate to apply a technique of analysis which ignored political principles, or treated them as rationalizations of economic or other interests. But if we go even a few years forward – to the Wilkes question – or a few years back – to the Jacobites, to 1688 – principles begin to

---

treachery, see Mr. B. Manning's contribution to '17th century revolutions' in *Past and Present*, No. 13, p. 70. Cf. p. 186 below.

1 Brunton and Pennington, *op. cit.*, p. 150. This did not prevent Dutton remaining on friendly terms with Cromwell and seeking his daughter's hand in marriage for his nephew.

2 J. and T. W. Webb, *Memorials of the Civil War in Herefordshire* (1879), II, pp. 349–53. The whole of Kirle's letter of 6 March 1643 is interesting.

3 Keeler, *op. cit.*, p. 22.

rear their inconvenient heads.[1] Here the Namier method is of more limited value, as its author specifically warned. Messrs. Brunton and Pennington analyse their M.P.s into family groupings, local groupings, economic groupings, patronage groupings, age groupings. (It may reasonably be argued that family and regional groupings were also economic groupings more often than Messrs. Brunton and Pennington recognize.[2]) But none of their groups are united by ideas. Yet there was in the House of Commons a group of republicans; perhaps some M.P.s even took their religion seriously enough to work together with men of like convictions?[3]

About the relation of M.P.s to the electorate questions must also be asked which would have been less relevant in 1760. Politics then was what went on at Westminster. But a civil war by definition transcends the limits of the old governmental institutions. The war was maintained not so much by the 500 M.P.s as by the citizens of London, Hull, Gloucester, Plymouth; by the freeholders of Buckinghamshire riding up to London to defend John Hampden; by the russet-coated captains of Cromwell's Ironsides; by the members of the sectarian congregations. Even if Messrs. Brunton and Pennington had established (as they have not) that there were no significant economic divisions between M.P.s on the two sides, they would have proved very little about the division in the country. The House of Commons was elected on the same franchise as had prevailed since 1430: naturally men of the same social types as in previous Parliaments were returned. Parliament contained a cross-section of the ruling class. The two houses were divided because the ruling class was divided. What needs analysis, if we are to understand the civil war, is the exact nature of this division; and, secondly, its relation to divisions in the country at large and in the electorate.

How did any particular M.P. get into Parliament? The contestants at Great Marlow were all gentlemen, but they represented such different interests that we need different categories to place them in. Whitelocke and Hoby 'stood for the liberty of the commons in the election', with the support of shopkeepers and labourers as well as of the burgesses and 'the ordinary sort of townsmen'; their opponent John Borlace,

---

1 I owe this point, as so much more, to discussions with Professor Richard Pares.

2 Keeler, *op. cit.*, p. 30; Manning, *Past and Present*, No. 5, p. 72.

3 'Mr. Pennington finds it difficult to understand the division into parties in the Commons because he ignores the ideas that underlie it' (Manning, *Past and Present*, No. 6, p. 90).

son-in-law of Attorney-General Bankes, was a great local landowner. Men feared that 'if they left Mr. Borlace out . . . he would not let them buy any wood of him, but do them many ill turns'. Bankes had to give Borlace the seat for his borough of Corfe Castle, vacated by the expulsion of Windebanke from the Commons.[1] In Essex 'it was said amongst the people that if Nevill [the royalist candidate] had the day they would tear the gentlemen to pieces'. The victorious candidates were of course also gentlemen: but gentlemen clearly with a difference. The defeated candidate thought that the 40s. freehold qualifications should be raised to £20. 'Then gentlemen would be looked up to'.[2] The only Royalist returned from Northamptonshire was M.P. for Higham Ferrers, a borough in the Queen's jointure.[3] In general it was a Royalist commonplace that corporations were 'nurseries of schism and rebellion'. Messrs. Brunton and Pennington give away a larger point than they appear to realize when they admit that, at the time of Pride's Purge, 'in the country generally there were undoubtedly the beginnings of a resistance by the small men, the propertyless and the oppressed', but 'little sign of a class division', in Parliament.[4] This means either that Pride's Purge bore no relation to events in the country, or that Messrs. Brunton and Pennington are looking for the wrong sort of connections.

V

Fortunately Mr. Pennington too has had second thoughts, or rather has pressed his investigations beyond Westminster into the depths of the country. The simultaneous publication in 1957 of excellent studies of the county committees of Staffordshire and Kent has very sensibly added to our understanding of social divisions in the provinces.[5] In each county two parties appeared in the course of the civil war. The compromise-peace party drew its main strength from the old ruling

1 M. R. Frear, 'The Election at Great Marlow in 1640', *Journal of Modern History*, XIV, No. 4, pp. 437–45; Brunton and Pennington, *op. cit.*, p. 167.

2 *C.S.P. Dom.*, *1639–40*, pp. 608–9. The writer added that raising the franchise 'would save the ministers a great deal of pains in preaching [away] from their own churches' – an interesting side-light on the political role of the pulpit.

3 Keeler, *op. cit.*, p. 57; cf. p. 64.

4 Brunton and Pennington, *op. cit.*, p. 182.

5 Ed. D. H. Pennington and I. A. Roots, *The Committee at Stafford, 1643–5*; A. M. Everitt, *The County Committee of Kent in the Civil War*.

families, concerned primarily with the preservation of their property
and dominant influence. The win-the-war party, in each county, was
led by members of leading families who were directly engaged in
military operations, but in general its members were of markedly lower
social origin. Inevitably it looked to London for a national lead and a
national military organization. Religious radicals gravitated towards
this group, but the conflict within county committees, which cor-
responds to the national rivalry between Presbyterians and Independents, was not primarily religious. Originally a dispute about
military tactics, it soon revealed itself as also a social quarrel. The old
ruling families were ousted from control of both counties in the middle
sixteen-forties.

In Staffordshire the conflict turned on the rivalry between the Earl of
Denbigh and Sir William Brereton. 'The adherents of Sir William
Brereton who in general favoured the most energetic and uncompromising prosecution of the war included more of the newcomers [to the
governing class] than did those of the Earl of Denbigh, who were
attracted by peace-making.' Brereton's victory was symbolized by the
replacing of one Governor of Stafford by 'a Walsall merchant accepted
as a "gentleman" ', 'who, though rich, was hardly in the same class' as
his predecessor. 'The bulk of the active members of the Committee'
also seem to have been relative upstarts. Some survived as county
families after 1660: most disappeared again.[1] In Kent the figure
corresponding to Brereton was Sir Anthony Weldon, a disappointed
courtier. In February 1642–3 baronets and knights composed 55 per
cent of the Kent Committee; in December 1652, 11 per cent. In the
Committee appointed after the formation of the New Model Army, 13
old members were dropped. Even when members of the old ruling
families remained on the Committee, they were being forced from the
controlling nucleus by men who 'looked to the state and thought
nationally'. The Accounts Committee, set up in 1645 to check and
supervise the activities of the Kent Committee, was also drawn from a
socially lower group. The old families tried to make a comeback in
1648, linking up with those other members of the ruling class who had
taken the King's side, and with whom relations had never been
completely severed. Defeated in this second civil war, the traditional
families withdrew or were excluded from the government of the
county, almost without exception. Henceforth, under protection of the

1 Pennington and Roots, *op. cit.*, pp. xxii–iii, lvii–ix, lxxiv, 349–56.

Army, Kent was run by lesser men, many of them with City connections.[1]

So far the evidence is inadequate for confident generalization: but in addition to Staffordshire and Kent, Mr. Wood and Professor Dodd have demonstrated that lower social types came into control of local government during the interregnum in Nottinghamshire and in most Welsh counties. South Wales had its 'Pride's Purge' before London.[2] The minute-book of Bedford corporation, recently edited by Mr. Parsloe, shows how successive coups d'état in the town roughly coincided with changes of government at the centre; the same appears to be true of High Wycombe.[3] The conflict between Presbyterians and Independents at Westminster looks very different in the light of such local studies.

The civil war, then, cannot be explained merely by looking at M.P.s. Men did not die and kill one another for four years over issues which can be satisfactorily analysed by a method evolved for a period in which there were no serious political disagreements. The civil war was fought about issues of principle which roused large numbers of men to heroic activity and sacrifice. To say that account should be taken of these issues need not lead us back to Gardiner's conception of 'the Puritan Revolution'.

The methods, the techniques of analysis employed by Messrs. Brunton and Pennington, and by Mr. Stone and Professor Trevor-Roper, seem to me in danger of giving a false emphasis which, unless very great care is taken to guard against it, would render their interpretations as lop-sided as Gardiner's, though on the opposite side. By their exclusive concentration on interests, whether economic, geographical, or those of patronage, the impression is given that all politics is a dirty game, struggles for the spoils of office, the 'ins' *versus* the 'outs', that principles are merely rationalizations. I do not believe that material conflicts are the only ones deserving serious analysis. This approach indeed brings its own refutation. The civil war did, after

1 Everitt, *op. cit.*, pp. 9, 25, 27.

2 A. C. Wood, *Nottinghamshire in the Civil War*, especially Chapter XI; A. H. Dodd, *Studies in Stuart Wales*, especially Chapter IV. Cf. also Sir J. F. Rees, *Studies in Welsh History*, p. 77.

3 Ed. G. Parsloe, *The Minute Book of the Bedford Corporation, 1647–64* (Publications of the Bedfordshire Historical Record Society, XXVI, 1949); W. H. Summers, 'Some Documents in the State Papers relating to High Wycombe', in *Records of Bucks.*, VII (1895), pp. 512–27.

all, take place, but Messrs. Brunton and Pennington supply no adequate explanation of that fact. Professor Trevor-Roper has to dismiss as 'futile' the deliberate waging of war for trade, colonies and markets by the Commonwealth and Protectorate.[1] Yet these policies were to be followed by successive governments for the next 175 years. The men of undeniable political principle, whose theories of democracy inspired the American revolutionaries, the Radicals and Chartists, and are still alive today, he dismisses as 'the lunatic fringe', who were able to become vocal only because of the degeneration of politics after 1643. This is not dealing very seriously with history.

VI

An earnest evangelical once expostulated with Baring-Gould about the chorus of 'Onward Christian Soldiers'. Dangerous concessions to ritualism, he thought, were made in the words

> *'With the cross of Jesus*
> *Going on before.'*

Baring-Gould accepted the criticism with due solemnity, and suggested that the low church gentleman might prefer to sing

> *'With the cross of Jesus*
> *Left behind the door.'*

'The Puritan Revolution' is dead and buried, and I do not want to resurrect it; but need Puritanism be left altogether behind the door? The importance of economic issues has been established; but we still have to find a synthesis which will take cognizance of this and yet give some explanation of why in 1640 not only M.P.s but a large number of other people thought bishops the main enemy; why there were so many conflicts before 1640 over the appointment of lecturers in town corporations; why, when the troops got drunk of a Saturday night in 1640, their animal spirits were worked off in the destruction of altar rails; why Cromwell's Army marched into battle singing psalms.

The following points, I would suggest, will have to be included in our ultimate synthesis:

---

1 Trevor-Roper, *The Gentry*, p. 43.

(i) A much more serious study needs to be made of the political effects of the 'industrial revolution' of the century before 1640. Professor Nef's valuable suggestions in his *Rise of the British Coal Industry* have not been properly followed up. The struggle over monopolies was not only of financial and constitutional importance; it was also of the greatest consequence for the future of capitalism in industry that there should be freedom of economic development. Further knowledge here might help us to a clearer understanding of the support which towns (except sometimes their ruling oligarchies) and the rural industrial areas gave to the parliamentary cause.

(ii) Valerie Pearl's *London and the Outbreak of the Puritan Revolution: City Government and National Politics, 1625–43*, published since this essay was written, has given us a useful analysis of politics in the City – the links between the ruling oligarchy of aldermen and the Court, which made the City government Royalist, and isolated it from the majority of the Common Council and of City voters, who were radical Parliamentarians. She has documented the fierce conflicts which led to the violent overthrow of the royalist clique in the winter of 1641, just in time to make the City a safe refuge for the Five Members. But there is still room for more work on London politics after 1643, and on political conflicts in other towns.

(iii) We should also, I believe, look more closely at colonial and imperial policies. Since Newton's book we all recognize the crucial importance of the Providence Island Company, but this was after all one of the smaller companies. The full political effect of disputes over colonial questions on the origin and progress of the revolution has never been fully worked out.[1] But when we find the Witney blanket-makers asking the House of Lords in 1641 to protect the rights and privileges of the Royal Africa Company, we can imagine how many people's lives were already affected by freedom of export.[2]

(iv) Professor Campbell and Dr. Hoskins have directed our attention to the rising yeoman;[3] but there has been no full analysis of his economic problems in relation to government policy, nor of those of the small clothiers and artisans generally. Yet traditionally these classes are

1 Cf. Manning, *Past and Present*, No. 5, p. 71. There are some valuable chapters on this subject in the Russian work quoted on p. 6, n. 1 above.

2 *Victoria County History of Oxfordshire*, II, pp. 247–8. Viscount Wenman, whose family had risen to a peerage through the Witney wool trade, represented Oxfordshire in the Long Parliament.

3 M. Campbell, *The English Yeoman*; W. G. Hoskins, *Essays in Leicestershire History*.

believed to have formed the backbone of the New Model Army, and most contemporaries agree in putting them solidly on the parliamentary side, at least in the south and east. There is a danger that in riveting our attention on the gentry we may underestimate social groups which were at least of equal importance once the old stable social structure began to crumble, and whose grievances helped to make it crumble.

(v) This brings us to a subject one mentions with diffidence – the people of England. Gardiner and the Whigs often assumed too lightly that Parliament represented 'the people', that it is easy to know what 'the people' wanted. But the modern tendency is again to throw the baby out with the bath water, and to leave out of account those who actually fought the civil war. Tenants no doubt often turned out to fight as their landlords told them, London demonstrations could be organized, the rank and file of the New Model Army were not all as politically sophisticated as the Agitators. Granting this, the evidence still suggests that in 1640 there was a real popular hostility to the old régime whose depth and intensity needs analysis and explanation, and whose influence on the course of events after 1640 we almost certainly tend to underestimate. The consumers and craftsmen who suffered from the high prices caused by monopolies, the peasants whom Laud's good intentions failed to protect,[1] and who thought the time had come to throw down enclosures in 1640–1; the ordinary citizens who resisted the Laudian attempt to increase tithe payments; the small men for whom the parson of the established church (*any* established church) was 'Public Enemy No. 1'; the members of the sectarian congregations of the sixteen-forties and -fifties whose naïve but daring speculations have still to be properly studied in their social setting[2] – it was these men, not M.P.s or 'the gentry', rising or declining, who bore the brunt of the civil war. It would also be interesting to have studies of those who fought for the King. But I suspect that in the Royalist areas the traditional 'feudal' machinery still worked, landlords brought out their tenants, the militia was officered by the gentry of the county. The New

---

1 It is significant that when the Levellers, the party of the small men, were using every stick to beat the Parliamentarian leaders, even going so far as to say that England used to be merrier before the Reformation, they never, to the best of my knowledge, argued that things had been better under Laud and Charles I. If the prosperity and 'social justice' of the sixteen-thirties had had any reality for the small men, it is very unlikely that they would not have used this argument.

2 But cf. P. Zagorin, *A History of Political Thought in the English Revolution.*

Model was an army of a new type.

(vi) On the gentry, let us admit that we still do not know enough. I personally believe that the contemporary analyses of Winstanley, Harrington, Hobbes, Baxter, and Clarendon are still the safest guides, and that Professor Tawney is more right than Professor Trevor-Roper. But we should stop generalizing about 'the gentry'. Professor Trevor-Roper himself points out the regional differences which made a gentleman with £150 a year in Devon comparable with one who had far more in the home counties.[1] We also need to know more about different types of estate management and leasing policies, about investments in trade and industry, before we can begin to see the way in which the rise of capitalism was dividing the gentry into different economic classes. We need more studies of individual families like Dr. M. Finch's admirable *The Wealth of Five Northamptonshire Families, 1540–1640;*[2] more documents like those of the Herbert and Percy families edited respectively by Dr. Kerridge and Mr. James.[3] We also need more regional inquiries like those of Professor Dodd and Messrs. Everitt and Pennington and Roots, and local documents like the minute-book of Bedford Corporation. Such local studies will divert us from exclusive attention to the small group of men at Westminster, and help us to see the deeper social currents on which the politicians were floating.

(vii) Professor Trevor-Roper has done a great service in drawing our attention to the significance of control of the state. But this was not important merely as a source of spoils, of windfall wealth for individuals. The state was an instrument of economic power, maintaining monopolists and customs farmers, fining enclosers, endangering property by arbitrary taxation; in different hands the same instrument was used to confiscate and sell land, to pass the Navigation Act which challenged the Dutch to fight for the trade of the world, to conquer Ireland and grab Spanish colonies. Yet the relation of individuals and groups to the state power still needs fuller investigation.

(viii) We also need far more understanding of ideas, especially at the

---

1 *The Gentry*, p. 52.

2 Publications of the Northamptonshire Record Society, Vol. XIX (1956).

3 Ed. E. Kerridge, *Surveys of the Manors of Philip, First Earl of Pembroke and Montgomery, 1631–2* (Wilts. Archaeological and Natural History Society, Records Branch, Vol. IX, 1953); ed. M. E. James, *Estate Accounts of the Earls of Northumberland, 1562–1637* (Surtees Society, Vol. CLXII, 1955).

point where they interact with economics. Over twenty years ago Mr. Wagner wrote a fascinating article on 'Coke and the Rise of Economic Liberalism'.[1] This line of thought needs fuller working out; it may prove as important as that summarized in Professor Tawney's *Religion and the Rise of Capitalism*. Contemporaries were influenced by legal theories little less than by religion: Lilburne held the Bible in one hand, Coke in the other. It is therefore important to take legal history out of the hands of the lawyers, as religious history has been taken away from the theologians, and to relate both to social development. Law deals with property relations, and liberty and property were the two things most strongly and consistently emphasized in the Long Parliament in 1640–1. The fact that after 1640 (and after 1660) Sir Edward Coke was regarded as *the* legal authority, whereas before 1640 his writings were suppressed by the government, shows the importance of clarity about the exact relation of his legal doctrine to the social and economic changes of the seventeenth century.

(ix) Finally, questions of religion and church government should not be 'left behind the door'. We must have a better explanation of their importance for contemporaries than the theory that Puritanism helps landowners to balance their income and expenditure, or encourages the bourgeoisie to grind the faces of the poor. Professor Haller has shown us how the Puritan ministers acted as organizers of something approaching a political party;[2] and the ministers were more interested in religion than economics. Puritanism means Vane and Milton and Bunyan as well as Alderman Fowke, who was 'not much noted for religion, but a countenancer of good ministers' and who was 'deeply engaged in Bishops' lands'.[3] We are in no danger today of forgetting Alderman Fowke and his like; we are in more danger of forgetting those who fought well because they thought they were fighting God's battles. We must remember too the vision of Bacon and George Hakewill and John Preston, of a freer humanity glorifying God by abolishing evil through profounder knowledge of the world in which men live. Bacon's influence in inspiring revolt against the past became widespread only after the political revolution of the sixteen-forties:[4] modern science entered Oxford behind the New Model Army. The

1 *Economic History Review*, VI, No. 1.
2 W. Haller, *The Rise of Puritanism, passim*.
3 Quoted in J. Stoughton, *History of Religion in England*, III, p. 148.
4 Cf. R. F. Jones, *Ancients and Moderns*, pp. 48–69, 122. For Preston, see pp. 216–47 below.

connections of religion, science, politics, and economics are infinite and infinitely subtle. Religion was the idiom in which the men of the seventeenth century thought. One does not need to accept the idiom, or to take it at its face value, to see that it cannot be ignored or rejected as a simple reflex of economic needs. Any adequate interpretation of the English Revolution must give full place to questions of religion and church government, must help us to grasp the political and social implications of theological heresy.

VII

One easy refuge is to say that it is all so complex that no interpretation at all is possible. The historian can only record the multifarious things that happened, but must not attempt to make sense of them. I believe this is to abdicate the historian's function. We need not accept Professor Trevor-Roper's interpretation to applaud his attempt to interpret. 'In humane studies there are times when a new error is more life-giving than an old truth, a fertile error than a sterile accuracy.'[1] Certain things we can say. 'The Puritan Revolution' failed. The City on a Hill was not built in England; the prelates came back in 1660, welcomed by many who had attacked them in 1640. The economic and political revolution succeeded to a much greater extent. The end of prerogative courts and of arbitrary taxation threatening security of property; sovereignty of Parliament and common law; the habit of continuous parliamentary government; effective rule of J.P.s and town corporations uncontrolled by Star Chamber or major-generals; end of monopolies; abolition of feudal tenures, but no security for copy-holders; conquest of Ireland; the Navigation Act and use of sea power for an imperialist policy – these were the lasting achievements of the years 1640–60, though some were not finally confirmed until 1688. There was much continuity of policy from the 'fifties to the 'sixties, and of administrative personnel.

But, whilst recognizing these facts, I at any rate should not wish to interpret them in crudely economic terms. Pym and the 'Presbyterians' were not a mere gang of capitalists, any more than Cromwell and the 'Independents' were a rabble of bankrupt gentlemen. And if we put it at its lowest, one could argue that to create the conditions for free capitalist development in England then did open up wide vistas for

1 Trevor-Roper, *History, Professional and Lay*, p. 22.

increasing production, for a Baconian relief of man's estate; whereas the régime of Laud and Charles I offered only a Spanish stagnation.

But my whole argument has been that we should not think *merely* in economic terms. The establishment of parliamentary supremacy, of the rule of law, no doubt mainly benefited the men of property. But on any showing the abolition of Star Chamber and High Commission and monopolies were to the advantage of the majority of Englishmen. And political ideas had outstripped constitutional achievement. The course of the Revolution itself led to the emergence of systematic democratic political theories, for the first time in modern history.[1] The theories of Vane, Milton, the Levellers, were not whispered in a corner; they had roused large numbers of men and women to political action. They were no more forgotten than was the public execution of a King of England in the name of his people. James II did not need reminding that he had a joint in his neck.

The epigraph to this essay shows how far an intelligent historian, who worked a century before Gardiner, could get simply by carefully studying social interpretations current in the seventeenth century.[2] What we need today, I suggest, is a return to these contemporary interpretations, integrated with the results of recent research into industrial history and modern studies of the relation between Puritanism and the rise of capitalism. Above all, we must widen our view so as to embrace the total activity of society. Any event so complex as a revolution must be seen as a whole. Large numbers of men and women were drawn into political activity by religious and political ideals as well as by economic necessities. This sense of the largeness of the issues, and some of my criticisms of current historical fashions, were expressed by no less a person than Oliver Cromwell when he asked:

> 'What are all our histories and other traditions of actions in former times but God manifesting Himself that He hath shaken and tumbled and trampled upon everything that He hath not planted? ... Let men take heed and be twice advised, how they call His revolutions, the things of God and His working of things from one

1 This is another subject deserving more space, on which much good work has recently been done in the U.S.A. Cf. D. M. Wolfe, *Milton in the Puritan Revolution*; W. K. Jordan, *Men of Substance*; P. Zagorin, *A History of Political Thought in the English Revolution*.

2 Cf. pp. 181–94 below for the very similar views of Clarendon.

period to another, how, I say, they call them necessities of men's creations.'[1]

We cannot all share Cromwell's intimate knowledge of the ways of the Almighty; but we can, I hope, agree with him that mighty revolutions should not be dismissed as the unfortunate mistakes of incompetent politicians, or as the product of the skill and greed of a few cunning men. No explanation of the English Revolution will do which starts by assuming that the people who made it were knaves or fools, puppets or automata.

1 W. C. Abbot, *Writings and Speeches of Oliver Cromwell*, III, pp. 590–2.

TWO

Social and Economic Consequences of the Henrician Reformation

Superstition is costly, and superstitious persons are either lavishly profuse, or slavishly ready to bestow their goods for very vanities which doe them no good, when by a right bestowing of their goods they might make them friends of the unrighteous Mammon and be received into everlasting habitations.

The Rev. John Tombes, *The Leaven of Pharisaicall Wil-Worship* (1643), p. 11.

I

THE Reformation in England was an act of state. The initiative came from Henry VIII, who wanted to solve his matrimonial problems. The King had the enthusiastic support of an anti-clerical majority in the House of Commons (representing the landed gentry and the merchants) and of the propertied classes in the economically advanced south and east of England. Overt opposition came only from the more feudal north (the Pilgrimage of Grace in 1536). The Reformation was not motivated by theological considerations: Henry VIII burnt Protestants as well as opponents of the royal supremacy. Some supporters of the Reformation were heretics; but the wide expansion of Protestantism in England may have been a consequence, not a cause, of the Reformation.

This was of course the most important outcome of the English Reformation. But it also had economic and social consequences, which played their part in preparing for the Revolution of 1640–9. The most obvious effect of the Reformation in England was the weakening of the Church as an institution. At the dissolution of the monasteries landed property bringing in a net annual income of over £136,000, and bullion, plate, and other valuables worth possibly £1–1½ million, were taken away from the Church and handed over to laymen of the propertied class.[1] To convey the significance of these figures we may recall that royal revenue from land never exceeded £40,000 a year before 1543.[2]

The Church's loss of economic power brought with it a decline in political power. In Parliament, the removal of abbots from the House of Lords meant that the clerical vote there changed from an absolute majority to a minority. Bishops ceased to be great feudal potentates and sank to even greater dependence on the Crown. Convocation lost its legislative independence. With monastic property the Church lost to laymen the right of presentation to some two-fifths of the benefices of the kingdom: this was ultimately to have momentous consequences.[3] The Church also lost much of that vast system of patronage – jobs for laymen no less than for ecclesiastics – which a shrewd observer noted as one of the main sources of strength of the Roman Catholic Church on the continent at the end of the sixteenth century.[4] In addition, the Church lost over £40,000 a year in first-fruits and tenths,[5] and judicial profits (restraint of appeals to Rome). These sums had been drawn out of the kingdom, and so did not benefit the English hierarchy directly: but they added to the wealth, power, and prestige of the international Church, and helped to build up a fund from which the highest dignitaries even of the English Church did not fail to benefit. The transfer of this regular income to the Crown again increased its relative economic power whilst diminishing that of the Church.

This then is the second major economic consequence of the English Reformation: the transfer of wealth and economic influence from the Church to the Crown, and the consequent political subordination of the former. Henry VIII, and later William Cecil, recommended a Reformation to Scotland for precisely this reason.[6] Much of the confiscated property was handed away by the Crown, but little enough of it returned to ecclesiastics or ecclesiastical bodies. The various projects for utilizing parts of the spoil for charitable, educational, or

1 A. N. Savine, *English Monasteries on the Eve of the Dissolution*, p. 100. The valuation of 1535 probably understates the value of the lands.

2 F. C. Dietz, *English Government Finance, 1485–1558*, University of Illinois Studies in the Social Sciences, IX, No. 3, pp. 80–2, 138.

3 See below, pp. 36, 41, 244.

4 Sir Edwin Sandys, *Europae Speculum* (The Hague, 1629), pp. 53–5.

5 Dietz, *op. cit.*, p. 221.

6 Ed. M. St. Clare Byrne, *Letters of King Henry VIII*, pp. 288–9, 314–16; Sir J. E. Neale, *Elizabeth I and Her Parliaments, 1559–81*, p. 74.

religious purposes came to very little: of the 26 new bishoprics which it was at one time proposed to create, only six were in fact set up, and one of these failed to survive. The subordination of the Church to the Crown remained a fact, and its subordination to the inheritors of its wealth became a possibility.

Who were the inheritors? Here we must distinguish between long-term and short-term consequences. It is clear that, in the first instance, there was nothing revolutionary about the Reformation land transfers, in England as in Germany. It was a shift in the balance of property within the landed ruling class, a land-grabbing operation of which the immediate beneficiaries were those who were politically influential at the time of the dissolution. Two out of every three peers were granted, or bought, monastic estates: peers, courtiers, royal officials and servants between them account for over two-thirds of the initial recipients.[1] In the seventeenth century it was agreed that nearly all the then members of the peerage held monastic lands.[2]

This was no social revolution. Nevertheless, it marked rather more than a mere shift of landed property, and of all the power and prestige that went with it, from clerical big landowners to lay big landowners. For those who were influential at Henry VIII's Court included many 'new men', members of the lesser gentry who had devoted themselves to the royal service: and the Pilgrimage of Grace showed clearly enough that sections of the old aristocracy were out of sympathy with Henry's policy. The Reformation land settlement was part of a shift of power within the landed ruling class, from the great feudal families, with their centrifugal traditions, to the aspiring gentry and new men who were coming up into their places through royal favour. The dissolution of the monasteries takes its place beside the statute of liveries in reducing the social influence of the old aristocracy.

For a monastery was in many ways an asset to the family which had endowed it. It gave the lord and his household free board and lodging whenever he required it. If it held its land by knights' service, this brought in revenue in the form of feudal aids. The founder's heir expected to be consulted before an abbot was elected: this naturally brought financial advantages.[3] These, and other less precisely

1 See the table, compiled by Savine, printed in H. A. L. Fisher's *History of England, 1485–1547*, p. 497.

2 T. Fuller, *Church History of England* (1842), II, p. 138; Sir Henry Spelman, *History and Fate of Sacrilege* (1846), pp. 218–30.

3 G. Baskerville, *English Monks and the Dissolution of the Monasteries*, pp. 49–54, 229–30.

definable fruits of feudal dependence, were lost at the dissolution, when many of the purchasers became tenants in chief of the Crown. Lord Berkeley is said to have lost 80 knights' fees in this way, 'to the value of £10,000 within the compass of few years'.[1] It was one of the many blows which that ancient family suffered in the sixteenth century. Peers and gentlemen had held many of the lucrative official posts which were at the disposal of monasteries. Moreover the religious life had offered an easy and profitable career to younger sons of well-connected families, and nunneries what Milton ungallantly described as 'convenient stowage for their withered daughters'.[2] The dissolution set the aristocracy new problems in raising marriage portions and dowries, at a time when prices were rising on the matrimonial market. It may have stimulated that tendency to marriage between aristocratic and merchant families which becomes noticeable at about this time.

Sir Thomas Smith observed in Elizabeth's reign that 'suche younger brothers as were wonte to be thruste into Abbayes, there to live an idle life, sith that is taken from them muste now seeke some other place to live in'.[3] The loss of monastic jobs was not compensated for, in England, by the development of a standing army officered by the gentry. Hence the portionless younger son of good family becomes the familiar problem child of Elizabethan literature. Hence too the prominence of poor younger brothers in the more speculative types of overseas adventure, whether in Ireland or in the New World. In this way too the dissolution contributed indirectly to the growth of free enterprise.

The monasteries, Fuller tells us, were 'a great cause of the long continuance of the English nobility in such pomp and power, as having then no temptation to torture their tenants with racking of rents, to make provision for their younger children'.[4] It has often been suggested that the purchasers of monastic lands introduced a new commercial spirit into agriculture; but this general weakening of the position of the old landowners would, as Fuller suggests, have worked in the same direction. Monasteries had also offered a cheap way of pensioning off superannuated civil servants or dependants of founders'

1 Fuller, *op. cit.*, II, p. 235.
2 J. Milton, *Prose Works* (Bohn ed.), III, p. 80.
3 D. B. Quinn, 'Sir Thomas Smith (1513–77) and the beginnings of English Colonial Theory', in *Proceedings of the American Philosophical Society*, LXXXIX, 1952, p. 552.
4 Fuller, *op. cit.*, II, p. 189.

families, who after the dissolution had swept away such 'corrodies' became a burden on the family (or the parish).[1]

So for a section of the aristocracy the Reformation brought economic loss, though not for the class as a whole. We should be very careful not to see anything 'anti-feudal' in this process. Indeed, in a sense the dissolution led to an intensification of feudalism, since it multiplied tenures in chief. Before the Reformation it was mainly great landowners, ecclesiastical and lay, who held by knights' service. But the splitting up of monastic estates scattered what Spelman called 'the leprosy of this tenure' throughout the kingdom.[2] The Court of Wards had to be established to deal with the spate of new financial business coming in to the Crown. Heraldic Visitations took on a new significance from Henry VIII's reign, not only because of the increasing number of *parvenus* but also because the monasteries had hitherto acted as genealogical depositories.[3]

II

Yet the monarchy was not permanently strengthened by the Reformation. The ecclesiastical property which passed to it was soon dissipated. Henry VIII built a great fleet and fought wars in France out of the proceeds of the dissolution; Elizabeth sold nearly all the remaining monastic lands to pay for the Irish war at the end of her reign. So the lands found their way on to the market; and the tax-payers did not have to foot the whole bill for national defence. The men of property benefited both ways.

In the short run, then, the Reformation strengthened the position of the lay landed ruling class as a whole, though it weakened some of those members of it hitherto most powerful. Even where the immediate recipient of monastic lands passed them on by sale, he almost certainly made a handsome profit on the transaction. The position of the Crown was temporarily strengthened, not only by monastic estates but also by the steady revenue from first-fruits and tenths and by the accession of political strength through the royal supremacy. It looked as though a sound economic foundation had been laid for English absolutism. But

1 Savine, *op. cit.*, pp. 225–67; Baskerville, *op. cit.*, pp. 58–66, 136.
2 Spelman, *op. cit.*, p. 233.
3 A. L. Rowse, *The England of Elizabeth*, pp. 247–8; J. Hurstfield, 'The revival of feudalism in early Tudor England', in *History*, New Series, XXXVII, No. 130, pp. 137–8.

we speak in abstractions: 'Crown', 'royal supremacy'. Edward VI's reign shows us these terms translated into social reality. 'The Crown' retained its initiative during the minority of the King: the 'royal supremacy' was used to continue the plunder of the Church for the benefit of Court aristocrats. Under Mary 'the Crown' was unable to undo the economic consequences of the Reformation. The process continued under Elizabeth, on a smaller scale but for the same ends: 'the Crown' was a funnel through which the wealth of the Church (bishops' lands in Elizabeth's reign) was drained off into the pockets of courtiers.

There were limits to the process, but they were not imposed either by the greed of the aristocracy or the willingness of the Crown to satisfy it. They were imposed by quite a different consideration. The Church's wealth and prestige could not be reduced beyond a certain point without seriously impairing its effectiveness as a buttress of the social order. The attack on Church property had been accompanied by the abolition of confession, penance and sale of indulgences, and by destruction of altars, windows, statues, etc., all of which reduced popular respect for the more mysterious powers of the Church, its sacraments, and saints. The limits were very nearly reached in Edward VI's reign, and this led all those who opposed social revolution to support the Marian reaction. Elizabeth's ecclesiastical *via media* was not entirely voluntary: she was left with very restricted ground for manoeuvre. By the time that James succeeded her, a positive policy of protection and support for the Church was the order of the day: 'no bishops, no king, no nobility'.[1]

It is indeed one of the many paradoxes of the English Reformation that in temporarily solving the economic problems of the ruling class it gave a stimulus to ideas which were ultimately to overthrow the old order. The Church was permanently weakened. Such authority as it henceforth held it derived from the Crown: bishops and kings stood or fell together. The critical ideas put about to justify the dissolution of the monasteries reverberated on long after the monks were forgotten. Henry VIII allowed the Bible to be translated into English, and a century later the soldiers of the New Model Army marched into battle against his successor singing psalms. In the short run it was good diversionist tactics to blame the monks and friars for all the economic

1 This version of the royal epigram is reported by Bishop G. Goodman, *The Court of King James I* (1839), I, p. 421.

ills the poor suffered: but when monks and friars had been replaced by lay landlords and poverty remained, new questions began to be asked.[1]

In all spheres, if we extend our vision to the middle of the next century, the long-term outcome of the Reformation was the opposite of that intended by the Machiavellians who introduced it. Charles I's Secretary of State, the near-papist Windebanke, pointed out to the representative of the Pope in England the historical irony of the situation. 'Henry VIII committed such sacrilege by profaning so many ecclesiastical benefices in order to give their goods to those who, being so rewarded, might stand firmly for the king in the lower house; and now the king's greatest enemies are those who are enriched by these benefices. . . . O the great judgments of God!'[2] The overthrow of papal authority by Henry VIII thus looks forward to the civil war and the execution of Charles I. The royal supremacy yielded place to the sovereignty of Parliament, and that to demands for the sovereignty of the people. The plunder of the Church by the landed ruling class stimulated the development of capitalism in England. The attack on Church property by the rich led to a questioning of property rights in general.

III

In the first instance, then, the wealth of the monasteries passed to a narrow group. Most of the properties were resold, and by the end of the century had come into the possession of gentlemen or monied men from the towns. The dissolution caused no social revolution. The social revolution that *was* taking place arose independently. It was caused by the rise of capitalism, notably in the clothing and extractive industries, and in agriculture.

In all sorts of indirect ways the Reformation contributed to this development. The dissolution indeed had become possible because

---

1 See H. C. White, *Social Criticism in 16th Century Religious Literature*, Chapters 3–5. Sir Thomas More had anticipated this danger. He saw that every argument which Simon Fish used against the idleness and unproductiveness of monks and clergy in *The Supplication of Beggars* could be turned against lords, gentry, and property-owners in general, who also do not live by the labour of their hands. He tried to convince 'landed men' that if the Beggars' demands were met, Fish would soon find new reasons 'that shoulde please the peoples eares, wherewith he would labour to have lordes landes and all honest mens goodes to be pulled from them by force and distributed among beggers' (More, *A Supplication of Souls*, in *Works*, 1557, pp. 304–5).

2 S. R. Gardiner, *History of England, 1603–42* (1884), VIII, p. 137.

the monasteries were ceasing to fulfil functions recognized by the propertied classes as useful. Their days of primacy in agricultural production were over: for the most part they had become parasitic rentiers. Economic initiative passed to the local gentry, who at the dissolution often purchased estates which they were already farming.[1] The rich had ceased to endow new monasteries. The main interest of those stories of corruption and immorality in the abbeys which were used to justify the dissolution is not as evidence of fact but as evidence of what public opinion was prepared to believe.

The original recipient of monastic property, if he sold, would receive a windfall lump sum, which he might fritter away as income, but which alternatively he might invest in improved farming methods. Many middlemen, merchants and others, bought in order to re-sell, making a profit in the process.[2] The ultimate purchaser was by definition a monied man, and so possibly a man of enterprise and ability. In nine cases out of ten he no doubt bought for reasons of social prestige rather than to make profits. But he had to recover his purchase money: he was likely to be a man of business habits, who would at least look to his profit and loss account more closely than his monastic predecessors. In this whole process we are considering very early beginnings. For one William Stumpe who converted Malmesbury Abbey into a factory, there were no doubt scores of Eliots and Cromwells and Fairfaxes who turned abbeys into country houses: and the Corporation of Lynn was equally exceptional in transforming an impropriate church into a factory.[3] But the important thing for our purpose *is* the exception, the new tendency. Glastonbury Abbey became a worsted manufactory, Rotherham College a malt-house. At Grimsby a friary was turned into a storehouse. In London, glass factories were established at the Black, White, and Crutched Friars, a storehouse at Greyfriars and at the Priory of St. John of Jerusalem; New Abbey, East Smithfield, became a biscuit factory and storehouse; the Minories was converted into an armoury

1 Savine, *op. cit.*, p. 261; cf. R. H. Hilton, *The Economic Development of some Leicestershire Estates in the 14th and 15th centuries*, pp. 33, 79–82, 87–91, 140.

2 Dr. Willan noted in his *Muscovy Merchants of 1555* 'how many of the property transactions [of merchants who were members of the Company] involved former monastic and chantry lands and houses, not only in the countryside but in the towns as well' (p. 51). Contrast H. Habakkuk, 'The Market for Monastic Property, 1539–1603', *Econ. H.R., Second Series*, X, pp. 362–80.

3 G. D. Ramsay, *The Wiltshire Woollen Industry in the 16th and 17th Centuries*, pp. 31–3; Spelman, *op. cit.*, pp. 240–1.

and workhouses. Immigrants settled in vacated monastic sites: Stowe dated the expansion of the City's population from the expulsion of the monks.[1] The Marian exiles brought back new industrial techniques.[2]

Many monasteries had been enclosing landlords, but on balance their methods of estate management had been conservative. The properties of St. Albans Abbey, valued at £2,510 at the dissolution, were worth 80 times as much to the lay inheritors a century later.[3] There is undoubtedly a connection between the land transfers, the advent of new purchasers anxious to recoup themselves, and the extension of enclosure for sheep farming.[4] We need not idealize the abbeys as lenient landlords to admit some truth in contemporary allegations that the new purchasers shortened leases, racked rents, and evicted tenants. William Stumpe was one of the many who did this.[5] 'Do ye not know,' said John Palmer to a group of copyholders he was evicting, 'that the king's grace hath put down all houses of monks, friars and nuns, therefore now is the time come that we gentlemen will pull down the houses of such poor knaves as ye be?'[6] Whether the purchasers farmed the land themselves, or leased it out to a man prepared to pay a higher rent, is immaterial for our purpose: the new tendency was accelerated, at any rate in the south and east of England.

We may also note the families whose wealth was raised by coal or iron which had previously been in the possession of monasteries – the Herberts, Lowthers, Cliffords, Riddells, Lilburnes, Sidneys.[7] The purchasers stimulated development by bringing fresh minds and fresh capital into the coal fields. The transfer of ecclesiastical properties seems to have had a similar effect on the metallurgical and salt industries.[8] Many lesser families acquired small realizable windfalls in

1 H. Ellis, *Original Letters*, Third Series, III, p. 35; E. J. Davies, 'The Transformation of London', in *Tudor Studies*, edited by R. W. Seton-Watson, pp. 305–6; J. Stowe, *A Survey of London* (Everyman ed.), pp. 114–15, 285, 387; Baskerville, *op. cit.*, pp. 241–2.

2 C. H. Garrett, *The Marian Exiles*, p. 336.

3 J. Stevens, *An Historical Account of Taxes*, pp. 188–9, 216.

4 Savine, *op. cit.*, pp. 176–7.

5 Ramsay, *op. cit.*, p. 32. But cf. Baskerville, *op. cit.*, pp. 47–8; 'Even if the monks had wished to be easy landlords, the patron in his own financial interests saw to it that they were not.'

6 *Victoria County History of Sussex*, II, p. 190.

7 J. U. Nef, *The Rise of the British Coal Industry*, I, pp. 142–7; II, pp. 438–45; H. R. Trevor-Roper, 'The Bishopric of Durham and the Capitalist Reformation', in *Durham University Journal*, March 1946, p. 46.

8 J. U. Nef, *War and Human Progress*, p. 429.

the shape of building stone or lead from abbey buildings, or timber from abbey lands. A further stimulus to production came from the retention in England of sums hitherto exported to Rome, and the consequent expansion of government expenditure, notably on ship-building and armaments. Monasteries had acted as deposit banks: their place had now to be filled by more enterprising institutions. When the government sold former monastic lands it was again largely to finance expenditure on armaments.

The cumulative economic effects of the exactions of the pre-Reformation Church were pointed out by William Tyndale. Wills, tithes, fees, mortuaries; 'Then bead-rolls. Item chrysome, churchings, banns, weddings, offering at weddings, offering at buryings, offering to images, offering of wax and lights, which come to their vantage; besides the superstitious waste of wax in torches and tapers throughout the land. Then brotherhoods and pardoners. What get they also by confessions? ... Soul-masses, dirges, month-minds, year-minds, All-souls-day, and trentals. The mother church, and the high altar, must have somewhat in every testament. Offerings at priests' first masses. Item, no man is professed, of whatsoever religion [i.e. religious order] it be, but he must bring somewhat. The hallowing, or rather conjuring of churches, chapels, altars, super-altars. ... Then book, bell, candle-stick, organs, chalice, vestments, copes, altar-cloths, surplices, towels, basins, ewers, ship [incense-holder], censer, and all manner ornament, must be found for them freely; they will not give a mite thereunto. Last of all, what swarms of begging friars are there! The parson sheareth, the vicar shaveth, the priest polleth, the friar scrapeth, and the pardoner pareth; we lack but a butcher to pull off the skin. ... If the tenth part of such tyranny were given the king yearly, and laid up in the shire-towns, against the realm had need, what would it grow to in certain years?'[1]

The economic case against the Church and its courts could be illustrated from any number of contemporary sources. The abolition of indulgences, pilgrimages, friars, and of a number of fees, created at least the possibility that money spent on such forms of conspicuous waste might be devoted to productive purposes. 'If it were against the commandement of God, to have images in the Churches,' said a Spaniard in Mexico to his English captive in 1556, 'then he had spent a

---

1 W. Tyndale, *The Obedience of a Christian Man*, in *Doctrinal Treatises* (Parker Society, 1848), pp. 237–40.

great deale of money in vaine.'[1] After the Reformation, a much smaller proportion of the English national income than, say, the Spanish, was required to maintain ecclesiastics who were unproductive consumers. Although monks and nuns were pensioned, monastic servants were thrown upon the labour market and helped to keep wages down, to the advantage of industry.

The fact that Protestantism was a cheaper religion than Catholicism became a seventeenth-century commonplace. Saints' days hindered men 'from the necessary works of their callings', said Nicholas Bownde in 1608; 'which hath moved the Reformed Churches . . . to cut off many that were used in time of Popery'.[2] In 1624 James Howell contrasted Protestant England with Catholic Spain in this respect: in Spain, he calculated, days amounting to more than five months in the year were dedicated to some saint or other and kept festival: 'a religion that the London apprentices would like well.'[3] Colbert succeeded in reducing saints' days in France to 92 *per annum* in 1666:[4] so Howell's estimate was not so wildly out. A late seventeenth-century English economist calculated that every holiday lost £50,000 to the nation.[5] That was the new attitude with a vengeance.

We need not inquire how satisfactorily the monasteries had functioned as agencies of poor relief, nor ask what had happened to the impotent poor in the 8,000 odd parishes in which there had been no monastery. Individual hospitality on the grand scale was falling into disuse by the time of the dissolution.[6] In the north of England the abbeys may still have had their uses: some of the rebels of 1536 appear to have thought so. But monastic charity was unorganized and indiscriminate, and may well have stimulated vagabondage and idleness. The causes of poverty and vagrancy lay in the deeper social transformation we have been considering, of which the transfer of monastic lands was but a small contributory part. But the dissolution did remove one possible piece of machinery for coping with the problem of poor relief on the new scale required. In Ireland the great Earl of Cork was able to convert two friaries into houses of correction, 'in which the beggarly youth are taught trade'; and in seventeenth-

---

1 R. Hakluyt, *Principal Navigations* (Everyman ed.), VI, p. 257.
2 N. Bownde, *The Unbelief of St. Thomas* (1817), p. 8.
3 J. Howell, *Familiar Letters or Epistolae Ho-Elianae* (Temple Classics), I, p. 217.
4 P. B. Boissonade, *Colbert*, p. 274.
5 H. Pollexfen, *A Discourse of Trade and Coyn* (1697), p. 50.
6 Baskerville, *op. cit.*, pp. 34, 278.

century France Colbert had schemes for using religious foundations to employ the poor.[1] On the other hand the Protestant social conscience, and the Protestant respect for labour, produced a new attitude towards begging by regarding it as a social problem, and no longer as either a holy state or a divine necessity.[2] The act for dissolution of the monasteries provided for the maintenance by the purchasers of traditional hospitality. But the lands changed hands many times, and might be subdivided. As the economic and moral climate changed, the charitable obligations laid on the purchasers were disregarded, and the real burden of the dissolution was placed on the poorest classes. With monastic property the new owners usually acquired the right to collect tithes and to present ministers: by the end of the sixteenth century five out of every six benefices in the country were in lay patronage. At the manorial level, a *cuius regio eius religio* system was established in England. This ensured that those divisions inside the landed class which developed later in the sixteenth century would be reflected in the clergy: the Puritan ministers could never have formed the influential group they did had it not been for the support of lay patrons.

IV

Finally the Reformation created a vested interest in Protestantism. This was comparable in its effects, it has been suggested, to the foundation of the Bank of England a century and a half later.[3] When the elder Sir Richard Grenville told Thomas Cromwell that he would like to buy monastic lands, in order that in religious matters his heirs might be of the same mind for their own profit,[4] he was giving naïve expression to an important truth. 'Butter the rooks' nests', Sir Thomas Wyatt said to Henry VIII when the latter was worried about the dangers of revolution, 'and they will never trouble you'. The wisdom may have come after the event; but that was certainly the effect of the dispersal of the lands.[5] It was a Lancashire proverb that the Botelers of Bewsey

---

1 D. Townshend, *The Life and Letters of the Great Earl of Cork*, p. 193; C. W. Cole, *Colbert*, II, pp. 499–501. Colbert was an ex-Huguenot.

2 Baskerville, *op. cit.*, pp. 31–2, 133; cf. below, pp. 195–215.

3 R. H. Tawney, *The Agrarian Problem in the 16th Century*, p. 383.

4 Rowse, *Sir Richard Grenville*, p. 35.

5 D. Lloyd, *State-Worthies* (1766), I, p. 89; cf. Fuller, *op. cit.*, II, p. 250; T. Hobbes, *Behemoth*, in *Works*, VI, pp. 186–7.

were the only landowners in the county whose Protestantism was not economically determined by the possession of monastic estates.[1]

The vested interest so created proved too strong for Queen Mary. Yet her attempt at restoration of monastic lands, and the Pope's refusal to confirm her acceptance of the Reformation land settlement, left a deep sense of insecurity, and a terror of Popery, in all holders of church estates.[2] In 1563 the Speaker of the House of Commons told Elizabeth that Papists aimed at 'the destruction of goods, possessions, and bodies' no less than at 'thraldom of the souls' of Englishmen.[3] Stephen Gardiner and Mary had reversed Henry VIII's policy of neglecting the old nobility for 'new men'. Elizabeth laid herself open to Catholic taunts that she revived her father's policy in this respect.[4] But the families which Mary had restored were solidly Catholic: the rising of 1569 was led by the great feudal houses of the north and directed against the new men. Mary Queen of Scots succeeded to the leadership of this party: her victory, a Member of Parliament declared in 1572, would mean that all our lands will be lost, all our goods forfeit.[5] The Reformation, the official historian of the Long Parliament noted, also engaged Elizabeth 'in a new Interest of State, to side with the Protestants against those Potent Monarchs of the other Religion'.[6] Much against her will, she had to support Protestant rebels in France and the Netherlands against their legitimate sovereigns; the men of 1640 learnt much from Huguenot and Dutch political theory. In the sixteen-thirties Archbishop Laud explained Lord Saye and Sele's Puritanism solely by the fact that 'the most part of my Lord Sayes estate ... consisted in Church means'.[7] Laud was wrong about Saye and Sele's property, as it happened; but he was right about the tendency. Fear that Charles I was going to attempt in England the policy of resuming church lands which he had initiated in Scotland and Ireland caused many gentlemen to support Parliament.[8]

1 R. Halley, *Lancashire: its Puritanism and Nonconformity*, I, p. 57.

2 Cf. G. Burnet, *History of the Reformation* (1825), III, pp. 380–1. This volume was first published in 1681, a critical year for Protestantism.

3 Neale, *op. cit.*, p. 106; cf. p. 213.

4 Sir John Harington, *A Briefe View of the State of the Church of England* (1653), pp. 46, 59.

5 Neale, *op. cit.*, p. 266; cf. pp. 282–3.

6 T. May, *History of the Parliament* (1647), I, p. 2.

7 Ed. J. R. Magrath, *The Flemings in Oxford* (Oxford Historical Society, 1904), I, p. 348 (the Rev. Gerald Langbaine to Christopher Dudley, 18 April 1640).

8 See my *Economic Problems of the Church*, Chapter XIV.

In 1641 it was undoubtedly fear of Catholicism that deprived the King, at various critical moments, of his natural allies, the peers: and it is reasonable to suppose that the hostility of these great landowners to Popery was not exclusively theological.[1] In the Civil War the King would gladly have called in Irish, French, or Spanish help, but his advisers feared lest acceptance of large-scale Catholic aid should bring with it an English Edict of Restitution, for even some Catholics held monastic estates. Great landowners like the Marquis of Newcastle or the Earl of Derby, for all their social conservatism, were held to an uncompromising Protestantism by their former church property.

Thus across all the divisions of the English Civil War there remained this firm bond of economic interest linking the gentry on the two sides. It was strong enough to make Protestant Royalist landlords in Ireland accept the victory of the English Parliament rather than fight side by side with Irish Papists;[2] it was strong enough to promote the Royalist landslide of 1659–60 the moment the Peace of the Pyrenees had set Catholic France and Spain free to intervene, jointly or separately, on behalf of the exiled Stuarts. Charles II told the Pope in 1670 that many landowners were restrained from declaring themselves in favour of Catholicism solely by fears for their property.[3] The same anxiety was used as an argument against a Roman Catholic successor by the proponents of the Exclusion Bill. A century and a half after the dissolution, James II, in introducing his Declaration of Indulgence, felt obliged to say explicitly that he had no intention of following the grant of toleration to Catholics by an attempt to recover monastic lands. It was still a real political issue, and had been for the intervening 150 years.

We can capture something of the anxieties of the time from Andrew Marvell's *Account of the Growth of Popery and Arbitrary Government in England*, published in 1677. Marvell is explaining how the Protestant religion is interwoven with the secular interest of 'the people', a word

---

1 Gardiner, *op. cit.*, IX, pp. 264–5; X, pp. 97–8, 175.

2 Even among Irish Roman Catholics the Reformation caused a split. During the Civil War the big Irish Papist landlords in the last resort preferred to be subjects to a heretic king, whose heresy guaranteed them security of tenure of their secularized church properties. It was the smaller Irish Catholics who supported the Papal emissary, Rinuccini, even to the point of repudiating Charles I (T. L. Coonan, *The Irish Catholic Confederacy and the Puritan Revolution*, p. 257, and *passim*).

3 C. H. Hartmann, *Clifford of the Cabal*, pp. 162, 193, 321.

which he uses in the Harringtonian sense to signify what we should more accurately call 'the middle class'.

'The Lands that were formerly given to superstitious Uses, having first been applied to the publick Revenue, and afterwards by several Alienations and Contracts distributed into private possession, the alteration of Religion would necessarily introduce a change of Property. *Nullum tempus occurrit ecclesiae*, it would make a general Earth-quake over the Nation, and even now the Romish Clergy on the other side of the Water snuff up the savoury Odour of so many rich Abbies and Monasteries that belonged to their Predecessors. Hereby no considerable Estate in England but must have a piece torn out of it upon the Title of Piety, and the rest subject to be wholly forfeited upon the Account of Heresie. Another Chimney-Money of the old Peter-Pence must again be paid, as Tribute to the Pope, beside that which is established on His Majesty: and the People, instead of those moderate Tythes that are with too much difficulty paid to their Protestant Pastors, will be exposed to all the exactions of the Court of Rome, and a thousand Artifices by which in former times they were used to drain away the Wealth of ours more than any other Nation. So that in conclusion, there is no Englishman that hath a Soul, a Body, or an Estate to save, that Loves either God, his King or his Country, but is by all those Tenures bound, to the best of his Power and Knowledge, to maintain the Established Protestant Religion.'[1]

Party divisions were forgotten in 1688 as rapidly as they had been in 1660: for again liberty and property seemed to be at stake. After 1688 'the Protestant interest' and 'England' came to be used as interchangeable terms.[2]

In the sphere of ideas too the economic changes resulting from the Reformation acted as a dissolvent. Men learnt that church property was not sacrosanct, that traditional ecclesiastical institutions could disappear without the world coming to an end; that laymen could remodel not only the economic and political structures of the Church but also its doctrine – if they possessed political power. Protestant theology undermined the uniquely sacred character of the priest, and elevated the self-respect of his congregation. This helped men to question a divine right to tithes, the more so when tithes were paid to

---

1 In *State Tracts* (1693), p. 73.
2 E.g. in Daniel Defoe's *An Appeal to Honour and Justice* (1715). 'Though I was a whore', Roxana boasted with Nell Gwyn, 'yet I was a Protestant whore'.

lay impropriators. Preaching became more important than the sacra-ments; and so men came to wonder what right non-preaching ministers, or absentees, had to be paid by their congregations. It took a long time to follow out these new lines of thought to their logical conclusions; but ultimately they led men very far indeed. By spreading ideas of sectarian voluntarism they prepared the way for the Revolution of 1640, and trained its more radical leaders.

In that Revolution episcopacy was abolished, bishops' and cathedral lands confiscated, the payment of tithes challenged. The radicals rejected not only Henry VIII's episcopal hierarchy but the whole idea of a state church. 'O the great judgments of God!' Windebanke had exclaimed when contemplating the paradoxical outcome of the Henrician Reformation. Henry VIII had denied the supremacy of the Pope; he had confiscated church property; and he had allowed the Scriptures to be translated into English. These challenges to the authoritarianism, to the wealth and to the propaganda monopoly of the Church opened doors wider than was perhaps intended. A century later the authority first of King, then of Parliament, was challenged in the name of the people; the social justification of all private property was called in question; and speculation about the nature of the state and the rights of the people went to lengths which ultimately terrified the victorious Parliamentarians into recalling King, House of Lords, and bishops to help them to maintain law and order. By that date Windebanke had died in the exile to which the Revolution had condemned him, but not before he had openly proclaimed himself a Catholic. So he paid tribute to the superior wisdom of the Church which, Protestants said, believed that 'ignorance is the mother of devotion'.

THREE

The Norman Yoke

My Nation was subjected to your Lords.
It was the force of Conquest; force with force
Is well ejected when the Conquer'd can.

Milton, *Samson Agonistes*.

Oh, where is the justice of old?
  The spirit of Alfred the Great?
Ere the throne was debas'd by corruption and gold,
  When the people were one with the state?
'Tis gone with our freedom to vote. . . .

William Hick, 'The Presentation of the
National Petition',
The Northern Star, 5 June 1841.

I
Lost Rights

THEORIES of lost rights, of a primitive happy state, have existed in
nearly all communities. The Fall of Man; the Golden Age; Arcadia; the
Noble Savage – all these in their different ways express a belief that
inequality and the exploitation of man by man have a historical origin,
and a hope that the period of equality which survived in popular
imagination may one day be restored. In England the peasant rebels of
1381 asked

  'When Adam delved and Eve span
  Who was then the gentleman?'

A century and a quarter later Henry VII's minister listed among the
enemies of tranquillity a character called Arrogancy, who said to the
common people, 'Ye be the children and right inheritors to Adam, as

well as they [the gentry]. Why should they have these great honours, royal castles, and manors, with so much lands and possessions, and ye but poor cottages and tenements?'[1] This 'old seditious argument', as it appeared to a Royalist, was still being used in 1641: 'We are all the sons of Adam, borne free; some of them say, the Gospell hath made them free. And Law once subverted, it will appeare good equitie, to such Chancellours, to share the earth equally. They will plead Scripture for it, that we should all live by the sweat of our browes'.[2]

Ruling classes tried to utilize the myths. The Fall of Man not only testifies to the existence of a happier condition before the introduction of private property and the state, but also shows that man is too sinful ever to maintain such a condition on earth. Paradise can be regained only in heaven, and meanwhile sin justifies inequality and social subordination. 'If Paradise were to be replanted on earth', wrote a bishop in 1653, 'God had never expelled man [from] Paradise'.[3] The argument was frequently used against Levellers and any other reformers who wished to improve man's estate.

This dual use of the legend of the Fall reflects the fact that economic advance in primitive society was necessarily accompanied by social inequality. This is recognized in countless other legends. Everything Midas touched turned to gold: so he lost all that he most dearly loved, and starved amidst plenty. Prometheus, the great inventor, brought fire down from heaven to man: but he also caused the opening of Pandora's box, containing 'the pleasures and licentiousness which the cultivation and luxury of the arts of civil life introduce by the instrumental efficacy of fire'.[4] So economic advance ended the Golden Age, and Prometheus 'robbed us of that happiness which we may never again enjoy so long as we remain buried in sin and degraded in brutish desires'.[5] Yet, Bacon reminded his readers, Hope was placed at the bottom of Pandora's box; and the moral he drew was that men's 'fond opinion that they have already acquired enough is a principal reason why they have required so little'.[6] Greed was the cause and luxury the consequence of

---

1 Edmund Dudley, *The Tree of Commonwealth* (ed. D. M. Brodie, 1948), p. 99.
2 Sir Thomas Aston, Bart., *A Survey of Presbitery* (1641), Sig. 1, 4v.
3 Godfrey Goodman, *The Two Great Mysteries of Christian Religion* (1653), p. 90.
4 Francis Bacon, *The Wisdom of the Ancients*, XXVI.
5 John Milton, *Third Academic Exercise* (c. 1629), in *Correspondence and Academic Exercises* (ed. Tillyard, 1932), p. 67.
6 Bacon, *op. cit.*

progress; it was sin to eat of the tree of knowledge; sin left us incapable of any Paradise except after death, the wages of sin. Yet Hope lay at the bottom of the box; the unprivileged were continually asking, with Gerrard Winstanley, 'why may not we have our Heaven here (that is, a comfortable livelihood in the Earth) And Heaven hereafter too?'[1]

In the sixteenth and seventeenth centuries it was generally agreed that there had been a state of primitive communism which was also a Golden Age, and that both had ended when private property and political authority were introduced. The Fox in Spenser's *Mother Hubbard's Tale* brought together many of these legends when he grumbled that

> '– *Now a few have all, and all have nought,*
> *Yet all be brethren, ylike dearly bought:*
> *There is no right in this partition,*
> *Ne was it so by institution*
> *Ordained first, ne by the law of Nature*
> *But that she gave like blessing to each creture,*
> *As well of worldly livelode as of life,*
> *That there might be no difference nor strife,*
> *Nor ought cald mine or thine: thrice happie then*
> *Was the condition of mortall men.*
> *That was the golden age of Saturne old,*
> *But this might better be the world of gold;*
> *For without golde now nothing wilbe got.*'[2]

Cobbett in 1824 used arguments very like those of Spenser's Fox.[3]

'Certaine hellish verses', attributed to Sir Walter Ralegh, are similar in theme:

> '*Then war was not nor ritches was not knowne*
> *And no man said then this or that ys my owne. . . .*'
> [*After war was introduced*]
> '*Then first the sacred name of king begann*
> *And things that were as common as the day*
> *Did yeld themselves and lykewise did obey. . . .*
> *Then some sage man. . . .*
> *Knowing that lawes could not in quiet dwell*
> *Unless the[y] were observed, did first devyse*

---

1 Ed. G. H. Sabine, *The Works of Gerrard Winstanley*, p. 409.
2 *Works* (Globe edition), p. 514.
3 *Advice to Young Men* (Morley's Universal Library), pp. 269–70.

The name of god, religion, heaven and hell'
[and posthumous rewards and penalties]
'... to keepe the worlde in feare
And make them quietly the yoke to bere
So that religion of itself a fable'

was devised to protect property and the social order.[1]

Those lines were dated 1603. Ten years later, George Chapman wrote of the Golden Age in a masque:

'Mine, and Thine, were then unusde,
All things common: Nought abusde,
Farely earth her frutage bearing.[2]

Enclosures and marriage, declared Thomas Randolph in 1638, were both deplorable human inventions, post-dating the Golden Age:

'I'th' golden age no action could be found
For trespasse on my neighbours ground:
'Twas just with any Fayre to mixe our blood.[3]

One of the great revolutions of radical thought, secularizing Winstanley's demand for heaven on earth, was Thomas Spence's claim in 1783 that

'The Golden Age, so fam'd by Men of Yore,
Shall soon be counted fabulous no more....[4]

In 1814, after the experience of the French Revolution, Saint-Simon wrote: 'The Golden Age of humanity is not behind us; it lies ahead, in the perfection of the social order.'[5]

The long life of the legend of Arcadia, and of the pastoral tradition in poetry, also testify to the strength, and the dualism, of legends of an earlier, more equal society. There was communism in Arcadia: Time 'ruin'd our state by sending of us kings', with whom came ambition, cruelty, oppression.[6] For sixteenth-century poets Arcadia became a

1 *Calendar of the MSS. of the Marquis of Bath (H.M.C.)*, II, pp. 52–3.

2 G. Chapman, *Dramatic Works* (1873), III, p. 117.

3 T. Randolph, *Poems* (1929), pp. 128–9; cf. Donne, Elegie XVIII.

4 Olive D. Rankin, *Thomas Spence and his Connections*, p. 63.

5 Saint-Simon, 'De la réorganization de la société européenne', in *Oeuvres de Saint-Simon et d'Enfantin*, XV, pp. 247–8.

6 John Chalkhill, *Thealma and Clearchus* (*c.* 1600?), in *The Caroline Poets* (ed. Saintsbury), II, pp. 382–4.

highly sophisticated escapist never-never land, inhabited by aristocratic shepherds and shepherdesses.[1] Nevertheless the emphasis
remained always on primitive simplicity, on real human relations
untramelled by property. Pastoral poetry was used to convey the purest
and simplest personal feelings, or to criticize the corruptions of an
over-sophisticated society, as in Spenser's *Shepherd's Calendar*,
Wither's *Philarete*, Browne's *Britannia's Pastorals*, or Milton's *Lycidas*.

Men had been suddenly reminded of the reality of primitive
egalitarian societies by the discovery of America: and travellers' tales of
'noble savages' stimulated thought about the origins of property and
society. More's *Utopia* was just such a traveller's story. It has been
suggested that John Ponet was inspired by Peter Martyr's *Decades of the
New World* to become 'the first to envisage a political philosophy based
on the noble savage' as well as one of the first English Protestants to
advocate resistance to monarchs on religious grounds.[2] Montaigne, the
greatest sixteenth-century primitivist, believed that 'the care to
increase in wisdom and knowledge was the first overthrow of mankind'.
In his essay 'On Cannibals', with his eye on the New World, he pointed
out that the use of metals, improved agriculture and trade, and the rise
of the arts and sciences, have been accompanied by the end of
communal ownership, by the differentiation of rich and poor, and by
economic and political subjection.[3] Montaigne's *Essays* were carefully
studied by the Leveller William Walwyn.

Here we are reminded of our theme, for Marchamont Nedham in
1650 and *An Historical Essay on the English Constitution* in 1771 both
observed that, in the words of the last named, 'this Saxon model of
government, when reduced to its first principles, has a strong
resemblance to the natural state of things, under which mankind was
found to live at the discovery of the New World by Columbus'.[4] Many
anthropologists have confirmed this resemblance, and extended the

---

1 C. S. Lewis, *English Literature in the Sixteenth Century, excluding Drama*, p. 334.
Sidney's *Arcadia* (1590) contains a grim reminder of the social realities: for the pastoral
existence of his ruling-class heroes and heroines is in continual danger from the
irruption of *real* peasants, with very different manners. *Arcadia*, appropriately enough,
was composed in a park made by enclosing a whole village and evicting the occupants
(Tawney, *The Agrarian Problem in the 16th century*, p. 194).

2 C. H. Garret, *The Marian Exiles*, p. 257. Ponet's *Short Treatise of Politike Power*
(1556) was reprinted in 1639 and 1642.

3 *Essays* (trans. Florio), World's Classics, I, p. 222; II, pp. 222–3.

4 P. 31; cf. Nedham, *The Case of the Common-wealth of England Stated*, pp. 83–4. For
the *Historical Essay* see pp. 86–7 below.

parallel to the Jews of the Pentateuch, and (as Hobbes did in the seventeenth century) to the Homeric Greeks. 'Back to the Golden Age', 'back to the free Anglo-Saxons', 'back to the Old Testament', 'back to the Noble Savage' are so many different expressions of the same demand: return to an earlier, more equal form of organization, before the development of private property and the state. 'No man', said Hobbes, 'can have in his mind a conception of the future, for the future is not yet. But of our conceptions of the past, we make a future'.[1]

The tradition of lost rights, and the hope of recovering them, has been expressed in many other ways. The most universal is the Sleeping Hero: the leader who has not really died, but will return one day to rescue his people. Often the Hero was associated with final unsuccessful resistance to foreign conquest. The memory of Arthur, sleeping in Avalon, and the conviction of his second coming were firmly held by Britons and Welsh seven centuries after Arthur had died fighting the Anglo-Saxon invaders. Harold was believed to have survived the Battle of Hastings, and his return to lead the fight against the Normans was long expected. Similar legends attached to the last leaders of Armenian resistance to Arab conquest in the seventh century, of Serbian and Montenegrin resistance to Turkish conquest in the fourteenth, to James IV after Flodden, and to Sebastian of Portugal, whose death in 1578 was followed by Spanish conquest of the kingdom.

There are stories of heroes sleeping in caves in Irish, Scottish, Welsh, Manx, Italian, Czech, German, Danish, and Swiss mythology. Similar legends, not so directly related to foreign conquest, were told of Charlemagne, Baldwin, Latin Emperor of the East, Frederick Barbarossa and Frederick II, Wenceslas, Mahomet Mahadim (grandson of Mahomet's successor, Ali) whom the Persians expected, Quetzalcoatl of Mexico, Stenka Razin.[2] Often these tales suggest that economic advance has been purchased at the cost of exploitation and suffering, in a way that reminds us of the legend of Prometheus: for the Sleeping Hero guards a treasure, which may turn to rubbish if it is sought with motives of greed. But one day it will be restored to the people.

In England, significantly enough, the last Sleeping Hero was the Duke of Monmouth, leader of the last armed revolt of the common

---

1 Hobbes, *Behemoth* (1679), in *Works*, VI, p. 259; *The Elements of Law*, p. 11. Cf. Morgan, *Ancient Society* (Bharati Library), pp. 85–96, 122.
2 For other examples see P. Worsley, *The Trumpet Shall Sound*, pp. 130, 134, 236.

people. The most widely influential of all such stories, influential both for hope and for passive waiting, were those which received canonization as official religions: especially that of Jesus of Nazareth, who will come again to build the New Jerusalem.

But official canonization could not remove the double edge from these myths. In times of crisis men would ask themselves 'Why wait? Why not begin preparing for the second coming now?' The economic crisis of the sixteenth and early seventeenth centuries bred Fifth Monarchism, a form of revolutionary anarchism. All existing institutions must be destroyed, so that there will be no obstacles to the reign of King Jesus. The four monarchies in *Daniel* were identified with Babylonia, Persia, Greece, and Rome: the Reformation, by overthrowing 'the ghost of the deceased Roman Empire, sitting crowned upon the grave thereof', stimulated prophecies that the Fifth Monarchy was at hand.[1] In the English Revolution Fifth Monarchist ideas mingled curiously with those of the Norman Yoke. John Rogers in 1654 wrote a pamphlet demanding 'new laws and the people's liberties from the Norman and Babylonian yokes, making discovery of the present ungodly laws and lawyers of the Fourth Monarchy and the approach of the Fifth'.[2]

II
Coke: The Law and Liberty

The theory of the Norman Yoke, as we find it from the seventeenth century onwards, took many forms; but in its main outlines it ran as follows: Before 1066 the Anglo-Saxon inhabitants of this country lived as free and equal citizens, governing themselves through representative institutions. The Norman Conquest deprived them of this liberty, and established the tyranny of an alien King and landlords. But the people did not forget the rights they had lost. They fought continuously to recover them, with varying success. Concessions (Magna Carta, for instance) were from time to time extorted from their rulers, and always the tradition of lost Anglo-Saxon freedom was a stimulus to ever more insistent demands upon the successors of the Norman usurpers.

1 See pp. 290–4 below.
2 J. Rogers, *Sagrir*, title-page, in E. Rogers, *Some Account of the Life and Opinions of a Fifth Monarchy-Man* (1867), p. 76; cf. the identification on p. 95 of the little horn of the Fourth Beast with William the Conqueror and his Norman successors, cut off for ever by the execution of Charles I in 1649.

Such was the theory. As a historical account of the Norman Conquest and subsequent history it leaves something to be desired. Anglo-Saxon society was already deeply divided into classes before William the Bastard set foot in England: and it was hardly the common people who won and profited by Magna Carta. But as a rudimentary class theory of politics, the myth had great historical significance. It was entirely secular, whereas most popular opposition theories before the seventeenth century had been religious.[1] It united the Third Estate against Crown, Church, and landlords, branding them as hereditary enemies of the people. It suggested that the ruling class is alien to the interests of the majority of the population. Even if they no longer speak French, whether or not they are of Norman descent, the upper classes are isolated from the life of the working population, to whose interests theirs are opposed. The people could conduct its own affairs better without its Norman rulers, whose wealth and privileges are an obstacle to equality. The nation is the people.

Some theory of this sort may well have had a continuous history since 1066, though it is not within the scope of this essay to discuss the Middle Ages. Less than fifty years after the Conquest, Henry I attempted to win support by confirming what were inaccurately called 'the Laws of St. Edward the Confessor'; and they helped to build up the mythology of a golden Saxon past which played its part in the struggles that won Magna Carta. The *Modus Tenendi Parliamentum*, a fourteenth-century document, purported to describe the method of holding Parliaments under the last Saxon King, as an example to be followed. Edward the Confessor was a very popular saint, so that any tradition attached to his name had a powerful emotional appeal, especially for the uneducated. There is evidence too of folk-memories of Alfred as a symbol of national independence, and as a model of valour, caution, and patience.[2]

In the seventeenth century men discovered the theory in *The Mirror of Justices*, a treatise probably written at the end of the thirteenth century by Andrew Horn, an opposition London fishmonger, later chamberlain of the City of London. It contains in fact very little about the Norman Yoke. Its aim was to emphasize the sanctity of law, against

1 There was originally an appeal to the popular cult of saint-kings in the demand for a restoration of the laws of St. Edward.

2 R. W. Chambers, *Man's Unconquerable Mind*, p. 92. Proverbs, those summaries of peasant wisdom, tended to be fathered upon Alfred. See for instance *The Owl and the Nightingale*, an English poem written about the time of Magna Carta.

false judges and even against the King. The law went back to 'the coming of the English'. Alfred had 44 unjust judges executed in one year. The laws should be in writing so that all could know them. Parliament should be held twice yearly. The treatise had what Maitland called 'curious leanings towards liberty and equality', and was strongly anti-clerical: one can see why it appealed to the seventeenth-century revolutionaries.[1] Ironically enough, in view of the later propagandist use to which it was put, *The Mirror* was written in French. Few Englishmen would be able to read, and those few would have learned the language of their conquerors. 'Jack would be a gentleman – if he could speak French' ran the proverb.[2] The *Modus Tenendi Parliamentum* was published under Parliamentary authority in 1641. *The Mirror* followed in 1642, with an English translation in 1646: so both works helped to form the thought of the Parliamentarians.

Both *The Mirror* and the *Modus* are examples of what Professor Galbraith has perceptively called 'the underworld of largely-unrecorded thinking'.[3] Opposition to the Norman Yoke was likely to be strongest in the illiterate: so the absence of evidence for the theory before the sixteenth century does not prove that it had no continuous existence. But it has been argued that the legend of a free Anglo-Saxon past arose as part of the mode of thought of an *urban* class which felt itself oppressed by feudal lords; such men became conscious of national unity as the market developed from the fourteenth century onwards. They projected their aspirations backwards, together with their dislike of those social superiors who prevented the realization of these aspirations in the present and therefore, it was assumed, had done so in the past.[4]

It is certainly true that, with the rise of an educated laity, aided by one of its most remarkable inventions, the printing press, our evidence for the theory increases. Sir John Fortescue, who has been described as 'the fifteenth-century English advocate of the middle class',[5] stressed

1 *The Mirror of Justices*, ed. W. J. Whittaker, with an introduction by F. W. Maitland (Selden Society, 1895).

2 J. Strype, *Life of Sir Thomas Smith* (1820), p. 232. We should not forget this fact in assessing *The Mirror*'s demand for the laws to be in writing.

3 'The *Modus Tenendi Parliamentum*', in *Journal of the Warburg and Courtauld Institutes*, XVI, p. 94.

4 P. Meier, 'Réflexions sur la langue anglaise', in *La Pensée*, No. 53, 1954, pp. 75–91.

5 R. B. Schlatter, *Private Property*, p. 72.

the continuity of English law in the same way as the London merchant who wrote *The Mirror*.[1] But a new note enters with Thomas Starkey's *Dialogue between Pole and Lupset*, written in the fifteen-thirties. Here Pole was made to urge the shaking off of the 'tyrannical customs and unreasonable bonds' imposed by the Conqueror 'when he subdued our country and nation'. 'This bondage' was 'unreasonable among civil people purposing to live in a just policy.' The argument was directed specifically against the feudal burdens of wardship and marriage. But Lupset later complained that the common law was written, disputed, and taught in French, which was a 'dishonour to our nation', witnessing 'our subjection to the Normans'. Pole called for a reception of Roman civil law, to wipe away 'the great shame to our nation . . . to be governed by the laws given to us of such a barbarous nation as the Normans be'.[2] The patriotic appeal was always a strong feature of the Norman Yoke theory.

We already have sharply opposed theories. One stressed the unbroken continuity of common law, which had carried Anglo-Saxon liberties into post-conquest England: the other, coming from the group of radical intellectuals around Thomas Cromwell in the revolutionary years of the Reformation, attacked the whole existing law as an alien imposition. Common to both versions was the conception of free Anglo-Saxon institutions. As the Reformation progressed, men like John Foxe, Archbishops Parker and Ussher looked back to Anglo-Saxon times for the pure primitive church, thus greatly stimulating Anglo-Saxon studies. For ecclesiastical corruption could be dated from the invasion of 1066, which the Pope had blessed.

Revival of interest in the Saxons was combined with an attack on the Arthurian legend. In its origins, as I have suggested, this was also one of the backward-looking myths embodying popular memories of lost rights. But in mediaeval England it had been taken up by the ruling class, and Arthur became the symbol of 'chivalry'. He was also much used in propaganda for the Welsh-sprung Tudor dynasty, and for James I after them: for the Stuarts claimed descent from Arthur through the Scottish line as well as through the Tudors.[3] The debunking of the legends associated with Arthur's name thus played its

1 *De Laudibus Legum Angliae*, Chapter 17.

2 Ed. K. M. Burton (1948), pp. 110–11, 117, 175. *The Dialogue* was a literary work: it does not necessarily represent the views of the spokesmen, though it probably is not far from them. Cf. John Rastell, *An Abridgement of the Statutes* (1527), Proheme.

3 R. F. Brinkley, *Arthurian Legend in the 17th century*, Chapter 1.

part in the growth of anti-absolutist sentiment in England. The work of demolition was done by Camden, Verstegan, Speed, Daniel, Selden. These antiquarians, together with Nowell, Lambarde, Harrison, Holinshed, and Hayward, were also sponsors of the free Anglo-Saxons. Most of them belonged to the Society of Antiquaries, founded about 1580, which had close associations with the Parliamentary opposition. Papers read before the Society early in James I's reign argued that the Anglo-Saxons had held popularly-elected Parliaments; and the Society did much to elaborate and popularize the doctrine of continuity. It is hardly surprising that it fell under royal disapproval and ceased to meet. The discrediting of the royal Arthurian legend, and its replacement by that of free Anglo-Saxon institutions, was thus of direct importance in the battle of ideas which preceded the Civil War.[1]

In 1581 the House of Commons imprisoned Arthur Hall for denying the immemorial antiquity of their House. But more than one constitutional conclusion could be drawn from Anglo-Saxon freedom. The opposition urged struggle to recover lost rights: the Rev. Dr. Blackwood, in his *Apologia pro Regibus* (1581), argued that William's power after the Conquest was absolute, and that any right which his conquered subjects retained in their property thereafter was by his grace. Blackwood compared the position of the American Indians after the Spanish conquest.[2] James I, before he came to the English throne, had claimed that Kings of England were absolute owners of all property in the realm. For the 'Bastard of Normandy', he declared in *The Trew Law of Free Monarchies*, 'set down the strangers his followers in many of the old possessors' rooms, as at this day well appeareth, a great part of the gentlemen of England being come of the Norman blood, and their old laws, which to this day they are ruled by, are written in his language, and not in theirs: and yet his successors have with great happiness enjoyed the crown to this day'.[3] 'The ancient laws of England', said Francis Bacon in 1596, were 'planted here by the

1 *Ibid.*, esp. Chapters 2 and 3; and T. D. Kendrick, *British Antiquity*, Chapter 6 *passim.*

2 *Opera Omnia* (1644), pp. 42–3. Blackwood was attacking George Buchanan's *De Jure Regni Apud Scotos.* Blackwood's treatise did not attract much attention until 1607, when it was quoted in Cowell's *Interpreter* and reprinted as anti-Parliamentarian propaganda.

3 *The Political Works of James I* (ed. C. H. McIlwain, 1918), pp. 61–3. James's argument was put forward in 1642 in the Royalist H. Ferne's *A Reply unto severall Treatises pleading for the Armes now taken up by Subjects*, p. 26.

Conqueror'. 'The Conqueror got by right of conquest all the land of the realm into his own hands', and redistributed it on his own terms.[1] The Conqueror's successors 'did ever hold' the crown by the title of conquest, Godfrey Goodman agreed. The Bishop, however, added, possibly with the wisdom that came with the abolition of episcopacy, that 'the greatest part of the English were descended from Normans, and in that right they might claim a liberty, that the Conquest is expired, and now they are to be governed by just laws'.[2]

The saintly but conservative Nicholas Ferrar accepted King James's version of the theory. Conquest by pious Normans had had a valuable disciplinary effect upon the dissolute Anglo-Saxons: indeed 'the enforcement of this example were most necessary perhaps for the present age, on which the inheritance of this debauched humour of our ancestors is evidently fallen, and like a snowball much increased perhaps in the descent'.[3] A far more important figure, Archbishop Laud, saw the appeal to the Saxon past as a stimulus to rebellion. Immediately after the Conquest, he thought, 'the Normans and French, which made spoil of the English, would endure no law but the will of the Conqueror'. They 'could not endure to hear of St. Edward's laws, though the subjects of England had as much freedom by them as any in Europe. . . . But after a descent or two . . . they became English', and by the time of Magna Carta the barons were appealing to the laws of Edward to protect their property against arbitrary taxation. 'So the Great Charter had an obscure birth from usurpation, and was fostered and shewed to the world by rebellion.'[4]

In Blackwood, James, Bacon, Goodman, and Laud we note the

---

1 Bacon, *Works* (1826), IV, pp. 82, 101–4. Bacon seems to have changed his mind under James I: in 1608 he wrote that 'the ancient laws and customs of this kingdom' were 'practised long before the Conquest' (*ibid.*, p. 309).

2 Goodman, *The Court of King James I*, I, p. 190.

3 *Ferrar Papers* (ed. B. Blackstone, 1938), pp. 181–2.

4 Laud, *Works*, VII, pp. 627–8. Mr. Pocock (*The Ancient Constitution and the Feudal Law*, pp. 54–5, 149–51) thinks that I exaggerate the extent to which the theory of absolutism based on conquest was used by the Royalists. He may be right: it is indeed difficult to find more than scattered pieces of written evidence for it. But why did the Parliamentarians find it necessary so regularly and consistently to attack a view which nobody held? See, for instance, Mason's contribution to the debate on the Petition of Right (Rushworth, *Historical Collections*, 1721, I, pp. 565–8). It was a discussion on the conquest theory that started Nathaniel Bacon on the researches that led to his *Historicall Discourse of the Uniformity of the Government of England* (see p. 66 below). I suspect that the conquest theory must have been prevalent at a rather low level of argument, perhaps in the sort of sermons that did not get into print.

supreme importance of the property question in these legal arguments.
If the King owed his title to conquest, and consequently owned all the
property in the realm, then he also had a right to arbitrary taxation. But
if the sanctity of property and representative institutions were part of
our inheritance, then we must struggle to preserve them. History was
politics. Liberty, property, and patriotism were inseparable. Elsewhere
similar causes produced similar results. The Bohemian Taborites
looked back to a Golden Age before Germans and towns had appeared;
in the Rhineland the early sixteenth-century *Book of a Hundred
Chapters* contrasted the communal life of the earliest Germans with
usurious ways introduced by the wicked Romans.[1] In France,
Hotman's *Franco-Gallia* (1573) urged a return to the ancient free
constitution as it had existed before the Roman conquest and in the
first generations of Frankish rule. In Sweden the cult of the Goths
fostered national consciousness.

John Selden and Sir Robert Cotton, both members of the Society of
Antiquaries, put their great learning at the disposal of the Parliamentary opposition, even after the Society had been suppressed.
Selden had to retract his *History of Tithes* (1618), in which he had
rejected the view that the Norman Conquest had brought a decisive
break in legal continuity.[2] In 1630 Cotton's famous library was
searched, not for the first time. Now, however, the government
decided that its manuscripts were too dangerous to leave in private
hands: henceforth Sir Robert could consult them only under official
surveillance. Cotton thought William the Conqueror left the Saxons 'in
no better condition than villeinage' and that 'he moulded their customs
to the manner of his own country, and forebore to grant the laws of the
holy Edward, so often called for'.[3] Another member of the Society, Sir
Henry Spelman, who founded a lectureship at Cambridge for the study
of Saxon antiquities, attacked the servitudes and incidents of feudal
tenures, introduced at the Conquest, as a stigma of bondage.[4] In 1646,
having won the Civil War, Parliament abolished them.

Before 1640 antiquarian studies were dangerous. In 1627 the
Dutchman Isaac Dorislaus was deprived of his newly-established

1 N. Cohn, *The Pursuit of the Millennium*, p. 227.

2 Selden, *Works* (1724), III, Part ii, p. 1333; see also his *Janus Anglorum* and
England's Epinomis (1610), and *Analecton Anglo-Britannicon* (1615).

3 *Cottoni Posthuma* (1679), p. 20. Note that Edward is still 'holy'.

4 *English Works* (1727), II, esp. pp. 40–6. Cf. Starkey, p. 55 above. For Spelman,
see Pocock, *op. cit.*, Chap. V *passim*. For feudal tenures see pp. 173–4 below.

history lectureship at Cambridge after the first lecture. For it had been on Tacitus, that favourite authority on Germanic liberties; and in it he had 'placed the right of monarchy in the people's voluntary submission', and had spoken in praise of the Dutch rebels against Spain.[1] A chasm was also opening between government and common lawyers. In the fifteen-nineties Spenser, like Bacon, echoed Starkey: the common law was 'that which William of Normandy brought in with his conquest, and laid upon the neck of England'.[2] Starkey had advocated the reception of Roman law. That was of a piece with the support which the men of property gave to the early Tudor monarchy and its prerogative courts. But as economic life grew more complex, the law itself was re-interpreted. Especially under the influence of Sir Edward Coke it was 'liberalized', adapted to the needs of an increasingly capitalist society.[3] Simultaneously the government, under attack from Parliaments representing landlords and merchants, began more and more to depend on the prerogative courts and the Church as instruments of its rule, to dispense with Parliaments and to over-ride the common law.

The theologians made their contribution as well as the antiquarians and lawyers. William Perkins, the great Puritan, had anticipated Dorislaus's view of the Conquest. William, Perkins thought, came in as an usurper and tyrant: his rule became lawful only because the people willingly submitted to him and because he was content 'to rule them by good and wholesome lawes'.[4] Perkins was much read in opposition circles.

So there were many converging reasons why Coke, by reviving Fortescue's doctrine of the continuity of English law and representative institutions, in a quite different social context, became the hero of the Parliamentarian opposition. Security of property depended on common law: 'the ancient and excellent laws of England are the birthright and the most ancient and best inheritance that the subjects of

1 Dorislaus was later assassinated by Royalists whilst in the diplomatic service of the English Republic.

2 Spenser, *A View of the Present State of Ireland*, in *Works* (Globe edition), p. 610.

3 D. O. Wagner, 'Coke and the rise of economic liberalism', *Econ. H.R.*, VI, pp. 30–44.

4 Perkins, *Works* (1609–13), I, p. 762. It was perhaps significant that Richard Harvey, who defended the historicity of the eponymous Brutus against the scepticism of the Presbyterian monarchomach Buchanan, attacked the Anglo-Saxons and Martin Marprelate with equal enthusiasm (see his *Philadelphos*, 1593, pp. 1–13, 97).

this realm have; for by them he enjoyeth not only his inheritance and goods in peace and quietness, but his liberty and his most dear country in safety.' Liberty, property, and patriotism: it has rarely been more succinctly put. Royalist theories of absolutism based on conquest threatened this inheritance. 'We would derive from the Conqueror as little as we could', was Coke's terse reply. 'The Grounds of our Common Laws', he told the House of Commons in 1621, 'were beyond the Memory or Register of any Beginning, and the same which the Norman Conqueror found within the Realm of England'.[1] Twenty-eight years earlier, as Speaker, Coke had told Elizabeth that a bi-cameral Parliament, including representatives of shires and boroughs, dated from Anglo-Saxon times.[2] The Norman Conquest had cut across the true tradition of development. Englishmen had been struggling ever since to recover the old freedom. Coke would have agreed with a member of the Middle Temple who said it was the object of Magna Carta to restore the ancient laws and customs, especially those of St. Edward.[3] Coke popularized *The Mirror of Justices*, which had been transcribed by a member of the Society of Antiquaries, and had long circulated in manuscript. He quoted it in the House of Commons in 1621.[4]

Charles I objected to Coke's history as much as his father had done to the Society of Antiquaries'. A defence of Anglo-Saxon liberties was also a defence of property against the state, against arbitrary taxation. The Parliamentary franchise itself was a property right: so the demand for the old constitution, for the supremacy of Parliament, was in effect a demand for a transfer of political power to the class which was now economically predominant. Charles would not allow the later parts of Coke's *Institutes* to be published, and they remained suppressed until the Long Parliament ordered the *Second Part* to be printed in 1641. Coke's interpretation of the law triumphed with Parliament's victory in the Civil War.

---

1 *Reports*, Part V, p. iii; *Third Part of the Institutes*, Proeme; Preface to *Reports*, Part VIII.

2 D'Ewes, *A Compleat Journal of the Votes, Speeches and Debates, both of the House of Lords and the House of Commons throughout the whole reign of Queen Elizabeth* (1693), p. 465.

3 Quoted in Faith Thompson, *Magna Carta: its rôle in the making of the English Constitution, 1300–1629*, p. 194.

4 Ed. Notestein, Relf and Simpson, *Commons Debates, 1621*, II, pp. 197, 211; IV, p. 136; V, pp. 36, 281; VI, pp. 39, 214.

The most famous statement of this interpretation was made by Pym in 1628, in the debate on the Petition of Right:

> 'There are plain footsteps of those Laws in the Government of the Saxons. They were of that vigour and force as to overlive the Conquest; nay, to give bounds and limits to the Conqueror. . . . It is true, they have been often broken, [but] they have been often confirmed by Charters of Kings, by Acts of Parliaments. But the Petitions of the Subjects, upon which those Charters and Acts were founded, were ever Petitions of Right, demanding their ancient and due Liberties, not suing for any new.'

The reference to the Petition of Right makes the political application direct and obvious. In the same debate Sir Dudley Digges emphasized that 'this so antient Common Law of England' was essential to the sanctity of property.[1] In 1642 Pym appealed to 'that contract which [William the Conqueror] made with this nation, upon his admittance to the Kingdome'.[2] When Civil War broke out appeals to the Saxon past became common form among Parliamentarian pamphleteers.

III
The Law versus Liberty

By the seventeenth century, then, paradoxically, those who believed that English institutions originated in the violence of the Norman Conquest were the conservatives: believers in the continuity of those institutions were revolutionaries. We must recall the general historical context. Representative institutions were everywhere in Europe (except in the revolutionary Netherlands) being suppressed. Catholic Spain was before 1640, and Catholic France after 1660, the model absolute monarchy. Charles I's court circle was as pro-Spanish as Charles II's was to be pro-French: and both were suspected of leanings towards Popery. So English patriotism, Protestantism, and the defence of representative institutions all seemed closely linked. The association of the enemies of all three with William the Bastard, the French conqueror blessed by the Pope, was good psychological warfare. It had also a certain historical logic. The Norman Yoke theory appealed to all

---

1 Rushworth, *op. cit.*, I, pp. 596, 527–8.
2 *A Declaration of the Grievances of the Kingdome, delivered in Parliament by John Pym*, in *Somers Tracts* (1750), VI, p. 161.

the under-privileged, in the first instance to the merchants and gentry who felt their property endangered by arbitrary government, arbitrary taxation, and the enforcement of feudal payments.

But the Norman Yoke theory also stirred far profounder feelings of English patriotism and English Protestantism. Herein lay its strength. Men fought for the liberties of *England*, for the birthrights of *Englishmen*. The monarchy, wrote Mrs. Hutchinson, was founded by the Norman usurper 'in the people's blood, in which it hath swum about five hundred years'.[1] Another republican, Sir Henry Vane, believed that the government which rose with the Norman Conquest was not founded on the public interest but on 'the private lust and will of the conqueror'. William and his successors 'lay as bars and impediments to the true national interest'. This was the cause ('upon a civil account') of the Civil War.[2] Yet for these Independent Grandees the enemy was only the monarchy. Mrs. Hutchinson, no less than Archbishop Laud, believed that after the Conquest, Normans and Saxons soon became one people. This people, she felt with Milton, had been specially favoured by God, who therefore deserved 'a greater return of duty from us than any other people in the world'.[3] So the patriotic theory of the Norman Yoke reinforced ('upon a civil account') the Puritan sense of destiny, so powerful in stimulating fighting confidence.

Nevertheless, there was here a great ambiguity. When Coke and Pym, Mrs. Hutchinson and Vane, spoke of the liberties of England, they were thinking, in the first instance, of the rights of the propertied. But the theory could be put to other uses. Defending the yeomanry, 'the ancient glory of England' against enclosure, Francis Trigge argued in 1604 that William the Conqueror had given common rights and other liberties to the rank and file of his army: so lords of manors had no right arbitrarily to take away what they had not given. 'Inclosers take upon them, as though they were not Lords of Mannours, but rather Kings, and doe make, as it were, a new Commonwealth and a new forme of governement'.[4] More radical revolutionaries than Coke and Pym were to speak of the birthrights of Englishmen, meaning thereby literally the rights of every adult male in the country. This

1 Lucy Hutchinson, *Memoirs of. . . Colonel Hutchinson* (ed. Firth, 1885), I, pp. 6–10.
2 Vane, *A Healing Question*, in *Somers Tracts* (1811), VI, p. 306.
3 *Loc. cit.*
4 F. Trigge, *The Humble Petition of Two Sisters: the Church and Commonwealth* (1604), sig. F–F5.

division among the supporters of Parliament, within the Third Estate, was as yet veiled by (among other things) generalized attacks on the Norman Yoke.

If we take this broader patriotic appeal into account, then even as history the Norman Yoke theory was not quite so absurd as some twentieth-century historians have assumed. If we go back far enough, the Anglo-Saxons *had* a tribal organization which was far freer than the unequal society and state which superseded it. The Norman Conquest accelerated class differentiation. 'Barons and knights until the later twelfth century were still essentially an alien occupying army ruling a conquered people. . . . All native villagers were regarded as unfree. . . . Freeholders, explained a lawyer in the reign of Henry I, should frequent the shire courts, but not villeins. . . . The peasantry . . . preserved the language and the traditions of the old English communities.'[1] The shire court was for centuries the real administrative centre, and from 1430 only 40s. freeholders enjoyed the Parliamentary franchise. We should bear this in mind when we come across the apparently wild use of the phrase 'Norman freeholders' by radicals in the English Revolution. It is a logical deduction from Trigge's assumption that they are the descendants of the rank and file of William the Conqueror's army.

Class divisions still seemed in some degree to coincide with national divisions. The names of Shakespeare's lower-class characters – Snug the joiner, Bottom the weaver, Snout the tinker, Starveling the tailor – are pure Saxon. So are those of the signatories of the Diggers' manifestoes. The point will force itself upon any student of seventeenth-century quarter sessions records. Wentworth's gibe at 'your Prynnes, Pyms and Bens, with the rest of that generation of odd names and natures',[2] was a social sneer.

Appeals to Anglo-Saxon precedent had the same advantages and disadvantages as appeals to the Bible. Texts and precedents gave something concrete to set against the authority of bishops and Kings. Men dared not yet appeal to reason and utility alone: authority must be challenged by counter-authority. Texts dating from earlier stages of civilization could be used to demonstrate the unlawfulness, or ungodliness, of institutions which had grown up in later centuries. Bishops were not to be found in the New Testament: away with them!

1 M. Gibbs, *Feudal Order*, pp. 58, 75.
2 *The Earle of Strafforde's Letters and Dispatches* (ed. W. Knowler, 1739), I, p. 344.

The law of England should be made to conform to the law of God: which meant that most existing laws should be abolished. 'I do not find anything in the law of God,' said Colonel Rainborough at Putney in 1647, 'that a lord shall choose 20 burgesses, and a gentleman but two, or a poor man shall choose none'.[1] Ergo, accept the Agreement of the People and manhood suffrage. In Saxon times, argued Thomas Scot the regicide at his trial, 'there was nothing but a House of Commons'; therefore the execution of the King on the authority of a single chamber was justified.[2]

The disadvantages of the appeal to Biblical or Saxon precedent are no less obvious. It is easier to reject institutions which cannot be found in the sacred texts than to agree on what should take their place. Men quoted those texts or precedents which proved what they wished to prove, and ignored those which made against them. The Bible was ambiguous, voluminous, contradictory, providing a text for every occasion: Anglo-Saxon precedent was unknown or doubtful. 'Afarre off it seems a Monarchy, but in approach discovers more of a Democracy', wrote Nathaniel Bacon of the old constitution; and he piously hoped that 'we may attain the happinesse of our Fore-Fathers, the ancient Saxons'.[3] But what was the Anglo-Saxon constitution? What had the effect of the Conquest been?

Here the course of events shattered the illusory unity which the theory had preserved among the opponents of Charles I's government. Two points of view emerged. The more conservative Parliamentarians argued, with that representative thinker, Philip Hunton, that 1066 had marked no decisive change. William had been voluntarily accepted by the people when the throne was vacant after Harold's death. The Conquest left untouched 'triall by twelve men, and other funda-mentalls of Government, wherein the English freedome consists'.[4] More radical thinkers agreed with the equally representative Henry Parker in admitting a breach in continuity at the Conquest, and stressed the subsequent struggle of the people. "Tis a shamefull stupidity in any man to thinke that our Ancestors did not fight more nobly for their free customes and Lawes, of which the conqueror and his successors had in part disinherited them by violence and perjury, then they which put them to such conflicts.'[5] Similarly Milton had

1 A. S. P. Woodhouse, *Puritanism and Liberty*, p. 56.
2 W. H. Terry, *The Life and Times of John, Lord Finch*, Appendix, pp. 571–2.
3 N. Bacon, *op. cit.*, Part I (1647), p. 111; Part II (1651), p. 307.
4 P. Hunton, *A Treatise of Monarchie* (1643), pp. 36–7.
5 H. Parker, *Observations upon some of his Majesties late Answers and Expresses* (1642), p. 3; printed in Haller, *Tracts on Liberty in the Puritan Revolution*, II.

written proudly in 1641 of 'our progenitors that wrested their liberties out of the Norman gripe with their dearest blood and highest prowess'.[1]

But it is significant that by 1644 Parker had fallen back on Hunton's less plausible but less dangerous theory;[2] and that Milton's description of the Saxons on the eve of the Norman Conquest in his *History of Britain* is extremely unflattering.[3] The challenge to the men of property came no longer from royal absolutism but from popular democracy. Hunton and Parker had seen the common law, as interpreted by Coke, as the true English inheritance; but the radicals came to regard the law itself as part of the Norman bondage.

Parliament's victory in the Civil War destroyed the Royalist doctrine that absolutism was justified by the Norman Conquest. Hobbes pointed out the folly of this line of defence, for it meant that the right of the monarchy was overthrown by military defeat.[4] In 1646 men in the New Model Army were asking 'What were the Lords of England but William the Conquerour's Colonels? or the Barons but his Majors? or the Knights but his Captains?'[5] Eight years later this was elaborated in a pamphlet written to justify the assumption of supreme power by the generals.

> 'Wheresoever Tyranny or mis-government arises, it may be removed by Force. . . . The Kings of England (as Successors, by

1 *Of Reformation in England*, in *Prose Works* (Bohn edition), II, p. 404. Before Milton finally fixed on *Paradise Lost* as the subject of his epic he had thought of some 'king or knight before the conquest' as 'the pattern of a Christian hero' (*The Reason of Church Government*, 1641, *ibid.*, p. 478). If it is true that the theory of the Norman Yoke, in its social significance, is closely akin to the Christian legend of the Fall, the change of subject is perhaps less great than appears on the surface. Among Milton's many projected topics for poems and plays on Anglo-Saxon subjects were Edward the Confessor's 'over affection to strangers'; 'Harold slain in battle by William the Norman'; 'a heroical poem . . . founded somewhere in Alfred's reign' (*Works*, Columbia edition, XVIII, pp. 241–4). Milton's first project, only apparently dissimilar, had been King Arthur repelling the *Saxon* invaders.

2 *Jus Populi*, p. 14.

3 Milton was inconsistent. In 1649 he had nothing but contempt for those who were 'ready to be stroked and tamed again into the wonted and well-pleasing state of their true Norman villeinage' (*Eikonoklastes, Prose Works*, I, p. 483); and in 1650 he wrote more favourably of the Saxons in his *Defence of the People of England*, quoting *The Mirror of Justices* (*ibid.*, pp. 172–4). This inconsistency reflects Milton's wavering political position between the Levellers and the generals.

4 *Leviathan* (Everyman ed.), p. 387.

5 *Reliquiae Baxterianae*, I, p. 51.

way of Conquest) have derived their Power for above 500 yeares from the Norman Sword, untill now that the people have again by conquest recovered their right ... out of the hands of Regall Power usurping it.' [So long as the army remained] 'in possession of absolute Conquest,' [the writer declared, it was] 'thereby declared by God to have right to the execution of the supreame power for the defence and ordering of the Common-wealth.'[1]

So the theory of conquest was turned against its inventors.

The most ambitious work produced during the Interregnum on the historical theory of the constitution was Nathaniel Bacon's *Historicall Discourse of the Uniformity of the Government of England*, published in 1647, with a *Continuation* in 1651. Bacon first became interested in the subject as a result of 'A Private debate concerning the right of an English King to Arbitrary rule over English Subjects as Successor to the Norman Conquerour, (so called)'.[2] Bacon argued that 'the entry of the Normans into this Island could not be by conquest', and he was aware of the dangers of idealizing the Anglo-Saxons.[3] But he emphasized the anti-democratic effects of the Conquest. 'Kings first (about the Norman times) joyning with the Lords for their joynt interest above the ordinary pitch had mounted each other too high to be Lords over free men.' 'The Norman way of government grew more Aristocraticall than the Saxon, making the Lords the cheif Instruments of keeping Kings above and people underneath.'[4]

This democratic aspect of the Norman Yoke theory had a great future before it. The re-statement of it adopted by the Levellers was that made by John Hare in *St. Edwards Ghost, or Anti-Normanisme*, written in 1642 but not published till 1647.[5]

England, said Hare, was a nation in captivity and vassalage to a foreign power and an alien aristocracy. 'If we contemplate the heraldry and titles of our nobility, there is scarce any other matter than

1 *The Extent of the Sword* (1654), pp. 2–3.

2 N. Bacon, *Historicall Discourse*, I, sig. A4; cf. Chap. LVI, 'A briefe survey of the sense of the Writers concerning the point of conquest', which unfortunately gives no names of modern authors.

3 *Ibid.*, I, sig. B4, pp. 155–8.

4 *Ibid.*, I, p. 317, II, sig. B3v. The 1665 edition of Bacon's work was suppressed by the government because of its hostility to the royal prerogative. It was reprinted in 1689.

5 Note that when the popular version of the theory first breaks into print, Edward's *sainthood* is emphasized. His hold over popular imagination probably owed much to that, even after the Reformation.

inventories of foreign villages.' Acceptance of this alien yoke was not 'suitable to the dignity or tolerable to the spirit of this our nation'. 'Even the barbarous Irish' had risen against a similar state of subjection, at risk to their lives and fortunes. Their violence need not be imitated, since 'it is but the carcass of an enemy that we have to remove out of our territories, even the carcass and bones of the Norman Duke's injurious and detested perpetrations'.

Hare's proposals were: (1) Deprive William of the title Conqueror; (2) Let the King abandon his claim by conquest; (3) Let the Norman nobility 'repudiate their names and titles brought over from Normandy . . . and disclaime all right to their possessions here as Heyres and Successors to any pretended Conquerours'; (4) 'All Lawes and usages introduced from Normandy' should be abolished and the laws of Edward the Confessor restored: the laws to be in English; (5) The language should be purified of Gallicisms. Unless this programme was realized, 'the alteration of the State will be to us but changing of usurpant Masters'.[1] Magna Carta was the work of the Norman aristocracy; Parliament itself had no legal basis until its Norman origins were disavowed.[2]

This was political dynamite. Hare did not specifically call for the expropriation of the aristocracy, but it was a clear enough consequence of his argument. He did advocate drastic reform of the whole legal system, speaking in 1648 of 'that generall and inbred hatred which still dwels in our common people against both our Laws and Lawyers'. And his attack extended to Parliament itself. He repeatedly emphasized that 'all our great Victories and Triumphs' in the Civil War were vain if Norman laws remained. The enemy was Normanism, not the King, and if 'our statesmen should profess themselves Normans, and so

---

1 *St. Edwards Ghost, or Anti-Normanisme* (1647), pp. 13–22. For the purposes of this essay I have ignored linguistic Saxonism, but it is an important subsidiary aspect of the patriotic Norman Yoke theory. Cf. Spenser's archaisms, the controversy over the importation of foreign words, and Verstegan's remark that the Normans 'could not Conquer the English language as they did the land' (*Restitution of Decayed Intelligence*, 1605, p. 222). Coke, advocating 'the general communicating of these laws in the English tongue', said 'Our English language is as copious and significant, as able to express any thing in as few and apt words, as any other native language that is spoke at this day' (Proeme to the *Third Part of the Institutes*). See also an article by P. Meier, 'Réflexions sur la langue anglaise', in *La Pensée*, No. 53, 1954. M. Meier draws attention to the fact that the series of linguistic revolts against Gallicisms always coincided with democratic and nationalist movements.

2 *Englands Proper and onely way to an Establishment . . .* (1648), p. 5.

persecute the assertors of the English liberty as enemies', they must be resisted to the death.[1]

In December 1648, preaching to justify Pride's Purge, Hugh Peter said that 'in the whole book of God he findes not any text of privilege of Parliament, which indeed came in with the conquest, and is now in the hands of the Conquerors'.[2] Such views would have horrified Coke and Pym. They witness to the breakdown of unity within the Third Estate. Anti-Normanism of Hare's type acquired a new significance when radical Englishmen, asserting English liberty on behalf of the disfranchised and unprivileged masses of the population, began to look beyond Parliament for the realization of their aspirations. A petition from 'above a thousand of the inhabitants of Essex', presented to Fairfax in June 1647, declared that, despite victory in the Civil War, 'we are now like to be Vassalaged and enslaved in the Norman Laws and Prerogative Clutches of an Ambitious Party in the Nation'. Their only hope was in the Army: no longer in Parliament.[3]

IV
The Levellers

With the Levellers, the most advanced democratic group which had yet appeared on the political stage in Europe, we enter upon a new phase of the theory. Appealing to the small proprietors in town and countryside – the vast majority of the population – the Levellers made use of a version of the Anglo-Saxon past; but they also moved forward to a conception of natural rights, the rights of man. It is a momentous transition: from the recovery of rights which used to exist to the pursuit of rights because they *ought* to exist: from historical mythology to political philosophy.

Parliament's victory, the Levellers thought, afforded 'an opportunity which these 600 years has been desired, but could never be attained, of making this a truly happy and wholly Free Nation'.[4] They expected to be delivered from 'the Norman bondage . . . and from all unreasonable Lawes made ever since that unhappy conquest'.[5] Among the abuses of

1 *Plain English* (1647), in *Harleian Miscellany* (1812), IX, p. 91; *Englands Proper and onely way*, pp. 2, 6.

2 Quoted in R. P. Stearns, *The Strenuous Puritan*, p. 328. Cf. Rainborough's remark quoted on p. 64 above, and the argument from conquest on pp. 65–6.

3 Rushworth, *op. cit.*, VI, p. 520.

4 *A Manifestation* (1649), in Haller and Davies, *The Leveller Tracts*, p. 277.

5 *A Remonstrance of Many Thousand Citizens* (1646), p. 19; in Haller, *op. cit.*, III.

the Norman power they included in 1647 the peers. 'When Parliaments were first begun', declared Overton, 'the Temporall Lords were very few or none': King and Commons legislated alone.[1] William the Conqueror and his successors, said another Leveller pamphlet, 'made Dukes, Earles, Barrons and Lords of their fellow Robbers, Rogues and Thieves'. The House of Lords had no authority which it did not derive from this tainted source. 'And therefore away with the pretended power of the Lords!'[2]

The Levellers fused Biblical and constitutional theories. All men, as sons of Adam, are by nature free and equal under God, whose law is written in the hearts of all men; also the Saxons exercised national sovereignty, under God, through representative assemblies, until the Norman Conquest. Each argument led to the same conclusion.[3] Lilburne began by accepting Coke's view that Magna Carta had embodied the Anglo-Saxon liberties, regained by struggle against the Normans. He quoted from *The Mirror of Justices* and from Coke's *Institutes* almost as often as from the Bible. But gradually his own experience in the courts convinced him that neither Magna Carta nor common law guaranteed those liberties which he wished to see established. Walwyn was always critical of the feudal barons' charter. It 'hath been more precious in your esteeme then it deserveth', he wrote to Lilburne in 1645. Magna Carta 'is but a part of the peoples rights and liberties', laboriously won back from Norman kings. Its importance was absurdly exaggerated when men called it 'the birthright, the great inheritance of the people'. On the contrary: people risked selling their natural rights as men in pursuit of chimeras like 'that messe of pottage'.[4] Overton, the third of the Leveller triumvirate, agreed that Magna Carta was 'but a beggerly thing, containing many markes of intollerable bondage';[5] and Lilburne came to see that, Coke notwithstanding, Magna Carta fell short of Edward the Confessor's laws, despite all the blood that went to its winning.

> 'The greatest mischiefe of all' [Lilburne wrote in 1646], 'and the oppressing bondage of England ever since the Norman yoke, is this: I must be tryed before you by a Law (called the Common

1 *A Defiance against all Arbitrary Usurpations* (1646), p. 16.
2 *Regall Tyrannie Discovered* (1647), pp. 86–92.
3 Ibid., *passim.*
4 *Englands Lamentable Slaverie*, pp. 3–5.
5 *A Remonstrance of Many Thousand Citizens*, p. 15.

Law) that I know not, nor I thinke no man else, neither do I know where to find it or reade it. . . . The tedious, unknowne, and impossible-to-be-understood common law practices in West-minster Hall came in by the will of a Tyrant, namely William the Conqueror.'[1]

The 'main stream of the common law' was corrupt.[2] Before the Conquest there were neither lawyers nor professional judges, 'but only twelve good and legal men, chosen in each hundred, finally to decide all controversies, which lasted till William the Conqueror subdued that excellent constitution'. At his trial in 1649 Lilburne told the jury that they were judges of law as well as of fact. 'You that call yourselves Judges of the Law, are no more but Norman intruders, and indeed and in Truth, if the Jury please, are no more but Cyphers, to pronounce their verdict.' On an earlier occasion Henry Marten told the jury to put their hats on in court, to demonstrate the fact that they were 'the chief Judges in the Court', and the judges inferior to them.[3]

Coke had wanted to establish the supremacy of judge-made law: the Levellers wanted the jury – men of small property – to define the law, rather than judges drawn from the ruling class and closely associated with the government. This was carrying re-interpretation of the law to a point at which Coke's achievement – absolute security for property – would have been reversed. We can see this if we consider what would have been the respective attitudes of judge and jury to security of tenure for copyholders, or to the monopolies of trading companies. 'Our very laws', said Wildman for the Levellers at Putney, 'were made by our conquerors.'[4]

In an argument between Hugh Peter and Lilburne in 1649, the former declared that there had been no true laws in England since the Norman Conquest. The Civil War struggles, contrary to Lilburne's view, were not 'for the continuation or preservation' of the laws, 'but to

1 *The Just Mans Justification* (1646), pp. 11, 13.

2 *Ibid.*, pp. 11–13. Cf. Milton's reference to 'Their gibberish laws, . . . the badge of their ancient slavery' (*The Tenure of Kings and Magistrates*, 1650, in *Prose Works*, II, p. 4); and John Rogers's 'The Norman iron yoke of corrupt lawyers' (E. Rogers, *op. cit.*, p. 53).

3 *The Tryall of Lt. Col. John Lilburne* (second edition, 1710), pp. 18n., 98, 106–8, 121.

4 Woodhouse, *op. cit.*, p. 65. Wildman extended his condemnation to mediaeval chronicles, 'because those that were our lords, and made us their vassals, would suffer nothing . . . to be chronicled' that made against them (*ibid.*, p. 66). This is throwing overboard the appeal to history with a vengeance!

be freed from them'. The laws, Magna Carta, the Petition of Right, Coke, Littleton, and the rest of the relics of heathenism, Popery, and tyranny, could now be replaced.[1] Lilburne was accused of mis-representing Peter's arguments on this occasion: but Peter declared in print that 'it is very advisable to burn all the old Records, even those in the Tower, the monuments of tyranny'.[2]

In 1649 a less influential but interesting figure, John Warr, devoted an entire pamphlet to *The Corruption and Deficiency of the Lawes of England*. They were 'full of Tricks, Doubts, and contrary to them-selves', as one would expect since they were of *Norman* origin. There was no real continuity from Saxon times, for the conquerors retained only 'those Parts of former Laws which made for their own Interest'. Those laws which 'do carry any Thing of Freedom in their Bowels . . . have been wrested from the Rulers and Princes of the World by Importunity of Entreaty or by Force of Arms'.[3] Warr indeed regarded the Saxons as alien conquerors no less than the Normans. He abandoned the appeal to history. 'At the Foundation of Governments, Justice was in Men before it came to be in Laws.' The people imposed laws on rulers, but the latter have twisted the laws so as to use them against the people. 'Many Times the very Law is the Badge of our Oppression, its proper Intent being to enslave the People.' Hence we must not make an idol of fundamental law, 'for what, I pray you, is Fundamental Law but such Customs as are of the eldest Date and longest Continuance? . . . The more Fundamental a Law is, the more difficult, not the less necessary, to be reformed.'[4]

Few Levellers attained to this clarity of thought. They tended more and more to appeal to reason rather than precedent: but they clung to the belief that reason had been embodied in the laws of the Anglo-Saxons. Robert Norwood thought that the Englishman's law had not only been enacted in the Parliament of 'King Ethelree' but also 'rooted by Heaven itself in the hearts of Englishmen'. The common law was identical with the laws of nature.[5] This comparison had got the Leveller spokesmen into difficulties in the Putney Debates of 1647.

1 Stearns, *op. cit.*, pp. 348–50, quoting Lilburne's account of what Peter said.
2 H. Peter, *Good Work for a Good Magistrate* (1651), pp. 32–3. Cf. the peasant habit of destroying manorial records in the riots of the 'forties: for very obvious reasons.
3 In *Harleian Miscellany* (1745), III, pp. 240–2.
4 *Ibid.*, pp. 240–5.
5 Robert Norwood, *An Additional Discourse* (1653), pp. 10–13. Cf. pp. 128, 284 below for Norwood.

Commissary Cowling argued that before the Conquest the franchise had been democratic, not a legal privilege attached to property; it was only the sword 'that had from time to time recovered our right'. Lt.-Col. Henry Lilburne replied that 'the Norman laws were not slavery introduced upon us, but an augmentation of our slavery before': and Commissary-General Ireton pointed out that no evidence had been produced to show that 'the ancient constitution', of which there had been so much talk, really was. He did not wish 'to derive all our tyranny from the Norman Conquest'. Rainborough agreed that it would be best to abandon constitutional history and 'consider the equality and resonableness of the thing'.[1]

The shift from arguments based on questionable history to arguments based on the rights of man can be illustrated most neatly in a story told by Aubrey. Henry Marten introduced a Remonstrance into Parliament, probably in 1649, in which he spoke of England being '*restored* to its ancient government of a commonwealth'. When challenged on his history, 'H.M., standing up, meekely replied that "there was a text had much troubled his spirit for severall dayes and nights of the man that was blind from his mother's womb whose sight was restored at last" – i.e. was restored to the sight which he should have had'.[2] Natural right was natural right, even if it could not be proved from history. 'Whatever our Fore-fathers were; or whatever they did or suffered, or were enforced to yeeld unto; we are the men of the present age, and ought to be absolutely free from all kindes of exorbitancies, molestations, or Arbitrary Power.'[3]

In fighting the Civil War Parliament had begun by appealing to the sovereignty of Parliament. But the radicals soon found that Parliament had replaced the King as an irresponsible, unrepresentative authority. In their conflict with the Presbyterians, not only the Levellers but also some Independents and republicans proclaimed that the people are superior both to law and Parliament: the President of the court which tried Charles I adopted that position. But 'the people' was ambiguous. In the mouths of the men of property, the phrase meant themselves. The Levellers wished to make it include the whole adult male population. Hence the Parliamentary franchise became a major object of contention between the two parties. At Putney, Ireton criticized the

1 Woodhouse, *op. cit.*, pp. 96, 118–21.
2 Aubrey, *Brief Lives*, ed. Clark, II, p. 47. Marten misquoted *John* IX in order to make his point. See p. 80 below.
3 *A Remonstrance of Many Thousand Citizens* (1646), pp. 4–5.

proposed extension of the franchise in the Leveller Agreement of the People because it 'takes away that which is the most original, the most fundamental civil constitution of this kingdom, and, which is above all, that constitution by which I have any property'.[1] 'The old constitution', for men like Ireton, meant law, property and a property franchise. The Levellers' appeal to abstract 'natural rights' was of no interest to such people. The law, both before and after Coke, safeguarded the rights of property rather than the rights of man.

So Hare, Warr, and the Levellers reversed the values of their betters. The law became the enemy, the symbol of Normanism, instead of being the surviving pledge of Anglo-Saxon freedom. William the Conqueror had had the laws written in French, so that 'the poor miserable people might be gulled and cheated, undone and destroyed'.[2] 'All the entryes and proceedings' in the law courts were in Latin, 'a language I understand not, nor one of a thousand of my native Country men'.[3] Interpretation of the law was left to the discretion of judges. And since they were 'but Norman intruders', were members of the ruling class themselves, they naturally interpreted in a sense hostile to the mass of the people. Mumbo-jumbo helped the propertied. Hence the Levellers demanded

> 'That all Lawes of the Land (lockt up from common capacities in the Latin or French tongues) may bee translated into the English tongue. And that all records, Orders, Processes, Writs, and other proceedings whatsoever, may be all entered and issued forth in the English tongue ... that so the meanest English Commoner that can but read written hand in his own tongue, may fully understand his owne proceedings in the Law.'[4]

The Bible, the book which decided men's destinies in the after-life, had been translated into the English language, with momentous

---

1 Woodhouse, *op. cit.*, p. 60. His failure to grasp the importance of their proposed extension of the franchise vitiates most of what Mr. S. Kliger has to say about the Levellers in *The Goths in England*, and leads him to make some remarkable statements about Ireton's devotion to democracy (see esp. pp. 261–87). But otherwise I have found his book useful.

2 *Regall Tyrannie Discovered*, p. 15.

3 Lilburne, *The Just Mans Justification*, p. 11.

4 *An Appeale from the degenerate Representative Body the Commons ... To the Body Represented, the free people* (1647), in D. M. Wolfe, *Leveller Manifestoes of the Puritan Revolution*, p. 192. An act for turning the law into English was passed in November 1650.

consequences. Now the law, which decided men's destinies here on earth, was also to be wrested from the custody of a clique of mandarins, and thrown open to the comprehension (and therefore control) of 'the meanest English Commoner'. The Reformation had cast down priests from their seats of power: legal reform was to cast down lawyers. Then the *English* commons could enter peacefully into their inheritance.[1]

The Levellers (like Hugh Peter and other radicals) wanted the laws rationalized and codified, 'made certain, short, and plain'. Lilburne would have abolished the 'Norman innovation' of courts at Westminster and had all causes and differences decided in the county or hundred where they originated. This, he held, had been 'part of the ancient frame of government in this Kingdome before the Conquerors dayes'.[2] Like the elevation of the jury over the judge, this is an appeal from the existing state power to surviving vestiges of the old communal institutions.

The Republic was established in 1649, but Normanism remained. There had been no fundamental change in the law or in the social relations which the law defended. The Levellers realized that they were attacking a *system*. 'Government we see none, but the old tyrannical Norman Government,' said a *Declaration* from Hertfordshire. 'All the people of this Nation are yet slaves, . . . being under the laws and government of William.' 'We protest against the whole Norman power'.[3] A similar *Representation* from 'the middling sort of men' of four Buckinghamshire hundreds also attacked 'the whole Norman power' – 'all Arbitrary Courts, Terms, Lawyers, Impropriators, Lords of Mannors, Patents, Privileges, . . . Tythes, Tolls, Customs, etc.'[4] Lilburne in 1649 expressed the opinion that Cromwell was 'more deserving punishment and death than the 44 judges hanged for injustice by King Alfred'.[5] No wonder the Levellers were forcibly suppressed. 'You must break them or they will break you,' cried Cromwell in this same year. In 1650 we find Whitelocke, Commis-

1 That is why so many of the radicals in the English Revolution hated the universities; they turned out men with specialized training who used it to exclude the common people from their mysteries, to their own exclusive profit.

2 *The Just Mans Justification*, p. 15. The demand was often repeated in later Leveller pamphlets. For examples see W. Schenk, *The Concern for Social Justice in the Puritan Revolution*, pp. 67–8, and W. Cole, *A Rod for the Lawyers* (1659).

3 Schenk, *op. cit.*, pp. 68, 80.

4 *Victoria County History of Buckinghamshire*, IV, p. 542.

5 Lilburne, *The Impeachment against Cromwell and Ireton* (1649), title-page.

sioner of the Great Seal, denying that the common law had been introduced by William the Conqueror, and suggesting that it was neither 'ingenuous nor prudent for Englishmen to deprave their birthright, the laws of their own country'.[1] 'The Law of England is the Law of God', Judge Jermyn even more surprisingly told Lilburne at his trial in 1649; 'the Law of England is pure, Primitive Reason, uncorrupted and unpolluted by human Humors, or human Corruptions, Wits or Wills.'[2] The law's victims thought otherwise. In 1651 prisoners petitioning for liberation said 'the law was the badge of the Norman bondage'.[3]

v

The Diggers

Many of the radicals used the theory to demand a clean sweep of all survivals of feudalism. All men were born free, wrote a Leveller partisan in 1646; and when 'that wicked and unchristian-like custom of villany [i.e. villeinage] was introduced by the Norman Conqueror', it violated both the law of nature and the law of the land.[4] Saxon churls, said Nathaniel Bacon, 'had as sure a title to their own liberties as the . . . Countrey Gentlemen had'.[5]

   That good bourgeois, Samuel Hartlib, who throughout the revolutionary years devoted himself tirelessly to the advocacy of every project that could improve economic production, pointed out that both copyholds and feudal tenures were obstacles to the development of agriculture, and hoped that these 'badges of our Norman slavery', although 'not in the power of the poor Husbandman to remedy', would be abolished by state action.[6] Feudal tenures, affecting mainly the rich, were abolished; copyhold, affecting mainly the poor, was not. Cultivation suffered in consequence, for their insecurity of tenure made copyholders reluctant to invest capital in agricultural improvements.

1 B. Whitelocke, *Memorials* (1853), III, pp. 260–73.

2 *The Tryall of Lt. Col. John Lilburne*, p. 20.

3 Whitelocke, *op. cit.*, III, p. 362. In 1653 a women's petition to Cromwell asked for the abolition of the 'Norman Yoke' of perpetual imprisonment for debt (Margaret James, *Social Policy during the Puritan Revolution*, p. 329). There were many similar petitions – e.g. B.M. 669 19/39, petition of November 1654.

4 *Vox Plebis*, p. 4.

5 N. Bacon, *An Historicall Discourse*, I, p. 56.

6 S. Hartlib, *The Compleat Husband-Man* (1659), p. 45. This tract is the second edition of *Samuel Hartlib his Legacie*, first published in 1652.

This point was noted by Moses Wall in May 1659, writing to Milton, who was also a friend of Hartlib. 'The tenure of land by copyhold, and holding for life under a lord, or rather tyrant, of a manor', Wall thought, showed that 'the Norman Conquest and Tyranny is continued upon the nation without any thought of removing it'.[1]

This was one consequence of the defeat of the Levellers, whose pamphlets called for the abolition of 'all base Tenures by Copies, Oaths of Fealty, Homage, Fines at Will of Lord, etc. (being the Conqueror's marks on the people)'.[2] Usually the Levellers would have been content if copyholders could have purchased the freehold, or have been guaranteed legal security of tenure. Others asked why, if copyholds came down from the Conquest, they could not be abolished without compensation now that the Norman monarchy and the feudal tenures of the gentry had gone? *Light Shining in Buckinghamshire* attacked the landed classes as a whole:

'Our Nobility and Gentry [came] even from that outlandish Norman Bastard, who first being his Servants and under Tyrants; secondly, their rise was by cruell murther and theft by the Conquest; thirdly, their rise was the Countries ruine, and the putting them down will be the restitution of our rights againe'.[3]

Thomas Tany, who believed that his parents had been poor 'through the Tyrannical power reigning in the Norman Yoake', thought that 'now our Lands being freed from the Norman subjection' by Parliament's victory in the Civil War, 'we may lawfully claim our Lands and Inheritance in the Common-wealth, as is due right: they by the Law of God and man do unto us belong, and unto us ought to be delivered'.[4] There is no evidence directly connecting Tany with Gerrard Winstanley and the Diggers, though he moved in very radical circles and was probably acquainted with William Everard.[5] But he certainly seems to be reproducing their views here. The Diggers' was the most comprehensive and drastic restatement of the social version of the Norman Yoke theory. Even 'the best laws that England hath', said Winstanley, 'are yoaks and manicles, tying one sort of people to be

1 Masson, *Life of Milton*, V. p. 602.
2 M. James, *op. cit.*, p. 94. Cf. the Quaker E. B., *A Mite of Affection* (1659), quoted by Schenk, *op. cit.*, p. 125.
3 Sabine, *op. cit.*, pp. 618–19. (This was not a Digger pamphlet.)
4 [T. Tany], *Theaureaujohn High Priest to the Jews, His Disputive Challenge to the Universities of Oxford and Cambridge* (1651), pp. 1, 8.
5 See pp. 128, 284 below.

slaves to another'.[1] Justifying their communal cultivation of the waste land at St. George's Hill, the Diggers declared to Fairfax and his Council of War in December 1649:

> 'Seeing the common people of England by joynt consent of person and purse have caste out Charles our Norman oppressour, wee have by this victory recovered ourselves from under his Norman yoake, and the land now is to returne into the joynt hands of those who have conquered – that is, the commonours – and the land is to bee held noe longer from the use of them [the commoners] by the hand of anye [who] will uphold the Norman and kingly power still.'[2]

The Diggers, that is to say, aimed at a far more radical revolution in agrarian relations. Copyhold was to be abolished, and peasants' lands freed from feudal services, just as the gentry's lands had been by the abolition of feudal tenures. 'Let all sorts have freedome by vertue of this Conquest over the Norman successor'. 'Our inclosures . . . were got by that murdering sword, and given by William the Conquerour' to the ancestors of the present landlords.[3] The confiscated estates of Church and Crown, and waste lands everywhere, should be set free for the poorest people to cultivate. Ultimately, private property in land would be abolished altogether; but communal cultivation was to be established peacefully, by voluntary associations built up from below. It was the most far-reaching programme put forward during the Revolution. If landlord supremacy could be destroyed, the Diggers believed, the democratic rural community was still strong enough to revive and flourish. But this radical programme was defeated. Feudal relations survived in rural England, to act for centuries as a brake on the development of democracy.

The Diggers' aim, Winstanley told Fairfax, was 'not to remove the Norman Yoke only', and restore Saxon laws. They wished to return to 'the pure Law of righteousnesse before the fall'. Here again we see the curious blending of the two myths: Paradise can be regained on earth only after Normanism has been overthrown. All laws 'not grounded upon equity and reason, not giving a universal freedom to all, but respecting persons, ought . . . to be cut off with the Kings head'. Laws

1 Sabine, *op. cit.*, p. 303.
2 *Clarke Papers*, II, p. 218; cf. Sabine, *op. cit.*, p. 408.
3 Sabine, *op. cit.*, pp. 307–8, 331.

made in the days of monarchy give freedom only to the gentry and clergy.[1] 'The Kings blood was not our burthen, it was those oppressing Norman laws, whereby he enslaved us, that we groaned under'.[2] Parliament could not be relied upon to make the necessary reforms, for the franchise itself was Norman. 'In the dayes of the Kings, none were to chuse nor be chosen Parliament men, or law makers, but Lords of Mannors, and Freeholders. . . . All inferior people were neither to chuse, nor to be chosen', for they were 'of the rank of the conquered ones, and servants and slaves from the time of the conquest'.[3] 'The violent people that are Free-holders, are . . . the Norman Common Souldiers, spred abroad in the Land; And who must be chosen? but some very rich man, who is the Successor of the Norman Colonels. . . . And to what end have they been thus Chosen? but to Establish that Norman power the more forcibly over the enslaved English, and to beat them down again, when as they gather heart to seek for Liberty'.[4] Even juries, so dear to the Levellers, seemed to Winstanley to be Norman.[5] 'This imprisoning and hanging of men is the Norman power still.' The privileges of market towns meant that freedom was withheld from the country people by 'a covetous Norman Toll-Taker'.[6] The laws were written in French and Latin 'to keep the common people ignorant of their Creation-freedoms, lest they should rise to redeem themselves'. The point, Winstanley thought, was not merely to get the laws in English, but to change their 'Kingly principles'; otherwise being able to read them would 'rather increase our sorrow, by our knowledge of our bondage'.[7]

The Digger programme was one of social revolution. The rich, naturally, would have none of it. From the moment of the execution of Charles I, conservatives began to group together again in search of a government which would guarantee property, a search which led ultimately back to a 'free Parliament' (elected on the old Norman franchise) and to the Restoration of Charles II. With remarkable prescience the Diggers issued their warning, just over three months after the proclamation of the Republic:

1 *Ibid.*, pp. 292, 288.
2 *Ibid.*, p. 308.
3 *Ibid.*, pp. 585–6. Cf. p. 277 below.
4 *Ibid.*, p. 259.
5 *Ibid.*, p. 333.
6 *Ibid.*, pp. 415, 506.
7 *Ibid.*, p. 587.

'If they get the foot fast in the stirrup, they will lift themselves again into the Norman saddle; and they do it secretly; for they keep up the Norman Lawes. . . . Therefore England beware! . . . William the Conquerours Army begins to gather into head againe, and the old Norman Prerogative Law is the place of their rendezvous: for though their chief Captain Charles be gone, yet his Colonells, which are Lords of Mannours, his Councellors and Divines, which are our Lawyers and Priests, his inferiour officers and Souldiers, which are the Freeholders and Land-lords, all which did steal away our Land from us when they killed and murdered our Fathers in that Norman conquest: And the Bailiffes that are slaves to their covetous lusts and all the ignorant bawling women against our digging for freedome, are the snapsack boyes and the ammunition sluts that follow the Norman Camp.'[1]

The warning proved to be correct. Winstanley's Norman power, aided by the 'corrupt interests of the lawyers and clergy', was too strong for the radicals. In 1657 a second chamber was established, to which 'the Off-spring of the Bastard of William the sixth Duke of Normandy' were called:[2] and in 1660 Norman King, Lords, and bishops came back to aid Norman lords of manors and freeholders in protecting their property and their Norman law.

VI
The Whigs

Thus in the revolutionary epoch we can trace four distinct interpretations of the Norman Conquest: (1) The Royalist doctrine justifying absolutism by conquest was killed by the Civil War; but its ghost walked the earth between 1660 and 1688, in the posthumous pamphlets of Filmer. Nevill and Locke both thought it worth the trouble of laying the spectre, though the events of 1688 did it more effectively than either.[3] (2) Coke's version we may call the Whig

1 *Ibid.*, p. 330. An anonymous pamphlet published in 1653, *No Age like unto this Age*, which appears to have been influenced by Digger ideas, referred to tithes as a Norman imposition. 'Five sorts of men uncapable to bear rule in this Commonwealth' included lawyers and lords of manors, who were 'of the Normans creating', as well as impropriators, who upheld 'the tyrannical power of Monarchy', Royalists, and 'the rich that is covetous' (pp. 17–22).

2 [Anon.], *A Second Narrative of the Late Parliament* (*so called*) (1658), p. 21.

3 H. Nevill, *Plato Redivivus* (1681), pp. 106–7, denies that the Norman Conquest made any difference at all; Locke, *Two Treatises of Civil Government* (Everyman ed.), p.

interpretation: the common law was the embodiment of Anglo-Saxon liberties; once the repressive institutions of the monarchy had been abolished freedom was 'by God's blessing restored'.[1] For the common law had adapted itself to the needs of a commercial society. Continuity and the sanctity of property: these were what the conservative Parliamentarians wished to emphasize. The theory of surviving Anglo-Saxon freedom and 'the myth of Magna Carta' are essential to the Whig interpretation of English history.[2] (3) The radical version of the Levellers suggested that the law itself legitimized inequality. They agitated for drastic legal reform, for the ending of all privileges. Magna Carta itself was but a beggarly thing: pre-Conquest equality could be recovered only by a wide extension of the franchise. Juries, not judges, should decide what the law was. Men should be tried locally, by neighbours, not at Westminster by professional lawyers. Some Levellers based their demands on natural as well as historical rights. (4) Finally, there was the most radical group of all, the Diggers, spokesmen for the dispossessed, who advocated a clean sweep of feudal survivals and the ending of private property in land. Looking both backwards and forwards, they believed that true equality could be established only by means of an attack on the institution of property as such. Their aim was 'to renew the ancient community of enjoying the fruits of the earth, and to distribute the benefit thereof to the poor and needy, and to feed the hungry and clothe the naked'.[3]

The Whig theory of continuity, having done service against the old régime, was then turned against attack from the opposite flank. When the Levellers claimed the rights of all Englishmen, the conservative Parliamentarians replied that those rights were enshrined in the *laws*. Thus Prynne, the victim of Charles I's arbitrary rule, defended the 'fundamental laws and liberties' left to the freemen and people by their

---

208. The view that William and Mary were sovereigns by conquest was condemned by both Houses of Parliament in January 1692.

1 The inscription on the Great Seal of the Commonwealth, 1651, devised by Henry Marten.

2 Cf. H. Butterfield, *The Englishman and his History*, p. 69. Harrington's *Oceana* (1656) contains a variant of this version. Harrington attached little importance to the Norman Conquest, since in his view society before no less than after 1066 was essentially landlord-dominated. But within this 'Gothic balance' representative institutions dating from Saxon times made the constitution 'no other than a wrestling match' between King, Lords, and people (*Works*, 1737, esp. pp. 64–8). See pp. 270–1 below.

3 Whitelocke, *op. cit.*, III, p. 18.

forefathers, against the Leveller attack on behalf of the natural rights of all men.[1] The Royalist journalist, Marchamont Nedham, said that the Levellers 'by placing the supreme power of making and repealing Lawes in the People, doe aime to establish a meere popular Tyrannie . . . to the destruction of our Laws and Liberties'.[2] Here the contrast between 'the People' and '*our* Laws and Liberties' is clear. Sir Matthew Hale, judge under Cromwell and under Charles II, and Coke's loyal disciple, thought it very important to maintain an unbroken pedigree for the English constitution and laws from Anglo-Saxon times.[3] Another eminent lawyer, Sir Roger Twysden, neutral in the Civil War, strongly emphasized continuity and defended legally limited monarchy against the absolutism of either King or people.[4] Lord Chancellor Clarendon criticized Hobbes's *Leviathan* on the ground (among others) that the laws of England were derived from immemorial custom, not from the will of a conqueror.[5] Bishop Bramhall in exile appealed to Magna Carta, Charles I at his trial claimed to be defending law and property. Whitelocke, Nedham, Prynne, Hale, Twysden, Clarendon, bishops, kings . . . from extreme right to left centre the ranks were closed against the radicals. Theories of the Norman Yoke in the decades after the Revolution were perforce very different from what they had been before.

After 1660, then, the third and fourth version of the theory temporarily disappeared from sight: the first finally after 1688. Men might disagree about whether the gentry of England were of Norman descent;[6] antiquarians and publicists continued to dispute about the exact nature of the Conquest: but most writers accepted the Whig view. Algernon Sydney did.[7] Defoe used the theory to ridicule the preten-

1 *The First and Second Part of a Seasonable Legal, and Historical Vindication and Chronological Collection of the Good, Old, Fundamental Liberties* (1655), p. 3.

2 *A Plea for the King and Kingdome* (1648), pp. 24–5. Nedham subsequently changed sides and wrote for the government of the Commonwealth.

3 *History of the Common Law* (3rd ed. 1739), pp. 70–109.

4 *Certaine Considerations upon the Government of England* (ed. J. M. Kemble, Camden Society), pp. 22, 99–103, 119–21, 133.

5 Clarendon, *A Brief View and Survey of the Dangerous and Pernicious Errors . . . in Mr Hobbes's . . . Leviathan* (1676), pp. 109–10.

6 Prynne, in his reaction of loyalty after the Restoration, attacked the view that the nobility were merely the descendants of the Norman conquerors (Butterfield, *op. cit.*, p. 75); cf. Hobbes, p. 83 below.

7 *Works* (1772), III, *passim*: conveniently summarized in Z. S. Fink, *The Classical Republicans*, pp. 158–61.

sions of the aristocracy to have 'come over with the Conqueror', whilst adroitly reviving the Cromwellian army's argument from conquest. If the right of the Stuarts derived from William the Conqueror, then since 1688 it had been superseded by the superior right of William the Liberator.

> 'The great invading Norman let us know
> What conquerors in after-times might do.
> To every musketeer[1] he brought to town,
> He gave the lands which never were his own.
> When first the English crown he did obtain,
> He did not send his Dutchmen back again. . . .
> The rascals, thus enriched, he called them lords,
> To please their upstart pride with new-made words,
> And Doomsday Book his tyranny records.
> And here begins our ancient pedigree,
> That so exalts our poor nobility:
> 'Tis that from some French trooper they derive,
> Who with the Norman Bastard did arrive.'[2]

The Conquest theory had ceased to be a threat and became a joke. Property is now so secure, Defoe skilfully hints, and William is so *bourgeois* a King, that there is no danger in *his* Conquest. White Kennett similarly referred jocularly to the Norman Yoke to make a topical point: 'Our good Forefathers . . . were invaded and subdued by a Pretender from France'.[3] By the mid-eighteenth century the Whig theory was unquestioned. The legal doctrine that all land derives from the King, Blackstone regarded as 'in reality a mere fiction', introduced by 'Norman lawyers' and 'monkish historians'. The law of nature, Blackstone thought, had been embodied in the pre-Conquest constitution.[4] The continuity of English law and institutions, as a peculiar and peculiarly admirable feature of English development, became a dogma of Whig historians, and has been uncritically accepted by many

1 Or archer (Defoe's note).

2 *The True Born Englishman* (1701), in H. Morley, *The Earlier Life and Works of Daniel Defoe*, p. 190. Defoe's purpose was to mock at racial theories, to show that 'We have been Europe's sink, the jakes where she Voids all her offal outcast progeny.' Cf. Rochester's sneer at the noble family 'who . . . ever since the Conquest, have been Fools' (*Poems*, 1953, p. 85).

3 W. Kennett, *A Compassionate Enquiry into the Causes of the Civil War*, in a Sermon preached on 31 January 1704, p. 7.

4 *Commentaries on the Laws of England* (1794), II, pp. 50–77.

who would not call themselves Whigs. Yet in origin it is doubly propagandist: it springs from Coke's theory used against Stuart absolutism, as modified by the need of the victorious Parliamentarians to defend their position against radical attack and to pretend that there had been no Revolution.

The few dissentients from the Whig view were no less partisan. One was Thomas Hobbes, always *sui generis*, who took a grim delight in reversing the values of the Parliamentary revolutionaries. From the Saxons, he said, it was possible to derive only 'examples of fact', no 'argument of right'; and the facts, Hobbes sorrowfully added, 'by the ambition of potent subjects, have been oftener unjust than otherwise'. The Saxons 'were a savage and heathen people, living only by war and rapine'. Their lords ruled absolutely over families, servants and subjects. These lords held courts by the King's writ, and were the King's counsellors; but they were summoned at his pleasure, and had had no right to oppose his resolutions by force. But our titles of honour, said Hobbes sardonically, recalling Hare and his friends, undoubtedly derive from the Saxons.[1]

Another dissentient was Dr. Robert Brady, a Tory and a defender of Stuart absolutism. The political impulse that took him to early English history is unmistakable. Yet his real scholarship led him to conclusions which most modern historians would accept: that the Commons were not represented in Parliament until 1265; before that date they had no 'communication in affairs of state unless they were represented by tenants *in capite*'.[2]

Only one point of the more radical interpretation of the theory of the Norman Yoke received prominence in the century after 1660: the Saxon origin of the jury, and the rights of juries as against judges. A crop of literature was produced on this subject by Bushell's Case in 1670, arising from a conflict between judge and jury in the trial of William Penn the Quaker. Penn himself defined the birthrights of Englishmen as: (1) Security of property, (2) The right to vote (though he said nothing about distribution of the franchise), and (3) The right

1 *Behemoth*, in *Works*, VI, pp. 259–60; *A Dialogue between a Philosopher and a Student of the Common Law of England*, *ibid.*, III, pp. 44, 152–3. Sir William Petty also gave the theory an original twist of his own: *Petty Papers*, I, pp. 17–21.

2 Brady, *Introduction to Old English History* (1694), Introduction. I have passed lightly over the controversies among antiquarians between 1660 and 1730, since they have been fully treated by Professor D. C. Douglas in his *English Scholars*, esp. Chapter 6. See also Pocock, *op. cit.*, Chapters VII–IX *passim*.

to serve on juries, all of which had descended from the Saxons.[1] Trial by jury was the only form of trial in Anglo-Saxon England, and was confirmed by the Conqueror, said a pamphlet of 1680 which was often reprinted.[2] (In passing we may note that the social significance of the jury was being transformed by economic developments. Juries used to speak for the village community: they were expected to have personal knowledge of the facts before the trial opened. In depersonalized capitalist society they came to be anonymous property-owners, selected because they did *not* know the facts.)

But there was one theme which we shall encounter later in radical thought, upon which Defoe, in his brutal commonsense way, un-expectedly touched. In *Jure Divino* (1706), he treats the Saxons as violent conquerors no whit better than the Normans:

> *'And thus began the Royal Saxon Line;*
> *In Robbery and Blood they fixed the Right Divine.'*

Defoe is still hitting at James II and his defenders, but his argument advances against prescription in general. The Saxons wrongfully dispossessed the Britons by 'the *Jus Divinum* of the Sword'. All property thus originated in violence:

> *'The very Lands we all along enjoyed,*
> *They ravished from the People they destroyed . . .*
> *And all the long Pretences of Descent,*
> *Are Shams of Right to prop up Government;*
> *'Tis all Invasion, Usurpation all;*
> *The strongest Powers get up, the weakest fall . . .*
> *Success gives Title, makes Possession just,*
> *And if the Fates obey, the Subjects must . . .*
> *Where then's the lofty Pedigree of Kings?*
> *The longest Sword the longest Scepter brings.'*[3]

William I was no better, if no worse, than his Saxon predecessors:[4]

1 *England's Present Interest Discovered*, in *Select Works* (1782), III, pp. 203–4.
2 Sir John Hawles, *The Englishman's Right* (1771 ed.), pp. 4–7. Hawles was Solicitor-General to William III. His pamphlet was reprinted in 1731, and at least four times between 1763 and 1771. Both Penn and Hawles believed that the jury existed in England before the Saxons.
3 D. Defoe, *Jure Divino* (1706), Book IX, pp. 205–7, 212, 217.
4 Rather better, Defoe thought, since William 'received the Crown by general fair Assent' and 'swore to the Laws, with all their Limitations', though he did not keep his oath (*Ibid.*, pp. 223–4).

> '*Whore in his Scutcheon, Tyrant in his Face . . .*
> *Upon his Sword engraved the Right Divine.*
> *Of all the Nations in the World there's none,*
> *Has less of True Succession in their Crown . . .*
> *Since if Hereditary Right's the Claim,*
> *The English Crown has Forty Times been lame.'*

Defoe's conclusion is

> '*That where th' Usurper reigns, the Tyrant must;*
> *He only justly holds a Government,*
> *That rules a People by their own Consent.'*[1]

That is all very well for Defoe: a bourgeois confident in his class's ability to control both Crown and people. But when we next meet this attitude towards the origins of property and political authority it will be deadly earnest, not heavy-handed fun. For it will be in the writings of Tom Paine.[2]

VII

The Radicals

The second half of the eighteenth century saw revivals of radical versions of the Norman Yoke theory.[3] In 1757 Lord Hawkesbury, whilst praising the skill of the Saxons in 'wisely constituting civil societies', and especially 'their military establishments', admitted that they were 'ridiculed for their ignorance and barbarity'.[4] That soon changed. In America Thomas Jefferson 'painstakingly collected every

---

1 Defoe, *op. cit.*, Book IX, pp. 219–20.

2 See below, pp. 90–5. In 1821 the radical reformer William Hone published a curious work entitled *The Right Divine of Kings to Govern Wrong*. It was a reprint of parts of Defoe's *Jure Divino*, with extensive additions. The passage on the Conquest adds nothing and omits much (pp. 49–51 of Hone's version correspond to pp. 215–25 of *Jure Divino*); but Hone has a long footnote on Alfred (whom Defoe ignored), praising especially his zeal for education. Otherwise Hone accepts Defoe's attitude towards the Saxons.

3 All that I venture to say in the following sections is put forward very tentatively, in the hope that others better qualified may criticize the lines of thought here suggested.

4 Charles, Lord Hawkesbury, *Constitutional Maxims extracted from a Discourse on the Establishment of a National and Constitutional Force* (reprinted by the London Corresponding Society in 1794), pp. 3–5. Hume's *History of England*, of which the relevant volume was published in 1761, took a similar position.

scrap of evidence to reconstruct the history of his "Saxon ancestors" ',
who, he believed, had realized his conception of political liberty.[1] In
England the *History of England* published from 1763 onwards by the
republican Mrs. Catharine Macaulay was an important landmark. She
said nothing very new, and the Norman Yoke was subsidiary to her
main theme; but she believed that the Civil War 'overturned the
tyranny settled by the Norman invader', and only regretted that in 1660
and 1688 Parliaments had failed to recur to 'the more wholesome
principles of the Saxon constitution'. Like Nathaniel Bacon, Mrs.
Macaulay stressed the fact that the Norman Conquest had concentrated property and political power in the hands of great landowners.[2]
Her book was a best-seller in radical circles. The Wilkesite agitation in
the immediately following years, and the American Revolution,
stimulated movements for Parliamentary reform which also helped to
revive enthusiasm for the free Anglo-Saxons. At the same time,
significantly, there was a decline in interest in Anglo-Saxon laws
among lawyers.[3]

The most comprehensive document on the radical side was the
anonymous *Historical Essay on the English Constitution*, published in
1771. This constitution, the *Essay* declared, was introduced by the
Saxons about 450 A.D. The English state was a federation of local
communities built up from below, finally established with a bi-cameral
national Parliament under 'Alfred the Great, a prince of the most
exalted merit that ever graced the English throne'.[4] Annual Parliaments were a right enjoyed for 1,200 years before the triennial Act of
1694 robbed us of them. Trial by jury dates from earliest Saxon times.
At all levels the government was democratic and representative, so that
'if ever God Almighty did concern himself about forming a government, for mankind to live happily under, it was that which was
established in England by our Saxon forefathers'.[5]

1 G. Chinard, *The Commonplace Book of Thomas Jefferson*, pp. 64–5. I follow the free
Saxons no further into America: they went far.

2 Catharine Macaulay, *The History of England from the Accession of James I to the
Elevation of the House of Hanover* (1766–83), V, p. 381; VI, p. 71; cf. I, p. 273; II, pp. 1–3;
III, p. 42; *The History of England from the Revolution to the Present Time* (1778), I, p. 5; *An
Address to the People of England, Scotland and Ireland* (1775), p. 9; *Observations on the
Reflections of the Rt. Hon. Edmund Burke on the Revolution in France* (1790), p. 30.

3 Holdsworth, *The Historians of Anglo-American Law*, pp. 34–6.

4 Pp. 3, 12–15, 22–33. *An Historical Essay* has been attributed, probably wrongly, to
the younger Allan Ramsay (H. Butterfield, *George III, Lord North and the People*, pp.
349–50).

5 *Op. cit.*, pp. 144, 165, 32.

But the Norman Conquest

> 'destroyed all the elective power, constitutionally placed in the people of England, and reversed the Saxon form of government which was founded on the common rights of mankind. . . . From this time, civil and religious tyranny walked hand in hand, two monsters till then unknown in England. . . .[1] Since the Conquest, our arbitrary kings, and men of arbitrary principles, have endeavoured to destroy the few remaining records and historical facts that might keep in remembrance a form of government so kind, so friendly and hospitable to the human species. . . . Whatever is of Saxon establishment is truly constitutional, but whatever is Norman is heterogeneous to it, and partakes of a tyrannical spirit.'

There has naturally been warfare ever since between these two forms of government.[2] The people at length recovered their elective power in Parliament, thanks to the 'immortal barons who rescued the constitution from Norman tyranny' by Magna Carta. The Civil War was fought because Charles I wished to reduce Parliament to the status of William I's Council; the M.P.s wished to raise themselves to the position of the Witenagemot.[3]

This *Essay* had a remarkable vogue. In 1776 it was used by Major Cartwright in his widely influential *Take Your Choice*: though Cartwright found in some other source the 'god-like sentiment' of 'the all-excellent Alfred' 'that it was just the English should remain as free as their own thoughts'.[4] The *Essay* was quoted *verbatim* in an address drafted by Cartwright and issued by the Society of Constitutional Information in April 1780.[5] In 1792 the *Essay* was serialized, without acknowledgment and with interpolations, in *The Patriot*.[6] The London Corresponding Society used its arguments to justify manhood

1 *Ibid.*, pp. 50, 43.

2 *Ibid.*, pp. 8–10.

3 *Ibid.*, pp. 68, 90, 103.

4 J. Cartwright, *op. cit.* (second edition, 1777), p. 119. The other source was probably Hume.

5 Butterfield, *op. cit.*, pp. 349–50.

6 Vols. I–III *passim*. One long interpolation (I, pp. 289–97) attributes the origin of the jury system to Alfred, and attacks imprisonment for debt. The favourite passage from *The Mirror* is quoted which describes how Alfred executed 44 unjust judges in one year. Elsewhere footnotes aim at sharpening the political attack on the aristocracy – e.g. the statement that the Conquest saw 'the origin of the immense, overgrown landed property of our race of Nobles and rich Commoners, a right founded in murder,

suffrage and annual Parliaments.[1] Its account of the Norman origin of the alliance between Church and state was still being repeated in 1807.[2]

From the publication of the *Historical Essay* Alfred begins to play a far greater part in the legend than previously. Robert Fabyan in 1516 had praised Alfred very highly, and restored to circulation William of Malmesbury's story that Alfred spent eight hours of the day on work, eight on prayer and almsdeeds, eight on sleep, eating and the needs of the realm.[3] Foxe made this story part of the patriotic legend.[4] Milton praised 'the most renowned King Alfred' on many occasions. But Robert Powell's *Life of Alfred* (1634) drew an elaborate parallel between the Anglo-Saxon King and Charles I, as Obadiah Walker was to do later between Alfred and Charles II.[5] Alfred was not yet an opposition figure. Indeed in the seventeenth century St. Edward had been the Anglo-Saxon King who mattered most, because his name was associated with the lost Anglo-Saxon laws. Yet Edward, the popular Saint-King, 'the superstitious prince who was sainted for his ungodly chastity', as a Puritan lady described him,[6] had never been an entirely satisfactory bourgeois hero. In the eighteenth century he was entirely eclipsed by Alfred, whose part in the legend was much more positive. Even Burke said Alfred was 'generally honoured as the founder of our laws and constitution'.[7] I cannot properly explain the rise of Alfred in popular estimation. Perhaps the fact that the monarchy was no longer the principal enemy made it easier to accept a royal hero, especially one without clerical and Papist associations. A *Life of Alfred the Great* by Sir John Spelman was published in 1709 and may have contributed. Spelman thought Alfred gave 'being and form' to the English state, and that he instituted trial by jury, hundred, and shire courts, and Parliament.[8] A third edition of Asser's *Life of Alfred* was published in

desolation, rapine, and proscription'. The House of Lords, and rotten boroughs, derive from this usurpation (I, p. 419).

1 See their 'Address to the Nation' in *A Narrative of the Proceedings at the General Meeting of the London Corresponding Society, 31 July, 1797*, pp. 19–20.

2 *Flower's Political Review and Monthly Register*, I, pp. 295–9.

3 R. Fabyan, *The newe cronycles of England and of Fraunce* (1516), Chap. CLXIII.

4 J. Foxe, *Acts and Monuments* (ed. J. Pratt and J. Stoughton), II, p. 27.

5 Brinkley, *op. cit.*, pp. 107, 116, and Chapter 3 *passim*. For Walker, see p. 89, n. 3 below.

6 Lucy Hutchinson, *Memoirs of . . . Colonel Hutchinson*, I, p. 6.

7 *Abridgment of English History*, in *Works* (1818), X, p. 294.

8 *Op. cit.*, pp. 94, 106–16, 157–8. Parliament, Spelman thought, was composed of bishops and thanes only. (Spelman, Sir Henry's son, died in 1643, and this edition was published by Thomas Hearne. An annotated Latin version by Obadiah Walker had appeared in 1678.)

1722 in Latin,[1] but there was no English translation until 1848. Another source may have been De Rapin-Thoyras, whose *Histoire d'Angleterre* (1724–7), which contains all the Alfred stories, was immediately translated into English and enjoyed a wide popularity.[2]

In 1723 Sir Richard Blackmore published *Alfred, An Epick Poem in Twelve Books*. This was an entirely fictitious account of the education of an ideal prince, dedicated hopefully to Prince Frederick. The poet's only original use of the legend was to remark that the Hanoverians came to England 'From the old seats, whence Alfred's fathers came'. Blackmore was cautious about the continuity of English constitutional history: Alfred 'was an excellent giver of laws, several of which, as I am informed, remain in force at this day'. But he throws interesting light on the conservative conclusions which could now be drawn from the formerly revolutionary myth. He wrote of George I:

> *'He shall the Kingdom rule by ancient Laws. . . .*
> *Thus he'll the headstrong Multitude restrain.'*

Sir Richard was very popular with the Whigs, and may have helped to make Alfred a more familiar name.[3] It was, however, probably from Spelman that Samuel Johnson derived the remarkable tribute which he paid to Alfred in *London* (1738):

> *'A single jail, in Alfred's golden reign,*
> *Could half the nation's criminals contain. . . .*
> *No spies were paid, no special juries known,*
> *Blessed age! but ah! how different from our own!*[4]

1 Earlier editions had been published by Archbishop Parker (1574) and Camden (1603).

2 English translation in 14 volumes, 1726–31, Vol. I, pp. 342–53; cf. II, pp. 135–201; XIV, pp. 391–468.

3 *Op. cit.*, pp. xli-ii, 289–90. Blackmore cited Obadiah Walker as the best source on Alfred. Sir Richard, who was versatile, had also written a couple of epics on the Arthurian legend (ingeniously adapted as an allegory of William III's invasion of England), as well as trifles of comparable length on *Eliza, The Nature of Man, Creation*, and *Redemption*. He claimed that he composed his poems in carriages and coffee-houses in the brief leisure moments of a successful career as a physician. The poems suggest that the claim was justified.

4 Cf. Spelman, *op. cit.*, pp. 14–15. Johnson's lines were to be quoted by radical reformers with political implications which would have shocked the near-Jacobite doctor. See e.g. *The White Hat* (1819), p. 140.

From the seventeen-sixties Alfred and the Anglo-Saxons advance together in popular estimation.[1] Mrs. Macaulay lived in Alfred House at Bath, and had a bust of Alfred over the door.[2]

The use of the theory of the Norman Yoke by the early Parliamentary reformers drew upon and closely followed orthodox seventeenth-century models. James Burgh quoted *The Mirror of Justices*, Camden, Verstegan, Whitelocke, Milton, Nathaniel Bacon, and many others. Cartwright used *The Mirror*, Coke, Sir Henry Spelman, Prynne.[3] Granville Sharp published extracts from Prynne's *Brevia Parliamentarii Rediviva*, and also used *The Mirror of Justices*, Fortescue, Lambarde, Coke, speeches in the Ship Money Case, and Brady. In 1780 the Society for Constitutional Information planned a pamphlet composed of extracts from, *inter alios*, *The Mirror*, Fortescue, Selden, Coke, Sydney, Blackstone, and the *Essay on the English Constitution*.[4] But suddenly a new note was struck – a note which had not been heard since the Levellers.

It rang out in Tom Paine's *Common Sense*, published in 1776. Discussing the title of the Kings of England, Paine wrote: 'A French bastard landing with an armed banditti and establishing himself King of England, against the consent of the natives, is, in plain terms, a very paltry, rascally original. It certainly has no divinity in it. . . . The plain truth is that the antiquity of English monarchy will not bear looking into.'[5] And he declared that although the English constitution 'was noble for the dark and slavish times in which it was erected', it was nevertheless 'imperfect, subject to convulsions, and incapable of producing what it seems to promise'.[6] The appeal to the past was again abandoned for the appeal to reason. Common sense showed the superiority of a republic to the rule of 'crowned ruffians'. The full implications of this attitude, proclaimed in the year of the American Revolution, were not made manifest until Paine's controversy with

1 Professor Butterfield noted 'Alfred' and 'Anglo-Saxon' as signatures to letters in the *London Chronicle* and *London Courant* in 1780 (*op. cit.*, p. 264). Cf. *Three Letters to the People of Great Britain* by 'Alfred' (1785 – an anti-government pamphlet), and *Alfred's Letters*, essays on foreign policy published anonymously by Sir J. B. Burges in 1793.

2 Alfred figures in three of six odes written for her by admirers on her forty-sixth birthday, in 1777 (*Six Odes Presented . . . to Mrs. Catherine Macaulay*, pp. 17, 35, 42–3). See also her *History*, VI, p. 109; VII, p. 486.

3 J. Burgh, *Political Disquisitions* (1774–5), Vols. I and II; Cartwright, *op. cit., passim*,

4 Butterfield, *op. cit.*, pp. 345–7, 351.

5 *Common Sense*, in *Political and Miscellaneous Works*, ed. R. Carlile, 1819, I, p. 16.

6 *Ibid.*, p. 7.

Burke over the French Revolution gave him wide influence among members of the working class.

In his *Abridgment of English History* Burke criticized those who 'would settle the ancient Constitution, in the most remote times, exactly in the same form in which we enjoy it at this day'. 'That ancient constitution, and those Saxon laws', he concluded, 'make little or nothing for any of our modern parties': it was neither practicable nor desirable to re-establish them.[1] In the *Reflections on the French Revolution*, Burke nevertheless emphasized the continuity through change of English institutions. 'All the reformations we have hitherto made have proceeded upon the principle of reference to antiquity.' Coke, Selden, and Blackstone were praised for proving 'the pedigree of our liberties'. Our inherited privileges, franchises and liberties, and not the abstract rights of man, were the safest constitutional guarantee.[2]

Paine's reply, in *The Rights of Man* (1791), was to reject the historical English constitution altogether. 'If the succession runs in the line of the Conqueror, the Nation runs in the line of being conquered, and ought to rescue itself from this reproach.' 'The Parliament in England, in both its branches, was erected by patents from the descendants of the Conqueror. The House of Commons did not originate as a matter of right in the People, to delegate or elect, but as a grant or boon.' Revolutionary France provided an object-lesson of the reverse process.[3] Norman rule was a tyranny founded on conquest. 'The exertion of the nation, at different periods, to abate that tyranny, and render it less intolerable, has been credited for a Constitution. Magna Carta . . . was no more than compelling the Government to renounce a part of its assumptions.' It 'was, as far as it went, of the nature of a re-conquest, and not of a Constitution: for could the nation have totally expelled the usurpation, as France has done its despotism, it would then have had a Constitution to form'.[4] 'May then the example of all France contribute to regenerate the freedom which a province of it destroyed.'[5]

1 *Op. cit.*, in *Works* (1818), Book II, Chapter 7, and Book III, Chapter 9, esp. pp. 351, 555.
2 *Op. cit.*, World's Classics, pp. 33–5.
3 *The Rights of Man*, Part I, in *Works*, I, pp. 49, 60.
4 *Ibid.*, Part II, *Works*, II, p. 46.
5 *Ibid.*, I, p. 47. In its essentials Paine's argument derives from Rousseau, and Rousseau's development is suggestive. In the *Discourse on Inequality* he posited a primitive Golden Age, from which men fell by the institution of private property: but in

This reminds us of Hare and the Levellers, and Paine, in his hostility to the oligarchy's state, reproduced points dear to Leveller propagandists. 'The whole of the Civil Government [in England] is executed by the People of every town and county, by means of parish officers, magistrates, quarterly sessions, juries, and assize, without any trouble to what is called the government.'[1] The French Revolution gave Paine something the Levellers lacked: an example of a historic constitution totally overthrown and re-made in the name of the people. Burgh had echoed the Levellers when he wrote: 'Antiquity is no plea. If a thing is bad, the longer it has done harm the worse, and the sooner abolished the better. Establishment by law is no plea. They who make laws can repeal them.'[2] That was disturbing enough. But Paine carried the point to an extreme which must have been profoundly shocking to admirers of the continuous British constitution. 'Government by precedent', he wrote, 'without any regard to the principle of the precedent, is one of the vilest systems that can be set up.'[3]

Paine's aim was to bring hereditary monarchy, the peerage, and indeed the whole constitution, into contempt; and here memories of Norman oppression were useful. 'Though not a courtier will talk of the curfew-bell, not a village in England has forgotten it.'[4] If that was at all true, it was a good reason for associating the foreign House of Brunswick and the rapacious aristocracy with the invading Bastard and his armed banditti. In the seventeen-nineties there were persistent rumours that Hanoverian troops were to be used against the reformers. The patriotic warning could be sounded with the same effectiveness, and the same justification, as when the Stuarts had been looking for foreign military support.

So Paine destroyed Burke's historical argument. Hereditary right derives from bastardy, property from theft, the state is founded by conquest, the constitution evolves by military violence. 'All hereditary government is in its nature tyranny', in its origins base and brutal.[5] But Burke's conception of a sacred constitution rooted in inheritance was not only inaccurate: it was also irrelevant. For Paine the argument from

---

the *Social Contract* he is concerned with the *future* foundation of a just, rational, and democratic society.

1 Paine, *Works*, II, p. 47.
2 J. Burgh, *Political Disquisitions*, II, pp. 296–7. Cf. p. 71 above.
3 Paine, *op. cit.*, II, p. 50.
4 *Ibid.*, II, p. 24.
5 *Ibid.*, I, p. 87; II, p. 27.

natural right was more compelling than that from history. The French Revolution showed that men could *reverse* the verdict of history, and throw off the dead weight of tradition and prejudice which, as Burke saw, protected the *status quo*.

Paine was not writing academic exercises: he was calling the dispossessed to action. The Levellers had proclaimed the rights of man in the English Revolution, and were promptly suppressed. Paine wrote in a situation little less revolutionary, and potentially far more dangerous to the ruling class. The most enthusiastic response to the French Revolution came from the victims of the industrial revolution, the small craftsmen and uprooted countrymen – just those classes among whom the tradition of lost rights lingered longest. To them the rights of man furnished a telling criticism of the constitution from which they were excluded. The tramp of their feet and the muttering of their illegal discussions is the essential background to Paine's writings. Despite savage repression, although men were sent to jail for selling it, 200,000 copies of *The Rights of Man* were distributed: a circulation beyond the Levellers' wildest dreams.

But for the radicals, Paine's book was a sword to divide. And the division reproduced that of the sixteen-forties and -fifties, only now the Industrial Revolution had brought into being a large and desperate working class; and this strengthened a preference for reform rather than revolution among propertied radicals. Thus the Rev. Christopher Wyvill of the Yorkshire Association wrote *A Defence of Dr. Price and the Reformers of England* in which he disavowed Paine's arguments as 'illtimed, impracticable, undesirable for England, and more likely to retard than to accelerate the recovery of our just rights'.[1] In May 1792 the highly respectable London Society of the Friends of the People warned the Society for Constitutional Information in Sheffield of the dangers of Paine's approach; in December of the same year they reaffirmed their constitutionalism in a formal resolution.[2] The far more plebeian London Corresponding Society in 1794 reminded the public that 'Alfred, justly styled the Great', had encouraged his people to have and to use arms; so that when three years later they also claimed that 'to restore the constitution to its original purity, and the people to their long lost rights' were their only objects,[3] their interpretation of

1 Wyvill, *Political Papers chiefly respecting the reform of the Parliament of Great Britain*, III, Appendix, pp. 67–70.

2 *Ibid.*, pp. 165–9, 175–8. Cf. similar sentiments in *The Patriot*, I, pp. 212–14, etc.

3 *An Account of the Seizure of Citizen Thomas Hardy, Secretary to the London Corresponding Society* (1794), p. 6; *Narrative of the General Meeting . . ., 31 July 1797*, pp. 22–3. For the Society's interest in military organization, see p. 85, n. 4 above.

constitutional action was at least ambiguous.

The extent of the division between the two wings of the reformers was most clearly revealed in the trial of Henry Yorke. Yorke was a moderate radical, who in 1795 was accused, and convicted, for inciting to unconstitutional action at a public meeting in Sheffield. Sheffield, we saw, had been warned against Paine in 1792, but in vain; in 1794 'every cutler' there was said to have his copy of *The Rights of Man*.[1] This is the background to the trial. Yorke subsequently deserted the reformers, and became an enemy of the French Revolution; but in this trial he seems to have conducted his defence with courage and ability. So the fact that his defence turned largely on his repudiation of Paine is significant.

'In almost every speech,' Yorke told the jury, 'I took essential pains in controverting the doctrines of Thomas Paine, who denied the existence of our constitution. . . . I constantly asserted, on the contrary, that we had a good constitution.' He had always defended 'that magnanimous government which we derived from our Saxon fathers, and from the prodigious mind of the immortal Alfred'.[2] 'If you never read the history of Alfred,' he said to one unfortunate witness, 'how can you say you have read a little into the constitution?'[3] Yorke promised to print his authorities for the Saxon constitution in an appendix, and it would have been interesting to see them; but his printer refused. They included the usual Fortescue, Camden, Coke, Sir Henry Spelman, and Blackstone.[4]

Yorke saw, and welcomed the fact, that 'a general wreck of the Gothic policy is taking place, and all the old and venerated governments of the world are passing gradually away'. Men had natural rights, which they retained in society. If these rights were denied, they would be claimed by violence. But Yorke hoped that violence could be avoided, since 'the constitution of this country, in my opinion, guarantees those rights', and all would be well if only that constitution 'were administered as I think it ought to be'.[5] The difference, in short,

1 *The Trial of Thomas Hardy* (1794–5), in *State Trials* (ed. T. J. Howell, 1818), XXIV, col. 1042 and *passim*.

2 *The Trial of Henry Yorke for a Conspiracy* (1795), pp. 84, 128. Yorke repeated Cartwright's point that 'good King Alfred', the illustrious founder of the constitution, had taught that Englishmen 'should be as free in their actions as their thoughts' (p. 104).

3 *Ibid.*, p. 67.

4 *Ibid.*, pp. 101, vii.

5 *Ibid.*, pp. 135–6, 24, 89–90.

between Wyvill and Yorke on the one hand, and those who agreed with Paine on the other, is that between reformer and revolutionary. Yorke, unlike Paine, believed that 'public force' was necessary, that government was 'coeval and co-extended with man'. Yorke spoke for 'all . . . men of any property',[1] Paine for all men. Yet Yorke, his mind sharpened by his battle against imprisonment and possible transportation, saw the crux of this disagreement in his and Paine's views of the constitution and of Anglo-Saxon society.

This difference of principle went right through the radical movement, though it was rarely stated as clearly as by Yorke. For so long as oligarchical corruption and violent repression still faced the reformers, the alliance between middle-class radicals and the emergent working class was a real one. The point of unity was the visible fact that the constitution in Church and state *had* degenerated from the heroic days of the seventeenth century, whose history the reformers knew so well. Hence the rallying cry of a return to the true principles of Saxon freedom could unite the two wings so long as those principles were not too closely defined.

The White Hat, a short-lived periodical of 1819, written by enlightened middle-class reformers, thus traditionally defined 'The Reformer's Creed': 'That our ancestors enjoyed, in its fullest extent, the right of framing laws for their own government by their representatives; and that at various periods of our history this right has been contended for and maintained against the encroachments of arbitrary power.' Before the Norman Conquest 'the power of the military was in the hands of the people', under elected officers.[2] 'The Commons is not the British Witena-gemot. It is not the representatives of the people, but the representative of an oligarchy.' And *The White Hat*, intimidated into silence by the government's gagging acts, defined in a farewell article its conception of its duty as being 'to unfold the principles of the British Constitution, to point out its corruptions', and to prepare the public mind 'for the change which must take place in the present state of the country'. It was again a definition of a reformist task.[3]

1 *Ibid.*, p. 122. In 1803–4 the pseudonym 'Alfred' was used by authors of anti-French recruiting pamphlets: see *Alfred's Address to the Ladies of England* (1803) and G. H., *Alfred's Letters* (1804).

2 *The White Hat*, I, pp. 124, 35–6.

3 *Ibid.*, p. 133. Another moderate reformer who referred to Anglo-Saxon liberties was Bentham. The Norman Conquest, he correctly pointed out, was not motivated by the principle of the greatest happiness of the greatest number (*Works*, ed. Bowring,

Side by side with this middle-class radicalism, however, the Painite plebeian tradition continued to develop in many variants. Most important perhaps for the working-class movement were the Spenceans. Spence himself makes little direct reference to the Norman Yoke. *The Restorer of Society* described contemporary land-lords as 'like a Warlike Enemy quartered upon us for the purpose of raising contributions, and William the Conqueror and his Normans were fools to them in the arts of fleecing. . . . Nothing less than the complete Extermination of the present system of holding land, in the manner I propose, will ever bring the world again to a state worth living in'.[1] And Spence's view of the origin of property, though generalized, has a strong affinity to the Norman Yoke theory. 'Societies, Families, and Tribes, being originally nothing but Banditties, . . . and the greatest Ruffians seizing on the principal shares of the spoils . . . introduced into this world all the cursed varieties of Lordship, Vassalage, and Slavery, as we see it at this day.'[2]

But it is not so much in his view of origins that Spence drew on the traditions expressed by the demand for a restoration of Saxon freedom. It was rather in his positive proposals. He conceived of the parish as a unit of self-government, and wished to set parishes free from the tyranny of the central state power. Then they could freely federate *from below*, in the way that *An Historical Essay on the English Constitution* described the Saxon constitution as coming into being. The Levellers had also valued highly the surviving communal institutions of the English village, and the jury: this emphasis was common to all radical versions of the Norman Yoke theory. Spence wanted parishes to become sole owners of the land. Even this conception of communal ownership had been anticipated by Gerrard Winstanley: and he linked it up closely with memories of the Saxon past.[3]

1843, VII, p. 196). The freedom of the Saxon system of local courts and juries 'was too favourable to justice to be endured by lawyers', and was replaced by centralized courts whose procedure was conducted in a language unknown to the majority of the inhabitants of the country. 'In British India, this state of things may, with a particular degree of facility, be conceivable' (*Ibid.*, II, pp. 151–2; V, p. 48. These passages date from the eighteen-twenties).

1 Letter V, 20 September 1800. This letter figured prominently in Spence's trial. See A. W. Waters, *The Trial of Thomas Spence in 1801*, pp. 46–7.

2 Attributed to Spence in the indictment at his trial (*ibid.*, pp. 78–9).

3 Cf. Morton, *The English Utopia*, pp. 118, 125–7. The demand for parochial or

What was implicit in Spence became startlingly explicit in Thomas Evans, Librarian to the Society of Spencean Philanthropists, who in 1798 had been secretary of the London Corresponding Society. In his remarkable *Christian Policy the Salvation of the Empire*, Evans declared that there had been 'three great eras from which to date the liberty of the world, that of Moses, that of the Christian, and that of Alfred'. Moses saw the establishment of an agrarian commonwealth, the Christian epoch was ushered in on the broadest republican principles.[1] Alfred, the great and good, again established in England the agrarian commonwealth, federating upwards through tithings and hundreds and counties.[2] Alfred was the third saviour of the liberties of the world: his exertions 'produced the present enlightened, free and improved state of European society'. His is the only constitution England ever had, if it is properly called a constitution. All the tyranny of the pagan Norman Conquest could not obliterate it: and ever since Englishmen have been struggling for its recovery: constitutional and arbitrary principles have been in continual conflict.[3] Now a fourth epoch was at hand. It was time that the feudal system, introduced by the pagan Norman Conquest, should be abolished; time to call upon those whose property originated in conquest for a restoration. 'They are not the nation, but the masters of the nation.' They should be pensioned off.[4] 'All the land, the waters, the mines, the houses, and all permanent feudal property, must return to the people, the whole people, to be administered in partnership' by the parishes. This 'is our natural situation, all our improvements lead us towards its accomplishment, it arises out of our old Saxon institutions and the part, the very small part, recaptured as it were from the Conquest at different times. . . .'[5] Whatever we may think of that as a statement of historical fact, it is a magnificent culmination to the myth. If Paine looks back to the

---

congregational independence of Church and state was in the seventeenth century the hall-mark of those sectaries whose views were really radical.

1 *Christian Policy the Salvation of the Empire* (second edition, 1816), pp. iii, 8. Both editions were published in the same year.

2 The London Corresponding Society, by a pleasing Saxonism, had organized its members in groups of ten, with a 'tithingman' at their head (*The London Corresponding Society's Addresses and Reports*, 1792, p. 9).

3 *Ibid.*, pp. 11–13, 22.

4 *Ibid.*, pp. 8, 16. Evans was prepared to give generous compensation. Dukes were to receive pensions of £40,000 a year, and others less on a sliding scale (p. 30).

5 *Ibid.*, pp. 14, 16–17, 25. The idea of reconquest seems to come from Paine. See above, p. 91.

Levellers, Spence and Evans look back to Winstanley: and all three look forward to theories of socialism.

It is difficult to assess the influence of the Spenceans. They appear to degenerate rapidly into a politically innocuous sect. And yet – the idea of an egalitarian rural community was an unconscionable time dying. Its ghost haunted the labour movement long after the reality had disappeared. From the earliest writings of Owen to the last disintegration of Chartism, and beyond, men thought they could escape from capitalism by building rural co-operative or communist communities. The hold of this dream over the nascent working class surely owes much to the traditions of Anglo-Saxon freedom, of lost rights and lost property which it was still hoped to recapture, and to those dying institutions which it was still hoped to revivify.

Paine's directly political approach was, however, the more obvious influence on the labour movement. For him William the Bastard was only one example among many of class tyranny: the remedy was not a restoration of lost rights, not a re-adjustment of the checks and balances of the constitution, but a transfer of sovereignty to the people. 'The SWINISH MULTITUDE', declared a committee of the London Corresponding Society in 1795, 'are well aware that it matters very little who are the HOG DRIVERS, while the present wretched system of corruption is in existence.'[1] Paine's works, reprinted in 1817, played a big part in moulding working-class thought. Godwin's influence must also have contributed to forming this semi-anarchist attitude. Godwin laid no stress on Anglo-Saxon liberties, but he referred contemptuously to 'the feudal system' as 'a ferocious monster devouring wherever it came all that the friend of humanity regards with attachment and love'.[2] And Shelley took it for granted that there had been 'a continual struggle for liberty on the part of the people, and an uninterrupted attempt at tightening the reins of oppression, and encouraging ignorance and imposture, by the oligarchy to whom the first William parcelled out the property of the aborigines at the conquest of England by the Normans'.[3]

The Black Dwarf in 1817 drew a familiar picture of the post-Conquest period of conflict 'between the people, who wished to be

1 *The Correspondence of the London Corresponding Society Revised and Corrected* (1795), p. 81. 'The swinish multitude' was Burke's notorious phrase, used against Paine.

2 *Political Justice* (1793), II, p. 31.

3 *Proposals for an Association of . . . Philanthropists* (1812), in *Prose Works* (1912), I, p. 275.

free, and the monarchs, who wished them to be slaves'. But the moral which this fighting plebeian journal drew was not so traditional.

> 'As the power is *always* on the side of the people when they choose to act, it followed as a matter of course that whenever a single point was put to the test of the sword, the people were always ultimately victorious. . . . The country has boasted of being free because Magna Carta was enacted, when the least share of penetration would have taught us that Magna Carta was only enacted because our ancestors were determined to be free.'[1]

Paine, Godwin, Shelley, the Spenceans, *The Black Dwarf*: they all concentrated on inspiring hatred and contempt for the oligarchy and its state, with a view to their overthrow, rather than on reminding Englishmen of their ancient liberties with a view to reform. But so long as the main enemy was the aristocracy and the unreformed Parliament, the fundamental cleavage which Yorke had so sharply described was not emphasized. *The Black Dwarf* in 1818 published Major Cartwright's 'Legacy to the Reformers', which restated his creed as he had learnt it nearly half a century earlier. The only note which could not have been found in *An Historical Essay on the English Constitution* was the statement that 'the constitution . . . necessarily existed anterior to all Law; and very long anterior to all recorded Law'.[2] For that opposes an ideal constitution to actual law, as Paine opposed the rights of man to the constitution.

VIII

The Working-class Movement

From the eighteen-twenties the emphasis shifts again.[3] The society of rural communities which nourished memories and aspirations centring round survivals of ancient institutions was in full dissolution. England's

---

1 No. 1, 29 January 1817, p. 1.

2 *The Black Dwarf*, extra number, 23 March 1818, p. 2.

3 It is with every reservation that I venture to suggest even an approximate date. Shifts in ideas are notoriously difficult to pin down, and my own knowledge of this period is insufficient for me to speak with confidence. Perhaps I have post-dated. The Norman Yoke does not seem to be important in the upsurge after 1815, and I have not found it as a vital part of the thought of any major radical or working-class reformer after 1800, except Cartwright; and his ideas had been formed far earlier. Thomas Evans was a secondary figure.

industrial expansion was rapidly increasing the number of a proletariat which retained no links with the land. The working-class movement was slowly working out its own theories. In the eighteen-twenties we meet the word 'socialism' for the first time. The great struggles before and after 1832 showed the profound division of interests between the middle-class radicals and the working-class majority of the population. Both Paine and Spence made their contributions to the thought of Chartism, but the Norman Yoke was not important in the theories of either: in those of the still more influential Owen it had no place at all. And Richard Carlile, who edited Paine's works and shared his contempt for arguments from constitutional precedent, threw overboard the last remnants of belief in Anglo-Saxon freedom. In 1820 he replied in *The Republican* to 'a friend to the primitive common law', who had argued that 'the old common law of England', as it had existed under Britons, Danes, and Saxons, guaranteed full religious toleration. 'This "primitive common law" ', declared Carlile, 'is no more than nonsense, and productive of nothing but common mischief'. Parliaments were not a primitive institution, but were established in 1265 by the armed violence of Simon de Montfort; 'and experience teaches that there is no other means of obtaining beneficial changes in the political state of our country'. 'What is called the Constitution of England is a mere farce and bye-word.'[1] It is the first occasion which I have encountered of Saxon constitutionalism being denounced as diversionary. Henceforward, radicals of the Painite tradition were increasingly to refer to the Norman Conquest merely as an example of the violent origin of class power, with little reference to the society that preceded it.

Carlile's point can be illustrated by the very popular poem which the Chartist Thomas Cooper wrote whilst imprisoned in Stafford jail for his political activities: *The Purgatory of Suicides* (1845), dedicated to Thomas Carlyle. The poet longed to see an England in which man should value love more than money, and should strive 'to make the Poor's heart-smile thy sole delight'. He expressed this dream in a

> *'Fond wish that, now a thousand years have rolled,*
> *To Alfred's land it might, once more, befall*

---

1 *The Republican*, II, pp. 198–9, 25 February 1820. I have not looked at the following periodicals: *Alfred and Westminster Evening Gazette* (1810), continued as *Alfred* (December 1810–11); *London Alfred or the People's Recorder* (1819); *Alfred* (1831–3).

That sun of human glories to behold –
A monarch scorning blood-stained gawds and gold,
To build the throne in a blest People's love!
It may not be! Custom, soul-numbing, cold,
Her web hath round thee from thy cradle wove:
Can heart of a born thrall with pulse of Freedom move?'

The memory of Alfred suggested the possibility of a future in which murder and war shall be abolished 'in Alfred's realm':[1] but it did not tell the poet how that future was to be won. Here we can see both the tenacity of the Anglo-Saxon tradition, and its powerlessness to furnish a programme of action. In the 'forties established institutions and ideas still seemed to the Chartist poet too strong to overthrow, and the people of England too servile to make a revolution. There remained the old naïve illusion of the peasantry, a popular monarchy which would protect the poor against the rich. Cooper became a Methodist preacher.

Yet for the middle class the free Anglo-Saxons were not dead. Indeed, the years 1820–80, the years of the Gothic revival, were in a sense their heyday. The middle-class radical tradition, whose thesis of the continuity of the constitution seemed to have been so triumphantly vindicated in 1832, became respectable in literary circles, and provided a real stimulus to historical research. *Ivanhoe* (1820) contains a rousing song against the Norman Yoke and some interesting linguistic speculations. Keats almost subscribed to Hare's views on the superiority of Anglo-Saxon elements in the English language.[2] Bulwer-Lytton's *Harold, Last of the Saxon Kings*, Kingsley's *Hereward the Wake*, and Tennyson's *Harold* are only the most obvious examples of many that could be given. Emerson called the Norman founders of the peerage 'filthy thieves'; Borrow 'hated and abominated the name of Norman'.[3] The most popular of the Victorian poets reduced to a truism that revolutionary discovery of the early Puritans:

'*'Tis only noble to be good.*
Kind hearts are more than coronets,
And simple faith than Norman blood.'

1　*The Purgatory of Suicides*, Book VII, stanzas xii–xiii, xxv. Cf. Hick's poem quoted as epigraph to this essay.
2　Scott, *Ivanhoe*, Chapter 27; Tillyard, *The Miltonic Setting*, pp. 107–16.
3　*English Traits*, in Emerson's *Works* (1882), III, p. 50; *Wild Wales*, Chapter 2.

In France the Revolution revived the corresponding French tradition, 'back to the free Gauls'. The *Manifesto of the Equals* (1796) began: 'People of France! During fifteen centuries you have lived as slaves!' The idea was probably taken from the Abbé Sieyès's *Qu'est-ce que c'est que le Tiers État?*[1] Thierry and Guizot accepted it, and the former also believed that the English Civil War of the seventeenth century had been waged between the descendants of Norman lords and the descendants of mediaeval villeins.[2] In Germany Klopstock and his disciples similarly idealized Tacitus's ancient Germans.[3] In England a whole school of historians turned to the Anglo-Saxon past to seek inspiration for the present – Kemble, Freeman, Stubbs, J. R. Green. The publication of the records of our early history, begun by the seventeenth-century antiquarians, was resumed under government patronage. In 1861, when Mr. Gladstone was accused of making a dangerously democratic constitutional innovation in asserting the financial supremacy of the House of Commons, he could retort with some confidence that he was merely 'restoring that good old constitution which took its root in Saxon times'.[4]

The Norman Yoke theory, then, was not only a stimulus to political action: it was also a stimulus to historical research. It is easy to decry the history written in the quest for the free Anglo-Saxons. The seventeenth-century antiquarians evolved the Whig legend which bedevilled our understanding of the past for two centuries. One sympathizes today with the shrewd scepticism of a Filmer, a Hobbes, a Brady, or a Hume, all of whom were political conservatives. Professor Butterfield has suggested that the historical knowledge of the Parliamentary reformers of the seventeen-seventies was at least 80 years out of date.[5] On merely historical grounds, Burke had a good case, and Paine was

1 I owe this point to Professor David Williams. St.-Just thought oppression had lasted for 1,200 years (*Discours et Rapports*, ed. A. Soboul, p. 150).

2 A. Thierry, *La Conquête de l'Angleterre par les Normands* (1825), III, p. 408.

3 R. Pascal, *The German Sturm und Drang*, p. 53.

4 Hansard, *Parliamentary Debates*, CLXII, p. 2249.

5 *Op. cit.*, p. 345. Granville Sharp had some realistic remarks about the 'disgraceful and uncivilised customs' of the Saxons in *A Representation of the Injustice and Dangerous Tendency of Tolerating Slavery* (1769), p. 112; but that note dies out in radical literature after the publication of the *Historical Essay on the English Constitution* two years later. I have not come across it again until 1833, when John Wade, the left radical author of *A History of the Middle and Working Classes*, denied that Anglo-Saxon society was the fount of English freedom: recent inquiries, he observed, had tended to lower the previous estimate of this period. It was 'an unfruitful waste of darkness and Vandalism' (pp. 1–5).

wise to shift the argument from historical to natural right. But it is too simple to dismiss the stimulus of the Norman Yoke as though it merely produced propagandist history. Alfred did not establish either bi-cameral parliaments or trial by jury as it existed in the eighteenth century. But there is a reality underlying the idea of Saxon freedom, in the traditions of a more equal society, and the surviving communal and democratic institutions of rural England. The degeneracy of the whole unreformed system of government in the eighteenth century was also a reality. To deny those facts, whether in the seventeenth or twentieth century, is as unhistorical as was the full-blooded theory of continuity.

It is possible to argue that the body of ideas associated with the Norman Yoke contributed something important to historical under-standing by focusing attention on the relation between force, property, and the origin of the state. Where it is most open to criticism is that it never arrived at a conception of history which sees society as a whole, with institutions and ideas themselves related to the social structure, and so of relative not absolute validity. The nearest that the eighteenth century got to this conception was in the *Historical View of the English Government from the Settlement of the Saxons in Britain to the Accession of the House of Stuart*, published in 1787 by John Millar, professor at Glasgow. Millar showed how the Anglo-Saxon Witenagemot had been transformed into the Tudor Parliament in consequence of great 'revolutions of property'. But Millar had advanced beyond the views of the 'free Anglo-Saxon' worshippers.[1]

Still, it was not entirely obvious in the mid-eighteenth century that Brady had been right. The greatest authority was Montesquieu: and he cited Tacitus to show that the English system of government had been 'discovered in the woods'.[2] As late as 1819 a respectable middle-class organ like the *Edinburgh Review* was aware that it was challenging Prynne and Brady, as well as the Tory Hallam, in asserting the pre-Conquest origins of the House of Commons. But it felt that the case was still open to argument, and it argued from the comparative history of the Germanic peoples in an entirely unemotional way, 'protesting in

1 See R. Pascal, 'Property and Society', in *The Modern Quarterly*, March 1938, pp. 167–79; R. L. Meek, 'The Scottish Contribution to Marxist Sociology', in *Democracy and the Labour Movement* (ed. J. Saville), pp. 84–102. Adam Smith, too, knew that feudalism as a social and political order, if not as a military system, existed in England before 1066 (*The Wealth of Nations*, World's Classics, I, pp. 457–8).

2 *De l'Esprit des Lois*, Book XI, Chapter 6. The phrase was often quoted – e.g. by the London Corresponding Society in a manifesto of 1796.

due form against any inferences which may be drawn' by Major Cartwright or the Hampden Club in favour of annual Parliaments and manhood suffrage.[1] The labours of the great Whig and Radical historians were helped rather than hindered by the prepossessions with which they started, and which they all too slowly threw off. Where would British history be without the honoured names of Camden, Selden, Prynne, Stubbs, Freeman, Green?

But by the time the Whig historians were getting seriously to work, the theory of the Norman Yoke had ceased to be of crucial significance for those who were challenging the existing order of society – Carlile, the Chartists and the working-class movement. Indeed, after 1832 (as after 1660) the theory of continuity became an anti-revolutionary theory: freedom slowly broadened down from precedent to precedent. The rural society which nurtured the backward-looking theory of the Norman Yoke was shattered by economic developments; the last vestiges of communal organs of self-government were wiped out by the same process and by reforms of local government. Only when Saxon freedom had ceased to be a rallying cry for the discontented masses did it begin to be enthusiastically taught in the lecture-rooms of Oxford. And ultimately, in the racial form which was rarely hinted at by the earlier revolutionaries, but on which the nineteenth-century historians laid more stress, the conception of a unique Germanic and Anglo-Saxon heritage of freedom could be perverted to justify German or Anglo-Saxon world domination.[2]

We may perhaps compare the part played in Russian history by Narodnik ideas. They sprang from a similar environment, from the village commune. They roused the peasants in opposition to the Tsarist régime and the power of landlords. They too stimulated an impressive school of historians, of whom Vinogradoff is the best known in England. But in Russia too, by the time popular ideas had reached lecture-rooms and text-books, they had become tainted with Slav racialism, and had been discarded by the working-class parties. For their roots were in a society which had been left behind by economic development.

So we must not be too severe in our condemnation of seventeenth-century antiquarians, eighteenth-century radicals, or even nineteenth-

1 *Edinburgh Review*, No. 63, pp. 25–7. Cf. Carlile's views quoted on p. 100 above.
2 See esp. C. Kingsley, *The Roman and the Teuton, passim*; and p. 109 below.

century Whig historians. They tried, of course, to have it both ways. It is logically difficult to believe simultaneously in degeneration and progress, though Rousseau did his best. The assumption that 'all States in the beginning are venerable',[1] and that the highest political task is to restore the original purity of the constitution, contradicts that other great revolutionary idea whose wide dissemination dates from the seventeenth century: the idea that the Moderns were as good as or better than the Ancients.[2] *The Patriot* published translations from Rousseau side by side with extracts from *An Historical Essay on the English Constitution*. The London Corresponding Society declared that 'the natural and imprescriptible right of the people to universal suffrage is founded not only in justice and true policy, but in the ancient constitution of the country'.[3] And many other examples could be quoted.

But on history the reformers could be challenged. Paeans in praise of the ancient constitution suited those who wished to preserve the *status quo*. Henry Yorke ended up, as Paine did not, a law-and-order man. But when Paine brushes history aside to rest his claims on natural right he is equally unsatisfactory. The rights of man are inevitably abstracted from the society in which they are conceived, and take the asumptions and property relations of that society for granted. The state of nature gives the right answers because it is peopled with abstractions from civilized society. Filmer, Burke, and Hegel reasonably insisted that all political institutions are, and that all political thinking should be, rooted in history. But the fact that such thinkers could pick holes in the doctrine of natural rights does not prove them more 'right' than the seventeenth- and eighteenth-century revolutionaries. We are taking the 'Tory' critique at its strongest point.

IX

Conclusion

Yet the theory of the Norman Yoke did not die: it was subsumed by theories of socialism. Paine and Spence, who used the Bastard and his banditti to re-emphasize that naked power lay behind the constitution,

1 *Vox Plebis* (1646), p. 1 (opening sentence).

2 Bacon started it, and down to Swift's *Battle of the Books* most of the leading figures in English literature were involved in the controversy. See especially R. F. Jones, *The Ancients and the Moderns, passim.*

3 *Narrative of the Proceedings at the General Meeting, 31 July 1797*, p. 19.

are the connecting links. They ridiculed the pretensions to sacredness of any institutions which perpetuate the rule of a propertied minority. We can see the fruits of this approach when Bronterre O'Brien tells us how 'our own ruling classes . . . wrung *their magna carta* from King John'.[1] The symbolism of the Bastard might have been extended from kings and peers to millowners, though I have come across no instances of this. Thomas Evans wanted to nationalize mines and houses, but only because he regarded them as forms of real property. An interesting moment occurred in 1819 when *The White Hat* attacked individualism, the 'anti-British notion' that a man's 'house is his castle, an asylum in which none dare to enter without his permission, even to instruct him in his duties. They think it would be . . . an insult to the housekeeper for the magistrate to dare to watch over his domestic rules. Yet these were duties enjoined on the magistracy in the days of glorious Alfred'. When one reflects how much of industry and agriculture was still carried on in small family firms, that the decisive relations between wage-labourer and employer were still regulated by the Master and Servant Acts, this could be read as a demand for state intervention in the labour market against *laissez-faire*. 'This domestic inspection to create domestic and national virtue, brotherhood, unity, and strength was . . . the spring of British glory.' We must aim at 'restoring the old Saxon government, founded on domestic legislation, general principles of integrity and unity'.[2]

I have found no other example of Alfred the state socialist. But good King Alfred's name was called upon in the campaign for shorter hours, because of his division of the day into three 8-hour periods.[3] Once theories of socialism had spread, however, the older conception lost its grip. After Carlile, 'demands for the restoration of Saxon rights' were also ridiculed by a writer in the Chartist *Cleave's Penny Gazette* in 1841.[4] They play no significant part in the thought of Hetherington, Bronterre O'Brien or Harney. Ernest Jones's *Notes to the People* passed lightly over 'the Norman land-robbery' because 'the people' had become

1 *Bronterre's National Reformer*, I, No. 3, 21 January 1837, p. 22 (Italics in the original). Cf. Hare, pp. 66–8 above.

2 *The White Hat*, pp. 79–80.

3 S. Webb and H. Cox, *The Eight Hours Day* (1891), p. 4; J. Rae, *Eight Hours for Work* (1894), p. 9. Round about 1900, the millenary, Alfred's name was in continual use. The Lord's Day Observance Society quoted him as the founder of the English Sunday, who put English laws 'on the foundation of God's Commandments'.

4 6 November 1841.

'repossessed of the land in the Civil Wars'; but he recalled Hereward the Wake as 'the last defender of England'.[1]

In so far as the theory of the Norman Yoke was used by Radicals, and even by some Chartists, it now tended to be restricted to a single point of attack: the landed aristocracy, political oligarchy, social privilege. 'Landlords, then, and landlords only, are the oppressors of the people,' declared Thomas Evans.[2] In the year of the first Reform Bill a poem in Hetherington's *Poor Man's Guardian* contrasted the great days of good King Alfred with those of William IV, and described the aristocracy as

> '– *A most tremendous host*
> *Of locusts from the Norman coast;*
> *A beggarly, destructive breed,*
> *Sprung from the* BASTARD'S *spurious seed.'*[3]

Cobbett was one of the many who referred the origins of English landownership to the Norman Conquest;[4] and the preface to the 1838 edition of Ogilvie's *Essay on the Right of Property in Land* said that 'the present reprint is submitted to the public at a time when the demands of the labouring classes are beginning to be heard from the deep degradation to which they have been submitted ever since the Norman Conquest'.[5]

In Harney's *Democratic Review*, in 1849, it was argued that

> 'this huge monopoly, this intolerable usurpation of the soil, had its foundation in force and fraud. . . . From the hour of the Norman Conquest . . . the whole history of the ancestors of the present usurpers of the soil is a crusade of confiscation, plunder, rapine and devastation. . . . The present aristocracy are the descendants of freebooters.'[6]

The most vigorous invective is to be found in *The Aristocracy of England*, published by 'John Hampden Junior' in 1846.

1 1851, I, pp. 104, 435–6; cf. pp. 173–4.

2 Evans, *op. cit.*, p. 15.

3 No. 55, p. 445, and No. 59, p. 479. Cf. No. 76, p. 615.

4 *Legacy to Labourers*, 1834, Letter II. Cf. *The Opinions of William Cobbett* (ed. G. D. H. and M. Cole), p. 55.

5 Ogilvie's *Essay*, which contains no reference to the theory of the Norman Yoke, was first published in 1781.

6 July 1849, p. 46: Alfred A. Walton, 'To the Trades of Great Britain and Ireland'. Cf. Harney's *The Friend of the People*, No. 28, 21 June 1851, p. 240.

'It is difficult to say which are the most revolting subjects of contemplation, the bastard king who led the way, the ready tools who deluged a whole land with innocent blood at his command, or the reptile swarms who, in the following age, stole in after them to deeds and usurpations equally detestable. Let the English people, when they hear of high blood, recollect the innocent blood of their fathers on which it fattened, and the spawn of miscellaneous, nameless and lawless adventurers, from whom it really flows.'[1]

After the decline of Chartism the theory of the Norman Yoke persisted among advanced Radical working men, free-thinkers and land reformers. But for them it was little more than an illustrative flourish. It was given a last lease of life by the revival of republicanism and the land reform agitation of the eighteen-seventies. 'The workers', declared Boon, who had been secretary and president of the Land and Labour League, 'are nothing but white wage slaves to the same classes who have always been licensed by the land robbers to rob and plunder their forefathers from the time of the Norman Conquest'.[2] 'William the Conqueror is the landlords' god, and the people of England are their slaves', said the republican William Harrison Riley, who was associated with the First International; 'William the Conqueror's landlords will find that they must give way to god's landlords, the whole people.'[3] It was to a meeting called by J. S. Mill's Land Tenure Reform Association in 1873 that Thorold Rogers declared 'The custom of primogeniture . . . was introduced into this country by William the Norman'. It 'is the symbol of the nation's slavery to the foreign conqueror, just as it is at the present time the means by which the owners of the great landed estates appropriate to themselves all, or nearly all, the forces of government'.[4] J. Morrison Davidson, an extreme radical republican who had contacts with the advocates of land nationalization, used the violence and greed of the Norman invaders as

1 P. 21. There are 336 pages in this vein, all highly quotable.
2 M. J. Boon, *A Protest Against the Present Emigrationists* (1869), quoted by R. Harrison in 'The Land and Labour League', *Bulletin of the International Institute of Social History*, Amsterdam, 1953, p. 176.
3 *British Slavery, a tract dedicated to all working men* (1870), a penny pamphlet.
4 *Report of the Public Meeting held at the Exeter Hall, London, 18 March 1873.* Cf. also F. Rogers, *How to Redress the Wrongs of the People* (? late 1860s), C. C. Cattell, *The Abolition of the House of Lords,* and *On Monarchy* (1872); C. Watts, *The Government and the People* (*c.* 1872); W. Maccall, *The Land and the People* (1873–4).

a stick to beat the modern aristocracy with; but he also went to some pains to explode the myth of the free and noble Saxons.[1]

From the late eighteen-sixties the Normans counter-attacked, for the first time. One W. Trapnell Deverell suggested that the Conquest had been 'a great boon to this country', because it welded together a race 'whose manifest destiny it is, under one form or another, to subjugate and civilize the habitable globe'.[2] In 1874 an anonymous defender of hereditary privilege argued, on evidence drawn from the London Post Office Directory for 1879, that virtually the whole Norman people had transferred to England after 1066, that their descendants equalled in number the descendants of the Saxons, and still formed the ruling and intellectual aristocracy of the country. Even a trade union leader like Joseph Arch was clearly of Norman stock.[3]

Our Old Nobility, written by Howard Evans in 1879, in interesting contrast to *The Aristocracy of England* a generation earlier, contains only one passing reference to the Norman Conquest. This, however, strikes a significant new note since it equates the conquered Saxons with 'mere Afghans and Zulus, who, by the divine right of triumphant scoundrelism, calling itself superior civilization, had to put their necks beneath the yoke'.[4] Robert Blatchford, in *Britain for the British*, argued that titles to land-ownership must be based on the Norman Conquest, or on theft by enclosure of common land; in either case 'he who has taken land by force has a title to it only so long as he can hold it by force. . . . The law was made by the same gentlemen who appropriated and held the land'.[5] The last semi-serious use I have found of the theory occurs, significantly enough, in 1911. The anti-landlord budget of 1909 provoked a last flicker of resistance from the House of Lords. A pamphlet produced on this occasion, entitled *Who shall rule: Briton or Norman?* argued from a series of maps that south-eastern England, the

1 Davidson, *The Annals of Toil* (Bellamy Library, n.d.), esp. I, pp. 46–51. Davidson was present at the formation of the Democratic Federation. He helped to popularize Winstanley's writings.

2 Deverell, *The Norman Conquest* (n.d.), p. 20.

3 (Anon.), *The Norman People and their existing descendants in the British Dominions and the U.S.A.* (1874), pp. 18–24, 47, 123–4. John Hare's ghost would be shocked to find his own among thousands of 'Norman' surnames listed in this book.

4 'Noblesse Oblige' (Howard Evans), *Our Old Nobility* (2nd ed., 1879), p. 252.

5 Blatchford, *Britain for the British* (1902), pp. 52–4. Blatchford took this point from Henry George, who assumed that landed property in England went back to the Conquest (*Progress and Poverty*, 1883, pp. 307, 325–6, 337, 345; *Social Problems*, 1883, pp. 65–6).

area of Tory dominance, is also Norman England. In that area 570 livings are in the gift of peers, 'and every one of these clergymen is more or less a political agent of the patron who placed him there. This is the rampart behind which Normanism lies entrenched.'[1]

So the theory of the Norman Yoke can be traced from the London burgher's *Mirror of Justices* – the first timid protest from 'the underworld of largely unrecorded thinking' – till the days of Gladstone and beyond. Its life roughly coincided with the rise and expansion of capitalist society. It originated to criticize the institutions of mediaeval society. It was a rallying cry in the English Revolution. When the battle for parliamentary reform began again in the late eighteenth century, the Norman Yoke once more did service. It declined when the Third Estate was no longer united, Chartism and socialism ultimately taking its place. Its last whimper, appropriately, comes at the most radical moment of the last Liberal government.[2]

The more revolutionary versions of the theory were those of the

---

1 Pp. 27–8, 40–2. The author used the pseudonym Cynicus, a name that in itself testifies to the decadence of the theory.

A separate essay might be written on the Church and the Norman Yoke. *The Mirror* was anti-clerical. Protestant reformers equated the Yoke with Popery. The first encroachment of the Pope on the liberties of the English Church was made under William the Conqueror, said Sir John Davies, a member of the Society of Antiquaries (Fuller, *Church History of Britain*, 1842, I, p. 266). (Thomas Evans drew on this tradition when he called the Norman Conquest 'pagan'.) Later the charge of Normanism was transferred to bishops: in 1641 both Archbishop Williams and Sir Simonds D'Ewes attributed the creation of bishops' baronies to the Norman kings, aiming only at their own financial and political advantage (Hacket, *Scrinia Reserata*, II, p. 173; ed. Coates, *Journal of Sir Simonds D'Ewes*, p. 31). After the Revolution, clerics like Stillingfleet and White Kennett blamed the Norman nobility and bishops for the impoverishment of the lesser (Anglo-Saxon) clergy, despoiled to enrich Norman monasteries (E. Stillingfleet, *Ecclesiastical Causes relating to the Duties and Rights of the Parochial Clergy*, 1698, I, p. xi; Kennett, *The Case of Impropriations*, 1704, p. 23). Kennett used the familiar phrase 'a badge of the Norman Conquest' to describe appropriations. For Winstanley, as for Cynicus, the clergy themselves (and tithes) are a rampart of Normanism; whilst the *Historical Essay on the English Constitution* stated that the Saxon mode of government was destroyed by a combination of the clergy with the Bastard. The clergy had had no place in Saxon Parliaments (Coke would have disagreed here), and therefore favoured William who owed to them his title 'the Conqueror'. 'The lives, liberty, and property of the people of England were surrendered into the hands of the Normans by the baneful influence of the clergy' (pp. 34, 43).

2 No last, there is none. A correspondence about pedigrees dating back to the Conquest, in *The Observer* in May 1954, revealed that anti-Normanism still had its vigorous spokesmen.

Levellers and Diggers, of Paine and the Spenceans. The long life of this backward look, I have suggested, is linked with the slowly disintegrating village community: its persistence into the Labour movement is a consequence of the centuries-long process by which, as capitalism developed, the producers were divorced – gradually and slowly, or violently and suddenly – from the means of production in land and industry. 'True Freedom', Winstanley had said, 'lies where a man receives his nourishment and preservation'.[1] As the peasants were driven from the land, as the ruined artisans were herded into the factories, they looked back nostalgically to the days when they had had some control over the forces which shaped their lives: to a lost freedom.[2] Only as the working class became conscious of its strength was the backward look replaced by socialist theories which put the golden age in the future. But perhaps some propagandist advantages were lost when the enemy could no longer be denounced as 'the French Bastard and his banditti'.

1 Sabine, *op. cit.*, p. 519.
2 Cf. D. Torr, *Tom Mann and his Times*, I, pp. 101–12, 174–9.

FOUR

The English Revolution and the Brotherhood of Man

If all Christian princes do not make opportune provision . . . ,
there is no doubt that the poisonous breath of this rebellion will
corrupt all peoples, far and near, wherever malcontents are found.

Memorial from Charles II to the Doge of Venice,
February 1650, in *C.S.P. Venetian, 1647–52*, p. 139.

Boast not, proud English, of thy birth and blood,
Thy brother Indian is by birth as good.
Of one blood God made him and thee and all,
As wise, as fair, as strong, as personal.

Roger Williams, *A Key into the Languages of America*,
quoted in Perry Miller, *Roger Williams*, p. 64.

I

THE Revolution which began in 1640 was an event of European
significance. The execution of Charles I in 1649 in the name of the
people of England led all European countries to sever diplomatic
relations with the English republic: the Tsar of Russia seized the
occasion to deprive English merchants of their exclusive trading
privileges. Foreign intervention on behalf of the old régime was
prevented only by the absorption of all the great powers in the Thirty
Years War, and by the war between France and Spain which continued
until December 1659. The English Revolution, unlike the French
Revolution of 1789 and the Russian Revolution of 1917, was able to
work out its problems free from direct foreign interference. This helps
to account for the 'lack of bitterness' in the Revolution, of which
English historians are apt to boast and which too many attribute to the
virtuous English character.[1] But the possibility of foreign intervention

---

1 Those who deny the existence of atrocities always leave Ireland out of account,
where massacres and deportation of the Irish population were normal techniques: but
plenty of savagery can be found in the fighting in England if we look for it.

was always present in the minds of the leaders of either side in the Civil War: and the speed with which Charles II was hurried back to England in 1660 sprang partly from fear that the Peace of the Pyrenees might make possible a conjunction of France and Spain to restore the King as an absolute ruler and not as a Parliamentary monarch.

Many of the leaders, and still more of the rank and file, thought of the Revolution which had begun in England as an international event. The Parliament which met in 1640, Samuel Hartlib thought, would 'lay the cornerstone of the world's happiness'. Hartlib himself aimed at 'the reformation of the whole world',[1] and others shared his consciousness of responsibilities to other peoples. It is the object of this essay briefly to consider the international repercussions of the Revolution, and to illustrate the sentiments of internationalism to which it gave rise.[2]

II

For many years before 1640 the radicals in England had seen their own struggle against a background of civil war and persecution in most countries of the Continent. An international conflict was taking place from which, they felt, England could hold aloof only at her peril. 'We forget the misery of the Church in other places', said Richard Sibbes; '. . . they pray, and call upon us, as farre as Prague, as farre as Heidelberg, as farre as France, that we would take notice of their afflictions'. 'Many Churches in France, and other places, are invaded by enemies, oppressed with cruelty, and deprived of liberty.'[3]

There were many attempts to found a Protestant alliance, at first with the blessing of the English government. In 1614 a Scottish minister was arrested in France whilst carrying to a Huguenot synod a proposal from James I for the union of all Protestant churches under the leadership of the King of England.[4] In the next year the famous

---

1 S. Hartlib, *A Description of the Famous Kingdome of Macaria* (1641), Preface; H. Dircks, *A Biographical Memoir of Samuel Hartlib*, p. 17.

2 Some of the evidence on which my conclusions are based has been printed in *The Good Old Cause*, ed. C. Hill and E. Dell, esp. pp. 143–45, 186–8, 197–211, 317–18, 339–40, 425–32. For this article I have tried to draw my illustrations from different sources.

3 R. Sibbes, *The Saints Cordials* (1629), pp. 216, 152. See also pp. 225–30 below, where similar passages from John Preston are quoted.

4 J. W. Stoye, *English Travellers Abroad, 1604–67*, p. 97.

theologian Paraeus of Heidelberg published his *Irenicon*, which aimed at uniting Lutherans and Calvinists under the patronage of the kings of Denmark and England.[1] The Elizabethan and early Jacobean governments regarded 'the Protestant interest' as the English interest, the 'Papist party' as that of Spain. In 1605 the great-nephew of Secretary Cecil could write to his great-uncle about William of Orange's daughter, widow of a Huguenot nobleman: 'She is a foreigner, but Protestant, and so depending of our state.'[2] Similarly Bacon wrote in 1624 that 'the party of the Papists in England are become more knotted, both in dependence towards Spain and amongst themselves, than they have been'.[3] But after the outbreak of the Thirty Years War in 1618 the English government recoiled from the idea of taking the lead of a European Protestant party. In 1622 the works of Paraeus were publicly burnt in England. Charles I gave no support to John Dury's attempt to revive the cause of Protestant unity in the sixteen-thirties: he had to look to the opposition. And so the European struggle became an issue in internal English politics.

Men like Preston and Sibbes and their followers saw a vast and co-ordinated Catholic conspiracy, aiming at the suppression of Protestantism and political liberty. Against this conspiracy the Dutch, the Huguenots, the Bohemian rebels, the Elector Palatine, and Gustavus Adolphus were in the most literal sense fighting the battles of their English brethren. It was with burning shame that such patriots saw the supine or hostile attitude of their government whilst these great issues were at stake. The governments of James I and Charles I pursued a timid foreign policy because they lacked money; but their financial difficulties arose from their inability to pursue a policy, at home or abroad, of which the tax-paying classes approved. The Duke of Buckingham, first minister successively to James I and Charles I, was described in a poem of 1628 as 'the agent for the Spanish state'.[4] Eleven years later the Earl of Northumberland, Lord Admiral, told the Earl of Leicester that Laud, Wentworth, and Hamilton, 'who are the Persons that do absolutely governe, are as much Spanish as Olivares'.[5]

1 M. Roberts, *Gustavus Adolphus*, I, p. 371.

2 Stoye, *op. cit.*, p. 45.

3 Bacon, *Works* (1826), III, p. 506. Cf. *ibid.*, p. 499: A war with Spain would be 'not for the Palatinate only, but for England, Scotland, Ireland, our king, our prince, our nation, all that we have'. This was written after Bacon fell from office.

4 *H.M.C., Third Report, Appendix*, p. 70.

5 Ed. A. Collins, *Letters and Memorials of State* (1746), II, p. 617, cf. p. 621.

These ministers and their sovereigns had an entirely different scale of values from that which put first the welfare of Protestantism and the commercial and colonial interests of England. Kings had a sense of international solidarity. Elizabeth hated executing Mary Queen of Scots, though she would have welcomed her assassination. Both Elizabeth and James disliked giving help to Dutch rebels, however Protestant, against their lawful sovereigns, however Catholic. This solidarity of rulers against social upheaval was suggested by Spenser in *The Faerie Queene*, when Burbon (the King of France) asked for help from the previously hostile Sir Artegall against a peasant revolt; and got it.[1] 'There is an implicit tie amongst kings', James thought, 'which obligeth them, though there be no other interest or particular engagement, to stick unto and right one another upon insurrection of subjects'.[2] James accordingly advised his son to count rebellion against any other prince a crime against himself; yet many Protestant subjects of Catholic rulers had to choose between rebellion and emigration or death.

So the religious disputes over foreign policy were not abstract theological disagreements, or differing warmths of sentiment: they were the expression of opposed philosophies of life. The one, the Royalist, put hierarchy, degree, social subordination first: kings are natural allies against their subjects, trade and industry exist for the benefit of the landed aristocracy and of the royal exchequer; a national religion is a useful means of preserving unity and obedience. 'The chief use' of the clergy, said Sir John Coke, Secretary of State from 1625 to 1639, 'is now the defence of our Church, and therein of our State'.[3] The other, the Parliamentarian, wanted above all to see the national wealth increased (in the first instance, through the enrichment of traders, privateers, and those producing for the market); it was utilitarian, not afraid of drawing on the energy and self-confidence of the unprivileged: in a negative sense it was egalitarian. It saw the international struggle not as a conflict of Protestant rebels against Catholic kings, but of God's cause versus the devil's, of conscience against authoritarian tyranny. It saw a régime which maintained itself by persecution facing one which trusted the independence of free men. And Charles Stuart was on the side of Antichrist.

1 Spenser, *Works* (Globe ed.), p. 353.
2 J. Howell, *Familiar Letters* (Temple Classics), I, p. 105.
3 *MSS. of the Earl Cowper* (H.M.C.), I, p. 90.

III

The Dutch Revolt played a similar part in the politics and thought of the early seventeenth century to that of the Spanish Civil War in the nineteen-thirties, only for a longer period. 'After my duty to mine own sovereign', said Sir Walter Ralegh, 'and the love of my country, I honour them [the Dutch] most'.[1] A regiment was recruited among English Catholic émigrés to help to suppress the revolt: all the chaplains were Jesuits, and Guy Fawkes was one of its officers. On the rebel side there were rarely fewer than 5,000 English volunteers. Many of these 'volunteers' were mercenaries; many dubious characters took advantage of continental wars to make piratical raids on Spanish colonies in America: it is easy to make jokes about the importance of plunder and piracy in the early history of Protestantism. But that is of the essence of the situation. We cannot draw rigid lines between those who acted out of religious idealism and those who acted out of economic calculation. Which prevailed when the merchants of London sent £500,000 to the rebel Dutch out of their own pockets – more than a year's government revenue? When in 1588 the City was asked to provide 15 ships and 5,000 men for defence against the Spanish Armada, the City fathers pleaded for two days to think it over; they returned with an offer of 30 ships and 10,000 men. It was private enterprise that beat the Armada almost in the government's despite: the fight for American colonies, from Drake to the Providence Island Company, was undertaken by private enterprise in face of government disapproval.

When John Rushworth proposed to himself to collect documents illustrating the history of the English Revolution, he found that he could only make sense of it by going back to the origins of the Thirty Years War. Clarendon chose 1625 as the opening date for his *History of the Rebellion*.[2] In the sixteen-twenties a great campaign developed in England to send help to Protestant Bohemia in the Thirty Years War. The lead was taken by Sibbes and his associates, together with Thomas Scott, a minister who had been silenced for his Puritan views. In his pamphlets Scott attacked the influential Spanish ambassador, defended Puritans and Parliaments, and pleaded for an alliance with the Dutch Republic against Spain and Austria. His support, Sir

---

1 W. Ralegh, *Works* (1829), VIII, p. 332.
2 Rushworth, *Historical Collections*, I, Preface; Clarendon, *History of the Rebellion* (1888), I, pp. 3–4.

Simonds D'Ewes tells us, came not only from 'the meaner sort that were zealous for the cause of religion' but also from 'all men of judgment'.[1] To such men, D'Ewes continues, the battle of White Mountain seemed the greatest blow the Church of God had received since the Reformation. They feared it would lead in the end to the subversion of Protestantism in England. All men that had any religion looked to the meeting of Parliament for a remedy.[2]

But Charles I tried to rule without summoning Parliament, whilst letting down repeatedly those whom the Commons regarded as natural allies – the Elector Palatine, La Rochelle, Gustavus Adolphus. When the latter marched into Germany and routed the Hapsburgs, the government, far from sharing popular joy, issued an order forbidding gazettes to print news of Swedish successes. Shortly afterwards newspapers were prohibited altogether: the news for which public opinion was hungry could only be spread by ballads, whose popularity increased rapidly. But soon the news ceased to be good. In 1632 Gustavus Adolphus was killed in action. 'More sad or Heavie Tydings hath not in this Age bene brought since Prince Harries Death to the true Hearts of England', wrote the man who 16 years later was to preside over the court which sentenced Charles I to death.[3] Thomas Beedome expressed prevalent feelings of guilt in praying that:

> 'This be the latest losse we may sustaine.
> And that no more of Heavens great Champions fall,
> Through our default, to so sad funerall.'[4]

Charles I, whose 'default' it mainly was, so far from feeling guilty, offered Spain a military alliance against Sweden and the Netherlands. Diplomatic relations were established with the Papacy for the first time since the Reformation. 'These priestly policies of theirs', wrote Milton in 1641, 'having thus exhausted our domestic forces, have gone the way also to leave us naked of our firmest and faithfullest neighbours abroad,

---

1 Sir Simonds D'Ewes, *Autobiography*, I, p. 158 f. The social division on foreign policy is confirmed by Secretary Coke (*Manuscripts of the Earl Cowper*, I, p. 108), by James Howell (*op. cit.*, I, p. 168) and by Bishop Hacket (*Scrinia Reserata*, pp. 113, 117, 160).

2 D'Ewes, *op. cit.*, p. 153, 162, 169.

3 Lady Newton, *The House of Lyme*, p. 135. Bradshaw's reference is to the death of James's eldest son in 1612.

4 T. Beedome, *Select Poems, Divine and Humane* (1928), p. 32. Many other poets could be quoted.

by disparaging and alienating from us all Protestant princes and commonwealths; who are not ignorant that our prelates, and as many as they can infect, account them no better than a sort of sacrilegious and puritanical rebels, preferring the Spaniard, our deadly enemy, before them'.[1]

But already as Milton wrote the scene was changing.

IV

When civil war began in 1642, there were many Englishmen and Scots who had had much experience of warfare. The Scottish Army of the Covenant was officered almost entirely by men who had served under Gustavus Adolphus. Among officers in the English Parliamentary Army, Essex, Fairfax, Skippon, and Monck had seen service in the Thirty Years War: individual Dutch, Swedish, German, and Huguenot soldiers fought on Parliament's side.

Many of the Parliamentary leaders stressed the international aspects of their cause, and its international obligations. Thus in September 1642 Pym, urging the two Houses to unite closely with Scotland in matters of church government, reminded them that the 'Jesuitical and prelatical faction' which had dominated Charles I's government had not only caused a crisis in England but had 'threatened ruin . . . to all . . . the reformed Churches'.[2] The peace propositions which Parliament offered to the King at York (June 1642), Oxford (February 1643), Uxbridge (November 1644) all demanded an alliance with the Dutch Republic and other Protestant states against the designs of the Pope and his adherents, and for the recovery of the Palatinate.[3] In 1643 General Leslie, commanding the Scottish Army, was reported as saying 'what a glorious thing it would be . . . if we manage to drive the Catholics out of England and follow them to France, and in imitation of the late King of Sweden unite with those of our religion there, and plant our religion in Paris by agreement or by force, and thence go to Rome, drive out Antichrist and burn the town that disseminates superstition'.[4]

Even stronger views were expressed by secondary figures. John

1 'Of Reformation in England', *Prose Works*, II, p. 400.
2 *A most learned and Religious Speech spoken by Mr Pym* (1642), p. 2.
3 Gardiner, *Constitutional Documents of the Puritan Revolution*, pp. 253, 266, 284.
4 Ed. J. G. Fotheringham, *The Diplomatic Correspondence of Jean de Montereul* (Scottish History Society, 1888–9), II, p. 550.

Goodwin, for instance, in a pamphlet published in the third month of the Civil War, reminded his readers that 'the action wherein the Church and people of God in the land are now engaged' was of great concern 'to all the Saints of God' in all the reformed Churches. If their cause prospered 'it will be the riches, strength and increase of them'; 'the heate and warmth and living influence thereof shall pierce through many kingdomes great and large, as France, Germany, Bohemia, Hungaria, Polonia, Denmarke, Sweden, with many others'.[1] Hugh Peter, in a sermon preached in 1645 before the Houses of Parliament, the Assembly of Divines, the Lord Mayor and Aldermen of London, declared: 'Me thinks I see Germany lifting up her lumpish shoulder, and the thin-cheekt Palatinate looking out, a prisoner of hope; Ireland breathing again, that not only lay bed-rid, but the pulse beating deathward: the over-awed French Peasant studying his long lost liberty, the Netherlanders looking back upon their neighbouring England, who cemented their wals with their blood, and bought their freedome, with many, many thousands of good old Elizabeth shillings. Indeed, me thinks, all Protestant Europe seems to get new colour in her cheeks.'[2]

Parliament's complete victory in the Civil War gave its supporters a new consciousness of a mission. Milton's defence of regicide was read in the Netherlands, France, Germany, Sweden, Italy, and by Greeks.[3] Hugh Peter was reported (by a hostile witness) to have preached a sermon before the Houses of Parliament on 22 December 1648, in which he declared 'This Army must root up Monarchy, not only here, but in France and other Kingdoms round about; this is to bring you out of Aegypt: this Army . . . must dash the powers of the earth to pieces.'[4] Cromwell himself was rumoured to have said that 'if he were ten years younger, there was not a king in Europe he would not make to tremble'.[5] Hugh Peter's sense of destiny was expressed by Andrew Marvell in 1650 when he wrote of Oliver Cromwell in his *Horatian Ode*:

1 John Goodwin, *Anti-Cavalierisme* (1642), pp. 49–50, printed in Haller, *Tracts on Liberty in the Puritan Revolution*, II, p. 267 f.

2 H. Peter, *Gods Doings and Mans Duty* (1646), pp. 24–5. The sentiment is similar to that expressed in a famous passage in Milton's *Second Defence of the People of England* (1654), in which he beheld 'the nations of the earth', 'from the columns of Hercules to the Indian Ocean', inspired by England's example, 'recovering that liberty which they so long had lost' (*Prose Works*, I, p. 220).

3 *Prose Works*, I, p. 278. Milton greatly desired to see Greece delivered 'from her ottoman oppressor' (Masson, *Life of Milton*, IV, p. 445).

4 Clement Walker, *The History of Independency*, Part II (1649), pp. 49–50.

5 Firth, *Oliver Cromwell* (World's Classics), p. 304.

'*A Caesar he ere long to Gaul,*
To Italy an Hannibal,
And to all States not free
Shall Clymacterick be.'[1]

Such sentiments came closer to reality when repeated on Spanish territory in 1651 by Admiral Blake, commanding the strongest fleet in the world. He was reported as saying in the public square of Cadiz that monarchy was a kind of government the world was weary of; he believed that all countries would soon annihilate tyranny and become republics. 'England had done so already; France was following in her wake; and as the natural gravity of the Spaniards rendered them somewhat slower in their operations, he gave them ten years for the revolution in their country.'[2] Such words spoken by such a man in such a place were ominous indeed.

V

So much for theory. What influence did the English Revolution have on other countries in practice? The English republican rulers were very anxious to influence European public opinion. A Declaration of Parliament (in French) justifying the execution of Charles I was approved by the House of Commons on 17 March 1649, for distribution on the Continent.[3] Milton was employed as official government pamphleteer for the Latin-reading public of Europe. From July 1650 a weekly newspaper entitled *Nouvelles ordinaires de Londres*, edited by William du Gard, 'printer to the Council of State', appeared every Thursday for despatch to the Continent. There were also occasional extended numbers (*Nouvelles Extraordinaires*), like No. 185, which printed the Instrument of Government in full. *Nouvelles Ordinaires* continued until January 1658, and enjoyed considerable popularity. Mazarin read and quoted it; and the periodical was

1 A. Marvell, *Poems* (1927), p. 90.

2 *C.S.P., Venetian, 1647–52*, pp. 169–70; *Clarendon State Papers*, III, p. 27. Blake's fleet, a Fifth Monarchist preacher proclaimed whilst the Barebones Parliament was in session, would carry the gospel 'up and down to the Gentiles' (L. F. Brown, *Baptists and Fifth Monarchy Men*, p. 24; cf. Sir Edward Peyton, *The Divine Catastrophe of the Kingly Family of the House of Stuarts* (1652). Sir Edward predicted the end of monarchy all over Europe).

3 G. Ascoli, *La Grand-Bretagne devant l'opinion française au XVIIe Siècle*, I, p. 75.

sufficiently in demand for a pirated edition to be published at the Hague in 1651.[1]

The soil of Europe seemed ready to receive revolutionary propaganda. Marx long ago pointed out that the mid-seventeenth century saw uprisings all over Europe: 1648, like 1848, was a year of revolutions.[2] Professor R. B. Merriman dealt with them in his *Six Contemporaneous Revolutions* (1938). His six were in England, France, Catalonia, Portugal, Naples, and the Netherlands. He might have added one in Sicily in 1647,[3] and an eighth, the revolt in 1648 of the Ukrainian Cossacks against the Polish government. In Turkey a rising of Janissaries led to a sultan's assassination in 1648. There were also peasant revolts in Austria (1648), Poland (1648–51), Sweden (1650–3), Switzerland (1653); and risings in many towns of Russia in the years 1648–50.

The Ukraine receives frequent mention in English newspapers of the time. In France the leader of the rebel Cossacks, Bogdan Khmelnitsky, was often compared to Cromwell.[4] A mysterious Scot, Maxim Krivonos (Wrynose), one of Khmelnitsky's fiercest lieutenants, attracted much attention abroad, and was believed by many to be an agent of the Commonwealth government.[5] I have found little evidence of English influence on events in Catalonia. With Portugal relations were closer. In May 1641 Charles I authorized the Portuguese ambassador, Antonio de Sousa, to recruit volunteers in England. But this was only a blind. The troops were in fact intended not to fight for the independence of Portugal but for a coup in Charles's favour in London. Notwithstanding the more than ambiguous behaviour of De Sousa on this occasion, three months later Parliament frustrated the King's intention of sending 4,000 Irish troops to help Spain to subdue Portugal.[6] In 1645 De Sousa published in London a vindication of his country entitled *Lusitania liberata ab injusto Castellanorum dominio*, which no doubt found sympathetic readers. But he continued to

---

1 C. Bastide, *The Anglo-French Entente in the 17th century*, pp. 152–7.

2 K. Marx, *Selected Essays* (trans. H. J. Stenning), p. 203.

3 See H. G. Koenigsberger, 'The Revolt of Palermo in 1647', *Cambridge Historical Journal*, VIII, pp. 129–44.

4 E.g. by P. Chevalier, *Histoire de la Guerre des Cosaques contre la Pologne* (1663).

5 E. Borshak, 'Early Relations between England and the Ukraine', *Slavonic Review*, X, pp. 142–4; B. F. Porshnev, 'The International Background of the Ukrainian War of Liberation, 1648–54' (in Russian), *Voprosy Istorii*, No. 5, 1954, pp. 44–58.

6 Gardiner, *History of England* (1884), IX, pp. 348–9; X, p. 10.

identify himself with the royal cause. His reports home treat the Civil War as the result of a revolt of the lower orders. Only pressure from Blake's fleet, and mutual hostility to Spain, brought Portugal to establish diplomatic relations with the Commonwealth: a treaty signed in 1654 gave English merchants a favoured position in Portugal and her Empire. But as late as 1668, when King Affonso of Portugal was dethroned, recollections of English experience two decades earlier caused high Portuguese officials to shrink from elected assemblies. Seven years earlier, in far-away Brazil, a popular revolt had led to unsuccessful demands for government by 'a type of Parliament', 'a new type of Parliament'.[1]

In Italy the main centre of interest for English Puritans and Parliamentarians had long been Venice, where earlier in the century Fra Paolo Sarpi had seemed almost one of themselves. The Venetian constitution was an object of admiration to opposition thinkers from Ralegh to Harrington and Marvell.[2] But it was in Sicily and Naples, not Venice, that revolts occurred in 1647–8. In the early seventeenth century Sicilians claimed that their Parliament and that of England were the only ones which still preserved their ancient rights and powers.[3] But I have found no evidence of contacts between England and the Sicilian revolt. Englishmen, however, seem to have taken a good deal of interest in Masaniello's rising in Naples. A speaker at a meeting in London in November 1647 said: 'The same business we are upon is perfected in Naples, for if any person stand up for monarchy there, he is immediately hanged at his door.'[4] An English barrister, Nathaniel Reading, is said to have been Masaniello's secretary during the insurrection.[5] Anthony Ascham's *Discourse, wherein is examined what is particularly Lawfull during the Confusions and Revolutions of Governments*, published in 1648, drew on Neapolitan and Spanish experience.[6] In 1649 T. B., 'a Gentleman who was an eye-

1 C. R. Boxer, *Salvador de Sá and the Struggle for Brazil and Angola, 1603–86*, pp. 390, 319; and information kindly supplied by Professor Boxer. The word 'Parlamento' in Portuguese could possibly refer to the French Parlement, but is more likely, Professor Boxer assures me, to refer to the English Parliament.

2 See Z. Fink, *The Classical Republicans, passim*.

3 H. G. Koenigsberger, *The Government of Sicily under Philip II of Spain*, p. 196.

4 *Portland MSS.* (H.M.C.), I, p. 441.

5 R. North, *Lives of the Norths*, I, p. 326.

6 Merriman, *op. cit.*, pp. 98–9, 108. Ascham, who had taken a prominent part in preparing the trial of Charles I, was subsequently murdered by émigré Royalists at Madrid whilst acting as agent for the Commonwealth.

witness', published a five-act tragedy on *The Rebellion of Naples*. His attitude was hostile, and he protested a little too much that no conclusions were necessarily to be drawn for England. In the following year James Howell brought out an English translation of Alessandro Giraffi's *The Revolutions of Naples*.

On the French Fronde, on the other hand, the influence of the English Revolution was great. The Parlement of Paris consciously imitated claims put forward by the English Parliament in 1640–1.[1] The authors of *The Hunting of the Foxes by Five Small Beagles* thought the cause of the Parlement the same as that of the Long Parliament.[2] Between 1643 and 1645 the Intendant of Normandy had frequently reported that Huguenot merchants were sending men and arms to support the Parliamentary cause in England.[3] In 1646 the instructions which the French ambassador to England received from his government betray anxiety lest the English and Scottish revolts might set a bad example to subjects of other princes. A republic, Mazarin stated, would be much more dangerous to French interests than a monarchy, since it would have far more popular support and so far greater financial and military power. By September 1647 Mazarin was worried about the danger of English revolutionary propaganda in France.[4] In fact English pamphlets were printed, in French translation, in the Netherlands, and illegally imported into France in that year; others appeared in 1649 hailing the English Republic. Pamphlets printed inside France itself during the Fronde reported fully on events in England, including the trial of Charles I, sometimes in sympathetic tones, occasionally threatening Louis XIV and his mother with the fate of the King of England.[5] Mazarin suspected the Frondeur leader Cardinal de Retz of

1 L. Battifol, 'Les idées de la révolution sous Louis XIV', *Revue de Paris*, II (1928), pp. 103–5.

2 In *Somers Tracts* (1811), VI, p. 47.

3 B. F. Porshnev, 'The English Republic, the Fronde and the Peace of Westphalia' (in Russian), in *Sredniye Veka*, III, p. 185. The article is based on unpublished French documents in Leningrad. Professor C. M. Williams of the University of New England tells me that Henry Marten had French officers and possibly troops in his regiment; but they may have come from Jersey, with which Marten had connections.

4 Ed. J. J. Jusserand, *Recueil des Instructions données aux Ambassadeurs et Ministres de France, XXIV, Angleterre*, I (1648–55), pp. 16, 35–8, 63; cf. p. 79.

5 E.g. *Epilogue, ou dernier appareil du bon citoyen sur les misères publiques* (1649); *Advis à la reine d'Angleterre et à la France* (1650); *Esprit du feu roi Louis le Juste* (1652). These and many other pamphlets are cited in Ascoli, *op. cit.*, I, pp. 73–104; and in B. F. Porshnev, 'Reactions of French public opinion to the English Bourgeois Revolution'

instigating and financing the publication of these pamphlets. Some of them were definitely republican in tone;[1] and placards were posted in Paris demanding a republic in 1649. 'The right of kings was disputed more than ever before' as a result of Charles I's fate, we are told by Milton's adversary Alexander Morus, Huguenot minister at Charenton. In a thousand public speeches and private conversations, he added, kings were attacked as though all of them were tyrants.[2] Many believed that the days of monarchy were numbered all over Europe. Other pamphlets urged French intervention to overthrow the English Republic before its example shook other thrones.[3]

The leading figures in the French government saw a direct parallel between events in England and in France. Mazarin observed that Charles I had hoped to save the situation by sacrificing Strafford, but had achieved the opposite effect. The Queen Mother took the hint, and told Madame de Motteville that Mazarin must be retained in office lest his dismissal lead to her suffering the fate of the King of England. Charles's execution, she said, was a blow which should make all kings tremble.[4] Mazarin regarded the Frondeurs as 'Cromwellians', who intended to bring about in France what had happened in England. He saw De Retz as the potential Cromwell. Cardinal De Retz on one occasion complained of this comparison to the Parlement of Paris, adding that Mazarin had compared Parlement itself to the English House of Commons.[5]

In 1650 or 1651 Sir Henry Vane, one of the most influential figures in the government of the English Republic, was sent over to make contact with De Retz. Vane carried a letter from Cromwell praising De Retz's 'defence of the public liberty'. The Cardinal, who was most impressed by Vane's ability, tries in his Memoirs to minimize his agreement with the heretical English revolutionaries; but he was in regular correspondence with them at least as late as 1653.[6]

(in Russian), in *Sredniye Veka*, VIII (1956), pp. 319–47. My debt to this last throughout this section is great.

1 Battifol, *loc. cit.*

2 Quoted in J. B. Bathery, 'Relations de la France avec l'Angleterre', *Revue Contemporaine*, XXII (1855), p. 163.

3 E.g. *Les intérêts et les motifs qui doivent obliger les princes chrétiens et autres états de l'Europe à retablir le roi de la Grande-Bretagne* (1649), quoted by Porshnev, *op. cit.*, pp. 335–6.

4 Ascoli, *op. cit.*, I, p. 97; Madame de Motteville, *Mémoires* (1824), III, pp. 206–10.

5 Marquis de Montglat, *Mémoires*, p. 243; ed. A. Chéruel, *Lettres du Cardinal Mazarin* (1883), III, pp. 971–2; IV, p. 62; Ascoli, *op. cit.*, I, p. 97.

6 De Retz, *Oeuvres* (1870–87), III, pp. 115–16; Firth, 'Thomas Scot's account of his actions as intelligencer during the Commonwealth', *E.H.R.*, XII, p. 120.

More significant was the link with the rebel Huguenot towns of Bordeaux and La Rochelle. In October 1651 the English Council of State was seriously discussing the dispatch of an expeditionary force to La Rochelle, at the request of the town. There were long negotiations about sending English troops 'to reduce France to the state in which England now is', as a hostile witness put it: to help to win for France 'the precious liberty' which the Commonwealth had established in England was the way the Frondeurs' representative expressed it to Parliament.[1] In 1651 the ex-Agitator Colonel Sexby and four others were sent by the Council of State to Bordeaux, where Sexby got in touch with the radical wing among the rebels. He translated the Leveller *Agreement of the People* into French, and offered it as the basis of a republican constitution for France, together with a declaration demanding protection of the poor against the rich. Sexby remained in France for two years. Pierre Lenet, principal agent of Condé in Bordeaux, had a scheme for a Calvinist republic, containing many imitations of England – an assembly of representatives of the people, juries, liberty of conscience, liberty and equality of citizens before the law. In May 1653 three deputies from Bordeaux were sent to London, and as long as the Barebones Parliament remained in session it seemed possible that an English army would be sent to Guienne. Two of the three delegates were subsequently hanged: the third prudently stayed in England.[2] In 1657 Sexby's *Killing No Murder* was published in a French translation.[3]

A propos of the appeal from Bordeaux John Rogers, the Fifth Monarchist, stated: 'We are bound by the law of God to help our neighbours as well as ourselves, and so to aid the subjects of other princes that are either persecuted for true religion or oppressed under tyranny. What mean our governors to take no more notice of this? How durst our army be still now the work is to do abroad? Are there no Protestants in France and Germany even under persecution? And do not the subjects of France that lie under the iron yoke of tyranny send and seek and sue unto us for assistance? Well, woe be to us if we help

1 Merriman, *op. cit.*, pp. 176–9; *Portland MSS.*, I, pp. 640 f., 647. The French representatives offered England free trade with Guienne, and a garrison port.

2 *D.N.B.*, 'Sexby', and references there; Merriman, *op. cit.*, pp. 181 sq.; C. Normand, *La Bourgeoisie française au 17e siècle*, pp. 401–2, 416, 421; V. Cousin, *Madame de Longueville*, II, pp. 283, 292–3, 465–75; C. Jullian, *Histoire de Bordeaux*, pp. 493–4; *Thurloe State Papers*, I, p. 245, possibly a letter from Sexby.

3 I owe this information to Professor Olivier Lutaud of the Sorbonne.

not the Lord (*Judges* v. 23) against the mighty; for it is the Lord has sent for us thither, and calls for a part of our army at least into France or Holland. . . . As it is against the law of nature for the King of France to be worse than an enemy to his own citizens and subjects, so it is as much against the law of God, should they supplicate us for assistance, to be worse than neighbours. . . .' Clearly such a revolutionary sense of international obligations was being criticized by 1653; for Rogers continues: 'Let not men dispute so much whether it be lawful to defend or strike in for another's liberty, if it were lawful to do so for our own, seeing we must love our neighbour as ourselves. If we love Christ in our own nation, why not in another?'[1]

Between England and the Netherlands relations had been closer. The Dutch revolt had received enthusiastic support from England, and in the seventeenth century the Dutch Republic was a model for 'the City of London and other great towns of trade', whose merchants, Hobbes supposed, 'were inclined to think that the like change of government here would to them produce the like prosperity'.[2] In 1639, when there was fear of invasion of England by a Spanish fleet, 'the Lord stirred up the Hollanders to fight for us', and they defeated the Spaniards in English waters, to the humiliation of the English Navy.[3] The Dutch fleet was helpful again during the Civil War in preventing Charles I from obtaining foreign military help. The Netherlands was the only country in which open approval was expressed of the execution of Charles I. In 1650 the House of Orange – closely related by marriage to the Stuarts – fell from power, and the States-General at once recognized the English Republic. Negotiations began between the two powers for a close alliance or even a union, on the lines of the union of 1652 between England and Scotland. But economic interests proved stronger than ideology. The rulers of England might be good Protestants and republicans: but they were also trade rivals, and the projected union was seen in Holland as a cool suggestion that English merchants should have free access to the Dutch colonial empire.

---

1 E. Rogers, *Life and Opinions of a Fifth Monarchy Man*, pp. 84–6. There were many similar protests, from Anabaptists and others, in 1653 (*Thurloe State Papers*, I, pp. 385, 501, 534).

2 Hobbes, *English Works*, VI, p. 168; cf. T. Mun, *England's Treasure by Foreign Trade* (1664), pp. 73–82.

3 Nehemiah Wallington, *Historical Notices* (1869), I, pp. 117–18. Wallington no doubt exaggerated the danger to England, but not the fears of English Protestants.

Negotiations broke down, the English Parliament passed the Navigation Act aimed against the Dutch carrying trade, and war ensued.

But there were strong parties in both countries who opposed the war. If the English 'could knock out Holland with one arm', said an English official, 'political expediency must prompt them to raise her with the other, for the honour and glory of republics in general'.[1] Once it was shown that the English fleet could not be defeated, the Dutch government was prepared to accept the Navigation Act; when Cromwell became Lord Protector he soon put an end to the war. 'It ought to be our principal aim', he told Dutch representatives in November 1653, 'to obtain security against [the] house of Austria, and to organize our affairs in such a way that we did not need to fear anybody's power, and that we could dictate the law concerning commerce to the whole world'.[2] The mutual interests of the two republics were shown by an agreement that the Dutch should expel the exiled Stuarts from their territories and that the House of Orange should be excluded from office in Holland.

In Germany, desolated by the Thirty Years War, there was no revolution; but there too English influence was felt. In quarrels between the Elector of Brandenburg and the Estates of Cleves and Mark, comparisons and arguments drawn from England were frequently exchanged. The Elector complained in 1647 that some leaders of the Estates had threatened publicly to treat him as the English had treated their King.[3] In a constitutional struggle inside Hamburg, which lasted from the sixteen-forties until 1712, the opposition often quoted the example of England in demanding popular sovereignty. In 1649 one of their leaders called for a 'league of free commonwealths', to be composed of England, the Netherlands, the Swiss cantons and the free towns of the Hansa and the Empire. The idea met with a sympathetic response from Strasbourg, Frankfurt, and Nuremberg.[4] In 1651 'one Dr. Seifrid, professor at Tubing[en] in the D. of Wirtenberg's country' wrote 'a base book to prove the King's murder lawful'. He was imprisoned, and the book was burnt. The

---

1 *C.S.P. Venetian, 1653–4*, p. 99.

2 Abbot, *The Writings and Speeches of Oliver Cromwell*, III, p. 124; cf. pp. 106–7.

3 Gerhard Schilfert, 'Zur Geschichte der Auswirkungen der englischen bürgerlichen Revolution auf Nordwestdeutschland', in *Beiträge zum neuen Geschichtsbild, zum 60 Geburtstag von Alfred Meusel* (ed. F. Klein and J. Streisand), pp. 127–8; F. L. Carsten, *The Origins of Prussia*, p. 235.

4 Schilfert, *op. cit.*, pp. 116–22.

author narrowly escaped a like fate at the hands of the indignant Duke; but – interestingly enough – 'he was saved by great intercession and banished the country'.[1] One would like to know who the intercessors were, and what were their reasons.

Finally, we may note the impact of the English Revolution on world Jewry. One of the essential preconditions for the millennium was held to be the conversion of the Jews,[2] so many of the sects with Fifth Monarchist tendencies interested themselves greatly in things Jewish. John Robins the Ranter had a scheme for leading 144,000 persons to reconquer the Holy Land. The first volunteers began by training on dry bread, raw vegetables, and water.[3] His disciple, the goldsmith Thomas Tany, taught himself Hebrew and announced in 1650 that he had been sent to proclaim the return of Jews of all nations to their native land, where Jerusalem would be built. Some years later he built himself a small boat 'to carry him to Jerusalem'. He set out in it for Holland 'to call the Jews there', but was drowned on the way.[4] Notwithstanding their extravagance, such views had some practical consequences. The Fifth Monarchists were enthusiasts for the readmission of Jews into England. As early as March 1651–2 Robert Norwood was urging that 'the Jews should be tolerated amongst us'.[5] In their turn, Fifth Monarchist doctrines had great influence on Jews all over the world. Carried to Smyrna by Puritan merchants, they paved the way for the rise of the pseudo-Messiah, Sabbathai Zevi.[6]

1 Elizabeth of Bohemia to Charles II, quoted in M. A. Everett Green, *Elizabeth Electress Palatine, Queen of Bohemia*, p. 431.

2 Marvell's allusion in 'To His Coy Mistress' was very topical.

3 J. Reeves, *A Transcendent Spiritual Treatise* (1711), pp. 5–14 (first published 1652); Lodowick Muggleton, *The Acts of the Witnesses of the Spirit* (1699), pp. 20–1, 44–6. See below, pp. 283–4.

4 T. Tany, *I Proclaime From the Lord of Hosts The Returne of the Jewes* (1650), single sheet; *Theaureaujohn His Aurora* (1655, written in 1650), p. 58; Muggleton, *loc. cit.* I am indebted to the kindness of Mr A. L. Morton for the first of these references. Tany adopted the name of Theaureaujohn at divine command on 23 November 1649. See p. 284 below.

5 Captain Robert Norwood, *Proposals for the propagation of the Gospel, Offered to the Parliament* (1651[–2]), p. 17. Norwood was an associate of Tany. See also Joshua Garment, *The Hebrews Deliverance at Hand* (1651), *passim*. Garment was another disciple of Robins.

6 Lucien Wolf, *Manasseh ben Israel's Mission to Oliver Cromwell*, p. xv.

VI

After the execution of Charles I, as the new ruling groups began to consolidate themselves in power in England, ideological considerations gradually yielded place to economic interests. In the Dutch War, international Protestantism was subordinated to the interests of England. A shrewd Frenchman writing in 1652 saw prophetically that Cromwell and the English Republic had set themselves aims unique in history – the political and economic subordination of the whole world.[1] When appeals were made to popular hatred of Catholicism in England, it was not in order to stimulate a European crusade against the Pope, but for a war to subjugate Ireland. Some of the Levellers opposed the government's Irish policy. Walwyn was reported as saying 'the cause of the Irish Natives in seeking their just freedoms, immunities, and liberties, was the very same with our cause here, in indeavouring our own rescue and freedom from the power of oppressors'.[2] 'What had the English to do in their Kingdome?' he asked. 'The Irish did no more but what we would have done ourselves, if it had been our case'.[3] An anonymous pamphlet published in 1649 attacked in the same sentence the way in which 'the Frenchmen dealt with the Waldenses' and 'the English hunted the poor Irish'.[4] When war was finally declared on Spain, it was in alliance with Catholic France, and its object was to grab colonies rather than to promote Protestantism.

Cromwell was reported as saying that under Charles I 'England had ruined the Protestant party in France'; and now 'England must restore it'.[5] Clearly Oliver was thinking primarily of the interests of the nation which he now ruled, not of the revolutionary cause as such. He apparently considered at one time obtaining the cession of Bordeaux to England.[6] This attitude became dominant after 1653. The 'Protestant interest' became once more an asset of English foreign policy. It was important, for instance, to persuade the Swiss Protestant cantons that England would protect their interests against the Hapsburgs better than France. They were offered English subsidies and support only

1 S. Sorbière, *Lettres et Discours* (1660), pp. 205–11.

2 *Walwyns Wiles* (1649), in Haller and Davies, *The Leveller Tracts*, 1647–53, p. 310.

3 T. Edwards, *Gangraena*, Part II (1646), p. 27; cf. T. Prince, *The Silken Independents Snare Broken* (1649), pp. 6–7.

4 *Tyranipocrit Discovered*, printed in *British Pamphleteers*, edited by G. Orwell and R. Reynolds, I, p. 105.

5 *The Journal of Joachim Hane*, ed. Firth, pp. xv–xviii.

6 Cousin, *op. cit.*, II, p. 359; cf. *Thurloe State Papers*, I, p. 320.

when they were actually engaged in war and in so far as they accepted English guidance. It was good for English prestige to have Protestants from all parts of the world – in Bremen, for instance – appealing to the Protector for help.[1]

This was a purely nationalist policy. Its agents were no longer revolutionaries like Sexby, but worldlings with City connections like John Thurloe and John Pell, Samuel Morland and George Downing – the latter both to be knighted by Charles II. 'It is an observation of that Excellent Prince, the Duke of Rohan', Morland tells us, 'that the Interest of the chief Magistrate of England is, by all means to become Head of the Reformed Party throughout Europe'. Cromwell, Morland thought, had done this after the Stuarts 'most treacherously betrayed the Protestant Cause'.[2]

Oliver sent a Huguenot minister, Stoupe, on a tour of France in the spring of 1654, to propose English protection to the Huguenots if they would unite to demand the restoration of their privileges. But they were not interested.[3] They probably guessed, as Thurloe later explained, that Cromwell wanted to draw the French Huguenots 'to a dependence upon him, and thereby keep an interest in France in all events and also do that which was most acceptable to his people as to all other Protestants in the World, whose cause and Interest he professedly asserted on all occasions and laid the foundation of becoming the head and Protector of them'. In December 1654 Oliver assured the French Ambassador that if the Huguenots 'should offer frivolously . . . to disturb the peace of France . . . he would arm against them'.[4] Foreign Protestants acted as vital sources of information for Thurloe's intelligence service:[5] similarly in negotiations for the readmission of the Jews into England in 1655 their value as intelligence agents carried at least as much weight as the religious arguments put forward for their admission, or the economic arguments against it.

Not, of course, that foreign Protestants got nothing from the

1 *The Protectorate of Oliver Cromwell*, ed. R. Vaughan (1838), II, p. 238, I, p. 336; Abbot, *op. cit.*, III, pp. 685 f., 710; *Thurloe State Papers*, II, pp. 492, 685–6.

2 S. Morland, *The History of the Evangelical Churches of the Valleys of Piemont* (1658), Sig. A 2v–3. Morland's book was written on Thurloe's instructions, and was dedicated to Cromwell. Sir Samuel had to withdraw it hastily after the Restoration.

3 G. Burnet, *History of My Own Time* (1897), I, pp. 130–1; Firth, *Journal of Joachim Hane*, pp. xii–xxvii.

4 S. von Bischoffshausen, *Die Politik des Protectors Oliver Cromwell*, p. 198; *Thurloe State Papers*, III, p. 61.

5 R. Vaughan, *op. cit.*, II, pp. 45–6 and *passim*.

connection. English diplomatic intervention on their behalf, backed by a mighty army and navy, could considerably alleviate the position of persecuted minorities. The best-known case is that of the Vaudois, dear to English Protestants because of the large place they occupy in Foxe's *Book of Martyrs*. Against their massacre in 1655 the Protector protested to the Duke of Savoy in burning words, probably drafted by Milton.[1] The English government threatened that Blake's fleet would intervene to seize Nice and Villafranca, and Milton wrote on the Protector's behalf to all the leading Protestant powers. Thurloe incited the Swiss to declare war on Savoy. But in fact it was the French government which gave effective help to the victims of the massacre, though its motive in so doing was no doubt to forestall England. £38,232 was raised in England by a public collection, started with £2,000 from the Lord Protector. But little more than half of this sum reached Savoy, and there were rumours of embezzlement. Milton's famous sonnet, with its appeal to God for vengeance, was a confession of earthly failure. But the employment of Irish troops against the Vaudois was used to justify the brutal transplantation of the Irish to Connaught.[2] The 'Protestant crusade' ceased to be a real aspiration: it remained a legend, useful when appealing to the patriotism of Royalist divines and Presbyterian parliaments;[3] useful too as an excuse for shipping disaffected troops to military service in the West Indies or on the Continent. Army officers in Jamaica in July 1655 conceived that 'the propagation of the gospel was the thing principally aimed at and intended in this expedition'.[4]

A man like George Fox, the Quaker, later an apostle of non-violence, felt that the Revolution had been betrayed. In 1657 he wrote a letter addressed to the Army leaders and the government, but intended 'for the inferior officers and soldiers to read'. In this he said: 'Had you been faithful to the power of the Lord God which first carried you on, you had gone into the midst of Spain, into their land, to require the blood of the innocent that there had been shed, and commanded them

---

1 Morland, *op. cit.*, p. 570.

2 Vaughan, *op. cit.*, II, p. 302, 310 f.; Abbot, *op. cit.*, III, p. 521.

3 Parr, *Life of . . . James Usher, . . . Archbishop of Armagh* (1686), p. 74; ed. J. T. Rutt, *Parliamentary Diary of Thomas Burton*, II, p. 313. The Presbyterian Sir Robert Harley prayed on his deathbed in 1656 for 'the ruine of Antichrist, for the Churches of God beyond sea, naming Savoy, Switzerland, Germany' (ed. T. T. Lewis, *Letters of the Lady Brilliana Harley*, Camden Society, p. xxviii).

4 *C.S.P., Venetian, 1655–66*, pp. 101–2; *Thurloe State Papers*, II, p. 681.

to have offered up their Inquisition to you, and gone over them as the wind, and knocked at Rome's gates before now, and trampled deceit and tyrants under. . . . And if ever your soldiers and true officers come again into the power of God which hath been lost, never set up your standard until you come to Rome.'[1]

VII

Some of the revolutionaries spoke not only of the brotherhood of Protestants, but also of the brotherhood of man. This goes back to Francis Bacon, whose conception of an industrial science which should be devoted to 'the relief of man's estate' had a profound influence on many supporters of Parliament.[2] But there were others. George Hakewill's spirited defence of the achievements of 'the moderns' against 'the ancients' helped to inspire a belief in progress before 1640, and so in the possibility of the improvement of society *by man*. Hakewill saw that, thanks to the mariner's compass and transoceanic trade 'the whole world' had been 'made as it were one Commonwealth, and the more distant nations, fellow citizens of the same body politic'; he described himself as 'a citizen of the world'.[3] John Preston, leader of the Puritan party until his premature death in 1628, often expressed this in purely religious terms. Labouring to do good to mankind is godliness.[4] Against this background Milton's pronouncements on human brotherhood can be seen not as unique utterances but as the culmination of a long tradition: 'Who knows not that there is a mutual bond of amity and brotherhood between man and man over all the world, neither is it the English sea that can sever us from that duty and relation.'[5]

---

1 Quoted by M. R. Brailsford, *A Quaker from Cromwell's Army, James Naylor*, pp. 23–5. Such passages create grave difficulties for the historians who believe that the Quakers were *always* uncompromising pacifists, even before the defeat of the revolutionary cause. Cf. a similar pamphlet, dated 1659, by another leading Quaker, Edward Burroughs, in his *Works* (1672), pp. 537–40.

2 B. Farrington, *Francis Bacon, Philosopher of Industrial Science*, Chapters V–VIII: R. F. Jones, *Ancients and Moderns*, esp. pp. 48, 65, 91 f., 122.

3 G. Hakewill, *An Apologie or Declaration of the Power and Providence of God in the Government of the World*, p. 323 and Preface. This was first published in 1627: I quote from the edition of 1635.

4 See below, p. 246.

5 *Prose Works*, II, p. 19. The passage comes from 'The Tenure of Kings and Magistrates', Milton's defence of regicide.

James Harrington, no Puritan, proposed in *Oceana* that England, after establishing the freedom of a commonwealth at home, should export it, her armies wielding the sword in the interests of God and mankind. 'If thy Brother crys to thee in affliction, wilt thou not hear him?' Oceana was 'not made for her self only, but given as a Magistrat of God to Mankinde, for the vindication of common Right, and the Law of Nature'. 'The late appearances of God to you', he told his countrymen, have not 'bin altogether for yourselves; he has surely seen the Afflictions of your Brethren, and heard their cry by reason of their Taskmasters'.[1] By the radical groups among the revolutionaries this conception of their international obligations was accepted without question. Gerrard Winstanley, the Digger, wrote a pamphlet which was signed by himself and forty-one others 'for and in the behalf of the poor oppressed people of England and the whole world'.[2] George Fox addressed one of his earliest pamphlets *To the World* and another *To all the Nations under the Whole Heavens*: his followers carried this out by undertaking world-wide missionary activity. Mary Fisher, who in 1657 set out to convert the ruler of the Ottoman Empire, later married a man of whom her highest praise was that he 'desired the good of all mankind'.[3]

The causes of the contemporaneous revolutions and upheavals of the mid-seventeenth century are no doubt to be found in the all-European crisis of that period.[4] But the example and ideas of the English Revolution certainly made their contribution to the political and social unrest in other countries of Europe. In their turn the risings elsewhere helped to build up the hopes not only of those revolutionaries who wished to export freedom from England, but also of those who thought the Kingdom of God was at hand. When both expectations were disappointed the disillusion must have been great, difficult though it is to trace except in individual cases. After Milton had destroyed his sight for God's betrayed and beaten cause, he devoted what remained of his life to the difficult but necessary task of justifying the ways of the Almighty to man. But he is one of the few who continued to expect a political solution. More typical was George Fox, who abandoned his bellicosity, and organized the Quaker sect on the

1 Harrington, *Works*, pp. 194, 200–3.
2 Sabine, *op. cit.*, p. 277.
3 M. R. Brailsford, *Quaker Women, 1650–90*, p. 280.
4 E. Hobsbawm, 'The Crisis of the 17th century', *Past and Present*, Nos. 5 and 6, 1954.

assumption that Christ's kingdom was not of this world. For Bunyan too *The Holy War* was no longer – as it had been for Fuller a generation earlier – a Crusade, nor did it involve the community as a whole: it was waged in the heart of the individual. The gradual collapse of their noble dreams for the rest of the world as well as for England must have had incalculably depressing effects on the morale of the radicals; and must have contributed to that moral disintegration which made the Restoration of Charles II so unexpectedly easy.

VIII

'What difference between Asia and Africa', asked Roger Williams, 'between Europe and America, between England and Turkey, London and Constantinople?'[1] Did the sense of brotherhood between man and man which we have been describing extend across the Atlantic and Indian Oceans as well as across the English Channel (and more successfully than across the Irish Sea)? Here we encounter difficulties. 'Three hundred years of European imperialism, which was ultimately to become an immense organization of hypocrisy, have', in the measured words of Professor Perry Miller, 'made us sceptical',[2] especially of professions of good will towards native peoples uttered by men engaged in dispossessing those peoples. Harrington himself has been seen, not altogether fairly, as a prophet of British imperialism. He certainly did not wish all peoples to enjoy equal freedom immediately.[3]

Clearly an element of hypocritical self-interest was there from the first. When in 1613 English merchants complained that treaties and contracts between Dutch merchants and rulers of states in the East Indies were invalid because extorted by force, their complaint was justified; but we may suspect their motives in making it. Similarly, we need not attribute to disinterested philanthropy the remarks which Lord Chancellor Hatton addressed to the Parliament of 1589. Spain, he said, was hated by the provinces subject to her, as the Indians, the Neapolitans, the Milanese, who will soon, he supposed, begin to throw off the yoke of their servitude and subjection.[4] Since Spain was trying

1 Roger Williams, *The Bloudy Tenent* (1848), p. 275.
2 P. Miller, 'Religion and Society in the Early Literature of Virginia', in *Errand into the Wilderness*, p. 102.
3 See below, p. 274.
4 Neale, *Elizabeth I and her Parliaments, 1584–1601*, p. 200; cf. Bacon, *Works* (1826), III, pp. 33, 455, 471–2.

to maintain a monopoly hold over trade with southern and central America, it was to the interest of English merchants and sea-dogs to enlist Indian help in their attempts to break open that monopoly. One should therefore be suspicious of expressions of concern about Spanish oppression of the American Indians in the mouths of Sir Walter Ralegh, or of King James in the charter incorporating the Virginia Company, or of John Pym, treasurer of the Providence Island Company. Subjectively they may have been genuine. But when an opponent of slavery on Providence Island began to assist negroes to escape, he was promptly rebuked by the Company. 'Religion', he was told, 'consists not so much in an outward conformity of actions as in truth of the inward parts'.[1]

Nevertheless, however dubious the motives of the propagandists, the propaganda against Spain had its effect. Kind-hearted Puritans with no investments in colonial enterprises were shocked to read in their geography books of 'the unparalleled cruelty of the Spaniards, who killed, burnt, and hanged above 50 millions of natives since their first plantation there'.[2] In 1621 a well-known London preacher, John Everard, was imprisoned by the Council for a sermon against Spanish cruelties in the Indies. There was thus a good deal of history behind the remarkable *Manifesto* which Milton wrote for Cromwell's government in 1655 to justify the declaration of war against Spain. It is, I believe, the first state paper ever to make a public grievance of the maltreatment of extra-European peoples by a great power. The Protector's government, Milton declared, properly used its naval power 'in avenging the blood . . . of the poor Indians, which . . . has been so unjustly, so cruelly, and so often shed by the hands of the Spaniards: since God has made of one blood all nations of men for to dwell on all the face of the earth. . . . All great and extraordinary wrongs done to particular persons ought to be considered as in a manner done to all the rest of the human race'.[3] Whatever we may think of the motives of the English government, with the blood of countless Irishmen still reeking on its hands, there is still great significance in having the principle of human brotherhood thus officially proclaimed as one which should guide the

1 A. P. Newton, *Colonizing Activities of the Early Puritans*, p. 149.
2 Ed. A. G. Reid, *The Diary of Andrew Hay* (Scottish History Society), p. 218.
3 *Prose Works*, II, pp. 335–6. Cf. a letter from Thomas Gage to Col. Edward Popham, June 1651, in *Leyborne-Popham MSS.* (H.M.C.), p. 101; and a paper of 1653 by Vermuyden, in *Thurloe State Papers*, II, p. 126.

actions of all states. Milton and very many English supporters of the government undoubtedly took the principle seriously.

IX

A desire for the conversion of infidels to Christianity was another claim frequently advanced by English colonists which today rightly arouses suspicion. Too often it merely served as a cover for aggression, subjugation, and extermination of extra-European peoples. It was apt to figure more prominently on company prospectuses in England than in the activities of the early colonists.[1] And it had its economic point. When the Indians were converted, observed Hakluyt, Purchas and many others, they would naturally wish to wear Christian garments, and that would be good for the English cloth trade.[2] American traders 'have won riches but not Souls', said the author of *The Whole Duty of Man* later in the century. 'The Gospel in one hand and a sword in the other has made many slaves, but I fear few Christians.'[3]

Yet Professor Perry Miller, whose sceptical words I quoted above, used them in an essay whose object was to show that the proposal to convert the Indians played a real as well as a propagandist part in the minds of those who ran the Virginia Company. And although this 'great and noble intention' collapsed, so far as Virginia is concerned, after the massacre of 1622,[4] further north there are cases in which Englishmen – only individuals and usually religious and political radicals – showed a genuine concern for the welfare of the native inhabitants. Roger Williams, for instance, contested the King of England's right to grant the colonists lands which belonged not to him, but to the Indians who hunted over them. He demanded that the Indians should at least receive compensation. Under his influence slavery was abolished in Rhode Island. The Quakers also have an excellent record of behaviour towards the American Indians, George Fox being one of the first Englishmen to declare publicly against slavery.[5] John Eliot, 'the

---

1 R. Hakluyt, *Principal Navigations* (Everyman ed.), VIII, pp. 110–20; P. Miller and T. H. Johnson, *The Puritans*, p. 403, quoting John Smith's *Advertisement for the unexperienced Planters of New England* (1631).

2 L. B. Wright, *Religion and Empire*, pp. 26, 48, 124–32.

3 *The Causes of the Decay of Christian Piety*, in *The Works of the Author of The Whole Duty of Man* (1704), p. 302.

4 P. Miller, *Errand into the Wilderness*, pp. 99–140.

5 Roger Williams, *The Bloudy Tenent of Persecution*, p. xiii; Perry Miller, *Roger*

Apostle to the Indians', preached to them in their own tongue and translated the Bible into the dialect of the Massachusetts Indians in 1658. He was largely financed from England, where in July 1649 Parliament had instituted the Society for the Propagation of the Gospel in New England, and had ordered collections to be made in every parish in England. The preamble to this Act is a remarkable declaration of responsibility towards the Indians. The proceeds of the collection were sufficient to maintain Eliot as one of the Society's first salaried agents. A concern for the welfare of the 'ignorant Nations of the Earth' was one of the lessons Richard Baxter had learnt by 1664, thanks to the activities of Eliot and the Society for the Propagation of the Gospel. For the cynical it is worth recording that the treasurer of this Society, Baxter's friend Henry Ashurst, was a wealthy war profiteer and one of the principal traders to America.[1] As early as 1649 at least one Englishman attacked merchants who pretended their object was to convert the heathen but in fact engaged 'in robbing of the poore Indians of that which God and nature hath given them; . . . and although their dealing concerning the Indians goods bee bad, yet they deale worser with their persons; for they either kill them, which is bad, or make them slaves, which is worse: I know not what to say concerning such impious proceedings with them poore innocent people'. The author goes on to link exploitation at home with colonial oppression and war abroad: the rich oppress the poor, and use them to 'robbe the poore Indians' or to 'kill our neighbour Tyrants slaves' when (because of some supposed injury) war is declared and we 'send some of our slaves to kill some of their slaves, and then one innocent shall kill another'.[2]

After 1653 it was clear that no continental country was going to follow England's example. At home the conservative Parliamentarians slowly brought the radical revolutionary movement under control. Colonial adventures in Ireland and the West Indies, commercial wars against the Netherlands and Spain, all helped to divert the interests,

---

Williams, pp. 58, 61–4; G. P. Gooch, *English Democratic Ideas in the 17th century*, pp. 86, 273.

1 *Reliquiae Baxterianae*, p. 131; R. B. Schlatter, *Social Ideas of Religious Leaders, 1660–88*, p. 184 f.

2 *Tyranipocrit Discovered*, in *British Pamphleteers*, *op. cit.*, I, pp. 90–1. Cf. Milton's reference in 1642 to 'the great merchants of this world' who 'abuse . . . poor Indians with beads and glasses', 'the false glitter of their deceitful wares' ('The Reason of Church Government', in *Prose Works*, II, p. 473).

dissipate the forces and betray the ideals of those who had believed that an international revolution was to usher in the brotherhood of man. By the end of the sixteen-fifties the revolutionary groups had been broken up, or, deciding that God's kingdom was unattainable in this world, had relapsed into quietist and pacifist religions. It was 130 years before the common people of France, and longer before the common people of England, were able to express their sentiments and aspirations as freely as had been done in England between 1640 and 1660. Nevertheless, during those two decades, words had been spoken and principles proclaimed which were never to be forgotten. Despite all the hypocrisy which sullied the principles of internationalism and human equality, it is worth recalling when and by whom they were first enunciated as a programme possible of attainment on earth. 'I believe', wrote a New England Puritan in 1647, 'that the light which is now discovered in England ... will never be wholly put out, though I suspect that contrary principles will prevail for a time'.[1] He proved right on both points.

1 Ed. I. M. Calder, *Letters of John Davenport*, p. 82.

FIVE

The Agrarian Legislation
of the Revolution[1]

Do not All strive to enjoy the Land? The Gentry strive for Land,
the Clergie strive for Land, the Common people strive for Land;
and Buying and Selling is an Art, whereby people endeavour to
cheat one another of the Land.

> Gerrard Winstanley, *A New Yeers Gift for the Parliament and
> Armie*, January 1650, in Sabine, *op. cit.*, pp. 373–4.

The very Arcanum of pretending Religion in all Warrs is that
something may bee found out, in which all men may have interest.
In this the Groome has as much interest as the Lord. Were it for
Land, one has 1,000 acres, the other but one: hee would not
venture so farr as hee that had a 1,000. But Religion is equall to
both. Had all men Land alike by a Lex Agraria, then all men would
say they fought for Land.

> Selden, *Table Talk*, 1927, p. 121.

I
Introduction

THE Civil War was more of a class war than orthodox English theory
allows. The geographical division of north and west versus south and
east is also an economic and social division between the economically

---

1 This essay is based largely on the researches of Professor S. I. Arkhangelsky, of
the University of Gorky, U.S.S.R., published in two volumes – *Agrarnoye Zakono-
datelstvo Velikoy Angliyskoy Revolyutsii*, I, *1643–1648* (Moscow–Leningrad, 1935) and
II, *1649–60* (Moscow–Leningrad, 1940). I am extremely grateful to Miss M. E. Gow,
who devotedly translated the whole of the first volume and most of the second, in the
hope, now unlikely to be realized, that Professor Arkhangelsky's work might be
published in volume form. In trying to summarize Professor Arkhangelsky's conclusions I have added quotations from some sources not available to him, and have
expanded certain points: but I have followed his ideas in the main.

backward areas, conducting a relatively self-sufficient economy, and those districts influenced by the demands of the London market, where agriculture and tenurial relations were being commercialized. The adherents of the King were principally the 'feudal' landowners of the north and west, and the higher members of the ecclesiastical hierarchy, together with their tenants and dependants. In all parts of England, moreover, there were gentlemen who were disturbed by the riots against enclosures, the possibility frequently voiced of a social as well as a political revolution, the 'appeal to the people' in the Grand Remonstrance. Parliament drew its strength from the City, the port towns, the 'progressive' gentry and yeomen of the southern and eastern counties. Its triumph was determined in the last resort by the support of the big merchant capitalists of London, though immediately by the victories of the New Model Army. In shaping the legislation of the interregnum the ultimate controlling influence was that of merchant capital, though on short-run policy the separate interest of the army carried considerable weight. Although the immediate impetus to each new phase in agrarian policy was fiscal – the need for ready cash – nevertheless the moulding influence on policy and its execution was the power of big capital in the City, even when financial need caused government policy to outrun what the merchants would have desired, as in the sales after the coup of December 1648 by which the army took over power.

The social background to the agrarian legislation can perhaps best be approached by a quotation from *The Wealth of Nations*:

'In every great monarchy of Europe, the sale of the crown lands would produce a very large sum of money, which, if applied to the payment of the public debts, would deliver from mortgage a much greater revenue than any which those lands have ever afforded to the crown. In countries where lands, improved and cultivated very highly, and yielding, at the time of sale, as great a rent as can easily be got from them, commonly sell at thirty years' purchase; the unimproved, uncultivated, and low-rented crown lands might well be expected to sell at forty, fifty, or sixty years' purchase. The crown might immediately enjoy the revenue which this great price would redeem from mortgage. In the course of a few years, it would probably enjoy another revenue. When the crown lands had become private property, they would, in the course of a few years, become well improved and well cultivated. The increase of their produce would increase the population of the country, by augmenting the revenue and consumption of the people. . . .

The revenue which, in any civilised monarchy, the crown derives from the crown lands, though it appears to cost nothing to individuals, in reality costs more to the society than perhaps any other equal revenue which the crown enjoys. It would, in all cases, be for the interest of the society to replace this revenue to the crown by some other equal revenue, and to divide the lands among the people, which could not well be done better, perhaps, than by exposing them to public sale.'[1]

Smith was assuming that Crown lands in England were generally forest, since by his time other lands had mostly been sold; but what he said would have been true of most Church and Crown lands in the early seventeenth century.

It was 'for the interest of the society' to 'divide the lands among the people', to mobilize capital that was being withheld from investment, and to improve production. The achievement of these objects was expedited by the Civil War. First, Church and Crown lands, and those of many Royalists, were confiscated and sold. This led to a general liquidation of assets – 'spoiling' of estates, stripping them of timber, buildings of lead, melting down of plate, and so on. Secondly, there was something like an all-round foreclosing on mortgages, the greatest care being taken of the interests of delinquents' creditors at all stages of sequestration, composition, and sale. Thirdly, wealth was transferred from one class to another. The financial measures directed most severely against the Royalists had the effect of expropriating the debt-ridden, extravagangly-living sections of the aristocracy and gentry; and their wealth flowed through the Parliamentary financial organs by means of state contracts and grants into the pockets of the commercial class. Fourthly, the agrarian changes of the period ultimately enriched one section of the community by reducing the standards of consumption of the mass of the population. Racking of rents, raising fines, enclosure, all the familiar techniques of improved estate management, increased landlords' revenues, either by curtailing the consumption of the old-established tillers of the soil, or by evicting them and replacing them by capitalist farmers who could afford the new agricultural methods.

The interregnum was a period in which these processes – long in motion – were enormously accelerated, especially by the intervention

1 Adam Smith, *The Wealth of Nations* (World's Classics), II, pp. 470–1. See also Maurice Dobb, *Studies in the Development of Capitalism*, esp. Chapter 5.

of the state (taxation, contracts, confiscation, and sale of lands). The rewards men sought for political services were money, or a position in which money might be acquired, or land from whose management money might be made. Capital was accumulated: small and scattered sums were concentrated into sufficiently large units (in fewer hands) to take the form of capital. Wealth which otherwise would not have been productively employed was converted into the form of money – i.e. into the form in which it can be invested.

Moreover, many merchants were interested in the estates of 'backward' landowners, not merely as a source of immediate capital, but also as a long-run field for investment in production for the expanding market, whether for food or wool, or in the hunt for minerals: this in addition to the traditional attractions of land, as the source of political power and social prestige, in what was before 1640 still a predominantly 'feudal' society. 'And if once Landlords,' said Winstanley of purchasers, 'then they rise to be Justices, Rulers, and State Governours, as experience shewes.'[1] Many such purchasers wanted to improve the cultivation of land along capitalist lines, so as to maximize the national wealth, and with it their own. Hence the abolition of feudal tenures, wardship, and purveyance, which removed obstacles to the free devising, purchase and sale of land, and to long-term rational estate management.

The agrarian legislation of the interregnum shows us the varying means by which these objectives were secured. Sequestration came first. When estates were sequestrated the revenues from them were paid in to the state receivers, the sequestration officers appointed by the county committees. The policy of sequestration need not necessarily have led to confiscation and sale of the estates of Crown, Church, or delinquents: and in so far as sale involved the tying up again of large sums of capital in land, it was opposed by the merchant interests (many of whom of course already leased Church and Crown lands before 1640). Pressure for sale came throughout from all ranks in the army, concerned to have their wages paid, later especially from the Levellers, overlapping with the rank and file of the army, who represented the desire of the peasantry for a parcelled sale. Opposition to sale came throughout from the House of Lords and the 'Presbyterian' section of the House of Commons, from motives of social conservatism. They were prepared to sacrifice bishops' lands as an additional insurance

1 Sabine, *op. cit.*, p. 258.

against the restoration of the hierarchical power. ('Chose à mon sens de grande consideration', Bellièvre wrote at the end of September 1646, 'et qui engage la ville [the City] contre leur Roy'.[1] 'By this means', Baillie added a fortnight after the passing of the ordinance of 16 November 1646, 'we gett the Bishops' lands on our backs, without any grudge, and in a way that no skill will get them back againe.')[2] Further than that they refused to go, and there were no more state sales until after Pride's Purge. This was due mainly to the hostility of the conservative section of the Parliamentarians to any tampering with the sacred principle of private property and to fear of the levelling tendencies of the army, partly to a desire to utilize dean and chapter lands for the better maintenance of an established church – as against the voluntaryism of the democratic sectaries, which would deprive the ruling class of its control of that vital medium of publicity and propaganda, the pulpit.

These general points may be illustrated by an examination of the legislation of the period.

II
Sequestration

The driving motive to sequestration was always fiscal. This is clear from the start. There was much overlapping in personnel between the sequestration committees and the commissioners for assessment in the counties.[3] Sequestration was first introduced to meet immediate financial needs – either by sequestrating the estates of particular individuals or by measures aimed at particular counties.[4] These sequestrations went at first to meet current expenses within the county concerned.[5] The beginnings of the process were piecemeal and *ad hoc*. It was not until 27 March 1643 that what had already become fairly common practice was summarized and generalized in an ordinance.

1 Ed. J. G. Fortheringham, *The Diplomatic Correspondence of Jean de Montereul* (Scottish History Society, 1898), I, p. 274.

2 R. Baillie, *Letters and Journals* (1775), II, p. 411. Such statements appear to conflict with Tatham's theory that 'no deep design existed', and that 'the importance of the question was only gradually appreciated' (*E.H.R.*, XXIII, p. 101).

3 Cf. *C.J.*, V, pp. 398–9.

4 *C.J.*, II, pp. 961, 973, 977.

5 For instance, *C.J.*, IV, pp. 168, 302, 444; V, pp. 29, 399, 410; *L.J.*, IX, p. 342; B. Whitelocke, *Memorials* (1853), I, p. 444; and cf. C. H. Mayo, *Minute Books of the Dorset Standing Committee, passim*.

The fact that this ordinance was passed just at the time when negotiations were started with the King at Oxford suggests that the dominant party in Parliament had no desire for a compromise settlement. Sequestration struck at the basis of the social power and prestige of those, delinquents and Papists, who had supported the King. As the area subjected to Parliament was extended to the counties of the north and west of England, so new Royalists and Papists came under sequestration. A like fate awaited those in the Parliamentary counties who refused to pay taxation.[1] Further sequestrations followed after the Second Civil War.[2]

But though the driving force behind this policy was fiscal, it was shaped by social factors of which Parliament cannot have been unaware. The sequestration committees in the localities stepped in to prevent tenants retaining rents in their own hands. They were empowered to lease the estates 'as the . . . Land-Lord . . . thereof . . . might have done',[3] at rents improved as much as possible. Personal estate was sold, delinquents being given ten days in which they might have the first option of purchasing their own goods. Revenue collected from the estates was paid in to the treasurer at war at the Guildhall. The revolutionary significance of these committees of county magnates has never been sufficiently stressed. Comparable powers had been used for similar purposes in the past – for instance, in dealing with recusants; but the scale on which they were now used was unprecedented. The committees had power to examine upon oath all persons who might give information of delinquents or their estates. The local sequestration committees had power to fine, the central committee to imprison, the recalcitrant: all local authorities, later all military authorities, had to assist the sequestrators when called upon. The sequestrators themselves had power of forcible entry.[4] Within their areas these committees were omnipotent.

In course of time it proved necessary to strengthen the supervisory powers of the central over the local committees. Complaints poured in to the willing ears of the Lords that these great powers were being abused.[5] So an ordinance of 25 May 1644 imposed an oath on

1 Whitelocke, *op. cit.*, I, p. 528; *C.J.*, II, p. 977.
2 *Ibid.*, V, pp. 587, 592, 604, 628, 681; VI, p. 67; *L.J.*, X, pp. 333–4, 515; *C.C.C.*, I, pp. 128, 134; Whitelocke, *op. cit.*, II, p. 350.
3 Ed. C. H. Firth and R. S. Rait, *Acts and Ordinances of the Interregnum*, I, p. 107.
4 See a petition in *L.J.*, VI, p. 583, for a picture of sequestrators at work.
5 See previous note, and *L.J.*, VI, p. 500; *C.J.*, III, pp. 156, 447.

sequestrators that they would honestly without fear or favour execute the ordinance: 'active, able, trusty men, who will diligently attend to this service', were to be added to the sequestration committees where necessary, Parliament to be notified of their names. (This was presumably to strengthen the committees with more active if socially less distinguished members than the guinea-pigs nominated by earlier ordinances.[1]) Henceforth committees were required to meet not less than twice a week and to keep strict accounts, to be presented quarterly. Money tended to stick to the sequestrators' hands: immediate payment of arrears was demanded under threat of a fine of 2s. 6d. in the £. The ordinance annulled any postponement of sequestration of delinquents' and Papists' estates made without Parliament's consent, and county committees were forbidden to lend sequestrated goods without similar authority. John Madden was appointed solicitor for sequestrations, to supervise the whole operation.

Further ordinances passed in August 1648 continued the same centralizing process, calling for the submission from the counties of full accounts and inventories of estates which either were or had been in the committees' hands.[2] The immediate stimulus to this measure seems to have been the violent seizure of the receipts of sequestration in certain counties by unpaid soldiers. The House of Commons frequently pledged itself to consider at an early date the accounts of all sequestrated properties and to carry out a general revision of the whole process of sequestration; but this did not happen till after Pride's Purge and the abolition of the House of Lords.

Sequestration, then, seems to have begun at the initiative of the powerful revolutionary committees in the counties, anxious both to raise money and to preserve landed property intact. Then the House of Commons saw its financial possibilities, and with the concurrence of the Lords tried to rationalize and standardize the process, controlling it from London in order to check corruption or favouritism. The committee at Goldsmiths' Hall was continually bullying the local sequestration committees to wring more money out of the sequestrated estates, and not to lease at undervalues. The Gloucestershire committee, for instance, reported in 1648 that annual receipts from delinquents' estates had increased from £1,020 to £1,622 6s. 8d., in spite of the miserable condition of the county, ruined by free quarter.[3]

1 Cf. pp. 19–21 above.
2 Firth and Rait, *op. cit.*, I, pp. 1179, 1186.
3 *C.C.C.*, I, p. 81.

Other county committees proved less successful, 'few being willing to stock ground for so short a time as we can grant and in such uncertain times', the Cornish committee explained. 'What is let is at so low a rate as only to defray taxes, annuities, and other charges usually encumbering the estates.'[1] Nevertheless, the effort was clearly being made. On 17 October 1647, under pressure from the army, and to avoid having to commit themselves to a policy of general sale, Parliament ordered rents from the sequestrated lands to be improved to the utmost value.[2] There can be no doubt that on the whole rents on the sequestrated lands were forced up.[3] Sequestration became the means by which money income and personal estate, forcibly confiscated from the Royalists, went to finance the force that expropriated them. Recusants, who had been treated so leniently by Charles I,[4] fared especially badly. At the instance of the House of Lords they were brought under the sequestration ordinance; later, Papists who had been in arms were forbidden to 'compound'.[5] As the whole process was controlled from the City, the big business men who were state contractors tended to find their own demands satisfied before those of the soldiery. So a new factor arises: the demand of the army that the land fund shall be increased in order that their wages may be punctually paid.

III

Composition

The logical sequel to sequestration would have been the sale of the sequestrated estates: but the pressure of vested interests working through the 'Presbyterians' and the House of Lords, and anxiety to preserve the inviolability of private property, prevented this until Pride's Purge had cleared the way. Instead, pressure of local financial need seems to have given rise spontaneously to the taking of composition fines from delinquents. There is significantly little legislation on the subject. An ordinance of 16 August 1643 authorized compositions in Kent. This was extended to other parts of the country merely by resolutions and declarations of the House of Commons.[6]

1 *Ibid.*, I, p. 116. Note the regard for creditors' interests; cf. *ibid.*, I, p. 99 – similar complaint from the Durham committee.

2 *L.J.*, IX, p. 582.

3 Chesney, *Trans. R.H.S.*, 4th series, XV, p. 200.

4 Cf. Rushworth, *Historical Collections*, II, p. 247.

5 *C.J.*, IV, p. 530.

6 For example, *C.J.*, III, pp. 540, 572; IV, pp. 534, 560; *C.C.C.*, I, p. 39. But cf. Husband's *Collection, 1642–6*, p. 751 – an order of the two houses empowering the committee at Goldsmiths' Hall to tender the covenant to the compounding delinquents (1 November 1645).

The committee for compounding at Goldsmiths' Hall, as it subsequently came to be called, was set up by the Commons alone, as a joint committee of members of the House and citizens of London to raise money for the Scots.[1] It is perhaps not altogether without significance that the headquarters of this great financial organ was the hall of the bankers of the day. Its functions were to raise money generally, and the exploitation of the sequestrated estates and composition were at first only one part of its activity. The committee at Goldsmiths' Hall treated with City companies for a loan;[2] wrote to the Lord Mayor of London to hasten the collection of assessments in the City.[3] Among the interlocking financial departments the committee at Goldsmiths' Hall was omniscient: it knew, for example, that the assessment had been raised without clamour in Bishopsgate ward, 'though the people are very poor', because the assessment committee there sat often and could equalize the rate and summon the refractory.[4] Yet in setting up this vast financial and administrative power the concurrence of the Lords had not been sought.

The reasons for this are fairly clear. The Lords, with the assistance of a conservative group in the House of Commons, fought a steady rearguard action all through. They had amended and delayed the sequestration ordinances,[5] and afterwards protected cavaliers from their operation, the latter looking to the peers as their natural defenders.[6] They similarly blocked all proposals for the sale of delinquents' lands, and the policy of compounding was a second-best adopted by the forward party in the country and in the lower house out of sheer financial necessity. The Lords accepted the inevitability of composition as a lesser evil than sale, to prevent which they exerted all their tactical ingenuity. At the end of 1646, in order to defeat a demand from the Commons for sale of delinquents' estates, they drew a herring across the trail by impugning the legality of the committee at Goldsmiths' Hall.[7] 'Whereas', ran the declaration they issued on 1 February 1646–7, 'divers Delinquents have formerly and still do address themselves unto some Persons sitting at Gouldsmiths Hall,

1 *C.C.C.*, I, p. v; cf. *C.J.*, IV, pp. 451–2.
2 *C.C.C.*, I, p. 44.
3 *Ibid.*, pp. 35, 39.
4 *Ibid.*, p. 82.
5 *C.J.*, III, pp. 21, 208–9; *L.J.*, VI, pp. 180–3.
6 *C.J.*, III, p. 148.
7 *Ibid.*, IV, p. 342; V, p. 51.

and they have and do daily enter into Agreements for the taking off
such Sequestrations as are duly laid upon them by Ordinance of
Parliament: the Lords in Parliament do Declare, that all such
Compositions made by those Persons sitting at Gouldsmiths Hall with
such as are under Delinquency, are not authorised by any Ordinance of
Parliament; and that the Committees for Sequestrations within the
several counties of England and . . . Wales ought not to obey any Order
from the Persons sitting at Gouldsmiths Hall, for the taking off or
suspending any Sequestrations, upon the Pretence of the Delinquents
having made his Composition with them, until such time as a
Committee or Commissioners to that Purpose be settled by Ordinance
of Parliament, and the Composition made with such Committee or
Commissioners be likewise ratified by Ordinance of Parliament.'[1]

This was an effective bargaining weapon. The Commons pointed
out that if composition had never received legal sanction, the Lords
had recognized it in practice by asking for considerable sums of money
from Goldsmiths' Hall for their own expenses, and by interceding with
the committee on behalf of their Royalist friends. An apparent
difference between the Houses would give great encouragement to the
enemies of Parliament, and might cause 'great Disturbances, and
Dangers of Broils, . . . in a Matter wherein so many are interested in
their Estates'.[2] The result was the ordinance of 8 February, by which
the committee was reconstituted, this time with 15 peers on it as well as
30 commoners and 10 representatives of the City.[3] Five diehard peers
in a House of 18 protested even against this 'in regard the Number of
Commoners were double in Number to the Lords', but in fact the
Lords had won a valuable point, even though the Lower House
amended their proposal that two peers should be necessary to the
quorum of the committee into 'three Members of Parliament'.[4] The
Lords had diverted attention from the proposal to sell lands; they had
won a say in the direction of the policy of composition; and the
ordinance also secured that money so raised should be expended only
by ordinance of both Houses.

Quite apart from its financial usefulness, the process of compounding had its attractions for the monied men. Goldsmiths' Hall played the

1 *L.J.*, VIII, p. 696; cf. pp. 590, 678. This declaration was to be printed, published,
and sent to the county sequestration committees.
2 *C.J.*, V, pp. 71–3.
3 Firth and Rait, *op. cit.*, I, p. 914.
4 *L.J.*, VIII, p. 708.

role of bailiff in a general foreclosing. At composition allowance was always made for the claims of creditors, and the summary procedure of the committees, backed up by the armed forces, was much more difficult to evade than the cumbrous processes of the debtors' law. In August 1645 Sir David Watkins told the House of Commons that 'Those who now come in to compound are fined ½ or ⅔ of their estates, and as they are mostly ⅓ of it in debt, they have little or nothing left'.[1] His figures may be exaggerated, and many a delinquent escaped at two years' purchase 'according to the true Value of his Estate before these Troubles began'.[2] But of the general indebtedness there can be little doubt.[3] In order to compound, delinquents frequently had to sell part of their estate privately, and so land came on to the market without any interference with the sacred rights of property. Lands thus privately sold were not restored in 1660.

Between 1644 and 1652 £1,304,957 was received from compositions.[4] But the delinquent's trials did not end at Goldsmiths' Hall. He had next to go on to Haberdashers' Hall to pay his fifth and twentieth, and still remained liable to free quarter and to the heavy commonwealth taxation – the decimation tax of 1655 being aimed directly at him. 'These tymes of libertie and distraccon', moreover, made tenants 'incredibly forgetfull, and manie would denye to pay anie rent'.[5] There was necessarily, therefore, a very great deal of transfer of lands by private sale between 1645 and 1660 though statistics are unobtainable. In November 1655 Major-General Goffe noted casually in a letter to Thurloe that in Sussex 'there are so many of the delinquents dead, and soe much of their estates sould, that I feare the revenew raysed by the [decimation] taxe in this county will not bee very considerable'.[6] Such sales, moreover, would be made in a glutted market. In the private sales which Professor Arkhangelsky listed from the *Calendar of the Committee for Compounding*, more than half of the purchasers specified were creditors. Dr. Chesney reached the same conclusion.[7]

1 *C.C.C.*, I, p. 23.
2 *C.J.*, IV, p. 237; cf. *Fairfax Correspondence* (ed. G. W. Johnson), I, pp. 294–5. In 1648 this was raised for participants in the Second Civil War to a quarter of the value of their estates (*C.J.*, VI, p. 5; cf. p. 73, and *C.C.C.*, I, p. 128).
3 Chesney, *op. cit., passim.*
4 P. Hardacre, *The Royalists in the Puritan Revolution*, p. 66.
5 Steward's note, June 1646, quoted in Lady Newton, *The House of Lyme*, p. 188.
6 *Thurloe State Papers*, IV, p. 208.
7 This estimate, and many of Professor Arkhangelsky's conclusions about purchasers may need revision in the light of Mrs. Thirsk's two important articles, cited

Everything possible was done, moreover, by Parliament and the committee at Goldsmiths' Hall, to extract ready cash from the compounder. He had to pay half his fine down and give security for the remainder, which was to be paid within six months. Failure to pay the second half meant a fresh sequestration until all was paid with interest.[1] As he had not been receiving his rents for some time before compounding, and could not receive them until he had compounded (and then might well find his lands had suffered during sequestration) the delinquent had almost inevitably to raise a mortgage on his estates in order to supply himself with any cash at all. Many delinquents were given permission to sell part of their estates before compounding for the rest. This process was authorized by a general resolution on 1 October 1650, subject to the permission of the commissioners for compounding.[2] Naturally delinquents did all in their power to delay payment of this second half of their fine,[3] or gave in false particulars of their estates, concealing portions of them,[4] abetted not infrequently by tenants. ('The inferior people are so overawed by the malignant gentry that they make no conscience of wilful perjury, and publicly profess that they will not offend their landlords, come what may.')[5] But all these temporary expedients were of no avail when the Royalist cause was finally defeated: the delinquent did not get his pardon under the Great Seal until he had completed the second half of his composition. He was liable to imprisonment as well as fresh sequestration for not completing

---

on p. 4, n. 1 above. In revising this essay, originally published in 1940, I have not attempted to do more than indicate points at which such reconsideration appears necessary.

1 For instances, see *C.C.C.*, I, pp. 41, 69, 83, 119, 125, 128, 132, 135, etc.; *C.J.*, V, p. 622; VI, p. 44; VII, p. 106.

2 *Ibid.*, VI, pp. 476–7.

3 Cf. *Mercurius Pragmaticus*, 14–21 September 1647: 'All you that forbeare the paiment of the remainder of your Compositions know that there is an Ordnance passed, which commands you to come and discharge it with all speed, or else to bee sequester'd. This is a terrible Gun-shot; but withall I advise you that have not yet beene catcht with the compounding Rat-Trap, to keep off and remember that there is to be a Treaty betwixt the King and the Generall Officers with Commissioners from the Parliament upon the Proposals of the Army, not admitting so much as a Scottish Louse to creep into the Affaire (God be thanked:) In which Proposalls is a great mitigation towards Delinquents that have not yet compounded; but those that have been a Simpling that way already, for ought I know may goe whistle, being to bee left to the mercy of the Crocodiles of Goldsmiths Hall, that devoure Gold as Ostredges doe Iron' (p. 6).

4 *C.J.*, IV, pp. 375, 637; V, pp. 464–5, 478.

5 *C.C.C.*, I, p. 61.

composition.[1] And lynx-eyed officers, hungry for their wages, to be paid out of what they could discover, probably squeezed out a number of 'concealed' estates during the 'fifties, as did delinquents' creditors.

In the Lord Mayor's pageant of December 1659, written by Thomas Jordan, 'Filcher, a cheat' observed that:

> *'Your roaring cavalier,*
> *Who, when he had the chink*
> *Would bravely domineer,*
> *In dicing, drabs, and drink;*
> *Go ask him now for money,*
> *And he hath none at all;*
> *But cryes, "'Tis in my compting-house*
> *In Haberdashers' Hall".'*

Moll Medlar, in the same pageant, underlined the point:

> *'I was bred a gentlewoman,*
> *But our family did fall*
> *When the gentry's coin grew common,*
> *And the souldiers shared it all.'* [2]

The general effect was twofold: First, much land passed by private sale into the hands of those with ready cash; secondly, those lands which delinquents retained were insufficient to maintain them at anything approaching their old standard of living without a vast amount of rationalization and improvement of cultivation. Either way led to the breaking down of traditional relationships between lord and tenant, by racking of rents, raising of fines, enclosure. 'Papists and malignants compound', said Richard Heyricke in a sermon preached in 1646, 'and they oppress their poor tenants that have engaged themselves in the public cause for the Lord against their lords'.[3] Selden noted this process of commercialization: 'When men did lett their lands under ffoote, the tenants would fight for their Landlords, so that way they had their retribution, but now they will doe nothing for them, may bee the first, if but a Constable bid them, that shall lay the Landlord by the

---

1 *Ibid.*, p. 119.

2 Ed. F. W. Fairholt, 'Lord Mayor's Pageants', *Early English Poetry and Ballads* (Percy Society), X (1843), pp. 215, 221.

3 R. Heyricke, *Queen Esthers Resolve*, quoted in Halley, *Lancashire: its Puritanism and Nonconformity*, I, p. 421.

heeles, & therefore tis vanity & folly not to take the full value'.[1] A civilization in which power was calculated in terms of men was being replaced all over England by one in which it was calculated in money.[2] And here too the Parliament's victory played its part, in that improved policing by the army (especially the major-generals), abolition of the Scottish border, slighting of fortresses, disarming of the turbulent gentry of the Royalist areas, all contributed to end social feudalism and so to diminish the value of tenants who did not pay economic rents but would on occasion fight for their lord. England was made safe for commercialism.

The problems, economic and moral, raised for landowners by this transition are familiar to students of seventeenth-century literature. 'I know and have seen them that have been highly obliged to some gentlemen, yet to gain £5 they would cut their throats,' wrote Sir John Oglander to his descendants, some time before 1652. 'Never think to bind them to thee by benefits.' 'Let no man's love, friendship or favour compel thee or draw thee to forgo thy profits', he had observed earlier. '£10 will do more than most men's love.'[3] In 1654 William Blundell was setting his spiritual adviser a variety of cases of conscience in relation to leasing policy, and receiving consoling replies.[4] After the Restoration John Moore gave his son advice almost identical to that of Sir John Oglander: 'Serve God and make much of your own; and as these new leases fall out, raise your old rents according to my directions, that you may have something to live on like other neighbour gentlemen.' Like Oglander, Moore emphasized that feudal relations had lost their former usefulness to landlords: 'Thus you may see what you must expect from a tenant, . . . as use them never so well'.[5]

IV

Obstruction by the Lords

In sequestration and composition, the initiative had always come from the House of Commons, the Lords reluctantly accepting what financial necessity dictated. But they kept up a steady rearguard action, and

1 *Table Talk* (1927), p. 67.
2 Cf. Tawney, *Agrarian Problem in the Sixteenth Century*, p. 2.
3 Ed. F. Bamford, *A Royalist's Notebook*, pp. 247, 231.
4 Ed. T. E. Gibson, *A Cavalier's Notebook*, pp. 254–60.
5 Ed. T. Heywood, *The Moore Rental* (Chetham Society, 1847), p. 119; cf. Roger North, *Lives of the Norths* (1826), I, pp. 34–6.

allowed nothing to slip past that would seem in any way a preliminary to a general sale of delinquents' estates. They successfully insisted that not the sequestrated estates themselves but only revenues from them should be given as security for loans. The House of Commons frequently discussed a general sale of delinquents' estates, but could never overcome the hostility of the Lords.[1] Absentee peers were beaten up to vote down such motions.[2]

In this opposition the Lords found themselves in alliance with 'the Lord-like men of the City, the Aldermen, and with other rich men in all places of the Country'. On 10 July 1645 the Sheriff of London informed the House of Commons that up to 10,000 horse and dragoons could be raised on the credit of an ordinance for the sale of delinquents' lands.[3] But later the conservative element regained strength in the City. On 9 September 1646 the Common Council agreed to a loan of £200,000 if it was raised by 'doubling' on the security of the excise and bishops' lands.[4] The Commons thanked the Common Council for their 'ready Affections' (at 8 per cent) and added delinquents' estates as an additional security, 'which shall first happen' – i.e. the sale of bishops' or delinquents' lands. The insertion of delinquents' lands was intended as the thin end of a wedge ensuring ultimate sale. The Lords countered by deleting 'which shall first happen', and substituting for it 'which of these shall be first desired by the Lord Mayor, Aldermen, and Common Council of the City of London, and agreed on by both Houses of Parliament'. The ordinance was finally passed on 13 October without either amendment: the original proposal of the Common Council was restored.[5] Again in May 1647, during the debate on the security for a loan of £200,000 for the Irish Army, the House of Lords insisted that receipts from delinquents' compositions should be added to the security. For by this time the Lords had resigned themselves to composition as a lesser evil; and to earmark compositions would create vested interests which

1 *C.J.*, III, pp. 556, 563, 570, 578, 603; IV, pp. 163, 186, 200, 225, 246, 342, 556, 608, 613, 627, 650, 676–7, 710; V, p. 51; *L.J.*, VII, pp. 580, 713; VIII, p. 442.

2 *Ibid.*, VII, p. 565.

3 (Anon.), *Englands Troublers Troubled* (1648), p. 2; *C.J.*, IV, p. 203.

4 'Doubling' meant that a creditor who already had lent the state £x and was beginning to despair of repayment could by advancing a further sum equivalent to his first loan receive new and better security – usually landed – for £2x + interest (see W. H. Shaw, *A History of the English Church*, II, pp. 212–13). Many estates given as security were in consequence earmarked when they subsequently came up for sale.

5 *C.J.*, IV, pp. 665, 667; Firth and Rait, *op. cit.*, I, p. 884.

would oppose a general sale of delinquents' lands. The Lords' proposal was obstinately resisted by the Commons, who could not agree to add Goldsmiths' Hall to the security, 'because it is the only Power and Means for raising Money if there should be any extra-ordinary Occasion'. After a conference the Lords gave way, but the Common Council came to their rescue and compelled the Commons to abandon their former resolution (by a majority of 104 to 91). They agreed that half of the compositions should be given as security. The Commons, rather than surrender on compositions, were anxious to offer as security the lands of those delinquents who were exempted from pardon, the 'fomentors of this war'; but this the Lords would not have. The omission, the Common Council thought, would not hinder 'the Raising of the said Monies'.[1]

The Lords were clever; but events were pressing. In July 1646 Mr. Reynolds told the upper house that if they rejected the bill for sale of delinquents' estates they must bear all the responsibility for the consequences. 'If Ireland be lost . . . if the Armies be not paid Arrears, and so not disbanded; if the creditors that have lent Monies for the Public Affairs be not satisfied', the Commons 'did and would hold themselves blameless'.[2] The history of the next three years is foreshadowed in Reynolds's warning. The Lords and the City could play the game of Parliamentary obstruction, but the power of the army was in the last resort decisive. In continually thus thwarting its demands the Lords were digging their own graves.

v

Bishops' Lands

As early as 9 July 1641 the House of Commons had voted that bishops' lands should be confiscated to the King.[3] Fourteen bishops had their estates sequestrated; but they were sequestrated only as individuals by virtue of their delinquency, not in consequence of their office.[4] It was only military victory that ensured the extirpation of episcopacy: no king, no bishop. By this time the Lords had resigned themselves to the sale of bishops' estates, and indeed took the initiative in pressing for this as a

1 *L.J.*, IX, pp. 161, 170; *C.J.*, V, p. 163.
2 *L.J.*, VIII, p. 442. Robert Reynolds was member for Hindon, Wiltshire. He subsequently purchased lands widely himself, and was knighted at the Restoration.
3 *C.J.*, II, p. 204.
4 *Ibid.*, IV, p. 275.

lesser evil than sale of delinquents' estates (September 1645).[1] The City, traditionally anti-episcopal, also approved. The immediate need leading to the ordinance of 9 October 1646 was for money to pay off the Scots. The ordinance of 13 October allowed bishops' lands as security for a loan of £200,000 and repeated word for word a suggestion of the Common Council that these estates should be 'made over unto such Feoffees, for the speedy Sale thereof, and such Treasurers for the Receipts of the Monies, as may give best satisfaction to the Lenders'.[2] In fact the trustees of bishops' lands appointed by the ordinance of 9 October were all aldermen or common councillors. The whole business of sale was in the hands of City merchants, and as trustees and contractors (created by the ordinance of 17 November) they took a large part in the legislative work, presenting petitions to the House of Commons, serving on committees, acting as information bureau and board of experts.[3]

'Doubling', that magnificent dodge for ensuring that to him that hath shall be given, really determined in advance the circle of purchasers,[4] and many were the complaints of the 'poor and decayed citizens' who, because they could not afford to double, lost even that which they had invested. The Common Council was so disturbed that it even proposed that £30,000 should be repaid to them to pacify them.[5] Outside London the grievance was even greater. 'The Londoners have herein beene too hard for all the Cuntry', Edward Roberts wrote to Henry Oxinden. 'They only will herby hedge in theyr owne debt and make gaine by others, as if this beneficiall ordenance had been only calculated for the meridian of London. . . . Before any man could write into the cuntry and prepare the money, they have clapt up all the £200,000'.[6] No attempt was made to extend the circle of purchasers, unless by the Lords, who wished to fix the price of the lands at eight years' purchase: the House of Commons, dominated by fiscal considerations, successfully held out for ten.[7] The ordinance of 17

1 *L.J.*, VII, pp. 565–73, 580.
2 *C.J.*, IV, pp. 655–67; Firth and Rait, *op. cit.*, I, pp. 884, 880.
3 *C.J.*, V, pp. 15, 57, 132, 276–8, 333, 338, 344, 604, 610; VI, p. 39; *L.J.*, X, pp. 112, 129.
4 See p. 153 above, n. 4,
5 *C.J.*, V, pp. 163, 509; VI, p. 89.
6 Ed. D. Gardiner, *Oxinden and Peyton Letters, 1642–70*, p. 96. See pp. 92–6 *passim* for evidence of keen competition to buy bishops' lands.
7 *C.J.*, IV, pp. 699–724; *L.J.*, VIII, pp. 560–9.

November gave immediate tenants a period of thirty days in which they had pre-emptive rights, but in the absence of credit facilities, and with no arrangements for purchase by deferred payment such as were made in the French Revolution, only those who had ready capital would be likely to be able to avail themselves of this. (The first half of the purchase money had to be paid within eight weeks after signing the contract, on penalty of a fine equal to one-third of the purchase price: this in a period of economic crisis when many tenant farmers were having difficulty in paying their rents.[1]) Later ordinances did not repeat even this empty gesture.[2] In this respect the land policy of the Long Parliament was less thoroughgoing than the Constituent Assembly's policy of deferring payment for nationalized ecclesiastical property for a number of years, which led to much subdivision and to collective purchases by peasants. But the conception of 'national property' was beyond the vision of the leaders of the Long Parliament.

A feature of ecclesiastical landholding before the Revolution was its conservatism and its long leases. Tenants must not expect such good pennyworths from lay landlords, argued a pamphlet attributed to the Bishop of Rochester.[3] The ordinance of 9 October 1646, in addition to converting all the lands sold into free and common socage, also provided that leases exceeding three lives or twenty-one years might be annulled (as well as those made since 1 December 1641). The same provision was made later in the ordinance for the sale of dean and chapter lands. The surveys which preceded sale, moreover, and the transference of the land itself, gave an excellent opportunity for testing tenant rights, in which all the advantages were on the side of purchasers anxious to recover their capital. Surveyors had power to administer oaths to tenants and others, and to imprison those who refused to testify. If tenants refused (or were unable) to present written evidence of their title, the estate was sequestrated and sold, with a right of appeal to the Parliamentary committee for removing obstructions in sale. Where tenants refused to present their titles and remained refractory while the land was sold over their heads, they might be committed to prison.[4]

1 Firth and Rait, *op. cit.*, I, p. 1019 (ordinance of 24 September 1647).

2 Similarly, it appears only in the first ordinance for sale of delinquents' lands; cf. *C.J.*, VII, p. 160.

3 (J. Warner), *Church Lands not to be Sold* (1648), pp. 19–20. For further evidence see Fuller, *Church History* (1655), IV, p. 178; and my *Economic Problems of the Church*, pp. 6–8, 36 and references there cited.

4 Firth and Rait, *op. cit.*, I, pp. 1229–30; cf. *C.J.*, IX, pp. 71, 175.

The loan secured by bishops' lands was regarded by contemporaries as a good investment, and doubling as a means of realizing debts feared desperate.[1] Figures given by Tatham suggest that purchasers were mainly Londoners or provincial gentry, and this is confirmed by other evidence.[2] Some of them may have been speculators buying to sell again at a profit; but what matters from the social and economic point of view is precisely this breach with tradition, this jerking up to the standards of the market.

The importance of the economic aspect of the sale of bishops' lands comes out in the Isle of Wight negotiations with the King in 1648. Charles regarded the sale of Church lands as sacrilege: the most he would consent to was leases for lives or 99 years, 'reserving the old Rents or other moderate Rents for the Maintenance of those to whom they did formerly belong'.[3] The House of Commons insisted that the abolition of episcopacy could not be guaranteed without sale; and anyway it had already begun.[4] Charles was prepared to surrender episcopacy almost in its entirety as a religious institution, but that was not what Parliament was most interested in. 'It was not the apostolical bishop which the bill desired his majesty to remove, but that episcopacy . . . formerly established by law . . . a burden to the persons, purses, and consciences of men.'[5] In answer to the legal argument of Parliament Charles at last abandoned the artificial terrain on which all questions in dispute had hitherto been discussed. 'Precedents in Cases of Conscience', he said, 'cannot satisfy: they only proving that such Things were done, not the Lawfulness of them.'[6] Charles sealed his own fate by tying it up with the lands of 'my church, my crown, and my friends'.

VI
Influence of the Army

From the beginning of the war the troops were interested in the land

1 'The stryfe wes, who should come in with his money soonest' (Baillie, *op. cit.*, II, p. 411); cf. *Fairfax Correspondence*, I, p. 323.

2 *E.H.R.*, XXIII, p. 102. Mrs. Thirsk's articles quoted on p. 4 above suggest that this conclusion may need to be modified.

3 *L.J.*, X, p. 622.

4 Whitelocke, *op. cit.*, II, p. 431; cf. *C.J.*, VI, p. 62; *L.J.*, X, pp. 569–71.

5 Whitelocke, *op. cit.*, II, p. 460. This echoes phrases used by D'Ewes in 1640: see his *Journal* (ed. Notestein), pp. 140, 245, 466.

6 *L.J.*, X, p. 605.

problem, which so directly affected the payment of their wages. Unpaid soldiers laid forcible hands upon the receipts of sequestration. The fierce demands and open mutinies of the summer of 1646 undoubtedly played their part in bringing about a sale of bishops' lands.[1] Composition was from its introduction associated with the needs of the army.[2] Officers sometimes collected composition monies on behalf of the committee at Goldsmiths' Hall for their own payment,[3] or were paid on the spot from county sequestration and composition monies.[4] As Goldsmiths' Hall financed the army, it was natural that the army in its turn should be much interested in the affairs of Goldsmiths' Hall.[5] From the first organization of the New Model Army to its entry into London in August 1647, a long and accelerating stream of petitions to either House of Parliament aired army opinions of how the land fund should be utilized.[6] Not only was the sale of delinquents' lands suggested, but officers also demanded the dismissal of certain county committees and the taking of accurate accounts from them. Parliament occasionally took action upon these individual demands, but proceeded to no general measures. At the end of 1646 and through 1647 there is much evidence that many sections of the army had proceeded to direct action to satisfy their needs. Reports of mutinies for pay and of plundering came in from all parts of the country.[7] And this point was always stressed in the arguments used by the forward party in the House of Commons to try to persuade the 'Presbyterians' and the House of Lords to agree to a general sale: 'the subsistence of the army much depending thereupon'.[8]

It was to divert this rising economic revolt in the army, which the Levellers might have led into more dangerous channels, that Cromwell and the grandees put themselves at the head of the army mutiny in May 1647. Pressure by the united army in that year ensured, first, the checking of accounts of officers' and soldiers' arrears and the appearance of debentures; secondly, a partial settlement of arrears,

1 Whitelocke, *op. cit.*, II, pp. 53, 58.
2 *C.J.*, III, p. 627; IV, pp. 307, 342, 602.
3 For example, *ibid.*, V, p. 391.
4 For example, *ibid.*, IV, p. 325; *L.J.*, VIII, p. 199; *C.C.C.*, I, p. 47.
5 *C.J.*, IV, p. 342; *C.C.C.*, I, pp. 36–7.
6 For example, *C.J.*, IV, pp. 171, 314, 404; V, pp. 61, 120, 141, 173, 182, 211; *L.J.*, VII, p. 680; IX, pp. 56, 95, 110; *C.C.C.*, I, p. 59.
7 *C.J.*, V, pp. 124, 161; *L.J.*, VIII, p. 507; IX, pp. 172, 180; Whitelocke, *op. cit.*, II, p. 85; *Fairfax Correspondence*, I, p. 335.
8 *C.J.*, IV, p. 342.

mainly those of officers. A few sales of the estates of individual delinquents were even authorized. But that was all that the movement achieved for the time being: the defeat of the Levellers and the dispersal of the Army Council meant that the latter's demand for dean and chapter lands as security was not immediately followed up. 'The Case of the Army' had also demanded a resale of bishops' lands, alleging that they had been sold corruptly and below their value. The campaign of petitions revived in November 1648, again headed by the officers who feared mutinies.[1] On 20 November the Remonstrance of the Army asked Parliament 'to lay aside that bargaining Proposition with Delinquents', and demanded 'That no delinquents be partially dealt with'.[2] But the sinister threat could not be carried out without the coup of 6 December, which was in effect a defeat of the City oligarchy by the army. For the City companies had closed their purses, refusing loans whilst the assessment remained heavily in arrears; the City had organized its own militia; it aimed at suppressing the army, which in addition to its own economic demands was beginning to speak for a revolt of the smaller property owners of the provinces against the tyranny of the capital and the capitalists, and was being supported by a party in London and the suburbs which looked to it to free trade.[3] After the occupation of London by the army, money was seized from Weavers', Haberdashers', and Goldsmiths' Hall; this, Fairfax explained to the Lord Mayor, was what the army had been ordered by Parliament to do in the counties which had not paid their assessments.[4]

In opposition to the New Model Army, 'Presbyterians' and City had tried to appeal to the separate interests of the 'Reformado' officers and soldiers, those who had been demobilized (without pay) at the reorganization in 1645. They hung about London in quest of their arrears;[5] like the New Model, they asked for the sale of delinquents' estates.[6] The 'Presbyterians' in Parliament came to listen more sympathetically to their demands in the summer of 1647, as the threat from Fairfax's Army grew more apparent.[7]

Not that Fairfax's Army represented an undivided interest. The

---

1 Cf. Carlyle's *Cromwell* (ed. Lomas), I, p. 392.
2 Rushworth, *op. cit.*, VII, p. 1331.
3 Whitelocke, *op. cit.*, II, pp. 400–3.
4 W. Maitland, *History of London*, I, p. 418.
5 *C.J.*, V, p. 209; *L.J.*, IX, p. 281; *C.C.C.*, I, p. 54.
6 *C.J.*, V, p. 47.
7 *Ibid.*, V, p. 206.

debates in the Clarke Papers show a clear class division between the propertied officers, of whom Ireton was the spokesman, and the Levellers, equally determined to preserve private property, but desiring a fair deal for the small man. The gulf was widened by the generous gifts of estates to the army commanders whilst the rank and file went hungry and unpaid. But most fruitful of division were debentures, the expedient of 1647 for keeping the common soldiers quiet. Public faith bills had long been used to satisfy creditors of the government, contractors, or officers: all these were men of means who could afford to wait for their money. But the common soldier needed ready cash, and could not eat paper. In consequence the debentures (which could be realized in land) almost immediately became the object of outrageous speculation, officers buying them up dirt cheap from their hungry troops. From 23 June 1649 debenture holders were allowed to 'double' upon dean and chapter lands.[1] And debenture holders could combine to keep the price of land down, thus gaining advantages over and above the discount at which they had bought the debentures.[2] The ordinance of 20 July 1648 backed the debentures by solid security and facilitated their circulation despite all prohibition.[3] Thus when these lands came to be sold after Pride's Purge, most of the purchasing power was already accumulated in the hands of a relatively small circle of officers, and again the purchasers were indicated before the sales took place; this despite the attempt to restrict purchase to 'original creditors' and exclude their assigns.[4] After Berry's regiment had used its debentures jointly to purchase a crown manor, the major and five other officers bought all the rest out some two and a half years later. Apparently they gave £1,000 less than cost price for it, though it is not quite clear whether this secured them the whole manor. The conditions of the market greatly favoured those who had ready capital

1 Firth and Rait, *op. cit.*, II, p. 154.
2 See S. J. Madge, *Domesday of Crown Lands*, Pt. IV, Ch. 3, for interesting documents illustrating control of the market by a ring of officers.
3 Firth and Rait, *op. cit.*, I, p. 1173. The sale of debentures had been legalized in April 1648 (*ibid.*, I, p. 1127).
4 Chesney, *op. cit.*, p. 203. The author of *The Levellers Vindicated* (p. 7) said that debentures were 'good for nothing but to sell to Parliament mens Agents, who have set them a work to buy them for three shillings, or four shillings in the pound at most'. . . . The grandees 'make themselves and their adherents the sole possessors of the late Kings Lands for little or nothing: and for ought we know, the moneys they buy our Debentures withall, is the money the Nation cannot have any account of'. Walker used this pamphlet, *History of Independency*, II, pp. 248–9.

– in this instance the officers as against the rank and file.[1] In Parliament in 1657 Colonel Sydenham said, *à propos* of grants of land to soldiers: 'They are poor, and if you assign lands to them, they must sell again.'[2] Thus unlike the otherwise similar assignats of the French Revolution, the circulation of debentures had the effect of restricting, not widening, the circle of those who secured land. This made the restoration of these lands relatively easy in 1660.

After May 1649 the government was in effect run by the army grandees (for the Levellers had been defeated as well as the 'Presbyterians'). Parliament's committee of the army played a big part in deciding how money was to be raised, and hence in determining the policy of sale of delinquents' lands.[3] In the act of 16 July 1649 for sale of Crown lands it was left to the Army Council (which now included officers only) to propose trustees to be approved by Parliament.[4] Eighty-one per cent of the dean and chapter lands sold under the Act of 30 April 1649 was earmarked for the army and its officers. The Acts for the sale of forest lands similarly reserved a part of the proceeds for a group of named officers.

Individual officers, moreover, were active in 'discovering' 'concealed' estates. This method of earning one's arrears seems to have been common from the earliest days of composition. The House of Commons frequently made appropriations from the receipts of estates still to be discovered, usually to officers,[5] sometimes to speculators. In July 1645 a Mr. Morgan and his partners were granted half of the estates discovered by them, and urged to continue their investigations.[6] In August 1646 the House of Commons discussed setting up a commission to discover estates concealed or undervalued by compounding delinquents. Delinquents who revealed their own 'concealments' were allowed to compound for them at one quarter.[7] After 1649, when Crown lands were purchasable by debentures, the officers' zeal in discovering such lands is understandable. After 1 July 1654 any person giving information of concealed Church lands had the right of pre-emption.[8]

1 Sir James Berry and S. G. Lee, *A Cromwellian Major-General*, pp. 95–105.
2 Ed. J. T. Rutt, *Parliamentary Diary of Thomas Burton*, II, p. 240.
3 *C.J.*, VI, pp. 390, 476–7.
4 *Ibid.*, VI, p. 189.
5 *Ibid.*, IV, pp. 325, 404, 661; V, pp. 454, 464–5.
6 *Ibid.*, IV, p. 221.
7 *Ibid.*, IV, p. 637; *Thurloe State Papers*, I, p. 531.
8 Firth and Rait, *op. cit.*, II, p. 895.

Whether by accident or design, therefore, the conditions under which lands were sold after 1649 (debentures) made as little for parcelling as the conditions which prevailed at the sale of bishops' lands (doubling). The conditions of sale themselves made against the creation of a population of small proprietors, and worked all in the interests of a relatively small group of people – the monied men of the City, the squires and self-made men who officered the New Model Army. In May 1650 the Royalist Colonel Keane in his journey to the west of England noted that most of the officers had received satisfaction out of Crown and dean and chapter lands, but the rank and file were discontented at the continued non-payment of arrears.[1] Nor did the sales merely set up barriers between grandees and rank and file within the army: they also helped to isolate the army from the smaller people in town and country with whom it had been so popular in 1647. Crown lands were assigned to pay the arrears only of those who were in the army in 1647, 'which was done', said Ludlow, 'by the influence of the officers of the army that was in present service, whereby they made provision for themselves, and neglected those who had appeared for the Parliament at the first and had endured the heat and burden of the day'.[2] Similarly, the proposed sale of Needwood Forest brought representations from the grand jury of Staffordshire showing the misery that would befall thousands of the poor if the forest were enclosed.[3] Officers, on the other hand, petitioned for the acceleration of the sale as necessary if their arrears were to be paid.[4] Again in the Parliament of 1657, the argument advanced against the plea of those with right of commonage in the forests was the overwhelming pressure of the needs of the army.[5] The two interests were irreconcilable: there were many reasons why the army lost the confidence of the common people and could so easily be disposed of in 1660.

1 C.S.P. Dom., 1650, p. 154.
2 Ludlow, Memoirs, ed. 1894, I, p. 232.
3 C.S.P. Dom., 1655, p. 32.
4 Ibid., 1655–6, pp. 363–4.
5 Burton's Parliamentary Diary, II, pp. 238–44. Many more influences worked together to the same end than can be listed here. Thus the economic crisis of 1649–51, the government's determination to fight its way out, to challenge the Dutch for the trade of the world by the Navigation Act, followed by the Dutch and Spanish wars: all this meant that the needs of the fleet as well as of the army were instrumental in forcing the later sales of delinquents' and forest lands.

VII

Sale

Political and military events were not without their effect on agrarian legislation. Just as, earlier, Baillie's hopes of being able to convert the English Parliament to Presbyterianism had ebbed and flowed with the successes of the Scottish Army, so the demands for sale of lands were raised after the victory of Marston Moor and grew more insistent after Naseby. But only the estates of a few named individuals were sold then by special ordinance. The Lords prevented a general sale by throwing bishops' lands to the wolves in 1646, but as we have seen the struggle recommenced in 1647–8. In the autumn of 1648 there was a campaign of petitioning and counter-petitioning about dean and chapter lands: the common council wanted these lands to be reserved for augmenting the salaries of ministers, whilst petitions from the general council of the army and from Norfolk demanded them as security for the payment of the army. Finance was the determining but not the only factor: the issue of established and controlled Church versus the democratic voluntaryism of the sects was also of great social importance, and the City fathers did not need to read *Gangraena* to understand how much more satisfactory from their point of view was a Presbyterian discipline than the anarchy of toleration. If dean and chapter lands should be disposed of otherwise than for the maintenance of the ministry, the Scottish Commissioners told Parliament in December 1647, 'it will prove a great Discouragement to faithful Pastors, make their Subsistence to depend upon the Benevolence and Charity of their Hearers, and give Occasion to the People (where Ministers are wanting for Lack of Maintenance) to follow after Sectaries and Tub-preachers'.[1] Yet, ultimately, it was the Common Council's demand for adequate security in the changed political circumstances that led to the sale of dean and chapter lands on 30 April 1649.[2] Three Acts for sale of delinquents' estates followed in 1651 and 1652.

Bishops' lands (like the estates of the monasteries a century earlier) seem to have gone primarily to City business men and speculators, secondly to gentlemen. The same seems roughly true of dean and chapter lands. The most interesting feature that emerges from illustrative tables of purchasers which Professor Arkhangelsky has drawn up is that curiously few gentlemen seem to have bought

1 *L.J.*, IX, p. 599.
2 *Cromwelliana* (1810), p. 55.

delinquents' lands, which went mostly to Londoners and officers, whereas a very much larger number bought the lands of deans and chapters (which they may no doubt have leased before), with a corresponding decline in the percentage of London merchants purchasing this category of land.[1] The Church was fair game, but dog does not eat dog. Even after Pride's Purge the gentlemen in the Rump had qualms about tampering with lay property, and it took fifteen months' anxious debate before the first Act for the sale of delinquents' estates was finally passed. Altogether, delinquents' lands were made security for a loan of £1,050,000 – a sum five times as great as the loan backed by bishops' lands in 1646.

But the important point to make is that in each case the circle of purchasers was very restricted. The average price at which an individual purchase of bishops' land was made was over £900:[2] Professor Arkhangelsky found evidence of only four below £100. Details of sixty-three sales of dean and chapter lands which he collected from various sources show an average purchase price of over £1,500. Only two were below £100. In days when the wages of an agricultural labourer might be £4 10s. a year, when a yeoman was well off who had more than £40 per annum, it is clear that there can have been very few peasant purchasers. (Though of course many purchasers resold, and there might have been greater subsequent parcelling if the Restoration had not intervened.) There are no instances of collective purchase by peasants such as we find in the French and Russian Revolutions. Where we meet with collective purchase, it is of a delinquent's estate by his creditors.[3] There are agents or jobbers like Wildman, Crouch, Foxley, Rushworth, making purchases all over the kingdom. This all fits in with the literary evidence of men like Walker and Holles, which, though it may be exaggerated, cannot therefore be ignored. Crown lands and fee-farm rents form rather a special category, as they were offered in the first place to debenture holders,

---

1 But see Mrs. Thirsk's articles, *passim*, on this point. She has shown that many of the delinquents whose estates were confiscated and sold managed to repurchase them before the Restoration, just as many French aristocrats recovered theirs before 1815 (A. Gain, *La Restauration et les Biens des Émigrés*, 1928, esp. I, pp. 57–88). Musgrave suggested that M.P.s, solicitors and agents for cavaliers were the main purchasers (J. Musgrave, *A True and Exact Relation*, 1650, p. 41).

2 Tatham, *op. cit.*, pp. 104–8.

3 *C.C.C.*, III, p. 2351.

and that meant that the purchasers were mostly officers or speculators. They might also be forgers.[1]

Purchasers' interests were well safeguarded by the many ordinances and acts for 'removing obstructions' to sale. They received delinquents' land free of all incumbrances 'and of all suits and questions that may arise or be moved upon pretence of Sale at undervalues'.[2] In the case of Church lands, 'if it be required by the purchaser or purchasers of any of them . . .', ran the ordinance of 17 November 1646, 'one or more Acts of Parliament, or Letters Patents under the Great Seal of England by Authority of Parliament, shall hereafter pass . . . for the further assuring of the premises' upon payment of the usual fees.[3] Fee-farm rents were sold in full ownership. The new conservatism that accompanies the establishment of the protectorate coincides with the exhaustion of the land fund, the 'satiation' of the monied purchasers. In 1655 the Venetian secretary reported, of a proposal to tax land which had been purchased too cheaply: 'it may easily cause trouble'.[4] The alternative (so long as the army remained undisbanded) was the decimation tax.

'How much hath sir John Stowel lost?' asked Fuller in 1660. 'How many new gentlemen have started up out of the estate of that ancient knight? What hath the lord Craven lost?'[5] Examination of the three Acts for sale of delinquents' estates shows that nearly eighty per cent of them were described as gentlemen.[6] Of 625 sales which Professor Arkhangelsky traced in the Calendar of the Committee for Compounding, 262 were in the four northern counties; eighty per cent of the sales were of lands north-west of a line drawn from the eastern boundary of Dorset to the western boundary of Nottinghamshire – in the economically backward area from which the main strength of the

---

1 *C.S.P. Dom. 1655*, pp. 7–13; Burton, *op. cit.*, II, p. 239; and cf. Madge, *Domesday of Crown Lands*, Pt. IV, Ch. 4. See also Mrs. Thirsk, 'The Sales of Royalist Land', *passim*.

2 Firth and Rait, *op. cit.*, pp. 531, 539; cf. II, pp. 179–80 – same provision for Crown lands.

3 *Ibid.*, I, p. 892; cf. II, p. 91 – same provision at the sale of dean and chapter lands. Cf. also Ludlow, *Memoirs*, I, p. 235, for contemporary views of the security of purchasers of dean and chapter lands.

4 *C.S.P. Venetian, 1655–6*, p. 211.

5 T. Fuller, *Mixt Contemplations in Better Times* (1830), p. 241.

6 Approximately the same percentage of compounders were gentlemen, paying ninety per cent of the total sum (Professor Arkhangelsky's figures, drawn from the *Commons' Journals* of 1646–8). Delinquents worth less than £200 had been exempted from composition.

King's armies had come. Church and Crown lands sold, on the other hand, were preponderantly in the south and east.

Influence of Creditors

The City early acquired a decisive influence in all the land transactions of the period. The treasurers at the Guildhall, who handled all the receipts of sequestration, were citizens of London; London merchants were also prominent in all the official positions – foeffees, trustees, and contractors for sale – of the new financial departments created by the sale of lands; loans were raised in the City on the security of sequestration and composition monies, later on the proposed sales.[1] And there is plenty of evidence that the sequestration officials, both in London and in the counties, had ample opportunity for turning a dishonest penny. There is much complaint of leasing at undervalues to such persons. The ordinance of 14 April 1648 authorized contractors for the sale of bishops' lands to purchase such lands with their unpaid arrears of salary.[2] Many officials of the committee for compounding speculated in land.[3]

Throughout the greatest respect was shown for the interests of state creditors. One of the earliest cases of individual sale was of a recusant's estate, to satisfy the debt owing to Thomas Pendleton and other boot-makers; clothing contractors, saddlers, received payment out of compositions.[4] Messrs. Pennoyer and Hill, whose debt of £9,402 5s. for clothing and arms looms large in the Parliamentary debates, were assigned lands from the sequestrated estates of the Earl of Worcester and other delinquents, pending the time when Parliament should 'in a general Way put Delinquents Estates to sale';[5] the ordinance for the sale of the Earl's lands in London and Middlesex was passed on 12 September 1646, only because they did not yield the revenue necessary to pay the state creditors to whom they had been handed over.[6] Other state creditors were paid out of composition monies, e.g. twenty-seven

---

1 For example, *L.J.*, VII, p. 713; *C.J.*, IV, p. 608.
2 There was a similar clause in the act of 31 July 1649 for sale of dean and chapter lands.
3 Chesney, *op. cit.*, pp. 190–2.
4 For example, *C.J.*, IV, pp. 404, 534; V, p. 3.
5 *Ibid.*, IV, p. 186.
6 *L.J.*, VIII, p. 490.

merchants in December 1645.[1] The contemporary petitions for these lands to be devoted to educational purposes have now rather an ironical ring.

The proposal to sell bishops' lands came after consultation with the Commissioners for the Customs, the Merchant Adventurers, the East India and Eastland Companies, from a Parliamentary committee on which City representatives were prominent.[2] The ordinance of 24 July 1648 guaranteed repayment from the sale of bishops' lands first of all to various state creditors.[3] From August 1649 purchasers of bishops' lands were permitted to pay the whole purchase money in 'Gold-smiths-Hall Bills or Weavers-Hall Bills'.[4] Public faith bills became an object of speculation like debentures. Creditors who 'doubled' were allowed lower rates of purchase, but many who could not afford to 'double' were long left unpaid.

> 'What was the public faith found out for,
> But to slur men of what they fought for?'[5]

The indebtedness of many delinquents was notorious.[6] Parliament looked carefully after the interests of their private creditors, at sequestration, composition, and sale. In 1645, when sale of delin-quents' estates was first mooted, the City asked that creditors should not be allowed to suffer, and a committee of the House of Commons was set up to work out a separate explanatory ordinance dealing with debts owed by or to delinquents whose land was to be sold.[7] An Act passed in August 1650 permitted a mortgagee to compound in place of the mortgagor.[8] Milton took advantage of a debt owed to him by his late father-in-law to compound for, and take possession of, lands which his mother-in-law regarded as hers.[9] There appears to be no evidence for

1 *C.C.C.*, I, p. 29.
2 *C.J.*, IV, p. 650.
3 Firth and Rait, *op. cit.*, I, p. 1175.
4 *Ibid.*, II, p. 237.
5 S. Butler, *Hudibras*, Part II, Canto 2; Chesney, *op. cit.*, pp. 194, 206–7. As early as 1646 public faith bills were selling in London at 14s. or 15s. in the pound (Gardiner, *Oxinden and Peyton Letters*, p. 96; cf. Walker, *History of Independency*, II, p. 207).
6 See R. H. Tawney, 'The Rise of the Gentry', *Economic History Review*, XI, No. 1, *passim*.
7 *C.J.*, IV, p. 225; cf. p. 613.
8 Firth and Rait, *op. cit.*, II, pp. 402–3. For an example, see Hon. H. A. Wyndham, *A Family History, 1410–1688*, pp. 225–6.
9 Masson, *Life of Milton*, IV, pp. 236–46, 336–41.

supposing that the Rump safeguarded the interests of creditors any less meticulously than the Presbyterian majority had done in the sixteen-forties, surprising though this may seem to those who believe that the Independents represented the declining gentry, driven to revolt by the burden of their debts.

Informers of 'concealment' were usually either state creditors (including officers) or private creditors of delinquents. Dr. Chesney showed the advantages creditors had for 'discovering' delinquents' estates, or for doing a private deal with their debtor. 'It is only occasionally', he says, 'that we learn of a delinquent that he has no creditors to betray his concealments'.[1] Where long leaseholders were expropriable on Church lands exceptions were sometimes made – to enable them to pay their creditors.

IX

Improvements

Sequestrated estates were leased from year to year, and every effort was made by the House of Commons, Goldsmiths' Hall, and county committees to see that rents on Church, Crown, and delinquents' lands were kept racked up to the utmost pitch.[2] On 20 October 1648, the officers of Weymouth and Portland garrisons were still unpaid £500 due to them: Dorset Committee proposed to raise this sum by 'improving' the rents of sequestrated estates.[3] Often it proved more profitable for local committees to lease sequestrated lands to their original owners, who would be interested in preserving and improving the estate. This practice, as one committee-man wrote, caused 'much sadness among the well-affected'.[4] Pressure for cash returned was intensified after 1649, with the reorganization of the committee for compounding and the replacement of county sequestration commit-tees and their officers by nominees of the commissioners for compounding.[5] The object of the purge was clearly to remove undesirable local agents and increase central control. The Act of 25 January 1649–50 ordered sequestration officials to 'consider how the same estates may be improved to the best advantage of the

1 Chesney, *op. cit.*, p. 189.
2 *C.J.*, V, pp. 4–5; *L.J.*, IX, p. 582; X, p. 334; *C.C.C.*, *passim*.
3 A. R. Bayley, *The Great Civil War in Dorset*, p. 334.
4 Hardacre, *op. cit.*, p. 63, quoting *C.S.P. Dom., 1648–9*, p. 48.
5 Firth and Rait, *op. cit.*, II, p. 331.

Commonwealth'. There is evidence of competition among would-be lessees,[1] as well as indications of refusals by tenants to pay the higher rent. Delinquents in difficulties also tended naturally to try to squeeze the utmost out of their estates. When Viscount Stafford's estate was sequestrated his tenants petitioned for relief from taxes, because after their landlord had compounded their lands had been 'raised to extreme rack-rents . . . and were charged with taxes, etc.'[2] One of the objects of the surveys taken before sale was to note possible improvements and ascertain tenant rights: hence the wide coercive powers given to surveyors. Instances can be given of such noting of improvements. Thus the surveyors of Richmond Little Park 'have not made any reprise for the fencing or keeping up the pales of the said parke in regard wee have valewed the same as it may bee improved and not in relation as to have valewed it stored with Deere'.[3] The Lord of the manor 'may set and let all manner of voyd and wast grounds belonging to the said mannor to any man by coppie paying a fyne to the Lord and a yearely quit rent to the king which custome being good the Commons aforesaid may bee improved to a good yearelie value; which wee thought fit to insert as a thing of good and great concernement for the purchaser to looke after'.[4]

Everywhere there was much enclosure of parks and forest, with scant regard to the rights of commoners.[5] An Act of 19 June 1657 told surveyors of forests 'to examine and inform yourselves, what Cottages have been Erected, contrary to the Laws in Force, upon the said Soyl of the Commonwealth, and by whom, and by what pretence the same have been Erected, what Rents or Services they pay, or ought to pay, and certifie, which and how many of them you judge fit to continue or be demolished'.[6] Legislation as usual followed practice: surveyors had been asking themselves these questions as early as 1650. In that year the surveyors of Duddleswell noted cottages which 'are incroached and very prjudicial to the said parke, and rather to bee pulled downe then continued, and therefore we have put noe value upon the same'. Most of them had disappeared by 1658, whereas the Earl of Dorset, 'who pduceth noe evidence whereby he claimes to hould' an enclosure in the

---

1 For example *C.C.C.*, III, pp. 2231–2, 2364; V, pp. 3269–71.
2 *C.C.C.*, III, p. 2085.
3 Surrey Archaeological Society's *Collections*, V, p. 98.
4 *Ibid.*, V, p. 96.
5 Cf. *C.S.P. Dom.*, *1655*, p. 308. (Enclosure by John Parker, see p. 174, n. 6, below.)
6 Firth and Rait, *op. cit.*, II, p. 1116.

same park, remained in possession.[1] In many places tenants complain of purchasers 'exacting such a rate . . . as they cannot bear without utter ruin'.[2] They beg that 'their rents may be continued at the same rates';[3] that 'rents lately increased from £200 to £400' may be reduced, or their farms be taken back into the commonwealth's hands.[4] In 1641 Peard had calculated that dean and chapter lands could be improved tenfold in value;[5] and we have seen how long leases on these lands were annulled. Everywhere the conditions of sequestration, composition, and sale made for economic pressure on tenants. An intercepted letter of 14 December 1653 reports that tenants of Church and Crown lands 'doe perfectly hate those who bought them, as possibly men can doe; for these men are the greatest tyrants every where as men can be; for they wrest the poore tenants of all former immunitys and freedoms they formerly enjoyed'.[6]

The standards of the market were spreading over all England. Josiah Child, giving evidence in 1669 before a committee of the House of Lords on the fall of rents and decay of trade, still looked back to the racking up of rents in 1651 and 1652 and thought that this must share a part of the blame.[7] In Durham, also after the Restoration, the Bishop reported that 'the purchasers have made the tenants so poore that they are not able to renew their farmes'.[8] It was noted in 1660 that Church and Crown lands had increased in value, and that the revenue from the custody of royal parks had risen ten- or twenty-fold by comparison with the period before the Civil War.[9]

x

Tenants and Copyholders

All this was at the expense of tenants and copyholders – mostly small people ill able to defend their interests. We meet with their variously

1 Sussex Archaeological Society's *Collections*, XXIII, pp. 302, 304.
2 *C.C.C.*, III, p. 1925. These petitioners claim to have farmed the estates for many years and to be well-affected.
3 *Ibid.*, IV, p. 2856.
4 *Ibid.*, IV, p. 2731.
5 Shaw, *op. cit.*, I, p. 59.
6 *Thurloe State Papers*, I, p. 633; cf. Chesney, *op. cit.*, p. 194.
7 *H.M.C. Eighth Report, Appendix*, Part I, p. 134.
8 Ed. G. Ornsby, *The Correspondence of John Cosin*, Part II (Surtees Society, 1872), p. 31; cf. pp. 23–4.
9 *C.S.P. Dom., 1660–1*, p. 286.

effective protests in the documents. In the 'forties they did not come off too badly. Hobbes said the House of Commons attacked the bishops so fiercely 'because they meant to make use of their Tenants'[1] (among whom there were of course many rich lessees). As long as the war lasted some consideration was shown for the smaller tenants. The threat of the formation of an independent third party (the Clubmen) seems to have been an incentive to the formation of the New Model Army, and the demands of this more democratic force had some effect in keeping the interests of the smaller men to the fore. But in the long run the economic advances of the interregnum were made at the expense of the small man, not shared by him.

In the disturbed economic conditions of the sixteen-forties many tenants seem to have secured reductions of rent from the sequestration committees, through sheer inability to pay. But the House of Lords defeated an attempt to make statutory a reduction by one-third of the rents of all tenants on sequestrated lands who accepted the new régime.[2] Later instructions to sequestration committees said more cautiously, 'to such tenants as shall willingly yield conformity to the said ordinance, you shall abate so much to their rack-rents, where the lands are set at an improved value (and not otherwise) as you shall think fit, ... not exceeding a fourth part of such improved rents'.[3] The sequestration ordinance declared that docile tenants would be 'considered', 'protected and saved harmless'. This was a political manoeuvre rather than the trumpet blast of a new social revolution.[4]

The Commons frequently appointed committees to consider the interests of tenants, especially such as were victimized by delinquent landlords,[5] but no legislation emerged. The question was resumed with apparent vigour after 1649.[6] But this seems to have been mainly a sop to extra-Parliamentary opinion. In May 1650 the judges going on circuit had been charged to let the people know that such an act was under consideration, 'which they accordingly did, and found the thing was well resented; the House to be moved therefore that the Act may be

---

1 Hobbes, *The History of the Civil Wars in England* (1679), p. 120. Walker makes a similar remark about tenants of delinquents (*History of Independency*, II, p. 204).

2 *C.J.*, III, p. 21.

3 *Harleian Miscellany* (1812), IX, p. 538.

4 Firth and Rait, *op. cit.*, I, p. 108.

5 *C.J.*, IV, pp. 557, 571, 684; V, pp. 33, 331, 356, 514, 530.

6 For instance, *C.S.P. Dom., 1649–50*, pp. 199, 514; *1650*, p. 149; *1651*, p. 16; *C.J.*, IV, pp. 240, 393, 501, 513; Whitelocke, *op. cit.*, III, p. 158.

again taken into consideration'.[1] Again nothing came of it, if we except a clause in the Act of General Pardon and Oblivion (24 February 1651–2) that 'nothing in this Act contained shall be interpreted to the Disadvantage or Prejudice of the Tenants of any Delinquent Land-lord, whereby they may not receive Redress of their Grievances, as the Parliament shall think fit to declare and ordain'.[2] As Parliament never did think fit, that was small consolation.

The ordinance for the sale of the bishops' lands said 'due respect' was to be paid to the rights of tenants: one suspects that tenants wealthy enough to protect themselves at common law would get this even without Parliament's pious declaration, and that the simpler and poorer tenants would hardly be helped by it. The ordinance of 21 November 1648 provided that the title-deeds of all tenants on bishops' estates should be examined. The same is true of the pre-emptive facilities granted to immediate tenants – they would benefit those tenants who had ready capital, and be largely illusory to those without it. Sub-tenants were given no right of pre-emption. When on 13 November 1649, on petition from the council of officers, Parliament forbade immediate tenants to purchase with debentures during their thirty days – otherwise 'a greater Benefit will be afforded to the immediate Tenant, and a lesser Benefit to the original Creditor, than is intended them by the Act'[3] – then the only hope the small ex-soldier had of purchasing his estate vanished.

Equally unsuccessful was the prolonged agitation carried on by the left-wing parties for a reform of the law in the interest of small producers, especially for stabilization of copyholds and the fixing of copyhold fines.[4] The surveys of the manor of Duddleswell show that of the 60 copyholders of 1650, 14 had disappeared by 1658, and their copyholds had passed to 15 newcomers, only 3 of whom bore surnames previously met with in the manor; 15 other holdings had changed in size.[5] The village population was fluctuating. It was naturally not to the interest of landlords whom Parliaments in the 'fifties largely repre-sented to do anything that would increase the security of tenure of copyholders and cottagers. We have given indications earlier of what might be the fate of cottagers. In the Duddleswell survey of 1658 the

1 *C.S.P. Dom., 1650*, p. 149.
2 *C.J.*, VII, p. 93; Firth and Rait, *op. cit.*, II, p. 576.
3 *C.J.*, VI, p. 323.
4 *Ibid.*, VII, p. 130.
5 Sussex Archaeological Society's *Collections*, XXIII–XXV.

only cottage remaining of ten mentioned in 1650 was the largest, that of John Taylor, who had built it himself and improved the land at his own expense, 'out of which considerations we have vallued the premisses as aforesaid': the surveyors felt they had to apologize for leaving it, though 'erected upon the soyle of the Common wealth . . . contrary to the Laws in force'.[1] In 1656 the ownership of the Forest of Dean was vested in the Protector, who 'expelled near 400 cabins of beggarly people living upon the destruction of the wood and timber'.[2] Cromwell had won his early reputation as Lord of the Fens by protecting the victims of enclosers and improvers; but times had changed.

On the one hand, a restored landlord might be expected to commence an offensive against tenants who in his absence had fought for or recognized the Parliament;[3] poor men pay cavaliers' compositions, said John Cook.[4] If a delinquent did not compound, on the other hand, all tenant rights were checked at the survey which preceded the sale of his estate. The position of small tenants seems to have deteriorated after 1649, with the war won and the Leveller and Digger movements suppressed. The Act of 1656 for the abolition of military tenures abolished fiscal feudalism upwards only, between landlords and the state, not downwards between landlord and tenant. The final defeat of the agitation for enfranchisement of copyholders was signalized by the rejection in the same Parliament of a 'bill for ascertaining of arbitrary fines upon descent or alienation of copyholds of inheritance'.[5] When the abolition of military tenures was confirmed in 1661, the Act specifically provided that it should not 'alter or change any tenure by copy of court roll or any service incident thereunto'. Thus landlords secured their own estates in absolute ownership, and ensured that copyholders remained evictable. Thanks to this and to the device of the 'strict settlement', land ownership 'lost much of that insecurity which had detracted from its social value in Tudor times and in the Civil Wars'.[6] Confirmation of the abolition of feudal tenures had

1 *Ibid.*, XXIV, p. 192.
2 *E.H.R.*, XXI, p. 450. For the effects of the land transactions of the Interregnum on the position of commoners in the Forest of Dean, see C. E. Hart, *The Free Miners*, pp. 195–207.
3 For instance Whitelocke, *op. cit.*, II, p. 107 (Committee appointed to draw up instructions for judges sent on circuit to settle these disputes). See also p. 151 above.
4 John Cook, *The Poor Mans Case* (1648), pp. 71–2.
5 *C.J.*, VII, p. 433.
6 D. Ogg, *England under Charles II*, I, p. 64.

been the first concern of the Convention Parliament after hearing the Declaration of Breda. This estimate of its importance was confirmed a century later by Blackstone, who thought it a greater boon to property-owners than Magna Carta itself.[1]

But these advantages were not shared by copyholders. Arbitrary fines, heriots, reliefs, courts leet and baron – all these remained. It was 'somewhat unequal', Lord Guilford remarked after the Restoration, that 'lesser tenures . . . were left exposed to as grievous abuses' as tenants-in-chief had been previously. 'Small tenements and pieces of land, that have been men's inheritances for divers generations, to say nothing of the fines, are devoured by fees'. So he advocated abolition of copyhold. His lordship was concerned exclusively for copyholders who were gentlemen, naturally;[2] but a fortiori humbler men would have even less chance of defending themselves against 'grievous abuses'. The Parliament of 1656 saw the last attempt to check enclosure as well as the last attempt to protect copyholders.

During the interregnum feudal rights were sometimes exploited with new vigour by sequestration committee,[3] returned delinquent or purchaser. With the same effect, the Act of 19 June 1657 provided for the enclosure of divers formerly royal forests and established the proportions in which land was to be divided out, according to the number of cattle which the tenant could produce documentary proof of his right to pasture. Many of these rights were customary, and documentary proof would not always be forthcoming: and in any case the standard was not an equitable one.[4] In the result, in Ashdown Forest 26 gentlemen received 1,259 acres (averaging 48½ apiece) and 192 others got 3,170 acres (16½ apiece).[5] 'The principal end' (of enclosure of forests), the Council of State was told in 1654, 'is advantage to husbandry and tillage, to which all commons are destructive'.[6] All this must have contributed to the great increase of vagrancy in the 'fifties.

1 Sir W. Blackstone, *Commentaries on the Laws of England* (1794), II, p. 77.
2 North, *Lives of the Norths*, I, pp. 34–6.
3 Cf. Firth and Rait, *op. cit.*, I, pp. 1179–83.
4 Cf. G. Winstanley, Epistle Dedicatory to *The Law of Freedom in a Platform* (1652), on overstocking of commons by 'the new (more covetous) Gentry'.
5 Sussex Archaeological Society's *Collections*, XXIV, pp. 197–209.
6 *C.S.P. Dom., 1654*, pp. 71–2 (Proposals by Dr. John Parker and Edw. Cresset). Parker was probably the purchaser of Greenwich Park, where 60 acres lately enclosed from Blackheath were causing trouble – see p. 169, n. 5 above.

Of course there was opposition: enclosure was laid open, timber destroyed. In the early sixteen-forties Parliament was comparatively lenient in face of direct action which might be aimed against Royalist landlords. But with the rise first of the Clubmen, then of the Leveller movement, its attitude stiffened: in March 1645–6 the House of Lords granted Lord Berkeley's request for military assistance against rioters who had thrown open 300 acres of his land, called, significantly, 'the New-Gained Grounds'.[1] In June 1647 rioters in Hatfield Chase said, 'if we cannot get our Common by Law, we will get it by Club Law', and alleged that they had the support of Fairfax's Army.[2] There seems to have been a political point even in the destruction of timber. On 23 February 1649–50 the Council of State observed that the impunity of the looser and disordered sort of people in stealing wood and timber encouraged them in other designs.[3] Four years later the Council of State, on petition from the ex-Royalist Lord Broghill, called on J.P.s to use troops to maintain enclosures in the forest of Frome Salwood.[4] There were continual disturbances in the Forest of Dean.[5] The struggle against tithes, especially impropriated tithes, runs parallel to the struggle against enclosures, an attempt to recover communal wealth privately appropriated. There is an economic basis to the voluntaryism of the sects, and during the years 1647–9, when dean and chapter lands were not made available for satisfaction of army arrears on the claim that they were needed to augment ministers' salaries, propaganda against 'hireling priests' had an easy weapon.

XI

Conclusion

In comparison with the French Revolution, the English Revolution stopped half-way. The Levellers were defeated, there was no law reform, copyholders were at the mercy of landlords, and Charles II came back with the goodwill of a large section of the revolutionaries of 1640. Why? The answer is to be found, Professor Arkhangelsky thinks, in the close connection of English capitalism with the land. Past history

1 *L.J.*, VIII, p. 200–1. Lord Berkeley claimed to have enjoyed possession for thirty years.
2 *Ibid.*, IX, pp. 428–9.
3 *C.S.P. Dom., 1650*, p. 10.
4 *Ibid., 1654*, pp. 337–8.
5 For instance, *C.J.*, VII, p. 648.

prevented the owners of impropriations from looking favourably on the democratic movement against tithes. New purchasers were as anxious as old landlords to maintain the common law, the 'law of the land' in two senses, a law for landlords as well as a national law. Even in the Barebones Parliament, where there were 'not so many lords of manors', and where there was a strong minority which would have liked to produce a 'Code Cromwell' – even there gentlemen and merchants predominated.[1] It was in fear of the movement for a new social revolution – against enclosure and tithes, for stable copyholds – that Winstanley's 'new (more covetous) Gentry' swung over to compromise with the old, through the hereditary protectorate and the Other House to the forms of the old monarchy and finally to the Restoration. The old order was not completely destroyed, and although new men moved on to the land, and the House of Commons acquired new powers, after 1660 the ghost of the deceased feudal order still sat coroneted at Westminster. But it was there on sufferance and in a subordinate position.[2] A decisive break had taken place. Traditional relationships had been broken down, rents were on the way to full commercialization, no Laud ever again fined enclosing landlords in the name of social justice. The origins of the new techniques of the eighteenth-century agricultural revolution are almost all to be sought during or just after the interregnum.

To summarize: during the interregnum, capital was mobilized, either by short-term 'spoiling' or by long-term improvements in the technique of management, whether by sequestration committee, purchaser, or returned delinquent. In all three cases a capital sum passed through the hands of the state into the possession either of capitalist contractors and creditors, or of soldiers, most of whom were bled by officers speculating in debentures. Moreover, when lands were transferred they either remained in the hands of purchasers anxious to recoup themselves, or after improvement at their hands were resold at a higher price to others, or returned to delinquents whose own impoverishment made it necessary for them to turn improving landlords. The moral of the Duchess of Newcastle's *The Tale of a Traveller* is that constant vigilance is needed if a landlord is to thrive.[3] The restored bishops had a concerted rent policy, which included the

1 H. A. Glass, *The Barbone Parliament*, pp. 62–3, 69–86.
2 Chesney, *op. cit.*, p. 210.
3 D. Grant, *Margaret the First*, p. 231.

conversion of leases for lives into leases for years, and whose object was the extraction of the maximum rent and fines from their estates.[1] So even where Royalists recovered their lands in or before 1660, they had to get on or get out. There was much mortgaging and reselling in the period from 1660 to 1688. The Duchess of Newcastle claimed that after his return her husband had to sell lands to the value of £56,000 in order to pay debts: after that he had to turn improving landlord.[2] After 1660, indeed, it became a social duty to get rich. The Duke of Albemarle, his physician tells us, realized that 'if the Wealth of the Nation came to centre most among the lower and trading Part of the People, at one Time or other it will certainly be in their Power and probably in their Desires, to invade the Government'. This was the more likely if the nobility made themselves 'contemptible and weak, by the Number and Weight of their Debts, and the continual Decay of their Estates'. So the self-made Duke resolved 'to become as great an Example to the Nobility of honourable good Husbandry, as he had been before of Loyalty and Allegiance'.[3] In this new commercial world the King is the most obvious example of the type of big landowner who could not adapt himself: Crown lands had almost all been sold before James II went on his travels. Conformably to the new economic order, the King ceased to be a landlord living of his own, and became a salaried official.

1 Ed. J. C. Hodgson, *Northumbrian Documents of the 17th and 18th centuries* (Surtees Society, 1918), pp. 213–15, 226, 234–8; Clarendon, *Life* (1759), II, pp. 184–6.

2 Ed. Firth, *Life of the Duke of Newcastle*, pp. 78–9; Grant, *op. cit.*, pp. 199, 229–33; cf. Henry Oxinden of Barham (*Oxinden and Peyton Letters*, pp. xvii, xxxviii). Further research is required into this point before we can be quite sure of the full significance of Mrs. Thirsk's researches, as indeed she herself recognizes. Roger Coke suggested that the effort to recover his lands in the sixteen-fifties often left a Royalist's family in financial difficulties after the Restoration. Many may have been forced to sell their estates again before the end of the century (R. Coke, *A Detection of the Court and State of England*, 1694, II, pp. 101, 105, 375–6).

3 T. Skinner, *Life of Monck* (1724), p. 384.

PART TWO

Men and Movements

SIX

Lord Clarendon and the
Puritan Revolution

There was never yet a good history written but by Men conversant
in Business, and of the best and most liberal Education.

Clarendon – *Essay on an active and on a contemplative life.*

I

IT is a healthy corrective to nineteenth-century conceptions of 'The
Puritan Revolution'[1] to turn to the rich and sonorous pages of
Clarendon's *History of the Rebellion and Civil Wars in England.* For
Clarendon, himself a leading actor in the Civil War, believed that
'Religion was made a Cloak to cover the most impious designs' of the
Long Parliament, who 'took none of the points in controversy less to
heart, or were less united in, than in what concerned the Church'.[2]
Forty years ago Sir Charles Firth went so far as to say that Clarendon's
History 'has the fundamental defect, that it is a history of a religious
revolution in which the religious element is omitted'.[3] Today we cannot
be so cheerfully confident that we know better than contemporaries.
Clarendon may have underestimated the religious sincerity of his
opponents: but he had no motive for decrying religion as such. He was
himself a genuinely pious man who, in his years of exile, wrote
Contemplations and Reflections upon the Psalms of David which run to 400
folio pages; and throughout his political career he was especially noted
for his devotion to the Church of England and its hierarchy.

Edward Hyde descended from a Wiltshire landed family. By his own

---

1 See above, pp. 4–6.
2 *The Continuation of the Life of Edward, Earl of Clarendon* (1759), III, pp. 977–8;
Clarendon, *History*, III, p. 477.
3 Firth, *Essays, Historical and Literary*, p. 119.

account he was in his youth something of a social climber and a snob. He married with extreme prudence, connecting himself with the court favourite, the Duke of Buckingham. Later he became a protégé of Archbishop Laud. But his education as a lawyer brought him into contact with the opposition. He had no use for the corruption of Charles I's court or the perversion of justice for political ends. So when the Long Parliament met Hyde took the lead in attacking prerogative courts and subservient judges, and in the overthrow of Strafford. But he was a reformer, not a revolutionary. He opposed the exclusion of bishops from the House of Lords, and the tendency of the House of Commons to appeal to public opinion for support. He feared popular influence on the formation of policy, and entered into an understanding with the King, whom he urged to take his stand on 'the law of the land' against revolutionary aggression from Parliament and populace. He followed this line consistently as Charles I's adviser during the Civil War, often winning unpopularity from military leaders by his anxiety to make a compromise peace.

But after the Royalist defeat in the war, and the execution of the King, Hyde came into his own. For the republican government, he tells us, 'was manifestly odious to all the nobility and gentry of the kingdom',[1] and could be maintained only by an army which cost more in taxation than even its enthusiastic supporters were willing to pay. Hyde advocated a policy of waiting, deprecated Royalist revolts or efforts to obtain foreign military help; and was justified when divisions among the Parliamentarians led in 1660 to the restoration of King, bishops and House of Lords.

Hyde played an important part in the Restoration. His association with the opposition in 1640-1, and his known desire to end the Civil War by royal acceptance of the reforms of those years, guaranteed that Parliament would be restored with the King. The clock was not set back to 1639. After 1660, in fact, Hyde was criticized for his concessions to the King's former enemies, and for the important share which they were allowed in the government of which he, now Lord Chancellor and Earl of Clarendon, was a virtual head. Clarendon's moderate reformist position made him acceptable as the man of 1660. But even he was too old-fashioned to survive long in the new world which the rebellion had produced. Let the King come in, the republican Harrington is reported as saying, 'and call a Parliament of

1 *History*, V, p. 253.

the greatest Cavaliers in England, so they be men of estates, and let them sett but 7 yeares, and they will all turn Common-wealthe's men'.[1] They did not quite turn republican; but punctually within seven years the Cavalier Parliament chased the Chancellor back into exile. As long as Clarendon was in the government, said Charles II, 'it was impossible . . . to do those things with the Parliament that must be done, or the government will be lost'. Clarendon virtually admitted the political necessity of his sacrifice when he noted that, bad though this House of Commons was, 'there is no Hope ever to see another House so well constituted for Church and State'.[2] He lost office almost on the day when *Paradise Lost* first appeared in the bookshops.

After his fall Clarendon resumed work on his *History of the Rebellion*, which he had begun during his first exile, in 1646. It was thus the product of his maturest reflections, after his apparent victory of 1660 had been turned into bitter defeat. Consequently, though the work was in part an apologia for its author's policy, it was written without illusions. Clarendon had no sympathy whatsoever for the forces which had defeated the old order in England; but he had experienced their power, and wished to analyse and understand them. This is the source of the unique value of his work for historians today. Clarendon's interpretation of the Civil War in class terms was shared, with different emphases, by three of the most original thinkers among his contemporaries: Harrington, Hobbes, and Winstanley. But none of these had been at the heart of affairs as Clarendon had. Nor is Clarendon in any sense a doctrinaire adherent of a 'blind forces' theory of history. On the contrary: his *History* is justly famous for the 'characters' in it, the shrewd and subtle portraits of the leading figures, based on personal observation and insight.

Clarendon then was a sincerely religious man who denied that 'the Puritan Revolution' was about religion; a participant in the events he describes, who took full advantage of his opportunities for studying the personalities and motives of the leaders on both sides; a man whose own political programme seemed at one time triumphantly justified by the march of events, but who afterwards lost control of the forces which he alone had seemed to understand. *The History of the Rebellion* is his attempt to explain, to himself and to posterity, what the great conflict had been about.

1 J. Aubrey, *Brief Lives* (1898), I, p. 291.
2 *D.N.B.*; *A Compleat Collection of Tracts by . . . Edward, Earl of Clarendon* (1747), p. 8.

II

Although not, in Clarendon's view, about religion, it had in part been about Church government, since 'the government here established by the laws hath so near a relation and intermixture with the civil state'.[1] In 1641 Hyde 'could not conceive how Religion could be preserved without Bishops; nor how the Government of the State could well subsist, if the Government of the Church were altered'.[2] Episcopacy was 'a part of the government of England', and its abolition was 'the removing a Land-mark; and the shaking the very Foundations of Government'. But it was still a political act: bishops 'were looked upon as so many votes for the King'.[3]

Hyde therefore opposed the abolition of episcopacy as an institution, though his biographers suggest that he exaggerates, in retrospect, the importance which he attached to it in 1641. But he rejected theories of divine right, of King or bishops, and was very critical of the conduct of the Laudian hierarchy. His criticisms, however, were *social*, not religious. The bishops, who had monopolized so many government offices under Charles I, 'by want of temper or want of breeding, did not behave themselves with that decency in their debates towards the greatest men of the kingdom as in discretion they ought to have done'. So they incurred 'the universal envy of the whole nobility'.[4]

Clarendon was a thorough-going erastian, who disliked clerical interference in politics. The Church for him was a necessary bulwark of the state, which might be reformed peacefully, but which it would be dangerous to overthrow altogether. He thus describes the theological position of that great Royalist magnate, the Marquis of Newcastle, with a touch of irony but with no moral disapprobation: 'He loved monarchy, as it was the foundation and support of his own greatness; and the Church as it was well constituted for the splendour and security of the Crown; and religion, as it cherished and maintained that order and obedience that was necessary to both.'[5]

So Clarendon denied that the breach between the two sides was caused by disagreements about religion. He blamed rather the King's

1 *History*, V, p. 512.
2 *Life*, I, p. 81; cf. pp. 138–9; *Tracts*, pp. 427–8.
3 *Life*, I, pp. 96–7; *History*, VI, p. 100.
4 *History*, I, p. 117, cf. pp. 132, 272; B. H. G. Wormald, *Clarendon*, pp. 2–4, 10, 63, 114–15, 301–10.
5 *History*, III, p. 381.

attempt to arrest the five members, which destroyed all possibility of peacefully agreed reforms; and Parliament's Militia Ordinance which followed two months later. He delighted in pointing out that many who had been called Puritans fought for the King, and that men 'of most licentious lives' supported Parliament from a pretended fear of Popery.[1]

What then were, in Clarendon's view, the causes of the Civil War? He records the traditional constitutional grievances: but in each case he goes out of his way to emphasize their social effects. Refusal to pay unparliamentary taxation caused 'very many gentlemen of prime quality' to be imprisoned. The elevation of the upstart Duke of Buckingham 'equally offended the ancient nobility and the people of all conditions'. By Lord Cottington's exactions at the Court of Wards, 'all the rich families of England, of noblemen and gentlemen, were exceedingly incensed, and even indevoted to the Crown'. The verdict of the judges in the Ship Money case involved 'a logic that left no man any thing which he might call his own', and so alienated all the propertied classes. 'Persons of honour and great quality' were prosecuted in the Court of High Commission, 'which they called an insolent triumph upon their degree and quality, and levelling them with the common people'.[2]

In making these points Clarendon's concern is to explain how a revolutionary situation had arisen. He assumes that the lower classes are hostile to the government. But the latter had alienated those men of rank and wealth who were its natural supporters. Hence the almost unanimous opposition of the Commons (including Hyde himself) in the early months of the Long Parliament, the overthrow of the government, the prerogative courts, the bishops. But as 'landmarks' began to be cast down, so there came a regrouping of men of rank and property round the King:[3] and Hyde began to write manifestoes stressing the monarchy as the focus of social stability, law and order: as a landmark.

Clarendon makes no bones about describing the line-up in the Civil War as a class division. The estates and revenues of Charles I's troop of guards alone 'might justly be valued at least equal to all theirs who then voted in both Houses . . . and so made and maintained that war'.

1 *History*, II, p. 370; cf. I, pp. 505–12, 522–4, 568, 594.
2 *Ibid.*, I, pp. 6, 12, 199, 87, 125; cf. p. 32, and *A Brief View and Survey*, p. 53.
3 See p. 16 above.

The people in 'great towns and corporations' had a 'natural malignity': in contrast with 'those of quality' who were 'loyally inclined'. By October 1642 Oxford was 'the only city in England that [Charles I] could say was entirely at his devotion'; 'the King had no port to friend' through which he could import armaments from his foreign allies. In Yorkshire 'by much the greatest part of the persons of honour, quality, and interest' were for the King; but 'Leeds, Halifax, and Bradford, three very populous and rich towns (which depending wholly upon clothiers naturally maligned the gentry)' were Parliamentarian.[1] In Lancashire in 1643 'men of no name and contemned interest, by the mere credit of the Parliament and frenzy of the people, on a sudden snatched that large and populous county from their devotion to the great earl of Darby. . . . His ancient power there depended more upon the fear than love of the people, there being very many now in this time of liberty engaging themselves against the King that they might not be subject to that lord's commands.' The unfortunate Earl was ultimately tried 'by persons of ordinary quality' and executed at Bolton, 'a town of his own'. Manchester 'had from the beginning (out of that factious humour which possessed most corporations, and the pride of their wealth) opposed the King'.[2]

So we could go on. In the south-western counties 'most of the gentry' were Royalists, 'as they were in truth throughout the kingdom; yet the common people, especially in the clothing parts of Somerset' were generally Parliamentarian. In the Forest of Dean 'the gentry, who for the most part were well affected' were opposed by 'very wealthy' yeomen, who were 'most forward and seditious'. Similarly in Sussex 'some of the well-affected gentry' offered to raise troops for the King in 1643. But 'the common people of the county' rallied to Parliament, and shut the Cavaliers up in Chichester. There the citizens could not be trusted to do guard duty: it had to be performed by 'the officers and gentlemen of quality, who were absolutely tired out'.[3] Everywhere Parliament had enthusiastic rank-and-file support: that of the Royalists was at best half-hearted. Even in Shropshire, Cheshire, and North Wales, 'the common people were more devoted to them

1 *History*, II, pp. 348, 226, 375, 461, 464; III, p. 13. Cf. the Duchess of Newcastle's reference (also *à propos* of the West Riding) to 'those parts of the kingdom which were populous, rich, and rebellious' (*Life of the Duke of Newcastle*, ed. C. H. Firth, n.d., p. 21). Cf. p. 16 above.

2 *History*, II, pp. 470–1; V, p. 184.

3 *Ibid.*, III, pp. 80, 129–30; II, p. 446.

[Parliament], and gave them all intelligence of what might concern them. Whereas they who were intrusted to govern the King's affairs had intolerable difficulties to pass through. . . . The difference in the temper of the common people of both sides was so great, that they who inclined to the Parliament left nothing unperformed that might advance the cause, and were incredibly vigilant and industrious to cross and hinder whatsoever might promote the King's: whereas they who wished well to him thought they had performed their duty in doing so, and that they had done enough for him that they had done nothing against him'.[1] In most counties, Clarendon complained, the Cavaliers had difficulties in getting supplies, because of popular hostility, and suffered from espionage on behalf of Parliament. 'The common people . . . were in all places grown to that barbarity and rage against the nobility and gentry . . . that it was not safe for any to live at their houses' who were known opponents of Parliament. In London 'the poorest and lowest of the people became informers against the richest and most substantial'.[2]

These class divisions were reflected in the composition of the rival armies. When in 1642 Parliament called on volunteers for military training, they were obeyed 'only in those corporations and by those inferior people who were notorious for faction and schism'. Clarendon speaks of 'the dismal inequality of this contention, in which always some earl, or person of great honour or fortune' fell on the Royalist side, whilst on Parliament's 'there was seldom lost a man of any known family, or of other reputation than of passion for the cause in which he fell. . . . Whilst some obscure, unheard-of, colonel or officer was missing on the enemy's side, as some citizen's wife bewailed the loss of her husband, there were . . . persons of honour and public name slain [on the Royalist side] . . . and more of the same quality hurt'.[3] 'The officers of the enemy's side were never talked of, being for the most part of no better families than their common soldiers.' Notwithstanding this social discrepancy, the noble earl had to admit that those whom he elegantly described as 'dirty people of no name' possessed a morale and a discipline far beyond that of their aristocratic enemies.[4] The fleet

---

1 *Ibid.*, II, p. 472; cf. pp. 172, 244, 310, 358–9, 448–9.
2 *Ibid.*, II, pp. 318, 329–30; cf. I, pp. 276, 501.
3 *Ibid.*, II, p. 23, III, pp. 20–1, 177.
4 *Ibid.*, II, p. 437; cf. p. 313, III, pp. 174–5, 222, IV, pp. 44–5; *A Brief View*, pp. 319–20. Cf. also Sir John Oglander: 'The King's side were almost all gentlemen, and

was brought over to Parliament by the common seamen, who arrested their Royalist officers.[1]

When Clarendon's *History* was published, his social analysis was challenged by Oldmixon. But Oldmixon's own account was almost identical. 'It is very true', he admitted, 'a major Part of the Nobility, and, perhaps, the Gentry, did side with the King'; but 'nothing is better known, than that the Nine in Ten of the Merchants, Clothiers and middling Yeomanry, sided all along with the Parliament'.[2] Oldmixon was wrong in suggesting that Clarendon simply put the rich on one side and the poor on the other. Clarendon, far more subtly, pointed out that men of new wealth were attacking the established ruling class. Listen to his account of Somerset. 'The gentlemen of ancient families and estates in that county were for the most part well affected to the King; ... yet there were a people of an inferior degree who, by good husbandry, clothing, and other thriving arts, had gotten very great fortunes, and, by degrees getting themselves into the gentlemen's estates, were angry that they found not themselves in the same esteem and reputation with those whose estates they had; and therefore, with more industry than the other, studied all ways to make themselves considerable. These from the beginning were fast friends to the Parliament', and they enjoyed 'an absolute implicit obedience' from 'the inferior sort'.[3] After Parliament's victory, those whom they made deputy-lieutenants in Somerset 'were for the most part clothiers and men who, though they were rich, had not been before of power or reputation there'.[4]

Any number of parallel passages could be given from contemporaries to demonstrate the accuracy of this analysis. Here is one written in 1645:

'There was no excessive number of powerfull gentry [in Gloucestershire], who for the most part care not to render themselves the slaves of princes, that they also might rule over their neighbours as vassalls: but the inhabitants consisted chiefly of yeomen, farmers, petty free-

---

of the Parliament's few. As one said, "The King shot bullets of gold for lead" ' (Bamford, *A Royalist's Notebook*, p. 109).

1 *History*, II, pp. 218–19.
2 (John Oldmixon), *Clarendon and Whitelock Compar'd* (1727), p. 129; cf. p. 142.
3 *History*, II, p. 296; cf. pp. 298–9, 316; III, p. 94. A letter of August 1642 confirms that 'In Somerset the Marquis of Hertford has all the prime gentry; only clothiers and freeholders were for Parliament' (*H.M.C., Fifth Report, Appendix*, p. 161).
4 *History*, II, p. 274.

holders, and such as use manufactures, . . . a generation of men truly laborious, jealous of their properties, whose principall ayme is liberty and plenty'. Such men 'continually thwart the intentions of tyrannie unto which they only are moulded, who detesting a close, hardy and industrious way of living, doe eate their bread in the sweat of other men. . . . Such is the predominant humour of gentlemen in a corrupted age.' On the Parliamentary side, 'some gleanings of the gentry, the yeomen, farmers, cloathiers, and the whole middle ranke of the people were the only active men. The gentlemen in generall denyed their concurrence'. 'The common people addicted to the King's service have come out of blinde Wales, and other dark corners of the land.'[1]

III

The results of the Civil War, in Clarendon's view, corresponded to this division. Local government passed into the hands of men of lower social status. Especially after the establishment of the Republic, 'a more inferior sort of the common people . . . who were not above the condition of ordinary inferior constables six or seven years before, were now the justices of peace', exercising 'great insolence over those who were in quality above them, and who always [had] had a power over them'. The nobility and gentry 'found themselves totally neglected'.[2]

The peaceful restoration of the King in 1660, then, Clarendon thought, was a reunion of the propertied classes in defence of social stability against military or popular violence. The King's party had come to consist of 'persons of all the considerable fortunes and families in the kingdom'. The decisive moment was that day in February 1660 when the militia was once more 'put under the government of the nobility and principal gentry throughout the kingdom', the commissions of 'persons of no degree or quality' having been revoked. Clarendon's manifestoes issued at the time speak repeatedly of the need 'to raise up those banks and fences which have been cast down'.[3]

1 John Corbet, *Historical Relation of the Military Government of Gloucester* (1645), in *Bibliotheca Gloucestrensis*, I, pp. 9–10, 16. Further confirmatory evidence is quoted in *The Good Old Cause* (ed. C. Hill and E. Dell), pp. 238–54, 277–9, 288–96, 367–9. See also Sir Edward Peyton, *The Divine Catastrophe of . . . the House of Stuarts* (1652), in *Secret History of the Court of James I* (1811), II, p. 413; and a letter from Whitelocke to Thurloe in Whitelocke's *Journal of the Swedish Embassy* (1855), II, p. 131.

2 *History*, IV, pp. 287, 315; cf. p. 455; V, pp. 262, 287; VI, p. 155. Clarendon's account is confirmed by the local studies quoted on pp. 19–21 above.

3 Wormald, *op. cit.*, p. 206; *History*, VI, pp. 176, 209, 218–19.

Episcopacy, we recall, had been a 'landmark'.

Clarendon afterwards professed to think the Restoration a miracle:[1] and historians have perhaps attributed too much to his skill in bringing it about. Indeed in the winter of 1659–60 he found it difficult to get in touch with the all-powerful General Monck, since Mrs. Monck (who really mattered) was 'so utterly unacquainted with all persons of quality of either sex' that no Royalist knew how to approach her.[2] So completely had the vulgar taken charge of English affairs!

After the landslide of propertied Parliamentarians to the King, many old Royalists who received no compensation for their Civil War losses felt themselves betrayed and neglected. They blamed Clarendon for their fate which, he rightly claimed, it was beyond his power to mitigate. Notorious former Parliamentarians bought themselves into positions of power in government, navy and civil service. The republican system of administration by committees and boards was continued, to Clarendon's disgust. The interests of trade occupied much of the government's attention. Bankers, despite their republican leanings, acquired a new importance by lending to the government. The Commons' control of finance was securely established. Clarendon complained that most of those who procured his downfall had been 'of Trust and Credit under Cromwell': his support, he believed, came from the peers. But by now the power of the House of Commons far exceeded that of the Lords.[3]

The old feudal England, which Clarendon had tried so hard to preserve by judicious reforms and concessions, had gone for ever. 'All Relations', he grumbled, 'were confounded by the several Sects in Religion, which discountenanced all Forms of Reverence and Respect' [social effects of religion again]. '. . . Parents had no Manner of Authority over their Children, nor Children any Obedience or Submission to their Parents; but every one did that which was good in his own Eyes. This unnatural Antipathy had its first Rise from the Beginning of the Rebellion; when the Fathers and Sons engaged themselves in the contrary Parties. . . . The Relation between Masters and Servants had been long since dissolved by the Parliament, that their Army might be increased by the Prentices against their masters' Consent. . . . In the Place of Generosity, a vile and sordid Love of

1 *Tracts*, pp. 726–34.

2 *History*, VI, p. 155.

3 *Life*, II, pp. 46, 275, 374, 433–5, 456–7; III, pp. 594–616, 710, 728–9, 869; *History*, VI, p. 175; *Tracts*, pp. 2, 87.

Money was entertained as the truest Wisdom, and any Thing lawful that would contribute to being rich.'[1]

That is not merely an old man's nostalgia for his lost youth: it is the helpless protest of an expiring civilization against the standards of its successor. Charles II adapted himself more easily to this bourgeois world. He 'had in his Nature so little Reverence or Esteem for Antiquity, and did in Truth so much contemn all old Orders, Forms, and Institutions, that the Objections of Novelty rather advanced than obstructed any Proposition'. Consequently 'these Dilapidations and Ruins of the ancient Candour, and Discipline, were not taken enough to Heart, and repaired with that early Care and Severity that they might have been'.[2] In other words, the prudent and intelligent Charles II had no intention of going on his travels again; his less adaptable (or more principled) minister travelled.

IV

Clarendon had a massive historical sense, rare in his generation. He believed that 'the Growth and Improvement of Arts and Sciences' were 'the most proper Subjects of History' no less than 'noble actions in peace and war'. He believed in the evolution of truth, and had no use for appeals to the authority of antiquity, whether in religion or in politics, unless the appeal was also backed by reason. He followed Bacon in arguing that belief in progress stimulated industry, whilst belief in the decay of nature and civilization begat fatalism and laziness. If 'we carry all the landmarks with us', he believed, his age could outdistance antiquity.[3]

In all these matters Clarendon, like Falkland, Chillingworth, and his other friends of the attractive circle which used to meet at Great Tew, was closer to the outlook of a Parliamentarian like Milton than to that of Charles I and Archbishop Laud.[4] It is easier, on the face of it, to understand his earlier co-operation with Pym and Hampden than his later association with Prince Rupert and George Goring. The clue is to be found in the acute social sense, one might almost say class-consciousness, which we observed running through Clarendon's

---

1 *Life*, II, pp. 39–41.

2 *Ibid.*, III, p. 605; II, p. 41.

3 *Tracts*, p. 182; cf. pp. 218–40, 409; Wormald, *op. cit.*, pp. 260, 271–4.

4 Clarendon almost echoes Milton's phrase about being a heretic in the truth – see *Tracts*, p. 409.

account of the Great Rebellion. 'In all well instituted governments', he declared, 'the heirs and descendants from worthy and eminent parents, if they do not degenerate from their virtue, have been always allowed a preference and kind of title to employments and offices of honour and trust'. That is from Clarendon's critique of Hobbes's *Leviathan*, where the *grand seigneur* castigated the former tutor for 'his extreme malignity to the Nobility, by whose bread he hath bin alwaies sustained'. Hobbes's belief in human equality and a career open to the talents seemed to Clarendon as wicked as the design of the Levellers and Agitators for 'the reduction of all degrees to one'.[1]

Property and inequality, Clarendon thought, were essential to society. 'Whatsoever is of Civility and good Manners, all that is of Art and Beauty, or of real and solid Wealth in the World, is the . . . child of beloved Propriety; and they who would strangle this Issue, desire to demolish all Buildings, eradicate all Plantations, to make the Earth barren, and mankind to live again in Tents, and nourish his Cattle where the grass grows. Nothing but the joy in Propriety reduc'd us from this barbarity; and nothing but security in the same, can preserve us from returning into it again'.[2]

Hyde was not so foolish as to think that the leaders of the Long Parliament wished to overthrow property or the dominance of the rich. But he did believe that their lack of respect for 'landmarks' encouraged the lower orders to make demands which threatened the social position of the aristocracy. He wished to consolidate the legislative gains of 1640-1, and believed that further revolutionary action would jeopardize the existing social order. He was rightly convinced that men of 'good fortunes and estates had all a great desire of peace'.[3] What he could not grasp was that the revolutionary leaders of the Commons were determined to transfer political power from King, aristocracy, and bishops to those men of wealth whom the lower house represented. It was thus far more than disagreement about whether Charles I could be trusted which separated Pym and Hampden from Hyde. Even if Charles I had accepted the legislation of 1640-1, many of his supporters would not have done so.[4] The leaders of the Commons felt they must advance further if they were to preserve what had been won. They also believed that they could ride the whirlwind: that they could

1 *A Brief View*, pp. 181-2. See p. 251 below.
2 *Ibid.*, p. 111.
3 Wormald, *op. cit.*, pp. 123-4, 139; *History*, IV, pp. 434-6; *Life*, III, pp. 781-3.
4 Alan Cole, 'Mr. Wormald's *Clarendon*', *Cambridge Journal*, V, p. 318.

use a popular army to defeat the Cavaliers without endangering their own social dominance. Clarendon, on the other hand, thought the lesson of history was that all rebellions end 'in a general detestation of the first promoters of them, by those who keep them company in the prosecution, and discover their ends to be very different from their profession'.[1]

In the event both were proved right, and both wrong. The proclamation of the Republic, the egalitarian demands of Levellers and Diggers after 1647, justified Hyde's social fears. But Cromwell was able to suppress the revolutionary democrats and to establish the power of property-owners, new and old. In one sense the Restoration seemed to vindicate Hyde's position, for the years 1642–60 were blotted out of the statute book: legally 'the Interregnum' ceased to exist. But great revolutions cannot be blotted out of men's memories. English society, government and Church were vastly different after 1660 from what they had been before 1640, and it was the events of 1642–53 which had ensured their transformation. Hyde's victory in 1660 was more apparent than real.

v

His weakness, as a politician and as a historian, was that he underestimated the passion for justice and equality which might animate ordinary men. His social analysis was acute: but he thought in terms of upstart *nouveaux riches* resenting old aristocracy, of greedy poor coveting the wealth of the rich. He dismissed as 'fanaticism' the flame which burned in a Milton, a Lilburne, a Winstanley. And so in the long run this great historian, who suggested that revolutions were caused by ignorance of history in the rulers, himself miscalculated at two crises of his political career. In 1640–1 he thought he could make an omelette without breaking any eggs: that Charles I and his opponents would be 'reasonable'. It has been argued that his attempts to rally 'constitutional' Royalists to the King in these years made civil war certain because it gave an army to those of Charles's advisers whose aims were not constitutional at all.[2] After 1660 Clarendon repeated his mistake, thinking that everybody who mattered had at last come round to his understanding of what was 'reasonable'. But blood, iron and 'fanaticism' go to the making of a revolution, as well as reason.

1 Wormald, *op. cit.*, p. 191.
2 *Tracts*, p. 485; Cole, *op. cit.*, p. 322.

Clarendon always rejected the argument that military success was evidence of divine favour: 'prosperity was never yet thought a good argument of men's piety, or being in the right'.[1] But his own social analysis of politics brought him very close to this view. He was only held back from it, I believe, by his conviction that there was a social order of which God approved (an idealized version of that which had existed in his youth) and which, in the last resort, God would intervene by a miracle to maintain. In 1660 God did so; but after 1667 He was less co-operative. Clarendon's social prejudices, in short, prevented his learning quite as much from history as he thought he had learnt: he never understood that people below the rank of gentlemen might genuinely believe that God favoured equality rather than inequality, and might be prepared to die to give effect to this moral conviction.

But, whatever his defects as a politician, Clarendon was a great historian. His profound social insight, tempered by acute penetration in analysing individual character; his lack of illusions, his scepticism, tempered by recognition of the fact of human progress even if he disliked the means which brought it about: all this fitted him to understand the conflicts of his age better than any contemporary, and most later, historians. But above all it is his style that we remember: that style which again reflects the idealized feudal society of his youth. It lacks the conversational urgency and directness, the utilitarian virtues, of the Parliamentarian pamphlets (especially the Levellers' and Diggers') whose forthright appeal to the man in the street prepared for the prose of Bunyan and Defoe. Clarendon's prose is thoroughly conservative – stately, leisured, opulent, hospitable, with a tang of allusive humour possible because the only readers he envisages are cultured gentlemen certain of their superiority to the common herd. Like the man himself, Clarendon's style is of the old world, the world of Sir Thomas Browne and Hooker, looking back to the Middle Ages: the future, in prose as in politics, lay with the ex-Parliamentarian civil servants Samuel Pepys and Andrew Marvell,[2] and with the ex-Cromwellian soldier John Bunyan.

1 Wormald, *op. cit.*, p. 324; *Tracts*, pp. 431–2, 544–5, 559–60.
2 See p. 330 below.

SEVEN

William Perkins and the Poor[1]

Alas man! What should we doe? The world is hard.

Worldling, in *A Fruitfull Dialogue Concerning the end of the world*, William Perkins's first work (1587), in *Works*, III, p. 477.

I

WILLIAM PERKINS has only recently come to receive from historians the attention that was given to him by contemporaries.[2] He was the first systematic Calvinist theologian in England who also had a clearly defined attitude towards social problems. I hope that a study of his theology and its outcome in social theory may help to throw some light on the historical significance of Puritanism.

Perkins's life almost exactly covered the reign of Elizabeth. He died in 1602, at the age of 44. It was the life of a don and popular preacher in Cambridge. He was at one stage associated with Cartwright and others in an underground *classis* in Cambridge, but there is no evidence that he took any part in the more directly political activities of the Puritans. From about 1590, when the radicals began to be subjected to severe

---

1 The reader may be interested in criticisms of this essay made by Mr V. G. Kiernan, printed in *Past and Present*, No. 3 (1953), together with my reply.

2 The 'rediscovery' of Perkins and his school has been the work especially of American historians. See Perry Miller, 'The Marrow of Puritan Divinity', in *Errand into the Wilderness*, Chapter III, and the same author's *New England Mind: the 17th century*, for Perkins's theology. For his social thought, see L. B. Wright, *Middle-class culture in Elizabethan England*, esp. pp. 170–86, which however deals with only one of Perkins's treatises; and M. M. Knappen, *Tudor Puritanism*, pp. 374–5, 411–12. There is a more comprehensive study of Perkins by Professor Wright in *The Huntington Library Quarterly*, Vol. III, No. 2. W. Haller, *The Rise of Puritanism, passim*, has a good deal to say about Perkins's influence. There is a brief life in *D.N.B.*

persecution, Perkins carefully dissociated himself from them.[1] Never-theless, he or his works were known to most of the great families from whom the leaders of the seventeenth-century opposition were to come. Treatises of his were dedicated, by himself or his editors, to the third Earl of Bedford, to Lord Russell of Thornhaugh, to the Countess of Cumberland (a Russell); to Henry Grey, Sixth Earl of Kent; to Robert, Lord Rich, father of the Earl of Warwick; to the family of Montagu of Boughton, many of whom were members of Perkins's College, Christ's; to Sir Edward Coke, Sir Christopher Yelverton, Sir John Savile; to Oliver St. John of Bletsho, and to Valentine Knightley.

Perkins's decisive influence was as a teacher. Ministers came to seek his 'advice and directions' from far and near.[2] His copious theological works presented a systematic Calvinism in clear and popular language, with a conscious application of its general principles to the life of the England of his day, and an equally conscious opposition to the first beginnings of Arminianism in England.[3] He made plain preaching a matter of principle, and was as popular with the townspeople as with the scholars of Cambridge. His is the dominant influence in Puritan thought for the forty years after his death. His books, all written with his left hand since his right was incapacitated, ran through innumer-able editions: 'it is a miracle almost', wrote Fuller, 'to conceive how thick they lie'. They were translated into French and Dutch, and even into Italian and Spanish.[4] Calvin, Beza, Perkins, are often cited as the trinity of the orthodox. Lilburne read Perkins in the spare hours of his apprenticeship: Walwyn knew some of his works by heart.[5] Most decisive of all was Perkins's establishment of a school of disciples in Cambridge, among whom we need only mention Preston, Sibbes, Ames, Cotton, Gouge, Thomas Goodwin to show their significance. When the last-named came up to Perkins's old College in 1613 he found that 'the whole town was then filled with the discourse of the power of Mr Perkins's ministry, still fresh in most men's memories'.[6] Through judicious use of the patronage of men like Lord Rich,

---

1 J. B. Mullinger, *The University of Cambridge*, II, pp. 323, 339, 473–4; C. H. and T. Cooper, *Athenae Cantabrigienses*, pp. 335–6.

2 Samuel Ward's 'Historical Notes', in *Two Puritan Diaries*, ed. Knappen, p. 131.

3 Perkins, *Works*, III, pp. 553–4.

4 Fuller, *Abel Redevivus* (1651), p. 436; *The Holy State* (1648), p. 84.

5 Ed. W. Haller and G. Davies, *The Leveller Tracts*, pp. 404, 362.

6 *Memoir of Dr. Thomas Goodwin* by his son, in Goodwin's *Works* (1861–3), II, p. lviii.

ministers of the Perkins school spread as a refreshing flood over East Anglia and the Midlands, and occupied key lectureships in London.[1]

In Perkins's theology, four points stand out. First, his obsession (shared with so many of his contemporaries) with the doctrine of justification by faith alone and the powerlessness of fallen man to work his own salvation.[2] Secondly, his conviction that there is a predestinate minority of the elect who can be quite sure of their election.[3] Thirdly, his anxiety to reduce to a minimum the conditions on which one can receive this assurance of salvation. It comes in the end down to little more than a serious-minded and conscientious *desire* to be saved. Salvation cannot be worked, but it can very nearly be willed.[4] Fourthly, we must note his horrified realization that 'the common sort of ignorant people' have no understanding of and positive dislike for the doctrines which their betters find so comfortable. They think, absurdly, that mere 'moral goodness' is more important than the inner consciousness of grace through which alone works acquire merit in God's sight.[5] Perkins did his best for the benighted lower classes, preaching for instance in the open air at Stourbridge Fair. But it is quite clear from the tone, the assumptions, the metaphors in his sermons that his chosen audience was the sober, hard-working, industrious middle class in town and country.

II

Perkins's theology is Calvinist, but it is a modified and adapted Calvinism:[6] Calvin himself might have disclaimed being a Calvinist of Perkins's latter-day type. Both Calvin and Perkins believed that social problems were ethical problems, for which theologians should provide

1 Haller, *op. cit.*, Chapters 2 and 3 *passim*.

2 See for instance *Works*, I, pp. 278–98, 328; III, pp. 63–4*. (The pages in Vol. III are renumbered from p. 265. Quotations from the first 264 pages I have marked with an asterisk after the page number.)

3 E.g., I, p. 563; II, pp. 19–24; III, pp. 270–3.

4 I, p. 438; II, pp. 19–24, 44, 629. In his confident youth Perkins used to 'pronounce the word Damne with such an emphasis as left a dolefull Echo in his auditours ears a good while after', but 'in his older age' he 'remitted much of his former rigidness' and preferred to preach God's mercy. The psychologist would no doubt be interested in the fact that Perkins died crying out 'Mercy, Mercy', 'which some standers by misinterpreted for despair' (Fuller, *The Holy State*, pp. 82–3).

5 III, pp. 493–500; cf. I, pp. 537, 631; II, pp. 290, 300; III, pp. 583, 595.

6 See Perry Miller, *Errand into the Wilderness*, esp. pp. 50–6. Contrast, however, Fuller, *The Holy State*, p. 82.

a solution. But the problems which Perkins faced at the end of Elizabeth's reign were different from those of Geneva in the fifteen-thirties. The century which separates the Reformation from the Civil War in England saw a series of vast changes, not only in economic life (depopulating enclosures, the 'first industrial revolution') but also in economic ideas, in ethics. Two sharply contrasted ways of life, two moralities, were in conflict: a traditional mediaeval catholic economic morality on the defensive, a Protestant and capitalist ethic on the offensive.

If we take our stand at the end of the seventeenth century, and contrast the newly-victorious ethic with orthodoxy at the beginning of the sixteenth century, we see how complete had been the trans-valuation of values. Labour, the curse of fallen man, has become a religious duty, a means of glorifying God in our calling. Poverty has ceased to be a holy state and has become presumptive evidence of wickedness. Indiscriminate alms-giving by the rich man in his castle had yielded place to a careful search for the industrious or impotent poor conducted by bourgeois churchwardens. Conspicuous waste has ceased to be a social obligation and is regarded as an anti-social vice. The sordid sin of avarice has been transmuted into the religious and patriotic duty of thrift. Whereas in 1500 the business man 'had practised extortion and been told that it was wrong; for it was contrary to the law of God', he was now 'told that it was right; for it was in accordance with the law of nature'.[1]

Calvin came at the beginning of this reversal of values. He abandoned the traditional absolute prohibition of usury (which theologians had whittled away by allowing exceptions) and permitted it in principle (though restricting it very stringently in a great many particular instances). So revolutions in thought are initiated. This slight shift of emphasis, in the busy clothing centre of Geneva, was enough. Calvinism and lenience towards usury were henceforth regarded as synonymous, however much individual ministers insisted on the distinction between legitimate interest and extortionate usury.

For Perkins, as for his respectable audience of Cambridge citizens and undergraduates, the poor presented one of England's major social problems. He inherited, and developed, a tradition of Protestant thought on the subject.

1 R. H. Tawney, *Religion and the Rise of Capitalism* (Pelican Edition), p. 152. My indebtedness to this work will be obvious throughout this essay.

III

The fundamental economic causes of the increase of vagabondage in sixteenth-century England are not in dispute. Great feudal households were being cut down. Some tenants were evicted, mainly by enclosure for sheep-farming. Others, driven below the poverty-line by loss of common lands, racking of rents and the general rise in prices caused by the influx of American silver, had to abandon their holdings. Inflation greatly accelerated the development of capitalist relations. Some capital accumulated from plunder of peasants, monasteries and the Indies was invested in production for the market by the employment of wage labour.

The ruling class in mediaeval society did not invest its surplus: it consumed it. The greater the lord, the more ostentatiously lavish his expenditure. His greatness, moreover, was reckoned in terms of his dependants – those who wore his livery and would maintain his cause on the battlefield or in the law court. There were therefore many reasons why he should dispense hospitality and charity to his dependants. Troeltsch speaks of 'the pleasure in giving away that which cannot be eaten, which is found in all social systems based upon a natural economy'.[1] But long after the rise of a money economy, largesse still remained profitable as well as pleasurable for a feudal landowner. It was good for his prestige; it was a form of social insurance; and, since he had no doubt whatever that his surplus came from the labours of his tenants, it was also sound economic sense to keep them alive in times of distress. In the absence of supplies of free labour, and of a developed national market, there was little incentive for him to invest in agricultural improvements. There is no need to make a virtue of his necessities: he had no inhibitions, when the time came, about evicting whole villages to make room for sheep. But that time came only when the English clothing industry had developed sufficiently to offer a promising market for his wool, that is to say when capitalist production was beginning to transform the English economy; and he himself was in effect switching over to new productive methods (or becoming a rentier leasing his land to farmers who would pay a rack rent). The outcry from moralists and publicists in the early sixteenth century shows how completely depopulating enclosure upset traditional standards of value. Looking back from the second half of the

---

1 *The Social Teaching of the Christian Churches*, I, p. 166. His point had been anticipated by Adam Smith (*The Wealth of Nations*, World's Classics, II, p. 442).

seventeenth century, David Lloyd could see what had happened: 'Noblemen in those days esteemed the love of their neighbours more than their fear, and the service and fealty of their tenants more than their money. Now the landlord hath the sweat of the tenant's brow in his coffers: then he had the best blood in his veins at his command.'[1]

The business man of the sixteenth century had a very different outlook from that of the feudal landlord. (I am speaking here not of a merchant prince like Sir Thomas Gresham, but of a numerically far more significant class – the small merchant or craftsman or farmer who was beginning to give employment to a wider circle than his own family and an apprentice or two, and to whom I believe Puritan social thought especially appealed.) To his prosperity the accumulation of capital for reinvestment was essential. His surplus was produced by hiring labour and selling the products of its workmanship: the amount of this surplus depended on his ability to keep wage rates down. So he grudged every penny spent over and above the minimum necessary to induce men to work for him. And since they chose 'voluntarily' to work for him, he felt no responsibility for them in hard times. If they did not like what he offered, they might go elsewhere: there was no shortage of labour in Tudor England. So his attitude towards charity was very different from that of the feudal lord. He stood to gain nothing from it, in this world, to which he attached any value. He saw simply a problem of poor *relief*, and it was not a problem for which he felt any personal responsibility. The real solution was to do nothing which would impede the accumulation of capital, the expansion of production, the extension of employment. If from the short-term point of view the switch-over to new methods seemed to create unemployment (by depopulation), in the long run not only unemployment but also the perpetual poverty of the mediaeval village could be cured by allowing the unfettered development of the productive forces of the country. It could be argued, I think, that Protestants occupied themselves with the problem of setting the poor on work not so much because that problem took a specially acute form in Protestant and industrially advanced countries, as because in those countries some men were beginning to have a dim vision of the possibility of getting rid of poverty altogether. Others saw that the expansion of industrial production would enrich employers. To both groups the immediate need seemed to be hard work and discipline.

1 D. Lloyd, *State-Worthies* (1766), I, p. 435.

In the meantime the poor must be prevented by coercive measures from revolting, and, by relief, from reaching a stage of destitution that would make them socially menacing. But the main problem was to transform the mental outlook of the lower orders so that they no longer waited at the rich man's gate for charity, but went out to offer their services on the labour market. Hence the sharp distinction drawn by the poor laws between the impotent but deserving poor and sturdy rogues. The precondition for the development of capitalist industry on a large scale was the existence of a pool of 'free' labour. The problem set by vagabondage and vagrancy was to force men who had been deprived of their independent means of livelihood to enter into 'free' contracts to work for a capitalist employer, and to accustom them to the habit of steady work throughout the year. A new pattern of social discipline had to be imposed.

Here indiscriminate charity, from the point of view of Puritans and employers alike, was a social menace. It prevented the poor from realizing their responsibilities and seriously looking for employment; it encouraged vagrancy, wandering bands of idle and potentially desperate men and women; it was bad for the poor themselves as well as for the rich. A letter to Burghley in 1596 describes the unwillingness and physical incapacity of rogues and vagabonds to work ('by reason their sinews are so benumbed and stiff through idleness, as their limbs being put to any hard labour, will grieve them above measure'). Employers were as unwilling to give them work as they were to accept it. The writer goes on to note the danger of revolt by men who 'stick not to say boldly, "they must not starve, they will not starve" ', who complain 'that the rich men have gotten all into their hands, and will starve the poor'.[1]

Not only was private charity incapable of coping with the problem, but it was undesirable that it should. Poor relief must be associated with, and subordinate to, the imposition of the new discipline: houses of correction, family means tests, the apprenticing of pauper children to a trade, whether they or their parents wished it or not. This necessitated a *national* programme, backed up by the power of the state, and administered by the employing class. From the labour legislation of 1349–51 onwards, the centralized power of the state had

1 Strype, *Annals of the Reformation . . . during Queen Elizabeth's happy reign* (1824), IV, p. 405. A sojourn in a house of correction similarly led to weakness and loss of earning capacity, sometimes to death. (See *Warwickshire Quarter Sessions Order Book, 1637–1650*, ed. S. C. Ratcliff and H. C. Johnson, pp. 13, 17, 29, 39, 53, etc.)

been advancing hand in hand with the power of the J.P.s as its local administrative agents: national regulation and control of labour came to be one of the more important of the new functions of government. Slowly, as a national market began to develop, the centre of gravity in the coercion of labour shifted from the manor court (the village community as the productive unit) to the monarchy (and subsequently the sovereign parliament) working through the local employer class.

This account foreshortens and schematizes the development of centuries. In the sixteenth century capitalist production was struggling forward in a society whose institutions and ideas were still largely pre-capitalist. The domestic system in industry, with the labourer not yet entirely divorced from the soil, is a characteristic phenomenon of this transitional stage before the industrial revolution. Men's ideas too were blurred in the sixteenth century, traditional attitudes outliving the social environment which had given them birth. We must beware of ante-dating the fully developed capitalist attitude. In the late sixteenth and early seventeenth centuries the situation is still confused and complex; but I believe that it is helpful to think of the new economic system, with its appropriate ideas about the position and duties of labour, striving to establish itself in a society whose own organization and ideas for the subordination of labour had broken down.[1] The conflict between the two sets of ideas was not absolute. Most landlords, their real income diminished by the price revolution, had to cut their expenditure anyway, so that the new attitude towards charity was not unacceptable to them. In so far as the poor law was concerned with preventing riots and revolts there could be complete solidarity between landowners and industrialists. Convocation never supported the Council of Trent's stand for individual almsgiving and the administration of relief by the Church. But it was, I believe, to the small employer that Puritanism especially appealed. The great feudal household, with its under-employed menials and hangers-on, had no labour problem; but the small craftsman or farmer offered harder work and less excitement to his prospective employees. He needed a body of ideas which would emphasize the dignity of labour for its own sake; which would be critical at once of the careless and extravagant rich and of the idle and irresponsible poor. He found both in Puritanism.

In attempting, so far, to look at the problem of poor relief in purely economic terms it will have been noted that we have failed to isolate

1 Cf. Gardiner, *History of the Great Civil War* (1901), I, pp. 226–8; Haller, *op. cit.*, pp. 116–17.

economics from ideas. 'Alms', 'industry', 'discipline', are ideological as well as economic concepts. Men's ideas about the way they and others should behave are shaped by their economic environment and way of life; but economic and moral theories also help to change that way of life and that economic environment. The reformers, from Luther onwards, attacked monks and beggars in the same breath. Bishop Jewell disapproved of monks because, 'for all they do nothing', they nevertheless 'riot lavishly of other folks' labours'.[1] They were parasitic rentiers. We shall later find Perkins making the same point.

But the economic complexity and confusion caused by the existence side by side of the two systems of production was for long reflected in ideas. The second Earl of Bedford, who is usually described as a 'Puritan', was accused by Elizabeth of making all the beggars in England by his charity.[2] Clarity, coherence and a new rigour were attained by Puritan social thought only in the last two decades of Elizabeth's reign, years of industrial depression. Such is the opinion of the historian of Tudor Puritanism. 'The chief formulator of the new teaching', he believes, was William Perkins.[3]

IV

Marx spoke of the poor laws as the means by which 'the agricultural people, first forcibly expropriated, [were] driven from their homes, turned into vagabonds, and then whipped, branded, tortured by laws grotesquely terrible, into the discipline necessary for the wage system'.[4] The Rev. William Perkins, on the other hand, said of one of these laws, the statute of 1597, that it was 'an excellent Statute, and beeing in substance the very law of God, is never to be repealed'.[5] This view was accepted by the succeeding generation. Even the gentle and Anglican Fuller thought that 'King Edward VI was as truly charitable in granting Bridewell for the punishment of sturdy Rogues, as in giving St Thomas Hospitall for the relief of the Poore'.[6] The Long Parliament, almost echoing Perkins's words, declared that the statute of 1601 (which

1 'Apology of the Church of England', in *Works* (Parker Society), III, p. 87.

2 Fuller, *The Holy State*, p. 285.

3 Knappen, *Tudor Puritanism*, pp. 411–12. It is Perkins's importance as systematizer and popularizer that I wish to emphasize. Similar views, though in a less sophisticated form, had been held by Edward VI (Burnet, *History of the Reformation*, 1825, IV, p. 85).

4 *Capital*, Vol. 1, ed. Dona Torr, p. 761.

5 *Works*, I, p. 755.

6 *The Holy State*, p. 144.

supplemented and extended that of 1597) was to be maintained in perpetuity.

Perkins, therefore, was not expressing an individual view whose harshness should surprise and shock us. He was giving his approval to legislation which was the culmination of over 60 years of experiment, and to an attitude of mind which was to survive for over three centuries.[1] But his prestige in Puritan circles gave to his approbation, on strictly theological grounds, of the poor law a crucial significance in that revolution of thought about the poor which took place in England between the Reformation and the Restoration. The fundamental reasons for this revolution, I have suggested, were economic. But it is very much nicer for a business man, finding himself under strong economic pressure to indulge in actions traditionally held to be sinful, to be told that those actions are in fact in accordance with the will of God. It is convenient to have these views expressed not only to the victims of your actions but also to third parties who might well sympathize with the victims, and to have them expressed from the pulpit with all the authority of a theologian like Perkins, obviously completely disinterested. So ideas lubricate economic processes.

Perkins's thought about society is not an excrescence on or an *ad hoc* addition to his theology, but an organic part of it. His ideas would indeed have been far less influential had this not been the case. Our view of the historical significance of Calvinism must also be based on an assessment of the theology as a whole, not merely of its social application. So if we can see Perkins's attitude towards the poor flowing from a total world view, this may throw some light on the exact nature of the relationship between Calvinism and the needs of the sixteenth- and seventeenth-century bourgeoisie.

Perkins's remarks about the statute of 1597 were made in *A Treatise of the Vocations, or Callings of men*, written between 1597 and 1601. In this he lays down a number of rules, the first of which is 'Every person of every degree, state, sexe, or condition without exception, must have some personall and particular calling to walke in'. Four types of person

---

1 Compare the views of the Head of the Poor Law Division of the Local Government Board, Mr. (later Sir James) Davy, as expressed to Beatrice Webb in December 1905. He wished 'to stem the tide of philanthropic impulse that was sweeping away the old embankment of deterrent tests to the receipt of relief' (Beatrice Webb, *Our Partnership*, p. 322. See *ibid.*, Chapter 7 *passim*, and Margaret Cole, *Beatrice Webb*, Chapters 9 and 10, for the discussions around the Poor Law in 1905–9. They were haunted by the ghost of Perkins.)

break this rule: (1) rogues, beggars, and vagabonds; (2) monks and friars; (3) gentlemen 'enriched with great livings and revenewes' who 'spend their daies in eating and drinking' and do not serve the Church or Commonwealth; (4) serving men, who should have some other particular calling, 'unlesse they tend on men of great place and state: for onely to waite, and give attendance, is not a sufficient calling'. They eat, drink, sleep, and game, producing nothing of profit to the commonwealth; and when their masters die and they are turned adrift they are useless.[1] Elsewhere Perkins adds a fifth type, more inclusive than the monks and friars of (2): Papists in general, who have added 52 saints' days to the 52 sabbaths appointed by God, 'and so spend more than a quarter of a yeare in rest and idleness'.[2]

In contrast to these various types of idle person, Perkins's ideal is the diligent small craftsmen, who 'rise early to their businesse, lest night overtake them'.[3] Even they, however, must see to it that their labour is profitable to society: those who manufacture or distribute useless commodities sin no less than unproductive parasites like astrologers and alchemists.[4] Work in industry, Perkins adds in a significant passage, 'is as good as land, because land may be lost; but skill and labour in a good occupation is profitable to the end, because it will helpe at neede, when land and all things faile'.[5] The vagabond class was drawn largely from evicted peasants: they were helpless in the new world of capitalist insecurity unless they had skilled labour power to sell.

'Art thou a poore man, and wouldest have sufficient foode and raiment for thy temporall life?' Perkins asked. And he replied, in words that have become more familiar since: 'Then first, set thy heart to seeke God's kingdome, follow the word, and labour therein for regeneration, and new obedience; and doubt not, but if thou be upright and diligent in thy lawfull calling, thou shalt finde sufficient for this life'.[6] Perkins, however, was far too much of a realist to leave it at that. He knew about vagabondage, he knew that grinding poverty led many Protestants to consult soothsayers and witches,[7] drove others to theft and the gallows.[8] So he put into the mouth of an imaginary interlocutor the

1 I, pp. 755–6.

2 III, pp. 512–13. Cf. p. 40 above.

3 I, p. 752.

4 I, p. 764. Perkins himself had been addicted to astrology and magic in his unregenerate youth (III, p. 653).

5 I, p. 752.

6 III, p. 191*.

7 III, pp. 506, 607–9, 615.

8 II, pp. 9, 438. Crimes springing from poverty, Perkins thinks, should be less severely dealt with.

reasonable question, 'if this bee the way to get sufficient, how comes it that we have so many beggars? . . .' His reply is like a flash of lightning in a dark sky: 'They are (for the most part) a cursed generation. . . . They joyne not themselves to any setled congregation for the obtaining of Gods kingdome, and so this promise belongs not to them'.[1]

This considered answer to a real and difficult social problem was no chance phrase. Perkins repeated it in other words on several occasions. 'Rogues, beggars, vagabonds . . . commonly are of no civill societie or corporation, nor of any particular Church: and are as rotten legges, and armes, that droppe from the body. . . . To wander up and downe from yeare to yeare to this ende, to seeke and procure bodily maintenance, is no calling, but the life of a beast'.[2] 'If every man must be subject to the power of the Magistrate for conscience sake, then all wandring beggars and roagues, that passe from place to place, beeing under no certaine Magistracie or Ministerie, nor joyning themselves to any set societie in Church, or Commonwealth, are plagues and banes of both, and are to bee taken as maine enemies of this ordinance of God ['These dreamers also defile the flesh, and despise governement, and speake evill of them that are in authoritie' – *Jude* 8]; and seeing a most excellent lawe is provided to restraine them, it is the part of every good subject or Christian to set themselves for the executing, strengthening, and upholding of the same'.[3]

I have quoted at length because this seems to me a crucial point. The argument is in part traditional. Pilgrims, wandering scholars, and other vagrants had their place in mediaeval society. But their numbers were small in relation to the stable nuclei of that society, village communities and gilds. In the sixteenth century, however, vagabondage was on a new scale: and there were no monasteries to feed the wanderers. 'Marryed under hedges, children born in Barns and under hedges, then baptized, so continue, to the shame of the Nation and of the Gospel': so Perkins's disciple, Richard Sibbes, was reported as saying.[4] Large numbers of such men, women, and children were members of no settled community, and consequently had no access to the means of grace, sacraments and sermons.

But the real breach with mediaeval Catholicism comes in Perkins's

1 III, p, 191*. The promise is that made in *Matthew*, vi. 33.

2 I, p. 755. Cf. III, p. 92*; also *Genesis*, iv. 12.

3 III, p. 539. Perkins uses the Geneva Bible. The text of the A.V. is slightly different.

4 J. R., *Proposals in behalf of the Poore of this Nation* (1653), p. 3.

attitude to the Church, which is Calvin's.[1] In one sense the Church is the whole of society: 'Church and state' for a Puritan means something more like our antithesis of society and state, or people and government. But for a Calvinist there is also a special sense in which only the elect are the true Church. 'No man', wrote Perkins, 'can believe himselfe to be a member of the Church, unlesse withall hee beleeve that he is predestinate to life everlasting'.[2] Now there was general agreement among Calvinist theologians, following St. Augustine, that the elect were a minority. Hence Perkins's traditional objection to 'the opinion of *Universall saving grace*; appertaining to all and every man. . . . For it puls downe the pale of the Church, and laies it waste as every common field. . . . If men should be tolde that whether they live in the market towne or no, there shall be sufficient provision brought them, if they will but receive it and accept of it, who would then come to the market?'[3]

This dual conception of the Church, as in a general sense the whole population, but in a particular sense the elect only, is an essential feature of Calvinist thought.[4] It explains the dominant rôle of the godly minority in running the Church, and the supreme importance of discipline. Everywhere in Calvinist churches the ruling groups, the elders, were overwhelmingly drawn from the propertied minority:[5] and the discipline turns out to be, among other things, the imposition and maintenance of standards of social behaviour agreeable to the employing class.

Now withdrawal from this Church, Perkins tells us, even the involuntary withdrawal of an evicted peasant, is evidence of divine disapproval. Beggars are '(for the most part) a cursed generation'. Some amount of property and worldly security appears to be a minimum condition without which salvation is impossible. Again this

1 Calvin, *Institutes of the Christian Religion*, trans. Beveridge (1949), II, pp. 288–9.

2 I, p. 298.

3 I, p. 295. The metaphors are illuminating: they help to define the class of person Perkins was addressing. Cf. I, p. 778.

4 For a very clear exposition, see *The Second Book of Discipline* of the Scottish Kirk (1578), Chapter I.

5 There is no room to prove this point by examples. I believe it is fairly generally accepted nowadays. But it follows from the Calvinist definition of the elect. They are the serious, educated minority, those who have sufficient leisure and learning to exercise themselves about whether they are saved or not. See Perkins, *Works*, I, pp. 438, 636–42; II, pp. 19–24, 44, 629. Cf. also Perry Miller, *Orthodoxy in Massachusetts*, p. 64.

conception of justification by success was to become a commonplace of Puritan thought; but Perkins was one of its earliest English exponents. Riches are good in themselves.[1] 'Men are to bee honoured for their riches.'[2] When Jesus told us not to lay up treasures upon earth he did not intend altogether to forbid the fruition and possession of goods and riches; but only covetousness and excess.[3] The words 'Take no thought for the morrow' do not mean that 'moderate care' is unlawful.[4] It is indeed a duty to save for one's children.[5] Usury is 'a sinne that cannot, nor ever shall be rooted out utterly': in certain circumstances it is lawful.[6]

I am selecting unfairly, for in each case Perkins qualifies heavily by insisting that riches are good *as they are used*, that men must desire them to glorify God, not for themselves. And he denounces engrossers, forestallers, usurers in the traditional manner. But I suspect that many good bourgeois in the congregations of Perkins and his followers would follow the same principles of selection as I have done: the new concessions would be noted, the traditional qualifications would be forgotten, as with Calvin's shift of emphasis in dealing with usury. 'The way of *Caine* is the high and broad way of the world.'[7] 'I doe nothing but that which everybody doth', cried Perkins's Worldling, explaining that it was competition, the blind forces of the market, not his greed, that drove up the price of corn.[8] And if 'the obedience of the Gospel . . . makes every man in his trade, office, and calling whatsoever it be, to prosper',[9] it was almost irresistible to argue backwards from prosperity to godliness. Perkins himself sold the pass. After stating that the master of a family may with a good conscience seek for that measure of wealth which is meet to maintain himself and his family in convenient food and raiment, he naturally asks how we are to judge what is sufficient. Not,

1 I, p. 769.
2 II, p. 150.
3 III, pp. 163–4*.
4 III, p. 177*.
5 III, p. 217*.
6 II, p. 116; I, p. 63.
7 III, p. 549.
8 III, pp. 466, 471.
9 II, p. 290. Weber and his disciples have been accused of 'grave anachronism' (e.g. by Laski, *The Rise of European Liberalism*, p. 34), since they generalized about Calvinism on the basis of late seventeenth-century examples of the permeation of the mediaeval doctrine of the calling by a capitalist spirit. They could, however, have found evidence of the process already at work in Perkins.

he replies, by the affection of covetous men, but by 'the common judgement and practise of the most godly, frugall, and wise men with whome we live'.[1] That was to allow bourgeois society to set its own standards. 'In the parish where I dwell, I am taken for an honest man', Perkins's own Worldling had boasted.[2]

The really poor, then, the expropriated vagabonds, are outcastes, outside the law and outside the Church. Their only hope of salvation (and nothing else really matters) is to be set on work, so that by diligence in a calling they may once again be restored to a disciplined (let us hope) community, to a settled congregation and to the promises of salvation offered to believers through the Church. In a real sense the way forward to a reintegration of English society lay through labour discipline and the development of production: the Spanish path of indiscriminate charity and contempt for labour was leading to stagnation. In the town of Mansoul, vagabonds acted as spies and agents for Diabolus.[3] Puritan social thought had an idealistic appeal as well as the sterner side I have emphasized: many good men genuinely, and with reason, believed that it was merely demoralizing to give alms to idle beggars. 'It is the good law of our Land, agreeable to the Law of God, that none should begge that are able to labour.' This law was unfortunately not enforced: Perkins called upon all Christians, and especially Christian magistrates, to put it into effect.[4] It should not surprise us to learn that, when Charles I's personal Government stirred up J.P.s to provide work for the poor, there was a more energetic response from the 'Puritan' eastern counties than from the rest of the country, even though those counties were the most dissatisfied with the general tendency of the King's policy.[5]

Setting the poor on work promoted their spiritual welfare as well as adding to the national wealth. By the same token indiscriminate alms-giving was far from being a virtue, as Papists taught and as mediaeval society had believed: for Calvin and his followers it was positively harmful. It was a 'good work' of the type which Protestant theologians regarded as worthless. It was formal, automatic, thoughtless. The

---

1 I, p. 769. *Frugality* was defined by Perkins's disciple William Ames as 'a vertue whereby we order our matters, with profit and benefit' (*The Marrow of Sacred Divinity*, 1642, p. 378).

2 III, p. 465.

3 Bunyan, *The Holy War*, in *Works* (ed. Offor), III, p. 348.

4 II, pp. 144–5; cf. III, 91–2*, 539.

5 E. M. Leonard, *Early History of English Poor Relief*, pp. 239–41, 258–66, 294.

Protestant ethic emphasized not the 'work', the external action, but the intention behind it.[1] The Puritan was anxious that his charity should serve a good end: not only that he personally should get value for his money, but that God's purposes should be served. Since God preferred industry to idleness, giving alms to a strange beggar might well be a sin. Relief should be given only after proper investigation: and it should take the form of employment, not of alms, to all except the aged and impotent. Indiscriminate charity was mere self-indulgence.[2]

The problem of creating a new mental outlook was not solely or even primarily a matter of re-educating the paupers themselves. The whip and the branding-iron, and the pressure of starvation, would no doubt have done the job in time. Nor was there any insuperable difficulty in persuading the rich to close their purses, or at least to divert their charity into new directions. The real problem was set by those above the poverty line and below the status of large-scale employer of labour – the artisan and peasant majority of the population. Such men and women had behind them centuries of communal solidarity in the struggle against nature, centuries of teaching on the virtues of Christian charity. In the latter half of the sixteenth century there must have been few peasants who could be confident that eviction and vagrancy might not be their ultimate fate. It is, therefore, easy to understand that in many areas there was considerable sympathy for sturdy beggars, and that constables had difficulty in enforcing the poor law. Few villagers, few artisans near the poverty line, would lightly believe that original sin was the sole cause of vagabondage, that men took to the road for the fun of the thing, that all beggars should be

---

1 Cf. III, p. 304. Cf. also Stockwood, in *A Sermon preached at Paules Crosse* in 1578: 'Almes . . . doth not consiste in the greatnesse of that which is bestowed, but in the minde and disposition of the giver. . . . All the large givings of the Papists, of whiche at this daye many make so great bragges, bycause they be not done in a reverent regarde of the commaundement of the Lorde, in Love, and of an inwarde being touched with the calamities of the needie, but for to be well reported of before men whilest they are alive, and to be praied for after they are dead, . . . are indeede no almes, but Pharisaicall trumpets' (pp. 106–8).

2 These points were made as early as 1552, in *A Treatise how by the Worde of God, Christian mens Almose ought to be distributed*, presented by Bucer to Edward VI. Contrast the older view, expressed two years earlier by Robert Crowley:

> 'Yet cesse not to gyve to all,
>   mythoute anye regarde;
> Thoughe the beggers be wicked,
>   thou shalte have thy rewarde.'
>   (*Select Works*, 1872, p. 16).

punished, that property was more important than life.[1] The common people's hostility to the wholesome doctrine of original sin is indeed one of the most regular complaints of Perkins and his Calvinist contemporaries in the ministry. A great deal of preaching was needed before truths so obvious to Puritan theologians would be accepted by the poorer members of their congregations.

So there was a double problem. First, to make parishes (and especially their richer members) aware of their responsibilities towards their own impotent poor. Secondly to make them (and especially their poorer members) discriminating in their charity. That was an additional reason for using the machinery of the parish for poor relief.[2] For only the Church could undertake the enormous task of re-education that was involved. The parson, and only the parson, could exhort and instruct his parishioners in these matters; and the government could tell the parson what to say.

But although the Church possessed an administrative machine capable of pursuing this task with a single directed will, that will seemed to the Puritans to be weak. They would have preferred some form of Presbyterian (or congregational) discipline. There you had a strong parochial discipline in whose supervision the minister (who might be old-fashioned, easy-going, lazy) was joined by lay elders, drawn from the employing class. A Presbytery would really know who were the idle and who were the industrious in the parish: it would be anxious to encourage the latter and discourage the former; and it would have the powerful sanction of excommunication at its disposal. The Presbyterian system, moreover, would have set parishes free from supervision by bishops, the nominated agents of the central government: yet it would have preserved, under new management, a national church, combining the advantages of local control by the rich with the possibility of national directives to impose the right standards on backward or recalcitrant regions. For men confident of their ability to dominate any machinery elected from below, the introduction of a

1 Cf. Edward Hext's letter to Burghley, September 1596: 'Most commonly the most simple country man and woman' of Somerset refused to co-operate in convicting vagabonds, even when they had been robbed by them, since 'they would not procure any man's death for all the goods in the world' (Strype, *op. cit.*, IV, p. 406).

2 Additional, that is, to the general reason that relief of the poor was thought of as a religious duty to which ministers should *exhort* their flock. Only gradually in the sixteenth and early seventeenth centuries did the power of the state step in behind the ecclesiastical machinery as poor relief was transformed from a voluntary offering to a tax; and churchwardens and overseers of the poor were subordinated to J.P.s.

Presbyterian system seemed to offer the possibility of a peaceful revolution.

I have no wish to exaggerate the importance of questions affecting the poor in the appeal of Puritan discipline. Contemporaries can speak for themselves. Sir Francis Walsingham, a shrewd and not unsympathetic observer, said of the Puritans: 'Because multitude of rogues and poverty was an eye-sore, and a dislike to every man; therefore they put into the people's head, that if discipline were planted, there should be no vagabonds nor beggars, a thing very plausible', though Walsingham himself did not believe it.[1] Lancelot Andrewes, no Puritan, noted in 1588 that the Calvinist refugee churches in London were able 'to do so much good as not one of their poor is seen to ask in the streets', and regretted that 'this city, the harbourer and maintainer of them, should not be able to do the same good'.[2] Many years later, in 1645, Hugh Peter, brought back from New England by the outbreak of revolution, preached a sermon before Parliament and the Assembly of Divines. 'I have lived in a countrey', he said, 'where in seven years I never saw beggar, nor heard an oath, nor lookt upon a drunkard: why should there be beggars in your Israel where there is so much work to do?'[3] That message from the Puritan promised land at once drew on an idea that had been current for two generations and seemed to prove its truth from experience.

A Presbyterian system was never established in England, for reasons that are social as well as religious. When power was ultimately seized by the House of Commons, it could only be preserved with the help of radical political groups drawn from artisans and small producers, who had no use for a Presbyterian discipline. But by that time the critical period of expropriation, and the most urgent need for inculcating labour discipline, had passed. A century of economic development had done much to root out the old mentality, both in the poor and in the rich. In the subsequent history of poor relief other considerations came to the fore.

---

1 Burnet, *History of the Reformation*, III, p. 535. See also *The Second Book of Discipline*, Chapter 13, on the economic advantages of discipline.

2 Spittle sermon, quoted in J. O. W. Haweis, *Sketches of the Reformation*, p. 282. Cf. *Cartwrightiana* (ed. A. Peel and L. H. Carlson), pp. 243–6.

3 *Gods Doings, and Mans Duty*, pp. 44–5.

V

Since we have glanced forward to the Civil War, however, one final point may be made arising from Perkins. His four unproductive classes were beggars, monks, idle rentiers, and their dependent servants. This recalls irresistibly Baxter's analysis of the two sides in the Civil War, concluding 'Free-holders and Trades-men are the Strength of Religion and Civility in the Land: and Gentlemen and Beggers, and Servile Tenants, are the Strength of Iniquity'.[1] Perkins, writing 40 years before the outbreak of civil war, in a society dominated by the landed class, was cautious but nevertheless clear in his condemnation. 'Such as live *in no calling*, but spend their time in eating, drinking, sleeping, and sporting' are guilty of disobedience and rebellion against God. They will plead that they have livings of their own, and lands left them by their parents: but that is no defence.[2]

Disobedience and rebellion against God: they are strong words. A Puritan minister could hardly utter a more powerful condemnation. Perkins does not go on to say that idle rentiers, like beggars, were cut off from the Church and so from the promises of God; though he does say that they serve neither church nor commonwealth.[3] But it may have occurred to some of his readers to reflect that the households of great landlords who had their own chaplains (whom they of course selected), and did not attend parochial worship, had in a sense separated themselves from the faithful. A Puritan petition of the fifteen-eighties asked that noblemen should be compelled to join with the nearest congregation, their houses 'being commonly not convenient . . . to have such Officers as ought to be in everie Church, and the want of mynisters yet being so great'. Peers should at least provide a sufficient living for their chaplains, and not take men from their congregations.[4] The judicious Hooker thought it would be 'repugnant to the majesty and greatness of English nobility' to bring 'equally high and low unto parish churches'.[5] Fifty years later, in 1645, when the attempt was

---

1 *Reliquiae Baxterianae*, 1696, I, p. 89. We may compare Jeremy Taylor's account of the Royalist Sir George Dalston of Cumberland, whose alms-giving was so munificent that on one occasion in the Civil War 'the beggars made themselves guard' to rescue him from the Parliamentarian enemy (*Works*, 1831, IV, p. 220).

2 *Works*, III, pp. 63–4.

3 I, p. 756.

4 Ed. A. Peel, *The Seconde Parte of a Register* (1915), I, pp. 168–9.

5 *Of the Laws of Ecclesiastical Polity* (Everyman edition), II, p. 475. Hooker's cosmic philosophizing around this simple point makes agreeable reading. Laud disapproved

being made to establish a Presbyterian discipline, the point raised difficulties, 'the Lords pressing to have their chaplains and families exeemed, as before, from ecclesiastick jurisdiction'.[1]

I do not wish to press this particular point too far, and there is no space to develop the general argument. I would, however, suggest that when we ask whether we should speak of 'a Puritan revolution' or 'a bourgeois revolution' in England we may be guilty of a false antithesis. For the fundamental concepts of Puritan thought *are* bourgeois. Perkins is the key figure in the systematization of English Puritanism: and the tendency of his thought is towards the exclusion from full membership of the Church, and so from active citizenship, of beggars and of rentiers and their hangers-on, who take no part in productive activity.[2] In the model Puritan society, New England, such exclusion would in fact have led to deprivation of political rights.[3] The logical consequences of this line of thought were never, so far as I am aware, fully drawn by Perkins or any of his followers: if they had been drawn verbally they could scarcely have been printed. But the mental attitude is unmistakable. It is shown, for instance, in the common depreciation of mere aristocracy of birth as contrasted with the aristocracy of the spirit. 'No man', wrote Perkins (and he went out of his way to include princes specifically), 'is to stand upon his gentilitie, or glorie in his parentage for nobilitie and great blood, but onely rejoyce in this, that he is drawne out of the kingdome of darknesse'.[4] Ungodly kings and property owners have 'a civil right' by God's permission, and so are not to be deprived without good cause 'yet of themselves they are but usurpers'.[5] Once these theses had become commonplaces, the good cause was found. The abolition of the monarchy and the House of Lords in 1649, the confiscation of Church, Crown, and Royalists'

---

only when families *below the rank of peer* made themselves 'strangers to the Mother-church' (*History of the Troubles and Tryal*, pp. 544, 560–1).

1 R. Baillie, *Letters and Journals* (1775), II, p. 149.

2 We may perhaps compare Saint-Simon's grouping together, as 'les industriels', of the productive classes, bourgeoisie, peasants, and workers (*Oeuvres Choisies*, 1859, III, p. 67).

3 Beggars of course had no vote in Perkins's England. Davy told the Poor Law Commissioners that he thought they should be disfranchised. He said nothing about disfranchising rentiers (M. Cole, *Beatrice Webb*, p. 97).

4 III, p. 293. Cf. I, p. 119, and Haller, *op. cit.*, *passim*, esp. pp. 86, 168–9, 178–9.

5 III, p. 191*. The inclusion of kings here is oblique and cautious, but unmistakable to the careful reader of the whole passage.

estates, would not have been possible without such intellectual preparation.

The full Calvinist discipline was never established in England. Faced with the alternative of sharing power with the social classes represented by the Levellers and the 'bloody Anabaptists', or with the House of Lords and the bishops, those whom we call Presbyterians showed no hesitation. 'The question is not, whether Bishops or no? but whether Discipline or none?' Baxter told the House of Commons in April 1660, in *A Sermon of Repentance*.[1] 'If it then should have been said to us', the Rev. Henry Newcome reflected after the event, 'well, you shall be eased of this power, and rid of the bloody Anabaptists, but you must have Bishops, and ceremonies again, we should have then said, with all our hearts'.[2] Calvinism broke in pieces when the godly were faced with the choice between lower-class sectaries believing in universal grace and perfection in this life,[3] and a sceptical aristocracy whose authoritarianism was Hobbist rather than Calvinist. A generation elapsed before Locke shored up a system out of the fragments.

Calvinism disintegrated in the Revolution it had done so much to make possible. Politically its achievements were wholly negative; but it moulded social thought in the Anglo-Saxon countries into patterns which still endure. 'Moses my servant is dead' was the text which James Montague, Master of Sidney Sussex, selected for his funeral sermon on Perkins. He no doubt applied the succeeding verses in the same chapter of *Joshua*, wherein God assured his chosen people that they would prosper and have good success whithersoever they went (even 'unto the great sea toward the going down of the sun') provided only they were strong, and very courageous, and observed 'to do according to all the law which Moses my servant commanded'.[4]

1 P. 43.

2 Ed. T. Heywood, *The Diary of the Rev. Henry Newcome* (Chetham Society), p. xxix. The same point is elaborated in Newcome's *Autobiography* (ed. R. Parkinson, Chetham Society), I, pp. 118–19.

3 The Quakers were only giving a new theoretical twist to the old belief which Perkins attributed to 'the multitude of our people', that they could be saved 'by their good serving of God, and their just and honest dealing among men' (III, p. 595; cf. also the references given in note 3 on p. 197 above).

4 Fuller, *Abel Redivivus*, p. 438. The text is from *Joshua*, i. 2. Montagu, head of a Puritan college, was also a member of a great Puritan family which had patronized Perkins (see p. 196 above). His nephew commanded the army of the Eastern Association in the Civil War.

EIGHT

The Political Sermons of John Preston

He spake so solidly, as if he knew Gods will.

William Noy, in Lloyd, *State-Worthies*, II, p. 208.

I

Preston's Life

JOHN PRESTON was born in 1587, son of a 'decayed' gentleman farmer of Northamptonshire. His father died when John was 12 years old, but (like Hobbes) he was educated by a wealthy maternal uncle, who was several times mayor of Northampton.[1] After a successful career at Cambridge, Preston contemplated various professions – trade, diplomacy, philosophy, medicine. The picture we get of him at this stage is of an able and ambitious young gentleman of declining family. But around 1611 he was converted by a sermon of John Cotton's: and henceforth devoted himself to divinity. He was a very successful tutor and lecturer, and also proved himself no mean academic politician, managing at the age of 27 to snatch the mastership of his college (Queens') for the Calvinist John Davenant from the greedy maw of George Mountain, Dean of Westminster and later Archbishop of York.

In 1615 Preston caught the eye of James I in a public disputation at Cambridge by his witty defence of the proposition that dogs can reason. He secured the patronage of Fulke Greville, Lord Brooke, and a court career seemed to be open to him. Already he was a leading figure in Puritan circles, and a kinsman of his who had married a relation of

1 Where not otherwise stated, biographical details come from T. Ball, *Life of the renowned Dr. Preston* (1885), or from the *Dictionary of National Biography*, or from I. Morgan, *Prince Charles's Puritan Chaplain* (1957). Ball's *Life* was probably written in the late sixteen-thirties. For Hobbes, see pp. 248–9 below.

Geoge Villiers suggested to the favourite that he might win support from the opposition by patronizing Preston. So he was made chaplain to Prince Charles (1621) at Buckingham's instance. Henceforth Preston devoted himself to promoting the interests of Puritanism by political manoeuvre. He even used to insist that his pupils must be eldest sons, and so likely to be socially influential.[1] He already had many enemies, who, his pupil and biographer assures us, were always lying in wait for him. In Cambridge he had been forced to preach in favour of set forms of prayer in order to be allowed to preach at all. So he learnt early to be ambiguous. But he also liked mystery for its own sake. Ball tells us that he went abroad in order to improve his Latin, so as to qualify for a chair in divinity. One would have thought the purpose innocent enough; but he went disguised as a gentleman, in scarlet cloak and gold hat band, followed by a spy sent after him by Lord Keeper Williams!

In 1622 Preston was appointed Preacher at Lincoln's Inn, 'where he was assured many Parlament men and others of his best acquaintance would be his hearers'.[2] Among the members of the society in his time were William Noy, Henry Sherfield, William Hakewill, Thomas Wentworth, Edmund Waller, Sir Ranulph Crewe, John Glynn, Harbottle Grimstone, Oliver St. John, William Lenthall, William Prynne. Among Preston's intimate friends were the Earls of Warwick, Lincoln, Pembroke, Bedford, Lord Saye and Sele, the second Lord Brooke, Sir Richard Knightley, Sir Thomas Crewe (probably), Sir Henry Mildmay, Lady Vere, Gilbert Pickering, Henry Lawrence. It is a nominal roll of the Puritan opposition. Preston also 'had formed a strong Party in the City', where in 1617 he had been sworn a member of the East India Company (gratis), and bought £400 worth of new joint stock.[3]

Preston and his friends were playing a deep political game. As early as 1621 Preston had written a paper opposing Prince Charles's

1 Ed. D. Parsons, *The Diary of Sir Henry Slingsby* (1836), p. 318.

2 Ball, *op. cit.*, pp. 56, 73–7. The Puritanism of preachers at Lincoln's Inn was notorious. One of them, Thomas Gataker, had even persuaded the lawyers of the Inn not to confer with clients or to give advice on the Sabbath.

3 P. Heylyn, *Cyprianus Anglicus* (1668), p. 157; *C.S.P., Col., East Indies, 1617–21*, pp. 98, 100. Typically, Preston invested in the East India Company because estates there were invisible, and 'he was not willing to be accounted rich', 'though he had great incombs from his pupils, and was not prodigal' (Ball, *op. cit.*, pp. 94–5). He sold all his East India stock in December 1624, at the same time as his friend the Earl of Lincoln (*C.S.P., Col., East Indies, 1622–4*, p. 488).

proposed Spanish marriage, which was 'copied out and spread among those of the Parliament they thought fit'.[1] The object of the group was to win the Duke of Buckingham over to a policy of opposition to Spain and of ecclesiastical reform at home. From 1621 onwards the favourite seems to have toyed with this as a possible line of policy. In 1622 Preston was made Master of the Puritan college of Emmanuel, thanks to another skilful piece of academic diplomacy and to the direct intervention of Buckingham. This incident created a national sensation, suggesting to the Puritans that they were dominant at court, and to the courtiers that Preston had sold out to them.[2] Next year Preston was made D.D. by royal mandate. In 1624, when the university authorities, the Arminian party and James himself wished to keep Preston out of a town lectureship in Cambridge, Buckingham offered him the vacant bishopric of Gloucester, and it is said that Preston was given his choice of any future bishopric. But he preferred the Trinity lectureship. Originally endowed by the voluntary contributions of the citizens for Richard Sibbes, by 1624 it had become the public lecture of the town. It was suggested that it was beneath Preston's dignity to accept a lectureship 'maintained by sixpences', but its sermons rivalled in popularity the more orthodox ones delivered at the university church.[3] So on this occasion, with Buckingham's help, Preston actually worsted the King.

For from 1624 the favourite was beginning to take the Puritan party more seriously. Secure in the affections of Prince Charles, he needed support in the country to reinsure against James, who opposed Buckingham's desire for war with Spain. It was in 1624 that Preston put forward, and Buckingham seriously considered, the abolition of deans and chapters, and the confiscation of their lands. This, Preston argued, would solve the financial problems of the Crown; Buckingham would 'not only surmount Envy, but turn the Darling of the Commonwealth', and the lands themselves would supply the means for bribing any opponents. The scheme was only frustrated, Hacket tells us, by the care of that devout churchman John Williams, who himself held the rich deanery of Westminster.[4] In March 1625 Preston was in

1 Ball, *op. cit.*, p. 60.

2 *Ibid.*, pp. 83–9.

3 *Ibid.*, pp. 98–101; Fuller, *The Appeal of Injured Innocence*, in *History of the University of Cambridge* (1840), p. 554. See Thomas Randolph, *Poems* (1929), p. 134. Laud tried to suppress the lectureship in 1630.

4 J. Hacket, *Scrinia Reserata* (1693), I, pp. 203–5.

attendance on Charles when James died, and he travelled in the same coach with the new King and the favourite to Whitehall. This 'gave great offence', since it was 'against the rules of the court'.[1] For the moment it looked as though Preston was to play a major political rôle. Williams, the main opponent of the scheme for abolishing deans and chapters, was dismissed from the Keepership of the Great Seal, after attacks on him from the Puritan group in Parliament. Buckingham offered the Seal to Preston.

But the struggle for influence at court was not a straight fight between Preston and the Puritan peers on the one hand, and Williams and Bristol on the other. Laud had succeeded Lancelot Andrewes (Preston's 'greatest Adversary'[2]) as head of a third party of ecclesiastical conservatives. Laud, like Preston and unlike Williams, wanted office and influence in order to pursue a policy of principle, though his principles were diametrically opposed to those of John Preston. So between Laud and Preston there could be no compromise. Buckingham 'rather used than loved' Preston, and thought that he had wholly won him over after the Emmanuel election.[3] After James's death, secure in the favour of Charles, Buckingham no longer needed the support of the Puritan party, to whom Preston remained obstinately faithful; and Charles unmistakably inclined to the Arminians. So Buckingham wavered in his support of the steadily anti-Spanish foreign policy favoured by the Preston group, and began to draw back from designs of ecclesiastical reform and plunder of the Church. Since Preston could not be bought over, the Great Seal went to Sir Thomas Coventry, who was tied to neither of the two parties.

The final show-down was forced on Buckingham and Preston – each of whom wished to avoid it by procrastinating – by the Puritan party at court – Warwick, Saye and Sele, Sir John Coke. It came one month after the fall of La Rochelle. The cause was Richard Montague, whose *Appello Caesarem* was under attack from the House of Commons and was defended by the Arminians. The Puritan lords pressed for a conference on Montague's book, at which they hoped Preston would rout Montague and his supporters, and so force Buckingham to declare himself one way or the other. It appears to have been the personal predilection of Charles for Laud and the Arminians that

1 G. Burnet, *A History of My Own Time* (1897), I, pp. 27–8.
2 Ball, *op. cit.*, p. 53.
3 Fuller, *The Worthies of England* (1662), II, p. 291; Ball, *op. cit.*, pp. 88–9.

forced the less theological Buckingham to throw the Puritans over. The offer of the Great Seal to Preston at this precise juncture seems to have been made in a last attempt to detach him from his associates. In February 1626 the Duke finally agreed to preside at the Conference; and after missing the first session Preston eventually appeared against Montague, though his performance was not up to the expectations of the lords who had egged him on.[1] In the week after the Conference, Laud had many long and confidential discussions with the Duke, who hitherto had been intimate with Laud only in the latter's dreams.[2] By March the Puritans realized that they had lost; and Eliot opened the attack on the favourite which led to his impeachment by the House of Commons. 'The business of religion is like to follow his [the Duke's] standing or downfall' was the terse summary of one of Joseph Meade's correspondents.[3] Preston and his friends were forced to abandon court intrigue and appeal to public opinion in the country, to Parliament.

Henceforth Preston was an opposition figure for what remained of his life. He thought of Lincoln's Inn as a refuge, just as Gray's Inn had been for Sibbes when he was driven out of Cambridge. But he also contemplated emigration – and rightly, for Laud 'would have found some way or other to remove him out of Lincoln's Inn'.[4] Earlier in his career Preston had suffered from sleeplessness, which on medical advice he had cured by smoking: but now tobacco was no help. In 1628 he died, at the early age of 41, of tuberculosis and overwork, in Sir Richard Knightley's house. His funeral sermon was preached by the veteran leader of the Puritan party, Decalogue Dod. 'Some men lived as much in seven years', Preston protested, 'as others did in seventy'.[5] Certainly he had sown good seed. The Feoffees for Impropriations, set up under his influence immediately after the breach with Buckingham in 1626, helped to build up a party of laymen and ministers which aimed, among other things, at capturing influence in Parliamentary boroughs.[6] Of the three Puritan heroes of the sixteen-thirties, Prynne was Preston's disciple, a Lincoln's Inn man; Burton, clerk to Prince

  1 T. Birch, *The Court Times of Charles I*, I, p. 86.
  2 Laud, *Works* (1853), III, pp. 182–3.
  3 Birch, *op. cit.*, I, p. 105. See below, pp. 223–4.
  4 P. Heylyn, *Cyprianus Anglicus*, p. 157.
  5 Perry Miller, *The New England Mind: the Seventeenth Century*, p. 374; *The Second Part of Old Mr. Dod's sayings*, p. 15, in J. Taylor, *Memorials of the Rev. John Dod*.
  6 For the Feoffees see I. M. Calder, *Activities of the Puritan Faction of the Church of England*, *passim*, and my *Economic Problems of the Church*, Chapter XI.

Charles's Closet, was probably a friend and certainly a disciple; Bastwick was an Emmanuel man. The leadership of Parliament in the early sixteen-forties was largely in the hands of what we have called the Preston group; his policy was consummated when dean and chapter lands were confiscated.

But Preston was not influential only as a politician. Professors Haller and Perry Miller have shown his crucial importance in the popularization of that covenant theology which was the most influential doctrine among seventeenth-century Puritans in England and America, and in building up an army of preachers in Cambridge. His sermons were edited posthumously by Sibbes, Davenport, Ball, and Thomas Goodwin, with dedications to all the great Puritan notables of his party. There is scarcely an eminent Puritan divine of the fifty years after Preston's death who does not refer to him as one of the greatest authorities. Archbishop Ussher was united to him by 'a most entire affection'.[1] He was quoted with approval by men as diverse as Johnston of Wariston, Richard Baxter, Thomas Goodwin, John Saltmarch, Hugh Peter, Henry Newcome, Oliver Heywood, and by Thomas Ward, one of John Mason's disciples.[2] In 1637 Sibbes and Preston were being read in an underground conventicle in Oxfordshire.[3] The pages of Clarke and Calamy testify to the continuing influence of Preston and his school as teachers. His works appear in every book-list of New England theology, Professor Perry Miller tells us, and were part of the essential reading of prospective ministers at Harvard.[4] Mary Prowde, later the wife of Isaac Pennington and mother-in-law of William Penn, was converted by reading Preston on prayer.[5]

II
The Covenant Theology

The essence of the covenant theology was that God had bound himself to the elect by an explicit bond, to stand by them if they would stand by

1 Nicholas Bernard, *The Life and Death of . . . Dr. James Usher* (1656), p. 83. The quotation is from Ussher's funeral sermon.

2 See p. 295 below.

3 E. R. Brinkworth, 'The Study and Use of Archdeacon's Court Records', *Transactions of the Royal Historical Society*, 1943, p. 114.

4 P. Miller, *The New England Mind: the Seventeenth Century*, p. 504; *From Colony to Province*, p. 221.

5 L. V. Hodgkin, *Gulielma: Wife of William Penn*, p. 4.

him. 'If thou walke before mee, and serve mee, and bee perfect. . . . I am willing to enter into Covenant with thee, that is, I will binde my selfe, I will ingage my selfe, I will enter into bond, as it were, I will not be at liberty any more.'[1] This was a means of overcoming the absolute decrees, of smuggling 'works' into Calvinism. God was omnipotent and therefore potentially arbitrary: but since he had been pleased to limit himself by covenant, his operations became predictable, comprehensible to human reason. Reason and science returned to the universe. The covenant theology emphasized God's love and mercy rather than the bleak arbitrary power of the absolute Calvinist deity. It established a relationship of contract between God and his elect to which the latter could appeal. Indeed the relationship is often expressed in terms which appear to us extravagantly legalistic. 'You may sue him of his bond written and sealed, and he cannot deny it'. 'Take no denyall, though the Lord may defer long, yet he will doe it, he cannot chuse; for it is a party of his Covenant.'[2] We must 'extort, . . . oppresse the promises, that as a rich man oppresseth a poore man, and gets out of him all that he is worth, he leaves him worth nothing, hee playes the extortioner with him; after that manner deale thou with the promises, for they are rich'.[3] It is a curious metaphor, and reminds us that Preston was 'the leading politician among the Puritan divines just when the union between religious reformers and lawyers was being cemented'.[4]

Thanks to the legal relationship of the covenant, one of the elect is no longer, in the last resort, subject to any earthly lord; his position is more akin to that of a partner with God in a business enterprise. God is 'willing to indent with us, as it were, to make himself a debtor to us'. The covenant 'implies a kinde of equality betweene us'.[5] If one is within the covenant one can be certain of salvation. But how can one know one is within the covenant? Here Preston, following Perkins, comes very near to accepting the will for the deed. 'If thou canst finde this now, that thou art able to take Jesus Christ . . . as a Lord and

1 *The New Covenant* (5th ed., 1630), p. 316. For all this section I am deeply indebted to Professor Perry Miller, especially his *The Marrow of Puritan Divinity*.

2 P. Miller, *The New England Mind: the Seventeenth Century*, pp. 389–90.

3 *The New Covenant*, pp. 477–8. This metaphor commended itself to Edward Leigh, M.P. for Stafford in the Long Parliament, who quoted it in his *Treatise of the Divine Promises* (4th ed., 1657), pp. 20–1.

4 P. Miller, *op. cit.*, p. 374.

5 *The New Covenant*, p. 331.

Saviour, thou art able to beleeve all the Covenant of Grace, thou art by that put into the Covenant'. And 'if ever thou art in covenant with God . . . thy election is sure . . . God will never alter it'.[1]

The effect of the covenant theology was to free men from the blind and incomprehensible eternal decrees of an unknowable God, and from the intolerable sense of sin which weighed so heavily on early seventeenth-century Puritans. It re-established moral obligation on a clearer, more rational basis. 'Every man hath a free-will to doe that, for the not doing of which he is condemned.'[2] Original sin is all but obliterated by the covenant. Good works are not the cause but they are the accompaniment of salvation. 'The way to grow in any grace is the exercise of that grace'.[3] Hence passivity is one of the greatest offences against God. Conscious effort, conscious morality, conscious struggle to make God's will prevail – such are the lessons of the covenant theology. The end of theology, Preston said, was action. He would apologize if in his sermons he stayed too long 'in the doctrinal part'.[4]

Sibbes expressed this demand for activity well when he wrote: 'We must not put all carelessly upon a providence, but first consider what is *our* part, and so farre as God prevents us with light, and affords us helps and meanes, wee must not be failing in our duty. We should neither out-runne, nor be wanting to providence. . . . Wee are *not our owne*, and therefore must not set up our selves. . . . When things are cleare, and Gods will is manifest, further deliberation is dangerous'.[5]

So we can understand why the Montague debate was so crucial. All concerned seem to have been fully aware of the political and social implications of the theological points they were discussing. 'Teach you this divinity?' cried Buckingham to Bishop Morton, who had defended the view that the elect cannot fall from grace. 'God defend us from following of it!' The Earls of Pembroke and Carlisle thereupon added that it was a most pernicious doctrine, and unfit for any people to hear.[6] The noble lords must have been unaware that perseverance in grace

1 *The New Covenant*, p. 390; *Life Eternal* (4th ed., 1634), Sermon XIII, p. 85; *The Breastplate of Faith and Love* (5th ed., 1634), pp. 8–9. For Perkins, see p. 197 above.

2 *The Saints Qualification* (2nd ed., 1634), p. 225.

3 *The Saints Daily Exercise* (5th ed., 1631), p. 35.

4 P. Miller, *The New England Mind: the Seventeenth Century*, p. 48.

5 R. Sibbes, *The Soules Conflict* (1635), pp. 362–4.

6 John Cosin, *Works* (1845), II, pp. 58–9. Reports of this Conference are suspect, since they emanate from Arminian sources. But Montague's defenders seem to have outmanoeuvred the Puritans.

had been laid down in the Lambeth Articles of 1595, and was explicitly stated in a catechism bound up with three out of every ten Bibles printed in England between 1574 and 1615, including the Authorized Version.[1] It was a doctrine which had fortified the Dutch Calvinists in their revolt against Spain, and one which Thomas Hobbes thought appealed especially to 'the generality of citizens and inhabitants of market towns'.[2] But when Saye and Sele asked for the decisions of the Synod of Dort on this subject to be accepted in England, 'No, no', quoth the Duke, 'away with it; we have nothing to do with that synod'. 'I have been assured by divers grave and learned prelates', he added, 'that it can neither stand with the safety of this church nor state to bring it in'.[3]

The Arminian view that grace was conveyed by the sacraments meant a reversion to the pre-Reformation doctrine of a mediating priesthood. Against it Preston felt compelled to defend the Calvinist proposition that none of the elect could fall into mortal sin after once enjoying grace. For this conviction was an essential component of the fighting morale, the obstinate courage in the Lord's cause, which Preston devoted so much of his life and energy to building up.[4] William Prynne's first work, published in this critical year 1626, sprang directly from the Montague controversy. It was entitled *The Perpetuitie of a Regenerate Mans Estate*. In it he attacked the view that grace could be conveyed to all men alike through the sacraments, and asked: 'If true grace . . . may be lost . . . who is there that would seek it? . . . Who is there that would suffer persecutions and afflictions?'[5] The questions are naïve enough; but Prynne's own career testifies to the courage in persecution and affliction which assurance of grace could give. Oliver Cromwell, we recall, was said to have inquired on his deathbed whether grace once enjoyed could be lost: and to have died happy when assured that it could not. 'For I know that once I was in grace', he said.[6] God must be held to his promises. Buckingham's rejection of this

---

1 J. Strype, *Annals of the Reformation . . . during Queen Elizabeth's happy reign* (1824), III, Part ii, pp. 238–42.

2 Hobbes, *English Works*, VI, pp. 194–6.

3 Cosin, *op. cit.*, II, pp. 35, 38, 61–3.

4 See below, pp. 241–2.

5 W. Prynne, *The Perpetuitie of a Regenerate Mans Estate* (1626), To the Christian Reader.

6 The attribution of this remark to Cromwell is uncertain. But many other examples could be given. See, for instance, Sir Simonds D'Ewes, *Autobiography and Correspondence* (1845), I, pp. 276–7, 286–7.

comfortable doctrine, and his acquiescence in the promotion of its enemies to key positions of control in the English Church, made it impossible for the Puritans to work with him any longer. A surrender here would, in their view, have been an even greater disaster to the Protestant cause than the rout at Rhé.

III

The International Situation

When Preston discussed in Cambridge *The Doctrine of the Saints Infirmities*, he noted that there were 'two things in the kingdom of grace, which when we looke on are apt to make us discouraged'. The first of these was our own weakness; the second was 'the Kingdome of grace abroad'. It was difficult for a man not to be discouraged when he observed how the latter 'goes downe the wind, and how the wicked prevail, and the godly are weak, and goe to the wall'.[1]

There are several points of interest about this passage. The first is the complete fusion of personal and public, domestic and foreign questions. The 'Kingdome of grace' is used as a conveniently imprecise phrase to describe the Protestant (or Calvinist) cause in international politics. Each individual member of the kingdom is profoundly, intimately, and directly affected by the welfare of the kingdom in other parts of the world. This is far more than 'an interest in foreign affairs'. A great battle between Christ and Antichrist, light and darkness, is being waged all over the world. It was impossible for one who aligned himself with Christ not to feel an active participator.

The sense of alarm manifest in so many of Preston's utterances is not something that he was trying artificially to stimulate. It already existed in the minds of his audience and he had to take account of it. It was in his sermons preached at court, not in those at Cambridge, that he felt called upon to describe and aggravate the danger.

To most Protestants the peril seemed very real in the sixteen-twenties. After sixty years of uneasy truce, a Roman Catholic counter-offensive had begun in Germany. Protestantism was being rooted out in its ancient home, Bohemia, and in the only Calvinist Electorate, the Palatinate. Powerful Imperial armies were advancing on Protestant north Germany. And the war appeared to be spreading. In 1621 the truce between the Netherlands and the Spanish Empire ended; and

1 *The Doctrine of the Saints Infirmities* (1637), p. 214.

226 PURITANISM AND REVOLUTION

the bastion of Protestantism and republicanism, which so much English blood and money had been expended to preserve, seemed to be in danger of destruction. Despite the rivalry of Dutch and English merchants, the independence of the Calvinist republic had a deep symbolic significance for all English Protestants.

Whilst the world was going up in flames, James I fiddled. He sent no troops to help his son-in-law, the Elector Palatine. He sent instead, according to the Spanish jibe, 40,000 ambassadors, one of whom Preston was asked to attend.[1] James thought that the conflict between Christ and Antichrist could be smoothed over by a marriage alliance between England and Spain. Prince Charles and the Duke of Buckingham went to Madrid on their ridiculous and risky courtship. When they returned disgruntled, Preston entered upon his brief period of influence.

But Buckingham thought of international politics in terms of states: Preston thought in terms of 'churches' or of peoples. It seemed clear to the Duke that a breach with Spain necessitated an alliance with France, the second great European power. The French government was engaged in reducing the liberties of its Huguenot subjects, and English help against La Rochelle was the French price for a marriage alliance. To Buckingham it seemed a fair and natural price; to Preston, who had just been prepared to contemplate a French marriage treaty as the lesser evil,[2] the French government seemed to be demanding the blackest treachery to 'the Kingdome of grace abroad'. His view was shared by many Protestant Englishmen, including the sailors in English ships lent to the French king for the siege of La Rochelle, who refused to serve against their Huguenot brethren.

The outlook then was gloomy. An overwhelmingly successful Papist advance in Bohemia and Germany, threatening Scandinavia; the Netherlands again with their backs to the wall, faced with a possible junction of forces by Spain and the Emperor; Protestants in France being deprived of their liberties. James appeased Catholic Spain; Charles I assisted Catholic France against the Huguenots. When the outcry in England caused a reversal of the latter policy, Buckingham's expedition to relieve La Rochelle was an isolated English exploit, no part of the great Protestant crusade of which the patriots dreamed: and it was conducted with an incompetence barely distinguishable from

1 Bell, *op. cit.*, pp. 93–5.
2 *Ibid.*, pp. 108–9.

treachery. This is the background to international affairs which we shall find in Preston's sermons, and to the desperate anxiety which lay behind them. For all was not well in England either.

IV

Court Sermons

In November 1626 Preston preached before the King at Whitehall a sermon variously entitled *The New Life* or *A Sermon of Spirituall Life and Death*. It was preached five months after Parliament had been dissolved for impeaching Buckingham, nine months after Preston's breach with him, and ten months after La Rochelle had surrendered to Louis XIII in consequence of English pressure and promises of future assistance.[1] The assistance had not been forthcoming: England was referred to in La Rochelle as 'the land of promise'. English trade with France was being interfered with. The French Ambassador was insulted by a London crowd, and a formal petition for redress was presented to the Council by merchants interested in the French trade, both in the month of Preston's sermon. In December 200 English and Scottish vessels, laden with wine, were seized at Bordeaux. In June 1627 the ill-fated expedition sailed to Rhé under Buckingham's command.[2] In November, then, no overt action had been taken by the English government. The sermon was 'preached when the Rochellers in distress accused us', noted Preston's biographer.[3] Pressure in favour of intervention, voiced in Parliament, was now making itself strongly felt among the trading community. The interests of 'the Kingdome of grace' and of the republic of commerce, not for the last time in English history, spoke with one voice; they were speaking very loudly when Preston entered the pulpit.

'A living member', he told the King and the courtiers, 'hath a fellow-feeling, yea, a quicke and exquisite sence within, when any member is pained and hazarded; therefore let us labour to find this character in ourselves, by being affected to our Neighbours, Brethren, and Churches abroad; by having bowels of compassion in us to melt over their condition, and to desire their safetie as our own. . . . We have reason to commiserate them for our owne sakes, for wee cannot stand alone, and God hath so ordered it in his providence, Luke 6. 38,

---

1 Gardiner, *History of England, 1603–42* (1884), VI, pp. 51–2.
2 *Ibid.*, VI, pp. 145–7, 171.
3 Ball, *op. cit.*, p. 155.

"Looke what measure we mete to others in their distresse, the same shall men measure to us in our necessities;" and how soone the fire may take here also wee know not. . . . Certainely God will recompence us with good if we doe it, with evill if we omit it. . . . We cannot doe God a more acceptable service than to helpe the Church, though for the present shee seeme to be under the cloud of his anger'.[1]

Here are all the elements of Preston's thought on international politics: his vivid sense of the unity of Protestantism, of the necessity on grounds not only of principle but also of self-interest for England to protect her brethren on the continent; and of the dangers of God's wrath if we failed to do our duty. The conclusion was even more stirring than the introduction:

'We may fall out and in at home, and the vicissitude of faire and foule weather within our own Horizon may passe away and blowe over, as I hope it will and I pray God it may: [Could Preston still have hopes of Buckingham?] yet in the mean time, if any of the Churches be swallowed up, you know that it is a thing that cannot bee recalled: and therefore let us do our best, and do it in time'.[2]

Turning directly to the King, Preston assured him that his subjects were persuaded that the royal desires and intentions were most real and firm, without any flattery. Nevertheless, a message from God might exhort, encourage, and confirm his majesty.[3] Let the King and his councillors, 'those who have greatest power and opportunity of doing good in this businesse', consider that excellent speech of Mordecai to Esther: 'If thou holdest thy tongue at this time, deliverance shall appeare to the Jewes from another place, but thou and thy house shall perish'.[4] 'So if any be impediments', resumed Preston, 'nay if they do not their best, I pronounce this in the name of the most true God, that will make it good sooner or later, They and their houses shall perish'.[5] Preston proceeded to draw upon the example of

1 *A Sermon of Spirituall Life and Death* (1630), pp. 23–4. This edition, dedicated by Prynne to Sir Nathaniel Rich, Richard Knightley, and John Pym, differs in some respects from the 'corrected' edition of 1634, edited by Thomas Goodwin and Ball.

2 *Ibid.*, p. 26.

3 This passage is not in the 1630 edition. I have taken it from *Sermons preached before His Majestie and upon other speciall occasions* (1634), pp. 51–2.

4 *Esther* iv. 14. Preston appears to have used the Geneva version. The marginal note to this edition tells us that Mordecai 'spake in the confidence of that faith, which all Gods children ought to have: which is, that God will deliver them, though all worldly means faile'.

5 *A Sermon*, p. 27. These words must have seemed prophetic when Buckingham was assassinated 21 months later. Some may even have recalled them on 30 January 1649.

Solomon and other kings, who permitted rebellions against God in their kingdoms and against whom God stirred up rebels. The application could be made to Louis XIII or Charles I according to the hearer's inclinations.

One is amazed at the plainness of the speaking, and yet at the skill with which each phrase is selected: in the most threatening passages a milder meaning is always possible, and the latter must have been accepted in Charles's flattery-ridden court. No wine-merchants were likely to be in the chapel at Whitehall; but as news of the sermon reached the City it would undoubtedly be appreciated, and different meanings would be given to the ambiguous passages.

Just under a year later, on the eve of the final disaster to Buckingham on the Isle of Rhé, Preston preached again at Court. His sermon was published under the title *A Sensible Demonstration of the Deitie*. After a preliminary sketch of the argument from the design of the universe to prove the existence of God, the preacher turned to the more congenial topic of the covenant of God with his people, and what it was incumbent upon the latter to do if God's wrath was to be averted. The political application was frank and direct:

'When the enemy is assaulting the Churches a far off, he is even then striking at the root of this Church and Commonwealth. . . . It's certaine that evil is intended against us, and will come upon us, except something bee done to prevent it. For there is a Covenant betweene God and us, and breach of covenant causeth a quarrell; the quarrell of God shall not go unrevenged. . . . If we will not beleeve his Word, yet shall we not beleeve his actions? Hath he not begun? Are we infatuate and see nothing? Doe we not see the whole body of those that professe the truth are besieged round about through Christendome? At this time are not present enemies not onely stirred up but united together, and we disjoined to resist them? Are not our Allies wasted? Are not many branches of the Church cut off already, and more in hazzard?'[1]

In explaining the débâcle it was beside the point to say that 'such an accident, and such a miscarriage of such a businesse, and such men, are the causes' [Perhaps Preston still had hopes of Buckingham even now]. 'But who is the cause of these causes?' he asked. . . . 'Are not these crackes to give warning before the fall of the house? Are not these the "gray haires" which Hosea speakes of, that "are here and there

---

1 *A Sensible Demonstration of the Deitie*, printed with *A Sermon of Spirituall Life and Death*, pp. 52–3.

upon us and we discerne them not?" Gray haires, you know, are a sign of old Age and approach unto death'.[1] As the causes of the disgraces and dangers that had overtaken continental Protestantism and England were not personal and accidental: so the remedies too are not merely personal. 'God is angry; and he is never angry but for sinne';[2] but the sins are the sins of society, of governments, even more than they are the sins of individuals. The regeneration must be social, national: and it is high time that the men in power set about this regeneration:

'It is apparent that God is about a great worke, yea, to make a great change in the world, except we doe as it were hold his hand by seeking and turning unto him, and by removing the things that provoke him: he doth not lay all these stones, and move all these wheeles for nothing, and yet who knowes what it is he is about, till it bee brought forth? . . . There are certaine times and seasons wherein God troubleth the Churches, and that very thing that distinguishes between Nations and Churches, to be saved or to be destroyed, is the very ability to discerne of those seasons.'[3]

In his sermon of the preceding November Preston had appealed directly to the King, expressing confidence in his good will and exhorting him to stand fast in his purposes. Charles was present at the later sermon too, but now there was no appeal to him. Individuals indeed are brushed aside, and the appeal was to the nation, the Church, the people. Two days after the sermon, news reached England of the final crushing disaster at Rhé, of the loss of 4,000 men and of the humiliating evacuation.[4] It is perhaps hardly surprising that Preston was prevented, by Laud, from preaching on the next occasion when it should have fallen to him. Both the words just quoted, and the fact that he was forbidden to preach again, attracted widespread notice. The sermon which he was not allowed to preach, his biographer tells us, was 'more talked of at Court *and in the citty* than any sermon that ever he had preached before'.[5]

The foreign danger was manifest. But was England secure from treachery in high places at home? You must consider the churches abroad, Preston told the House of Commons in July 1625; 'but for the

1 *Ibid.*, p. 53; cf. *Hosea* vii. 9.
2 *Ibid.*, p. 55.
3 *Ibid.*, pp. 56–7. It was *à propos* of this sermon that Bishop Neile said that Preston 'talked like one that was familiar with God Almighty' (Ball, *op. cit.*, p. 159).
4 Ball, *op. cit.*, pp. 158–9; Gardiner, *op. cit.*, VI, pp. 198–9.
5 Ball, *op. cit.*, pp. 159–61. My italics.

Church at home, you see the Lord hath begun to make a breach upon us'.[1] The reference was to the rise of the Arminian party to high favour at court, and to failure to enforce the recusancy laws. The unity of the faith, as Preston conceived it, was in danger. The more a family or a commonwealth is divided, the nearer it comes to perishing; 'and the more peace and Unitie, the more safety'.[2]

Parliament, Preston told the Commons, should punish sin, especially whoredom, idolatry and (straying from his text) injustice. Injustice was defined to include bribery or a respecting of persons in judgment which amounted to bribery, i.e. by failing to enforce the recusancy laws. Lest the point should not be quite clear, Preston reminded the House of the two great deliverances of 1588 and 1605 in exhorting them to contend for the faith against whoredom, idolatry, and superstition.[3] The Commons indeed were already at work preparing a Petition against Papists, who aimed at the subversion of church and state, depended upon foreign powers, and offered a dangerous basis of support for any demagogue who might put himself at their head. Among the reasons for the strength of the Papists were mentioned the non-enforcement of the penal laws, foreign protection, lack of a preaching ministry, inadequate censorship of Popish books.[4]

This is the background against which we must consider Preston's call to the magistrates to root out heresy. Neither Popish errors nor their authors should be suffered in the Church of God, Preston told the King to his face; and who should root them out but the magistrates?[5] To Lincoln's Inn Preston said that the magistrates should cut down Popery and whatever is an impediment to Christ's truth.[6] In Cambridge, with the Arminians directly in mind, he said 'We must do with heresies as men do with a fire in a town, leaving not a spark lest it stir up *novum incendium*, a new fire'.[7] The issue was directly political, and Preston and his audience knew it. In the existing state of international affairs the security of the state and of all the achievements

1 *A Sermon preached ... before the Commons-House*, printed with *The Saints Qualification*, p. 294.
2 *The New Covenant*, p. 160.
3 *A Sermon preached*, pp. 295–301.
4 Ed. Gardiner, *The Debates of the House of Commons in 1625* (Camden Society), pp. 18–20.
5 *The Pillar and Ground of Truth* (1630), p. 21.
6 *The Saints Qualification*, pp. 210–11.
7 *A Patterne of Wholesome Words* (1658), p. 278.

of the Reformation demanded the suppression of the Catholic fifth column. As for the Arminians, their offence was not their sweet reasonableness, their greater tolerance: it was that this tolerance was extended to Papists only. Laud persecuted Protestant dissenters with the greatest severity. The political implications of this in the given situation were clear and to Preston detestable.

v

God is Angry for Our Sins

A conspicuous feature of Puritan Calvinism was its cultivation of the sense of sin. Our consciousness of sin must be aggravated before we can hope for divine mercy. We come to faith in Christ through our sense of sin. In modern pulpit usage this desire to convict of sin is aimed at the individual conscience, to urge the individual to change his life. The Puritan preachers attacked the individual conscience too. But they thought, far more than their twentieth-century successors, in terms of *the Church*: a Church that was the nation, society. Sins were not merely individual but national. The remedies too must be national. This called for a change of heart in a number of individuals: but it might also demand a change of institutions, of personnel, of policy, in government. The Puritan denunciation of sin slipped easily into something that was very close to being a demand for a change of government.

In his sermon preached before the House of Commons on 2 July 1625, at a general fast in time of plague, Preston seized the obvious occasion. But his account of God's chastising hand led him beyond the plague to the topic that was never far from his mind, the danger to the churches abroad and to the Church at home: a danger of which sin was the cause. But what were the remedies?

'It is not our Armie by Land, nor our Navie at Sea, that shall secure us at home, or prevaile abroad, though it bee well that these things bee done, and therefore you doe well in contributing cheerfully to his Majestie, for the maintenance thereof, for the common good'; but prayers were more important than armaments. 'It is not our woodden walls that will guard us, it is not the Sea wherewith you are invironed, nor our policy, counsell and strength that wil secure us and defend us, but it is turning to the Lord, and cleansing the Land from the sinnes wherewith he is provoked that will do the deed.'[1]

---

1 In *The Saints Qualification*, p. 269. Cf. *Life Eternal*, Sermon XVIII, p. 175 (pages renumbered from Sermon X).

In the circumstances there is something almost insolent in this passage. 'You doe well in contributing cheerfully to his Majestie': that is Preston's off-hand reference, as though to a matter of minor importance, to the Commons' vote of two subsidies two days earlier. This vote, taken in conjunction with the debate which preceded it, was, in Gardiner's words, 'practically a vote of want of confidence' in the King's advisers.[1] The phrase 'for the common good' could hardly have been misunderstood by a House which had recently heard many suggestions that previous sums voted had not been properly accounted for. Among the sins of which the Commons were invited to cleanse the land, no one would fail to recognize the heresies of Richard Montague, whose *New Gag for an Old Goose* and *Appello Caesarem* had been discussed at length by the Commons and referred to a committee the day before Preston preached. Thus in two sentences Preston managed, by implication, to criticize the foreign and religious policy of the government, and to call on the House of Commons to set matters right.

This last point must be emphasized. It was the duty of the Commons to oppose sin within their sphere, the sphere of high politics. But it was also the duty of individuals to oppose sin whenever and wherever they met it: and never more than now. 'It is not only the great sins of the Land that are causes of Gods wrath, but the coldnesse of them that are otherwise good.'[2] Preaching in Lincoln's Inn, Preston outlined their duties to the future J.P.s, recorders, and lawyers in his congregation. The year is still 1625:

'The Church of God hath times and seasons, and the Common-weath hath some seasons and times when men should be set aworke to doe more than at other times; and you all know this is such a season,[3] wherein there should be a working of every one in their severall places . . . more than ordinarily.' – 'What is it you would have us to doe?' – '*Contend for the faith once delivered to the Saints*. . . . You must be men of contention, let the world say what they will of you. Let not pretence of indiscretion hinder you. . . . Discretion makes no man lesse active, but it gives his actions a better tincture. . . . It is the common Faith, therefore every Man hath interest in it . . . and should contend according to his place and power. . . . It were better there should be great offences committed in the Land, great and notorious crimes, than

---

1 Gardiner, *op. cit.*, V, p. 347.

2 *A Sermon preached before the Commons-House*, p. 284.

3 The assumptions behind a casual phrase like this tell us more about the political atmosphere of the time than any official document can.

there should be any losse in the matters of Faith, because where the opinions of men are set wrong, that is a principle that carries them still on'. Preachers, magistrates, every man in his sphere must contend for 'the common Faith'. It is an especial duty to fast and pray 'when there is a plague coming, when there are great enterprises in hand, when there is anything *plotting* for the advancement of the good of the Church'.[1]

Every man hath interest in, and a duty to contend for, the common faith: these are large claims, illustrative of the embarrassingly democratic tendency of Puritan Protestantism, at least in opposition. But no harm could be done by making them in Lincoln's Inn, to men who would in any case be called upon to play a part in the political life of the country. 'If thou be a rich man, if thou be a Magistrate, if thou be a man of such and such opportunities to serve the Lord and doe but a little, he will not accept it at all', just as a landlord will not accept from a tenant less than the whole rent due.[2] It was such men of status that Preston called upon to 'strive and contend for the advancing of Christs Kingdome, for the furtherance of the Gospel, for the good of mankind, for the flourishing of the Church, wherein our own good consisteth; and we should doe it earnestly, we should contend for it, contend with God in prayer, contend with our Superiours by intreaty, with our adversaries by resistance, with cold and lukewarme men by stirring them up'.[3]

The reference to opinions being set wrong can hardly be to anything but the influence of the Arminian party. Similarly 'our adversaries' must include Arminians as well as Papists: the adjuration to resist these adversaries considerably modifies the already ambiguous call to contend with our superiors by entreaty. If these points are borne in mind, and the whole passage is re-read without any prepossessions about what a Puritan preacher is likely to have thought and said in 1625, it is difficult to see how a man would have expressed himself differently if his object had been, under a strict censorship of the spoken and written word, to call his hearers to organize themselves for a political struggle against an internal enemy which might ultimately

1 *The Breastplate of Faith and Love*, pp. 236–9. I have italicized the word 'plotting', a remarkable one to use in the context. But cf. Sibbes, *The Saints Cordials* (1629), p. 82: 'We must plot for eternity'. The Bodleian copy of *The Breastplate* was presented to E. Ewer by Mrs. Hampden.

2 *Ibid.*, p. 158. Cf. *The New Covenant*, p. 560.

3 *Ibid.*, p. 241.

have to be pushed to the point of revolutionary violence ('great and notorious crimes').

It would be a gross over-simplification to say that such was Preston's conscious and deliberate intention at this date. But it would be equally mistaken not to take full account of the difficulties imposed by the censorship and of the need to probe below the surface meaning of words. 'Prudence', Preston told the House of Commons in this same year 1625, 'doth not abate diligence, but guides it in its worke. It teaches not to doe lesse, but to doe better'.[1] Preston himself was undoubtedly the most 'prudent' and 'discreet' of men, who used every possible means 'to doe better' in the cause of righteousness, which he here interestingly equates with 'the good of mankind'. We should not underestimate his political sagacity or his cunning. Certainly his advice was good, and it was taken. Among those who heard Preston urge them to be men of contention, employing a well-regulated boldness, were, very probably, Henry Sherfield, William Prynne, and Oliver St. John.

In another course of sermons preached at Lincoln's Inn, Preston argued that 'to every action, and to every purpose, there is a certaine opportunity; and be a man never so well fitted, yet if he misse of that opportunity, he shall not bring his enterprise to passe'.[2] Here Preston seems to be dealing with the individual in his private life. Yet in the next sermon he slips insensibly over to a discussion of political duties. The remarks which have a political bearing are still sandwiched between exhortations about private conduct, and by extracting the political passages I ruin the carefully woven texture of Preston's argument. Whether it is the brilliant *tour de force* of a man anxious to convey political advice without exposing himself; or whether it merely testifies to the complete fusion of questions of private and public morality in the minds of Preston and his audience, would be difficult to say. Probably both are true. In any case, the passage throws interesting light on the nature of Puritan thought. The reader must imagine that in the gaps which I have indicated the preacher switched to questions of personal morality.

'For all private actions, as well as for those that are publicke, there is a time. . . . The times for the severall changes to which every man, every Common-wealth, and every Citty is subject, these times God

1 *A Sermon preached . . . before the Commons-House*, p. 292. In the margin Preston's answer to an objection from the danger of too much boldness is summed up: 'Danger of Excesse must be prevented by a well regulating of our boldnesse' (pp. 291–2).

2 *The New Covenant*, p. 569.

hath assigned . . . and they are as bounds that cannot be passed.' God, however, keeps these times secret.[1] 'There is a time when (it may be) a mans voice or suffrage would have turned the scale of a businesse, that concerned much the Commonwealth or the societie where he lives: but when that opportunity is past, it can be recalled no more. . . . There is an opportunity of preventing a mischiefe to a Common-wealth or to a Kingdome': this too we may miss. If he misses his opportunity, temporal miseries will fall upon 'a man, a Kingdome, *or a King*'. 'There is a time that if a man speake, *hee makes himselfe a prey* to the wrath of men. . . . And there is a time wherein if a man doe not speake, he makes himselfe a prey to the wrath of God.'[2]

'You all know this is such a season': Preston had taken that for granted in the sermons he preached to the same audience in 1625.[3] If we make the same assumption in reading the above passage, then it becomes a call to political action, as well as to personal dedication to the service of God: or rather personal dedication to God's service may necessarily involve a man in political action. 'Godlinesse is that which is done to God; such things, and such qualities as have an eye and respect to him, such things please him'.[4] In this definition Preston put before his congregation of lawyers and country gentlemen the ideal of self-abnegating devotion to God's service. He concluded *The New Covenant* with words in which personal and political obligation are completely synthesized:

'The doing what we have to doe with all our might, and with all our diligence, is that which quickens us, and keepes our hearts in a holy preparation to take the times, and not to overslip and overpasse them.'[5] Again we may suppose that William Prynne took note.

The classic example perhaps of Preston's failure to distinguish between political and religious action comes in his advice about elections, in a treatise dedicated by Goodwin and Ball to Lord Saye and Sele. An election is just as much a religious exercise as is diligent work

---

1 *Ibid.*, pp. 591–4.

2 *Ibid.*, pp. 602–3. I have italicized the words 'or a King', so deftly slipped in, and so ambiguous in their meaning. The other italics are Preston's own.

3 See p. 233 above.

4 *The Breastplate of Faith and Love*, Sermon III, p. 188. Cf. the *Sermon preached . . . before the Commons-House*, pp. 294–6, in which opposition to bribery is discussed as a part of zeal for the Church and the faith (above, p. 231).

5 *The New Covenant*, pp. 611–12.

in one's calling. Since he was preaching in Cambridge, Preston started with College elections:

'So you should behave yourselves in your Elections to looke with a single eye to the oath by which you ought to bee guided; doe nothing for feare or favour of men, or for any sinister respect. I wish I could speake and give this rule to all the Kingdome at Parliament times; for it is an errour among men to think that, in election of Burgesses or any others, that [they?] may pleasure their friends, or themselves, by having this or that eye to their owne advantage or disadvantage that may arise from it; whereas they ought to keepe their mindes single and free from all respects, so that when they come to choose they might choose him whom in their own consciences, and in the sight of God, they thinke fittest for the place; and that you may doe so, you are to get a single and simple heart to doe it.'[1]

It is hardly necessary to emphasize how such an attitude as Preston advocates, natural though it seems to us today, would strengthen the independence of freeholders and burgesses against the pressures of landlords and courtiers which were a normal part of seventeenth-century elections: and so would help to make the House of Commons representative of new trends of opinion among the propertied classes.

VI
Destiny

Implicit in all Preston's sermons is the sense of a ruler of the universe who is working out his beneficent purposes through human agents. It is the supreme, almost the sole duty of the elect to endeavour to understand those purposes, to accept them, and to co-operate with them to the best of their ability. The conception clearly had a great consolatory force, and was held with increased passion, as the long European crisis of the sixteen-twenties developed. This crisis, indeed, was itself evidence that God was at work.[2] To his Lincoln's Inn congregation, after discussing the dangers of the Church 'and the confusion that is almost throughout all Europe', Preston argued: 'Put the case all were turned upside downe, as it was in the confused Chaos . . . yet as then when the Spirit of the Lord did but moove upon the waters, many beautiful creatures were brought forth, and the Sea

1 *Life Eternal*, Sermon XII, p. 67.
2 See the passage quoted on p. 230 above.

divided from the rest, that those waters that seemed then to spoyle all serves now to water all, and without it we cannot be: even so, were the Church in never so confused a condition, yet the Lord shall so order the things that seem to undo us that they shall bring forth something of speciall use.' Only we must be humbled, for there is cause so to be.[1]

This is more than an assertion that God will overcome our enemies, or he will bring good out of evil; it asserts that apparent evil is God's way of bringing his good purposes into effect. It accepts history, the world of politics: it is no escapist refuge. The worse the situation gets, the more likely it is that men will repent and take the necessary measures. If you do not show zeal in contending for the faith, Preston told the House of Commons in July 1625, God's anger against us will grow hotter. We shall be utterly destroyed unless we take decisive action.[2] To his humbler Cambridge congregation, in the same year, Preston said:

'Where there is an evident signe that God hath a controversie with a Kingdome and the Churches, and a signe of his wrath is proclamed from heaven, then every man must doe something. . . . If we looke backe upon that Generation of Queene Elizabeth, how are we changed! They were zealous, but here is another generation come in their roome that is dead and cold.' 'The light of those times remaine (sic), but not the heate!'[3]

The only danger is lest we should draw the wrong conclusions from God's chastisement, and sink in despair instead of being roused to action. 'What though the Candlestick bee removed out of the Palatinate, because they were luke-warme and falne *from their first love*? What if he should do it in *France*? What if in *England*? In the *Low Countries*? Should it seem strange to us? It is his manner so to doe!' Only Papists argue that temporal success proves the justice of their case[4] – a view that more successful later Puritans were rash enough to abandon. There will be no cessation, Preston continued, until the necessary transformation in men's hearts and action has been wrought. 'Doest thou thinke that thou art plowed longer than thou needest? It is

---

1 *A Profitable Sermon preached at Lincolnes Inne on Genesis XXII. 14*, in *A Liveles Life, or Mans Spirituall death in Sinne* (fourth ed., 1641), p. 93.

2 *A Sermon preached . . . before the Commons-House*, pp. 294–305.

3 *The Golden Scepter held forth to the humble* (1638), p. 12.

4 *Ibid.*, pp. 19–20. Note how England, at peace but threatened by an internal enemy, is slipped in between churches and countries experiencing direct Papist military attack.

but till the clods, thy stiffe spirit, bee broken.'[1] Here the personal and political trials are completely fused: for each the remedy is in our own hands. 'This life is the time of striving, of running, of acting; it is not the time of being rewarded.'[2]

Yet, though the remedy lies with us, we may be mistaken about it. Preston discussed this point fully with his Lincoln's Inn congregation. Men may pursue a course of action, genuinely supposing it to be that which God wishes, and yet find it frustrated and themselves disappointed. They are then apt, in their short-sightedness, to despair and think that all is lost. God's 'usuall course is, when men have pitched upon particular meanes, and thinke surely the businesse must bee brought to passe by this, or else all will faile: God many times useth not that, but a meanes which thou never thoughtest of'.[3] The solution, then, is not to despair, not to slacken – as men were no doubt inclined to do on occasions during the shattering defeats of the sixteen-twenties – but to set to work again with honest intentions and full confidence in God. God's 'blessing is dispensed, not according to thy meanes, but according to the uprightnesse of thy heart, according to thy workes'. 'Use the meanes and depend and trust in God for the bringing it to passe.'[4] Cromwell's 'Trust in God and keep your powder dry' was a translation of this into non-theological language.

God, after all, has many matters to attend to. When our prayers go unanswered, 'it may bee God heares thee, but it crosseth some other secret passage of his Providence. There are many things that God, the great Governour of the World, must bring together'.[5] It was indeed the danger of the Calvinist onslaught on the individual soul that it might lead to autocentrism, to parochialism, to a demand that God intervene directly to help an individual or a group. Preston, the sophisticated man of affairs, is urging his congregation to take the world view, to have a historical perspective. 'A man cannot see round about all the corners of Gods Providence.'[6]

In *The Saints Daily Exercise*, another course of sermons preached at

---

1 *Ibid.*, p. 29.
2 *The New Covenant*, p. 539.
3 *The Breastplate of Faith and Love*, p. 263.
4 *Ibid.*, pp. 265, 269. Note the remarkable phrase, for a Calvinist, 'according to thy works'.
5 *Ibid.*, p. 282.
6 *Ibid.* This helps us to understand why the ungodly prosper, and consoles us in adversity, pp. 283–96.

Lincoln's Inn, Preston made a direct political application of these principles. The date of these sermons is uncertain, but a reference in the passage I am about to quote must be to the disastrous intervention of Christian IV of Denmark in the war in Germany, ending in his rout at Lutter in August 1626, four months after Mansfeld had been defeated by Wallenstein at Dessau: 'Suppose we pray, that such a great Prince should raise the Churches, that such a warre, that such an enterprise and project may doe it; put the case the Lord will not doe it so, are wee then presently undone? And is there no help, because such a battaile is overthrowne, because such a King did not succeed, because such a Generall had not successe according to our expectation? It may be that is not the way. . . .'[1] 'God withholds blessings, that wee might have a greater edge set upon our desires, that wee might pray harder for them, that we might prize them more when we have obtained them.'[2]

God governs the world, as the head of a household governs his family. He brings things to pass by apparent accident and chance: his providence is indeed most manifest in such cases.[3] 'Therefore', declared Preston in Cambridge, 'say not, I am undone, or the Churches are undone, because Princes are not for you; because men helpe you not: for God can helpe you alone. Hee doth not need Princes'.[4] God's immediate government of the world is a remedy against the complaint of evil governors, since God acts through them even when they do ill.[5] This omnipresence of God means that we must do all in our power to walk with him: for he observes all that we do. He speaks to us by our consciences, by the motions of the spirit, by good counsel of friends, ministers, and others: and by the passages of his providence. 'To observe what the Lord saith to us in all these, is a great part of our walking with him.' 'When a man hath this full perswasion in his heart, not onely habitually, but actually, that the Lord lookes upon him in all that he speakes and doth, hee makes the Lord present with him.' This very dialectical solution to the problems of election and free will leads Preston back to political application. The 'presence of God makes a mans home and country and liberty to bee every where: hee is at home when hee is abroad, and at liberty when he is in prison'.[6]

1 *The Saints Daily Exercise*, pp. 58–9.
2 *Ibid.*, p. 65.
3 *The New Covenant*, pp. 160–3.
4 *Life Eternall* (Sermon VII), p. 126.
5 *Ibid.* (Sermon XVI), pp. 151–2.
6 *Ibid.*, pp. 159–64; cf. *The Breastplate of Faith and Love*, pp. 8–9.

God does not need princes. Preston said almost the same thing, a little more cautiously, to the House of Commons in July 1625. 'Indeed wee care for the favour of Princes, and think that they can hurt us, or doe us good; and therefore we are so intent about them, so busily occupied about them. But this would not worke on us so much if wee did beleeve that which I have now delivered unto you, that God onely is the Author of good and evill. . . . If the Creature were able to doe you good or hurt, I will be bold to say to you, that God were not God. . . . For on this ground we worship him alone, that hee onely is able to doe good or hurt.'[1]

The whole object of Preston's teaching was to forge steeled souls determined to walk with God, to care nothing for princes, and to fight for God's cause, if necessary alone: to face persecution and to feel at liberty in prison.[2] This emphasis was a product of his analysis of the political situation. 'Consider the present time of the Church', he said in one of his last sermons, 'consider how soone the things may come upon us, when we shall be put to it, for now things are *in praecipitio*, hasting downe to the bottom of the hill. . . . These times are growing and daily gather strength more and more; therefore let us strengthen our faith, and prepare for a tryall'.[3]

Men must harden themselves, prepare for the worst. Serving God in Caroline England was not likely to be an easy task. 'If you mean to follow Christ', Preston warned his Lincoln's Inn hearers, 'looke for a rainy day. It may bee it is a faire morning, but yet we know not what the evening will be'.[4] The godly were always a minority. They must be prepared to fight hard in difficult circumstances. Doubters may say 'The paucity of those that goe with us shew[s] that it is difficult, wee have no company, there are so few to bare us company; and not that onely, but the multitude of those that are against us, we goe against the crowd, against the righteousnes of the world; and where a multitude is against us there must needs be shame cast upon us, though they be in a wrong way'.[5] The minority in the right, moreover, were likely to be

1 *A Sermon preached*, pp. 261–2. Cf. Sibbes, 'What a shame is it for an heire of heaven to be cast downe for every petty losse and crosse: To be afraid of man whose breath is in his nostrils, in not standing to a good cause, when we are sure God will stand by us' (*The Soules Conflict*, 1635, To the Christian Reader, sig. A.4).

2 Haller, *The Rise of Puritanism*, passim.

3 Quoted in P. Miller, *The New England Mind: the Seventeenth Century*, p. 469.

4 *The Doctrine of Selfe-Deniall*, in *Four Godly and learned Treatises* (3rd ed., 1633), p. 225.

5 *Grace to the Humble as Preparations to Receive the Sacrament* (1639), p. 99.

men of substance, and this fact brought its own difficulties. Preston realized, like his teacher William Perkins, that 'the more men do possesse in the world, ordinarily, the less courage and resolution they have for the religion of God, as experience in Queen Maries daies hath shewed'.[1] Preston's audience, at Cambridge, at Lincoln's Inn, and at Whitehall, was largely composed of influential persons, whose support was essential for the victory of God's cause. They must be strengthened so that they held their convictions even dearer than their possessions. Before the King and his court in November 1626 Preston declared: 'A man that hath this life of grace in him, he will suffer any thing, he will lose his life, his credite, his goods, his libertie and all, rather than he will wound his conscience, and violate his inward peace and communion with God.'[2] That was clear, but discreetly general, as befitted the occasion. At Lincoln's Inn, Preston was more specific about the trials and temptations likely to await his generation:

'Many would be willing to doe much – but it may cost them their estates: then they favour themselves, and will sleepe in a whole skin. But if a case comes, that yee must stand against Popery and for justice against indirect courses, stand to it though persecution and imprisonment come'.[3] To the objection 'Yea, but I am alone, and therefore can do nothing', Preston replied that Luther was alone, and yet withstood the force of the whole world. The force of example was incalculable. 'Men are incendiaries to make one another wicked: be thou so to make others good.'[4] Making others good meant more than making them morally virtuous: it meant transforming them into 'new Creatures', freeing them from traditional shackles so that they could listen to the voice of God speaking in their consciences, by preachers, and by what is happening in the world around them. 'If we must be new Creatures, then pull downe all that is old.'[5] Preston spoke here of old ideas and prejudices within a man's soul; but a man who had achieved such a work of destruction within himself would have far fewer inhibitions about pulling down external institutions in order to build a better world.

1 Perkins, *Works*, III, p. 398.
2 *A Sermon of Spirituall Life and Death*, p. 11.
3 *The Doctrine of Selfe-Deniall*, p. 227.
4 *Ibid.*, p. 231.
5 *The New Creature: or, A Treatise of Sanctification*, in *The Saints Qualification*, p. 433.

VII

The Importance of Preaching

In this tense atmosphere of struggle, actual and potential, we can perhaps understand something of the significance which the Puritans attached to preaching. Preston described the preacher as 'an Embassadour or Minister who speakes to the people in stead of God in the name of Christ'.[1] Preaching was the normal way in which God conveyed his spirit into the hearts of men.[2] This is part and parcel of Preston's intellectual approach to religion. 'If the mind be right', he told his lawyers, 'the Will will follow; and if the Will follow, be sure the affections will follow'.[3] 'There is not a Sermon which is heard', declared Preston with the terrifying logic of Calvinism, 'but it sets us nearer Heaven or Hell'.[4] Anyone who hears a sermon therefore has the duty to 'make it your own by Meditation'.[5] Sabbath-breaking was always classed by Preston among the major sins, presumably because it interfered with the work of instruction and meditation which should take place on that day.

Ministers bear an even greater responsibility than members of their congregations. Their task is not to humour men but to cure them, to change the evil disposition of their nature.[6] They, of all men, must be prepared to stand out against the current of the times. They must not 'speak peace to whom God speaks not peace'.[7] The preacher therefore must, where necessary, adapt his preaching style to the simplicity of his audience.[8] Preston was, indeed, an outspoken practitioner and theorist of the plain style in preaching common to the school of Perkins.[9] His treatise, *A Patterne of Wholesome Words*, deserves more attention than it has received from students of seventeenth-century preaching.[10]

1 *A Patterne of Wholesome Words*, p. 320; cf. *The Saints Qualification*, p. 2, and Sibbes, *The Saints Cordials*, p. 440. Ministers receive their commission as ambassadors for the Church: that is why private men may not preach (*A Patterne of Wholesome Words*, p. 321).
2 *The Saints Spirituall Strength* (1637), p. 145; cf. *Life Eternall*, p. 162.
3 *The Breastplate of Faith and Love*, p. 204.
4 *A Pattern of Wholesome Words*, p. 288.
5 *Riches of Mercy to Men in Misery* (1658), p. 70.
6 *Sinnes Overthrow* (4th ed., 1641), p. 105; cf. *The New Creature*, pp. 462–72.
7 *A Patterne of Wholesome Words*, p. 301.
8 *Ibid.*, pp. 298–9.
9 See Perry Miller, *The New England Mind: the Seventeenth Century*, Chapter XII *passim* and p. 517.
10 Preston's name does not occur in the Index of W. F. Mitchell's *English Pulpit*

The preaching of the gospel was therefore of direct concern to the moral welfare of the nation. It was a task of political importance. In his sermon before the House of Commons in July 1625 Preston impressed upon his hearers the duty of advancing the ministry, of seeing that every flock had a shepherd: the Commons took his advice. Those areas of the kingdom which were to be strongly Royalist in the Civil War were notoriously lacking in a preaching ministry, and Preston sounded a note of alarm: 'Is it not a lamentable case to see how many perish for want of knowledge in Wales, in the Northern countries, and in many places besides?' 'Where doth Popery abound so much as in the dark places of the kingdom?'[1] This complaint was frequently reiterated in the years that followed.

Lamentable though the shortage of preachers was, Preston nevertheless thought that the ignorance of 'Countrey-people' was inexcusable. 'For though every Parish have not a Preaching Minister (which is a thing much to be wished) yet there is no Countrey but some light is sett up in it, whither they may resort if they will'.[2] It was meanwhile the duty of patrons to present, and of congregations to maintain, godly ministers: 'if yee will not be at cost for a good Minister, it is a signe you love your profit above Christ'.[3]

The preponderance of impropriations laid the Church at the mercy of the gentry, few of whom heeded Preston's admonition to put Christ above profit. Buckingham had rejected the scheme for confiscating dean and chapter lands, and applying some of the proceeds to the maintenance of a preaching ministry. A proposal to augment livings out of impropriations, made in the Parliament of 1625, came to nothing.[4] There was here a three-handed struggle between hierarchy, Puritans, and profit-loving impropriators. The two latter categories might be united in the same person, and often agreed on most other political issues. But on augmentation of ministers' stipends their interests were divided; and hierarchy and government were able to prevent a reconstruction of the Church by Parliamentary action,

Oratory from Andrewes to Tillotson. Two of Preston's works are mentioned in the Bibliography, but not *A Patterne of Wholesome Words*.

1 *A Sermon preached . . . before the Commons-House*, pp. 298–9.

2 *The Saints Qualification*, pp. 222–3. Laud was soon to punish men if they thus broke the law by attending sermons outside their own parish.

3 *An Elegant and lively Description, of Spirituall Death and Life*, in *Four Godly and learned Treatises*, p. 181; cf. *The Saints Qualification*, pp. 209–10.

4 Gardiner, *Debates in the House of Commons in 1625*, p. 22.

though they had no hope of undertaking it themselves.[1] After his failure with Buckingham, Preston inspired the Puritan attempt at extra-Parliamentary action, through the Feoffees for Impropriations. But it was not until 1644 that 'able and learned divines' began to be introduced into the northern counties, in the wake of Fairfax's army.[2] The series of acts and ordinances which followed, culminating in the setting up of the Commissioners for the Propagation of the Gospel in Wales and in the North Parts in 1650, testify to Preston's skill in picking on the issues of abiding political importance.

VIII
The Service of Mankind

Reading history through the wrong end of the telescope, we tend always to reduce the grandeur and sweep of Puritan ideas because we insensibly assimilate them to the ideas of later Protestant nonconformity. Nothing could be less helpful in trying to assess Preston's thought. This courtier and scholar was anything but the nasal-whining Puritan of hostile caricature. He pointed out, urbanely enough, that the Apostle Paul quoted profane poetry: 'Why may not we?'[3] He read Aquinas (at the barber's), Scotus and Occam. He took his metaphors from the stage.[4] His sermons often approached a dialogue form similar to Bunyan's,[5] and his style was always clear and vivid, packed with similes. These came from the world of science as well as of everyday life.[6] From the Protestant denial of Papal infallibility he drew for Charles I's benefit the fullest logical conclusion: 'Hence we may learne, to take up nothing meerely upon trust, nor to thinke things are so, onely because the Church hath said.'[7]

1 I have discussed this at some length in my *Economic Problems of the Church*.

2 Firth and Rait, *Acts and Ordinances of the Interregnum*, I, pp. 391–2.

3 *A Patterne of Wholesome Words*, p. 313. Preston, however, opposed the habit of plastering a sermon with quotations from authorities, as had been the custom 'when Popery overspread the earth'. 'Luther renewed the Doctrine of Christ and preached it purely' (*ibid.*, p. 316).

4 Ball, *op. cit.*, pp. 18–19; *The New Creature*, p. 348.

5 Cf. *The Churches Marriage*, in *The Golden Scepter held forth to the humble*, pp. 43–5; *Mount Ebal, or a Heavenly Treatise of Divine Love* (1638), esp. pp. 22, 34–9.

6 Cf. *The Christian Freedome* (1641), p. 4; *The Saints Qualification*, p. 45, where Preston discusses the difference between scientific truth (easy to demonstrate to the merest country yokel, given time) and faith, towards whose truths 'there is not onely a blindnesse in man, but an unteachablenesse and resistance'.

7 *The Pillar and Ground of Truth*, p. 19. Preston of course was not preaching complete scepticism: the Bible *is* infallible. Yet even here the elect know *by their own experience* that the Bible is true. Even God is liable to the same test: 'As he is described in the Scriptures, such have they found him to be to themselves' (*Life Eternall*, p. 64).

Since religion included politics, Preston's conception of God is of something this-worldly as well as other-worldly. The end of our life, he told Lincoln's Inn, was first to render glory to God and secondly to do good to mankind. And he emphasized that he meant *doing* good, not merely having benevolent intentions. 'Shall they be able to fare the better for your purposes, for your good resolutions? No, they fare the better onely for that you doe for them and to them; it is your actions that benefit men'.[1] (Such words would no doubt please that godly man of action, the Earl of Warwick, to whom the sermons were dedicated – if he read them.) Indeed, labouring to do good to mankind *is* godliness.[2] We are here at that union of Puritanism and humanism of which Milton is the finest flower. The service of mankind is the service of God: so conversely the achievements of mankind, the progressive discoveries of the arts and sciences, prove the existence of God, his care for his creatures.[3] Preston may have learnt that from Bacon; or he may have learnt it in the same school of experience as Bacon had done, as Winstanley was to do. If the service of mankind is the service of a God who reveals himself in scientific and technical advance, many could support the Puritan cause who did not share Preston's own deeply personal religion. It was one of the many ways in which the greater rationalism of the covenant theology broadened its appeal. God for Preston was essentially law-abiding: he 'alters no law of Nature'. The orderly and constant course of the universe is better proof of the existence of God than miracles. So 'faith addeth to the eye of reason, and raiseth it higher', it 'teacheth nothing contrary to sense and reason'.[4] Preston himself used the argument from design, and tells us that American Indians have it written on their hearts that there is a God.[5] Such passages reveal the deeply theological connections between Puritanism and early science.

Yet we are not yet in the world of eighteenth-century deism. As a

---

Only the unregenerate lack this experimental knowledge: and they are unable to believe (*The Saints Qualification*, p. 45).

1 *The Breastplate of Faith and Love* (Sermon VIII), p. 232; cf. p. 241.

2 *The deformed forme of a formall profession* (1641), p. 10. Cf. Sibbes: 'No Christian can warrant himselfe to be a good Christian, but he that labours to have the Commonwealth to flourish' (*The Saints Cordials*, p. 82).

3 *Life Eternall*, pp. 10–13. Preston gives the invention of printing as an example.

4 *The New Covenant*, p. 46; Miller, *The New England Mind: the Seventeenth Century*, p. 201.

5 *A Sensible Demonstration of the Deitie*, pp. 31–46; *The New Covenant*, pp. 159–60; *Life Eternall*, Sermon I, p. 13.

corrective to these passages which may seem too precociously suggestive, I conclude with words whose sombre eloquence sound a fitting note on which to leave John Preston, dying at the height of his powers at the age of 41. For here we are reminded of the traditional, elemental world in which the Northamptonshire boy grew up, the world of murder, pestilence, sudden death and *memento mori*, to which the Baconian vision still seemed very remote:

'As evidently as you see the heavens roll about every day, so plainely we may see, if wee will take it into consideration, mankinde hurried along with an unwearied motion to the West of his dayes; their posterity posting after them by an unrepealable law of succession. Our fathers you know are gone before, and we are passing, and our children shall follow us at our heeles: that as you see the billowes of the Sea one tumble on the neck of another, and in the end all are dashed upon the shoare: so all generations and ages in the end are split on bankes of death; and this is the condition of every man.'[1]

---

1   *The Cuppe of Blessing*, p. 591.

NINE

Thomas Hobbes and the Revolution in Political Thought

As he [Hobbes] said of the Law, that without this Sword it is but Paper; so he might have thought of this Sword, that without a Hand it is but cold Iron. The Hand which holds this Sword is the Militia of a Nation; and the Militia of a Nation is either an Army in the field, or ready for the field upon occasion. But an Army is a Beast that has a great belly, and must be fed; wherfore this will com to what Pastures you have, and what Pastures you have will com to the balance of Property, without which the public Sword is but a name or mere spitfrog. . . .

Nevertheless in most things I firmly believe that Mr. Hobbs is, and will in future Ages be accounted the best Writer, at this day, in the world.

James Harrington, *Works*, 1737, pp. 41, 259.

I

THOMAS HOBBES was born in 1588 and lived till 1679. His life thus extends from the defeat of the Spanish Armada to the beginning of the Popish Plot; from the year in which the independence of Protestant England was finally ensured to the period when a threat to restore Catholicism in England was less a political reality than the stunt of a Parliamentary party. The Revolution of 1640 occurred after Hobbes was 50 years old, when his main ideas had taken form. But they had been shaped by the intellectual forces of his world.

Hobbes was, as Aubrey put it, 'of plebeian descent'. His father was a country vicar, and by all accounts not a very learned one. But he died while Thomas was still young, and – as in the case of John Preston – the boy's education was financed by his uncle, in this case a prosperous glover and alderman of Malmesbury. His mother came of yeoman stock. They managed to send him to Oxford. From there he passed in

1608 into the service of the great family of the Cavendishes, as tutor to the future Earl of Devonshire. At one period – we do not know exactly when – Hobbes worked in close collaboration with Bacon, acting as his amanuensis. But with brief interruptions he remained in the service of the Cavendish family until 1640, when he fled to Paris and the Cavendishes began to gather an army for Charles I. In Paris, Hobbes was for a time tutor to Prince Charles. In 1653, after his return to England, Hobbes resumed his service with the Cavendish family.

Like many of the great landed families, the Cavendishes were in financial difficulties. 'His lord', says Aubrey delicately, 'was a waster'; and Hobbes wore out his shoes and got colds from wet feet by being sent 'up and downe to borrow money and gett gentlemen to be bound' for the second Earl of Devonshire.[1] Hobbes taught the Earl to keep accounts; but nevertheless his extravagance brought disaster on the family. After his death in 1628 Hobbes was out of the family's employment for three years whilst the widow was trying to restore some sort of economic order. So the glover's nephew learnt something of the economic hazards as well as of the external splendour of a feudal ruling house.

The contradiction is apparent. Hobbes, the small bourgeois, the clever boy making good at Oxford, is taken into the service of one of the most conservative of the great feudal families, which still ruled large tracts of the economically backward north of England. When Hobbes takes his noble pupils on the grand tour of Europe he meets the most advanced intellects of his time – Galileo, Descartes, Gassendi. He comes home to discuss their ideas with the Duke of Newcastle.

Hobbes's station in the world thus rendered him conscious of conflict, of the rifts in society which were plunging it into a civil war that would be fatal to his position as a hanger-on of the old order. In *Behemoth* he gives a convincing social analysis of the causes of the Civil War. In the *De Cive* and *Leviathan* his object is to prevent that conflict (or any other conflict) ever taking the extreme form of civil war. Hobbes's theory of sovereignty dates from the actual period of armed conflict in England.

So Hobbes, suspended between two worlds, is equally critical of both. His environment and mode of life may have aligned him with the old order politically; but none can deny the revolutionariness of his method, of his criticism, the boldness of his rejections. Even his

---

1 Aubrey, *Brief Lives*, I, pp. 322–3, 347.

reasons for rejecting revolutionary Puritanism have far-reaching implications: for his critical-sceptical approach cut right through the religious smoke screen which concealed divisions within the ranks whilst seventeenth-century Parliaments advanced on power.

II

What then was the Hobbesian revolution?

Hobbes found official political thought dominated by the idea that government was to be obeyed because ordained of God; and he substituted the theory that the state was instituted by man for his own convenience, and that it should be obeyed because the consequences of disobedience can be demonstrated to be more disagreeable than obedience, in almost all cases. That is to say, expediency, not morality, is for Hobbes the motive for political obedience.

Hobbes found opposition thinking dominated by the idea that government should not be obeyed when it conflicted with divine law, natural law, natural rights; and he showed that natural law, morality, and rights in society are derived from the state, and that it is impossible to obtain agreement among men on what constitutes divine, natural, or fundamental law except in so far as these have been defined by the sovereign. That is to say, he made power, not right, the key question in politics.

Finally, Hobbes abandoned the old games of text swapping and precedent hunting and substituted logical argument. That is to say, he made reason, not authority, the arbiter in politics. Paradoxically, it is the absolutist Hobbes who demonstrated that the state exists for man, that it is the product of human reason, and therefore that political theory is a rational science.

Despite his practical conclusions, then, the whole essence of Hobbes's approach to politics, his mental atmosphere and pre-suppositions, are 'bourgeois'. He postulates a society in which traditional static hierarchical feudal relations have broken down. In the mediaeval state the important questions had been those of personal status and privilege: the relation of lord to serf, of gild member to purchaser, of cleric to layman. But by the seventeenth century, society has dissolved into its component parts, who face one another not as members of estates or corporations but as egotistic individuals. This new individualism is reflected in religion: Hobbes's view of human nature is that of Calvinism or Jansenism; he has as little use as Calvin for the hierarchy of saints, the mediating priesthood, the round of formal 'works' by which the medieval Catholic hoped to save his soul. Hobbes sees society as a collection of atoms, in which the important relations are contractual, such as those between employer and workman, the Nonconformist and the minister whom he selects: the emphasis is on the individual, not on the social group. Hobbes's natural man is an individualist, like Robinson Crusoe or Adam Smith's economic man. Like Descartes, Hobbes believes he can generalize about the passions of all men by examining his own. His state is a mechanical contrivance, set up by contract. The contract idea which he adopts was almost the private property of the Puritan and revolutionary opposition, whether we consider the *Vindiciae contra Tyrannos*, which was the Bible of the Dutch revolutionaries and the French Huguenots, the covenant theology of John Preston, or the Solemn League and Covenant which bound together the Scottish and English opponents of Charles I.

Hobbes postulates the complete equality of natural man in 'the faculties of body and mind'. 'The inequality that now is, has bin introduced by the Lawes civill.'[1] 'Good Counsell comes not by Lot, nor by Inheritance; and therefore there is no more reason to expect good Advice from the rich, or noble, in matter of State, than in delineating the dimensions of a fortresse.' So the sovereign will give the hereditary aristocracy 'no further honour, than adhaereth naturally to their abilities'.[2] No egalitarian democrat could go further. How right Clarendon was to upbraid Hobbes for 'his extreme malignity to the Nobility, by whose bread he hath bin alwaies sustain'd'. The noble lord correctly pointed out that the Levellers concurred with Hobbes's view 'that no man may have priviledges of that kind by his birth or descent'.[3]

Man in the state of nature, for Hobbes, is an abstraction from the competitive world he saw about him: the fittest survive. Indeed, he goes out of his way to tell us that his state of nature is a logical abstraction rather than a piece of historical description.[4] Natural man is 'bourgeois' man with the policeman removed. The main objects which Hobbes makes to his state of nature are such as would occur to and appeal to the commercial classes: 'There is no place for Industry; because the fruit thereof is uncertain: and consequently no Culture of

1 *Leviathan* (Everyman ed.), pp. 63, 79.
2 *Ibid.*, pp. 187–8.
3 Clarendon, *A Brief View and Survey*, pp. 181–2. Cf. p. 192 above.
4 *Leviathan*, p. 65.

the Earth, no Navigation, nor use of the commodities that may be imported by Sea; no commodious Building; no Instruments of moving, and removing such things as require much force; no Knowledge of the face of the Earth; no account of Time; no Arts; no Letters; no Society.'[1] The setting up of the sovereign state is the only escape from the natural state of war:[2] but it also alone makes possible any of the achievements of civilization.

Man emerges from the state of nature by his own efforts, by self-help based on the use of reason. The laws of nature are 'precepts or general rules, found out by reason', and they lead to the elevation of the sovereign to save men from the state of war which is at once the state of nature and the condition of 'feudal anarchy'. 'To seek peace and ensue it' is for Hobbes the first law of nature, the clue to all success in politics; and peace, internal order, and security are the first necessities of existence for the commercial and industrial classes.

The overriding problem of seventeenth-century politics, which Hobbes was shrewd enough to see absolutely clearly, was, Who was to interpret conflicting customs – King or Parliament, Lords or Commons? The House of Commons represented the landed class; but since capitalism in England was largely rural, many M.P.s in the seventeenth century had an outlook very different from that of the government. As the Crown, in its financial extremity, resorted to arbitrary taxation, so the House of Commons, to protect property, resurrected the claims of fifteenth-century Parliaments to a say in control of policy. There were therefore conflicting precedents with which the conflicting claims could be supported. Most students of politics devoted themselves to antiquarian research to find arguments for their own side, or to the hopeless task of discovering which side was 'right'. Hobbes brushed all these cobwebs aside, and showed that such questions were not decided by 'right' but by power; what mattered was not arguments, but who was to decide between them. Custom, precedents, admittedly could produce contradictory conclusions: very well, then, the only important question was, Who was to interpret conflicting customs? This is the historical point of Hobbes's theory of sovereignty.

1 *Leviathan*, pp. 64–5. Cf. p. 89, and *The Elements of Law*, pp. 79–80.
2 It leads, of course, to wars between states; but the state of nature is worse than the condition of warfare between nations, which may indeed be profitable to rulers: 'But because they uphold thereby, the Industry of their Subjects; there does not follow from it, that misery, which accompanies the Liberty of particular men' (*Leviathan*, p. 65).

Hobbes agrees with almost all contemporary political theorists in seeing the rise of private property from a previously existing state of primitive communism as the cause and justification of the state. 'For before constitution of Soveraign Power ... all men had right to all things; which necessarily causeth Warre: and therefore this Proprietie, being necessary to Peace, and depending on Soveraign Power, is the Act of that Power, in order to the publique peace.'[1] As property is inherited, and we may not go behind possession (sanctified by the sovereign) to question *right*, so sovereignty itself passes by inheritance, and we have no right to question the arrangements made by our ancestors. Sovereignty and property stand or fall together, are maintained by the same laws of inheritance.

Here again Hobbes is transitional, and this part of his argument seems the weakest in the light of later and more sophisticated contractual theories. But we must remember when and for whom Hobbes wrote. A society which believed that all men inherited the consequences of Adam's sin, and that Anglo-Saxon precedent was relevant to its own problems, could hardly boggle at an original contract which bound posterity. Hobbes's combination of contract and inheritance would make sense to a seventeenth-century landowner, for whom an unchallengeable succession of property is the important thing. It is only after the new standards have triumphed that even land loses its feudal status and becomes a commodity, which can be bought, sold, and devised, and is secured by contract. This development is reflected in political theory by the transition from divine hereditary right to Locke's contractually limited monarchy. Hobbes is writing at an intervening stage, and his arguments are addressed to the contractualists, to those, like Selden, who held that 'a King is a thing men have made for their owne sakes, for quietness sake'.[2] There is already nothing divine about the sovereign's right: that is why Hobbes was so unpopular with the high-flying Church of England men.

Hobbes is also a spokesman of the new attitude towards poverty in capitalist society. The idea that poverty was a holy state had long been abandoned. Opinion was now shifting away from the sixteenth-century view that pauperism should be dealt with by Christian charity. That solution had been sufficient for the occasional victims of misfortune in the more static mediaeval society: it could not cope with the mass

1 *Ibid.*, p. 93. For primitive communism, see *English Works*, II, p. vi.
2 John Selden, *Table Talk* (1927), p. 61.

unemployment created by early capitalism and enclosure of arable lands for sheep farming. Hobbes saw that pauperism on the new scale was a problem for the state. 'And whereas many men, by accident unevitable, become unable to maintain themselves by their labour; they ought not to be left to the Charity of private persons; but to be provided for, (as far-forth as the necessities of Nature require), by the Lawes of the Common-wealth.' But even this subsistence minimum must not be rashly distributed. 'For such as have strong bodies, the case is otherwise: they are to be forced to work; and to avoyd the excuse of not finding employment, there ought to be such Lawes, as may encourage all manner of Arts: as Navigation, Agriculture, Fishing, and all manner of Manifacture that requires labour.' Emigration is also a remedy for unemployment. And with Malthus, Hobbes concludes: 'And when all the world is overcharged with Inhabitants, then the last remedy of all is Warre; which provideth for every man, by Victory, or Death.'[1] The function of the state in a competitive world, as Hobbes sees it, is the mercantilist one of building up power for wealth and wealth for power, and building up power and wealth for ultimate war, the final arbiter of wealth and power.

One final point about the contract. 'Whatsoever is not Unjust, is Just', says Hobbes. 'And the definition of INJUSTICE, is no other than the *not Performance of Covenant*.'[2] Justice is the keeping of contracts: no more. One consequence of this will be clear to anyone who is acquainted with the social problems of sixteenth- and seventeenth-century England. The burning question of the day was the position of the small proprietor, the copyholder or cottager, whose holding was frequently an obstacle to consolidation of estates, enclosure, racking of rents, and all the familiar methods by which one section of the gentry was enriching itself and sharing in the commercial and industrial boom of the century before 1640. The attack on the security of tenure of these small men, the mere idea that customary rents could be raised and that peasants unable to pay might be evicted, had seemed in the sixteenth century a breach with all that was right and proper, a gross violation of equity even when the letter of the law was observed. For most copyholders and cottagers held by customary right, at customary rents, not automatically enforceable at common law. There was no contractual basis for their claims. The aim of the improving landlord

---

1 *Leviathan*, p. 185. Cf. pp. 195–215 above.
2 *Ibid.*, p. 74; cf. *The Elements of Law*, pp. 63–5.

was to replace copyholds by leaseholds, copyholds for lives by copyholds for a fixed term of years; to substitute precise, limited, and determinable contracts for the indeterminate, traditional, customary rights of the mediaeval peasantry; to pass from status to contract. It had been a moral as well as an economic revolution, an intrusion of the alien standards of the market into a sphere hitherto unaffected by them.

By the middle of the seventeenth century, no doubt, the new morality of competition was becoming generally accepted. The last attempt to legislate against depopulating enclosures was defeated in Parliament in 1656. But the peasants' struggle for stable copyholds still went on, supported by the Leveller movement just before the publication of *Leviathan*. The last pamphlets against enclosure were published in the 'fifties. At least the new standards were regarded as a lapse from the old, a concession to the wicked covetousness of fallen man. But now here was Hobbes making contract the basis of morality! Justice is the keeping of covenants: no contract, no injustice. Nowhere is the fundamentally 'bourgeois' nature of Hobbes's approach to the state and to morality more apparent than in this, the foundation of both.

It should be noted, moreover, that though the basis is *contractual*, force is needed too to maintain contracts. Contracts are free, but must be maintained by force against the unfortunate. As that good Hobbist, Commissary-General Ireton, put it four years before the publication of *Leviathan*: 'Any man that makes a bargaine, and does finde afterwards 'tis for the worse, yett is bound to stand to itt.' 'They were couzen'd', replied the Leveller Wildman, 'as wee are like to be'.[1]

III

The 'bourgeois' characteristics of Hobbes's thought come out perhaps most clearly in his attitude to the Roman Church, and to non-rational elements in religion altogether. The point of the attack on the Kingdom of Darkness in Part IV of *Leviathan* is that Hobbes is defending the negative achievements of the Reformation, its break with priestcraft, its denial of the need for a hierarchy to mediate between man and God.

In the first three decades of the seventeenth century, in opposition to

---

1 *Clarke Papers* (ed. Firth, 1891–1901), II, p. 404. An enclosure agreement drawn up in 1702 by the freeholders of Eyam is an excellent example of a Hobbist contract: see W. E. Tate, 'Enclosure Acts and Awards relating to Derbyshire', in *Derbyshire Archaeological and Natural History Society's Journal* (1944–5), pp. 63–4.

pressure from the Puritans, the Church of England under Lancelot Andrewes and Laud had reverted to a kind of social Papistry. With no desire to return to the Papal allegiance, such men wished to elevate the dignity of the priest, to distinguish him from the mass of the congregation, to emphasize the formal and symbolic aspects of worship (prayer and the sacraments) as against the rational (preaching). 'There should be more praying, and less preaching', said Hobbes's patron, the Duke of Newcastle; 'for much preaching breeds faction, but much praying causes devotion'.[1] Hobbes had no love for Puritanism, for he held that the logical conclusion of its belief in the rights of the individual conscience was complete anarchy; but he was far too imbued with the new science to have any truck with the neo-Papist movement. In Part IV of *Leviathan* he is attacking 'ghost' ideas, in Ibsen's sense of the word; clearing away impediments to rational thought. He openly contrasts religion with science. He mercilessly attacks superstition and belief in magic, for the specific reason that they are the means by which priests establish their authority over the people. 'Who will not obey a Priest, that can make God, rather than his Soveraign; nay than God himselfe? Or who, that is in fear of Ghosts, will not bear great respect to those that can make Holy Water, that drives them from him?'[2] Claims to inspiration may be a cheat; and at best fear of hell and hopes of heaven are unsatisfactory as motives for political action.[3]

Hence Hobbes's Erastianism, which is as great as that of the majority of the House of Commons in 1640. The state must wield the vast power over men's minds which religion still possesses, just because of the infinite possibilities of disagreement and dispute which there would otherwise be. For 'the most frequent praetext of Sedition, and Civill Warre, in Christian Common-wealths hath a long time proceeded from a difficulty, not yet sufficiently resolved, of obeying at once, both God, and Man, then when their Commandements are one contrary to the other'.[4] It is in fact the question of sovereignty. Who is to decide? In the last resort, Hobbes thinks this is a question of power. The quarrel between the Puritans and Laud was only in appearance over doctrinal niceties, the position of the communion table, the priestly vestments. In fact two philosophies of life were in conflict, two

---

1 Duchess of Newcastle, *Lives of William Cavendish, Duke of Newcastle, and His Wife, Margaret*, ed. Firth, p. 124.
2 *Leviathan*, p. 369.
3 *Ibid.*, p. 76.
4 *Ibid.*, p. 319.

social orders: the mediaeval, the Catholic, the hierarchic, the feudal; and the modern, the Protestant-rationalist, the individualist, the bourgeois.

Yet whilst attacking the priesthood Hobbes has a clear perception of the uses of religion for keeping the vulgar in order. The ancient Romans 'obtayned in order to their end, (which was the peace of the Common-wealth), that the common people in their misfortunes, laying the fault on neglect, or errour in their Ceremonies, or on their own disobedience to the lawes, were the less apt to mutiny against their Governors. And being entertained with the pomp, and pastime of Festivalls, and publike Games, made in honour of the Gods, needed nothing else but bread, to keep them from discontent, murmuring, and commotion against the state.'[1]

Hobbes's definition of religion sufficiently indicates his view of its purpose, and his own complete Erastianism: '*Feare* of power invisible, feigned by the mind, or imagined from tales publiquely allowed, RELIGION; not allowed, SUPERSTITION. And [with a blatantly cynical nod to the decencies] when the power imagined, is truly such as we imagine, TRUE RELIGION.' Religion, in fact, is an instrument of government, 'In all things not contrary to the Morall Law, (that is to say, to the Law of Nature), all Subjects are bound to obey that for divine Law, which is declared to be so, by the Lawes of the Common-wealth.' 'An opinion publiquely appointed to bee taught, cannot be Haeresie; nor the Soveraign Princes that authorize them, Haeretiques.'[2] The calmness with which Hobbes describes on paper and rationalizes the practice of all governments in his day takes one's breath away. He alone had the courage to justify the *cujus regio ejus religio* principles on which every government acted.

It is not surprising, therefore, that the great enemy for Hobbes is the claim to inspiration, to direct revelation, to be able to work miracles. Here he is attacking the sectaries on the left as well as the Papists on the right; and in the process his rigorous logic undermines the whole Christian position. 'To say [God] hath spoken to him in a Dream, is no more than to say he dreamed that God spake to him. . . . So that though God Almighty can speak to a man, by Dreams, Visions, Voice, and Inspiration; yet he obliges no man to beleeve he hath so done to him that pretends it; who (being a man) may erre, and (which is more) may

1 *Ibid.*, pp. 59–60.
2 *Ibid.*, pp. 26, 153, 316.

lie.' 'All the Miracle consisteth in this, that the Enchanter has deceived a man; which is no Miracle, but a very easie matter to doe. . . . For two men conspiring, one to seem lame, the other to cure him with a charme, will deceive many: but many conspiring, one to seem lame, another so to cure him, and all the rest to bear witnesse; will deceive many more.'[1] Hobbes denies possession by devils, even in those cases where the devil was cast out by Christ. He also denies the existence of a local hell or everlasting torment.[2]

It is quite clear, in fact, that Hobbes does not really believe in Christianity, in any normal sense of the word 'belief', and merely accepts it as the creed authorized in the state in which he lived.[3] 'It was . . . almost impossible for man without the special assistance of God, to avoid both rocks of atheism and superstition.'[4] God saves the situation by direct revelation; but we have already seen how dubious Hobbes is about claims to revelation as such. He is no Pascal, using scepticism to build up a firmer faith; he uses the existence of faith to inculcate scepticism. 'Shall whole Nations', he asks, 'be brought to *acquiesce* in the great Mysteries of Christian Religion, which are above Reason; and millions of men be made believe, that the same Body may be in innumerable places, at one and the same time, which is against Reason', and shall it be impossible to educate them into the more sensible principles of the Leviathan?[5]

Hobbes sneers at arguments based only on biblical texts. Those who employ them 'by casting atomes of Scripture, as dust before men's eyes, make every thing more obscure than it is; an ordinary artifice of those that seek not the truth, but their own advantage'.[6] He develops his own case by logic and rational demonstration first, then proceeds to bolster it up by texts, 'with submission nevertheless both in this, and in all questions, whereof the determination dependeth on the Scriptures, to the interpretation of the Bible authorized by the Common-wealth, whose Subject I am'.[7] Individual interpretation of the Scriptures, carried to its logical conclusion, means as many truths and schemes of salvation as there are citizens: Hobbes wants uniformity in the interest

1 *Ibid.*, pp. 200, 238–9.
2 *Ibid.*, pp. 351, 244, 342.
3 *Ibid.*, p. 241.
4 *English Works*, II, p. 227.
5 *Leviathan*, p. 180.
6 *Ibid.*, p. 329.
7 *Ibid.*, p. 241.

of stability. But his method again diminishes respect for the sacred books. He himself indulges in some daring historical criticism of the attributions of authorship of books of the Bible.[1]

Rather unexpectedly, though less so if we consider the social roots of his theories rather than the form those theories took, Hobbes approves of Independency so long as it does not degenerate into sectarian anarchy.[2] But that is really only a measure of his indifference, of his approval of the Independent separation of politics from theology, of the tendency of Independency to approach deism and rationalism. For though Hobbes is prepared through indifference to defend political intolerance, still tolerance – at least of opinions not translated into actions – is more natural to him. 'But what reason is there for it?' he asks of persecution. 'Is it because such opinions are contrary to true Religion? that cannot be, if they be true. Let therefore the truth be first examined by competent Judges, or confuted by them that pretend to know the contrary.'[3] Here Hobbes links up with the sceptical or deist aristocrats of the Restoration period, with the whole drift of political thought to the sort of practical toleration *de covenance* realized after 1688, in which considerations of expediency and the welfare of trade played a far greater rôle than the passion for liberty of a Milton. 'Forasmuch as some ease to scrupulous consciences in the exercise of religion may be an effectual means to unite their Majesties' Protestant subjects in interest and affection...' ran the preamble to the Toleration Act of 1689, frankly. This is how Hobbes put it: 'There is another Errour in their Civill Philosophy... to extend the power of the Law, which is the Rule of Actions onely, to the very Thoughts, and Consciences of men, by Examination, and *Inquisition* of what they hold, notwithstanding the Conformity of their Speech and Actions: By which, men are either punished for answering the truth of their thoughts, or constrained to answer an untruth for fear of punishment.'[4] It is not the noblest strain in which to plead liberty of conscience, but it has proved perhaps the most acceptable political argument; and it is one for which the author of *Leviathan* has received insufficient credit.

1 *Ibid.*, pp. 204–5.
2 *Ibid.*, p. 380.
3 *Ibid.*, p. 376.
4 *Ibid.*, p. 374.

IV

The scientific spirit of Hobbes is most clearly shown in the structure of *Leviathan* itself. Dr. Strauss has argued that all Hobbes's fundamental ideas existed before he became acquainted with the scientific ideas of his contemporaries, that the scientific method is imposed on Hobbes's material and does not grow out of it.[1] Even if true, this does not affect my main contention – that *both* Hobbes's philosophy *and* the scientific method grew out of one and the same social environment, and so naturally could be fused. I do not think Dr. Strauss is altogether convincing when he argues that the scientific method *conflicts* in any way with what Hobbes is trying to say: certainly Hobbes thought he was establishing 'the science of justice', lack of which had brought about the Civil War.[2] The style and form of *Leviathan* were undoubtedly influenced by the new sciences: that is why the book is so important in the history of English prose. Its construction is beautifully logical. Once we have started, it is almost impossible to break the chain of Hobbes's argument without going back to the beginning. He is self-consciously rigorous in his use of words. All his terms are defined in Book I, and a close attention to those definitions disposes of some of the alleged contradictions in the later chapters. For 'when men register their thoughts wrong, by the inconstancy of the significance of their words, ... they register for their conceptions, that which they never conceived; and so deceive themselves'.[3]

Hobbes tries to reduce the rational process to calculation. 'For REASON, in this sense, is nothing but *Reckoning* (that is, Adding and Subtracting) of the Consequences of generall names agreed upon, for the *marking* and *signifying* of our thoughts.'[4] This is a kind of Benthamite calculus, borrowed from the counting-house and the merchant's ledger: as bourgeois as Benjamin Franklin.

Together with this goes a denial of all metaphysical absolutes. Hobbes's corroding scepticism worked a revolution of destruction in the world of thought parallel to that which was taking place in institutions and social standards. Hobbes has no use at all for conventional moral exhortations. 'For one man calleth *Wisdome*, what another calleth *feare*; and one cruelty, what another *justice*. . . . And

1　Leo Strauss, *The Political Philosophy of Hobbes, passim.*
2　*English Works*, VI, p. 363.
3　*Leviathan*, p. 13; cf. pp. 15, 20, 21, 369.
4　*Ibid.*, p. 18.

therefore such names can never be the true grounds of any ratiocination.' Standards are entirely relative, except for Leviathan's arbitrary absolutes. 'Whatsoever is the object of any mans Appetite or Desire; that is it, which he for his part calleth Good.'[1] And this moves over to politics. 'The doctrine of Right and Wrong, is perpetually disputed, both by the Pen and the Sword: Whereas the doctrine of Lines, and Figures, is not so; because men care not, in that subject, what be truth, as a thing that crosses no mans ambition, profit or lust. For I doubt not, but if it had been a thing contrary to any mans right of dominion, or to the interest of men that have dominion, *That the three Angles of a Triangle, should be equall to two Angles of a Square*; that doctrine should have been, if not disputed, yet by the burning of all books of Geometry, suppressed, as farre as he whom it concerned was able.' The laws of nature, therefore, are precepts or general rules, found out by knowing the consequences, by book-keeping, by counting the cost.[2] A man would be irrational, unaware of his own best interests if he did not observe them, just as a merchant would be a fool if, having once learned to keep accounts, he let his affairs get into confusion by failing to keep them.

There are various hints which suggest that Hobbes would agree with Rousseau in holding that no true commonwealth, in his sense of the term, has ever yet existed: that he was legislating for the future. In the chapter 'Of Dominion Paternall, and Despoticall', he wrote: 'The greatest objection is, that of the Practise; when men ask, where, and when, such Power has by Subjects been acknowledged. But one may ask them again, when or where has there been a Kingdome long free from Sedition and Civill Warre. . . . For though in all places of the world, men should lay the foundation of their houses on the sand, it could not thence be inferred, that so it ought to be.'[3] 'So, long time after men have begun to constitute Common-wealths, imperfect, and apt to relapse into disorder, there may, Principles of Reason be found out, by industrious meditation, to make their constitutions (excepting by externall violence) everlasting. And such are those which I have in this discourse set forth.'[4]

Hobbes knows that a new world has come into existence, to which

1 *Ibid.*, pp. 18, 24.

2 *Ibid.*, pp. 18, 52–3, 66.

3 *Ibid.*, pp. 109–10; cf. p. 93. Clarendon takes this up, naturally enough: 'He will introduce a Government of his own devising'. (*A Brief View* . . . , pp. 46–7).

4 *Leviathan*, p. 179.

the standards of the old order will no longer apply. No revolutionary himself, all the assumptions of his approach to politics are new, radical, and 'bourgeois' – though stripped of the religious swaddling clothes in which opposition thought was still clothed. Rousseau had only to insist that sovereignty must and could lie in the people alone, in order to convert Hobbes's political philosophy into a revolutionary creed that would overthrow the thrones of Europe.

V

Combined with this scientific spirit we find in Hobbes what was its almost invariable accompaniment in the seventeenth century – materialism. This is flatly stated in Chapter 1, 'Of Sense': 'The cause of Sense, is the Externall Body, or Object'. It is only 'not knowing what Imagination, or the Senses are' that allows some schoolmen to say 'that Imaginations rise of themselves, and have no cause; ... that Good thoughts are blown (inspired) into a man, by God'.[1] 'A wooden top that is lashed by the boys, and runs about sometimes to one wall, sometimes to another, sometimes hitting men on the shins, if it were sensible of its own motions would think it proceeded from its own will, unless it felt what lashed it. And is a man any wiser, when he . . . seeth not what are the lashings that cause his will?'[2] 'The words *In-powred vertue, In-blown vertue*, are as absurd and insignificant, as a *round quadrangle*.'[3] This is politics of course: 'For who will endeavour to obey the Laws, if he expect Obedience to be Powred or Blown into him?'[4] Hobbes regards no philosophical question as academic, but sees that the most apparently abstract theories lead to practical conclusions. He attacks idealism as such. 'The causes of this difference of Witts, are in the Passions; and the difference of Passions, proceedeth partly from the different Constitution of the body, and partly from different Education.' He expresses his disbelief in an eternal soul which can exist separately from the body; and so denies dualism.[5]

Hobbes has also a fascinating historical sense, the product no doubt of his early preoccupation with historical studies. He is aware that ideas are coloured by the society in which they arise: 'Leasure is the mother

1 *Ibid.*, pp. 3, 8.
2 *Works*, V, p. 55.
3 *Leviathan*, p. 17.
4 *Ibid.*, p. 369.
5 *Ibid.*, pp. 35, 337–8.

of Philosophy; and Common-wealth, the mother of *Peace*, and *Leasure*: Where first were great and flourishing *Cities*, there was first the study of *Philosophy*.'[1] He makes an extremely shrewd criticism of the quality of scholastic thought when he points out that much of it cannot be translated 'into any of the moderne tongues, so as to make the same intelligible; or into any tolerable Latine, such as they were acquainted withall, that lived when the Latine tongue was Vulgar'.[2] That shows a real appreciation of the connection between living thought and living language, an awareness of the social nature of language and thought.

Hobbes turns to history, as Bacon did, for the application.[3] A striking feature of his thought, linking it again with Bacon and seventeenth-century science, is its domination by the idea of motion, change, development. Like a modern biologist, he asserts, 'The constitution of a mans Body, is in continual mutation.' 'Life it selfe is but Motion', 'Felicity is a continuall progresse of the desire, from one object to another; the attaining of the former, being still but the way to the later.'[4] 'The knowledge of the nature of motion', he says, is 'the gate of natural philosophy universal', which Galileo opened.[5]

This motion, as is clear from the passages last quoted, is conceived as a dialectical process. So too is thought. 'When in the mind of man, Appetites, and Aversions, Hopes, and Feares, concerning one and the same thing, arise alternately; and divers good and evill consequences of the doing, or omitting the thing propounded, come successively into our thoughts; so that sometimes we have an Appetite to it; sometimes an Aversion from it; sometimes Hope to be able to do it; sometimes Despaire, or Feare to attempt it; the whole summe of Desires, Aversions, Hopes, and Feares, continued till the thing be either done, or thought impossible, is that we call DELIBERATION.' 'As the whole chain of Appetites alternate, in the question of Good, or Bad, is called *Deliberation*; so the whole chain of Opinions alternate, in the question of True, or False, is called DOUBT. No Discourse whatsoever, can End in absolute knowledge of Fact, past, or to come.'[6]

Ideas are important for Hobbes because they lead to action. But rational theory may always come up against the irrational in practice.

1 *Ibid.*, p. 364.
2 *Ibid.*, p. 40.
3 Strauss, *op. cit.*, p. 89.
4 *Leviathan*, pp. 24, 30, 49.
5 *De Corpore*, Dedication.
6 *Leviathan*, pp. 28, 30.

Hobbes has an overwhelming sense of the obstructive power of vested interests to dangerous truths. In his final apologetic conclusion he is anxious to show that 'there is nothing in this whole Discourse . . . contrary either to the Word of God, or to good Manners; or to the disturbance of the Publique Tranquility'; and that it will in fact encourage men to obey and to pay taxes willingly. And here Hobbes sums up all the bitterness of his cynicism, all the penetration of his social analysis, and all his confidence in the ultimate triumph of rational science: 'For such Truth, as opposeth no mans profit, nor pleasure, is to all men welcome.'[1]

VI

Despite his materialism, we may guess that Hobbes believed in a God. He needed one because he was a materialist, as all materialists did before the rise of a theory of evolution. If the universe is composed of a given quantity of matter (and of nothing else), if mind is merely organized matter, and if there is no conception of progress, of historical advance, of evolution, then some intervention from outside is needed to set matter in motion (i.e. to create the world) and perhaps to organize matter into mind (i.e. to create man). 'Nothing can move itself.'[2] This view of God became fashionable in the eighteenth century, under the influence especially of Newton: the universe is a machine which God has wound up and set going. God is an abstraction, another word for scientific laws; but he is also the first cause, the Creator at the very beginning.

For Hobbes, God is absolute law, and therefore absolute power: for all law is command. 'To those therefore whose Power is irresistible, the dominion of all men adhaereth naturally by their excellence of Power: and consequently it is from that Power, that the Kingdome over men, and the Right of afflicting men at his pleasure, belongeth Naturally to God Almighty: not as Creator, and Gracious; but as Omnipotent'. This is far enough from evangelical Christianity; but has its affinities with Calvinism. 'Though Punishment be due for Sinne onely, . . . yet the Right of Afflicting, is not alwayes derived from mens Sinne, but from Gods Power'.[3] Since God is absolute power and absolute law, he is

1 *Ibid.*, pp. 391–2; cf. *The Elements of Law*, p. xvii.
2 *The Elements of Law*, p. 154.
3 *Leviathan*, p. 191. This book was in proof before I read Mr. Warrender's *Political*

completely unknowable. His nature and purposes are alike inscrutable; or rather he has no purposes: 'God has no ends'.[1]

It is because God, and God alone, has irresistible power, that the sovereign is ultimately responsible to him, though absolutely free vis-à-vis his subjects. The sovereign cannot be unjust to subjects (for his law determines what is just); but he can commit iniquity (for God 'prohibited all Iniquitie by the law of Nature'[2]). The law of nature is God's will because it is a scientific law: that is merely another way of saying the same thing. So sovereigns infringe the law of nature at their peril: it is their *duty*, as well as their interest, to govern well. This is a point sometimes forgotten by those who speak as though Hobbes allowed no checks on his sovereign. Actions which 'tend to the hurt of the people in general' are 'breaches of the law of nature', actions in conformity to which are required of sovereigns 'under the pain of eternal death'.[3] God is the sanction behind the laws of nature. 'Whether men will or not, they must be subject always to the Divine Power. By denying the Existence, or Providence of God, men may shake off their Ease, but not their Yoke'.[4] To deny God is for Hobbes to deny science.

Hobbes, then, like all seventeenth-century materialists, needed God for his philosophical system. As a consequence of his system he felt himself obliged to accept the religion authorized by the sovereign of his own country. So he does lip-service to Christianity. But this is not to say that Hobbes was a disguised atheist pretending to believe in God for fear of the consequences. His expressed views were so heretical as to make this unlikely. Atheism in the seventeenth century was a pose, a revolt, rather than a philosophical system. That is why rakehelly aristocrats like Rochester were so liable to death-bed conversions. No one had yet reached the point of being able to say that God was a hypothesis of which he had no need.

So Hobbes's philosophical system contains two assumptions: (1) the universe has a rational structure: physical and chemical laws exist and correspond to something in the real world; (2) in each man there exists, at least potentially, the natural light of reason, which *ought* to be able to

---

Philosophy of Hobbes. Though I disagree with him on some points of emphasis, Mr. Warrender's seems to me easily the best book on Hobbes.

1 *Ibid.*, pp. 53, 193–5; *English Works*, I, pp. 10–11.
2 *Leviathan*, p. 112.
3 *The Elements of Law*, p. 142.
4 *Leviathan*, p. 190.

grapple with the world, to understand its structure, to ascertain and follow its laws. Science is the knowledge of those laws. The chief obstacle to the accumulation of scientific knowledge is that man has to depend on his fallible sense impressions. Man is the only rational being on earth; but he is liable to err, to abuse language, to surrender to passion – and to use the reasoning faculty to deceive others. All scientific laws are difficult to establish, but the science of politics is especially difficult because it deals with men, not things: human interests and passions are involved. Nevertheless, 'the skill of making, and maintaining Common-wealths consisteth in certain Rules, as doth Arithmetique and Geometry; not (as Tennis-play) on Practise onely'.[1]

So the attempt to found a science of politics is the attempt to define the laws which govern, or should govern, human behaviour in society. The ultimate sanction for these laws is divine but, once the watch has been set in motion by the great watchmaker, it has its own laws of motion which can be ascertained by human reason. 'And it would be an incomparable benefit to the commonwealth, if every man held the opinions concerning law and policy here delivered.'[2] Hence the sovereign has not merely a right but a duty to instruct his people in Hobbism. He must 'convert this Truth of Speculation, into the Utility of Practice', in order to get his laws obeyed. If men do not recognize their obligations, that they have made covenants, then they will not keep them or enforce their keeping on others: and that will be to their detriment as well as to the sovereign's.[3] It is almost like Rousseau wanting men to be educated up to a point at which their wills coincide with the general will. 'Geometry', as Hobbes put it, 'is demonstrable, for the lines and figures from which we reason are drawn and described by ourselves; and civil philosophy is demonstrable because we make the commonwealth ourselves'.[4] Politics is a rational science because, although God made the universe, man made the state. That very important statement of principle witnesses to the emancipation of politics from God's direct intervention. The proper study of mankind has become man.

1 *Ibid.*, p. 110.
2 *The Elements of Law*, p. xviii.
3 *Leviathan*, p. 197; cf. *The Elements of Law*, pp. 145–6, and Adolfo Levi, 'La Filosofia di Thomas Hobbes', *Biblioteca Pedagogica Antica e Moderna Italiana e Straniera*, LIV (1929), p. 328.
4 *English Works*, VII, p. 184.

VII

Hobbes lost the confidence of the Royalists after the publication of *Leviathan*. He returned to England and accepted the Commonwealth. His *De Cive* had found enthusiastic readers in England in the sixteen-forties; but on the whole Parliamentarian theorists, with the exception of Nedham and Harrington, had little use for a man with the reputation of an irreligious absolutist. Yet gradually a change set in. Opposition to government looks rather different when you have become the government yourself. Ireton already spoke at Putney in purely Hobbist terms of 'covenants made' to the Leveller proponents of manhood suffrage and equal natural rights. So too we find parsons abandoning the claim that tithes are due by divine right, and beginning to claim them by the law of the land. As the 'anarchy' of 1659–60 intensified, and with it the fear of Levellers, Anabaptists, and Fifth Monarchists, so more and more of the propertied Parliamentarians came to long for stability, law and order, the command of a sovereign – everything that Hobbes had to offer them. Richard Baxter, near-Presbyterian divine, had little in common with the republican Ireton, and less with Hobbes; yet in his *A Holy Commonwealth*, published in 1659, he occupied much ground that is common to both. Sovereignty is indivisible, dual power is fatal to the stability of a state, any government is preferable to anarchy or civil war; the sovereign must control political speculation if social subordination is to be preserved: such Hobbist maxims came home to many a Parliamentarian in 1659 who had ignored them in the palmy days of 1641. Did it, after all, matter whether the sovereign's surname was Cromwell or Monck or Stuart, whether he was a man or a body of men, so long as he protected law and order and property?

So conservative Parliamentarians made their way towards some elements of the Hobbist theory of sovereignty by 1660. Many Royalists arrived at similar conclusions by a different route. Matthew Wren used Hobbist arguments against Harrington as early as 1657. The more intelligent members of the returned aristocracy and gentry had lost faith in their traditional ideas, and were not captivated by the Puritanism which the successful Parliamentarians were hastily discarding. Scepticism flourished among these court groups adapting themselves to a society dominated by money relations rather than by personal loyalties. They had been restored because the victorious Parliamentarians needed them, or some of them. The idealists on both sides were sacrificed: hard-faced business men like Downing and

Ashley-Cooper inherited the earth. The process is commented on bitterly by Samuel Butler, one of the victims: 'Oaths and Obligations in Affaires of the world are like Ribbons and Knots in dressing, that seem to ty something, but do not at all. For nothing but interest does really oblige'.[1] That is the underlying basis of the cynicism of Restoration comedy: Bunyan's Mr. Badman was a Hobbist. After the Restoration, Macaulay said, Hobbism 'became an almost essential part of the character of the fine gentleman'.[2] Our most religious King protected his old tutor from his enemies; gave him a pension of £100 a year; and hung up his portrait in his private room at Whitehall.

But the union which brought about the Restoration of 1660 did not last long. The Hobbism of court sceptics and dramatists went too far: Charles II's Hobbism indeed did not exclude Hobbes's greatest enemy, Popery. Radical Puritanism had been rejected because too revolutionary, too democratic: yet religion still had its social uses. The Royal Society laboured to reveal God in science and bishops as scientists: the ruling class turned gradually to 'rational Christianity', deism, tolerance. The two great enemies were atheism and 'enthusiasm'. So we find Locke synthesizing Hobbes and Milton, science and religion; and leaving out everything that had made religion exciting, much that had made science politically dangerous. The materialism of Bacon and Hobbes was discarded, and with it their confident and exclusive reliance on the scientific method for the progress of human thought. Science was necessary to economic advance, religion to political stability. So religion and science were reconciled by limiting the sphere of each. Locke's synthesis performed a social function invaluable for his class. But it was woefully incomplete, for it left out the dialectical element of thought which the Puritan revolutionaries and the early scientists had grasped. It was the dogma of a static civilization.

1 S. Butler, *Characters and Passages from Notebooks* (1908), p. 292, and *passim*.
2 Lord Macaulay, *History of England* (1905), I, p. 161.

TEN

James Harrington and the People

Bee there a writing nere so high,
The writer while he lives may die,
Blasted by scorne or envy-bitten;
But if hee die for what is written,
The pen how lowe so ere it bee
For ever lives, and so doth hee.

Lines said to have been carved by Harrington into
the wood above his prison door, 22 September 1662.[1]

I

THE COMMONWEALTH OF OCEANA was published in October or
November 1656. But James Harrington had started writing it seven
years earlier, after the execution of Charles I. It reflects the problems of
the years 1649–56. Though cast in the form of a political romance, it
was intended as a serious proposal for immediate implementation.

England was in need of a constitution. The original objects of those
men of substance who opposed the King had been to establish
parliamentary control of central government and taxation, to secure
their own liberties and properties. But the years after the war had seen
the emergence of democratic groups which wished to extend the gains
of the Revolution from the gentry and well-to-do citizens to the whole
population. It was under pressure from these radicals that the King had
been brought to trial and the Republic proclaimed in 1649. But no
democratic constitution was established. The Levellers were forcibly
suppressed. Four years of an oligarchic Commonwealth were then
succeeded by the expensive military dictatorship of Oliver Cromwell.

1 Written in a Moscow copy of the first edition of *Oceana*, quoted by Yu. M.
Saprykin in *Sredniye Veka*, IX, p. 381.

Cromwell failed to come to terms with one Parliament in 1654, and another met in September 1656 which was to offer him the Crown. The conservative Parliamentarians – the mass of the gentry and the City – scared by the democratic hornets' nest they had stirred up, wanted a restoration of the law and of the old known institutions, provided their rule was made secure against any return of absolutism.

Harrington's *Oceana*, and the stream of lesser writings in which he defended and explained it in the next three years, was intended to place the English Revolution in historical perspective, to show that there was an irreversible drift towards republican forms in England, and that the only 'settlement' which would last was one along the lines he recommended. In 1656, a month or two after Parliament met, he offered his proposals to Oliver Cromwell.

Harrington's personal position was peculiar. Like Thomas Hobbes – whose *Leviathan* had appeared in 1651, and which Harrington greatly appreciated – Harrington had been a spectator of the Civil War, not a participant. He was a theoretical republican, especially admiring the Venetian constitution. But he was also a friend of Charles I, and in 1648 was in trouble for arguing in favour of accepting the King's terms. His main concern in *Oceana* was to find a constitution which would preserve the essential gains of the Civil War, and yet protect the republic against what he regarded as the dangers of excessive democracy.

Harrington, whose brother later became a Fellow of the Royal Society, was deeply influenced by the seventeenth-century scientific movement: like Hobbes he hoped to make politics a science.[1] Unlike Hobbes, Harrington believed that the key to politics lay in history. Indeed its historical character is the novel feature of Harrington's thought, and what gives it permanent value. A student both of European politics and of classical antiquity, he saw the English Revolution in the setting of world history. For him there had been three historical epochs. First, the ancient world, whose best form of polity was the republic, given by God to the Hebrews and known also to the Greeks and Romans: its decline set in 'under the yoke of the Emperors'.[2] The collapse of the Roman Empire was followed by the establishment of what Harrington called 'the Gothic balance' – a society in which political and military power were held by an

1 See p. 260 above.
2 Harrington, *Works*, p. 43.

aristocracy. They owned the land and controlled its cultivators (their tenants), and so dominated the army. The 'Gothic balance' had in its turn been upset, in most European countries, through the acquisition of property by those whom Harrington called 'the people', though we shall see that by 'the people' he meant what we should call 'the middle class' – yeomen, merchants, gentlemen. The recent growth of the City of London coincided, in Harrington's view, with 'the declining of the Balance to Popularity'.[1]

The rise of this new class introduced a third epoch. 'The people' had acquired most of the land, and therefore had become independent of the aristocracy and monarchy. Armies were paid with their money, raised by taxation. Europe now lay 'tumbling and tossing upon the bed of sickness' in 'the dregs of the Gothic Empire': constitutions had become 'no other than a wrestling match' between King, nobles, and people.[2] The crises and civil wars of the sixteenth and seventeenth centuries Harrington explained as attempts to redress the balance[3] – either by re-establishing aristocratic monarchy by military force, as in France, or by establishing a republic – as in the Netherlands, Switzerland, or Venice – which would give political as well as economic power to the middle class. 'Where there is a Bank', said Harrington, 'ten to one there is a Commonwealth'.[4] His brother, the later F.R.S., was also a City merchant.

The European crisis took special forms in England. Henry VII, insecurely enthroned by a section of the aristocracy, introduced a series of 'anti-feudal' measures. He reduced the power of the barons by confiscating their estates and cutting down the number of their retainers. Henry VIII dissolved the monasteries, and distributed their land among 'the people' – i.e. those who could afford to buy it. The cumulative effect of these measures and of the transfers of land in the sixteenth century, Harrington thought, was that England became a republic in all but name. Queen Elizabeth was the equivalent of a Doge of Venice. 'Converting her reign thro the perpetual Lovetricks that past between her and her People into a kind of Romance', Elizabeth 'wholly

1 *Works*, p. 389.
2 *Ibid.*, pp. 203, 68.
3 'Balance' was a familiar commercial metaphor in the seventeenth century: balance of trade, balance of the constitution, balance of property. The concept of a balanced monarchy was often in the mouths of Parliamentarians. It came as naturally to business men as did the notion of contract.
4 *Works*, p. 247.

neglected the nobility'.[1] The economic foundation on which the monarchy had rested was destroyed; and therefore what Harrington called 'the superstructure', the political forms, could not survive. 'A Government founded upon the overbalance of Property, is legitimately founded, and so upon Justice; but a Government founded upon the underbalance of Property, must of necessity be founded upon Force, or a standing Army.'[2] Charles I's failure to build up a standing army meant that nothing could save the monarchy. 'Wherefore the dissolution of this Government caus'd the War, not the War the dissolution of this Government'.[3] Men were absolved from all obligation to 'a Throne which had no foundation'.[4]

II

Most historians find this analysis impressive. But it has been challenged recently, on the curious ground that its author was a declining member of the lesser gentry who was whistling in the dark to keep his courage up, by arguing against the evidence that 'the people' (i.e. the gentry and middle class) had been increasing in economic power.[5] I find this view unconvincing for many reasons. First, Harrington was not a declining gentleman. He was the son of a younger son of a younger son of an Elizabethan knight. For such a junior branch he was exceptionally well provided.[6] But his family was one of the most aristocratic in England. From Harrington's great grandfather, we are told, were descended eight dukes, three marquisses, seventy earls, twenty-seven viscounts and thirty-six barons.[7] One Harrington married Henry VIII's bastard, and their son was Queen Elizabeth's godson; another Harrington was the close friend of James I's eldest son, Prince Henry; a fourth was guardian of James's daughter, the future Queen of Bohemia. (This one seems to have suffered the not unusual fate of being ruined by holding court office.) Yet another

1 *Ibid.*, p. 69.
2 *Ibid.*, p. 487.
3 *Ibid.*, p. 70.
4 *Ibid.*, pp. 74, 391.
5 Trevor-Roper, *The Gentry, 1540–1640*, pp. 46–7.
6 Ian Grimble, *The Harington Family*, pp. 190–1. Some further corrections of Professor Trevor-Roper are to be found in *ibid.*, pp. 14, 72–3, 77, 129. I have profited greatly by discussing Harrington with Mr. Grimble.
7 J. Wright, *Antiquitys of the County of Rutland* (1684), p. 52, quoted in Toland's Life of Harrington, *Works*, p. xiii.

Harrington was offered the care of Charles I's younger children in 1649, but he refused. James Harrington himself was a personal friend of Charles I, whom he attended in captivity. One of his critics, writing in 1657, accused him of 'blasting a long line of ancestors' by his republicanism, and warned him that he was stirring up 'the ill affections of all the noble families to whom you stand in alliance'.[1] The fate of the lesser gentry was no direct concern of this patrician family.

Secondly, Harrington was not inventing his facts – or if he was, so were the best thinkers among his predecessors and contemporaries. Harrington himself refers to Ralegh, Bacon, James I, Selden, Sir Henry Wotton among those drawing attention to the social changes on which he based his theory: we might add Sir Thomas Wilson, Spelman, Bishop Goodman, Quarles, Henry Parker, Ireton, Winstanley.[2] These are not the least distinguished social thinkers of the age: against them Professor Trevor-Roper can quote only a few unsuccessful individuals. Harrington hardly imposed the theory of the balance of property on his contemporaries. It rose almost to the status of an orthodoxy whilst its author was languishing in jail. 'What can be opposed', Hobbes asked, 'against the consent of all men, in things they can know, and have no cause to report otherwise than they are (such as is a great part of our histories) unless a man would say that all the world had conspired to deceive him?'[3] Surely what matters is not the subjective reasoning which led Harrington to formulate his theory (and of which we know nothing) but the fact that the theory 'took on'. A book, in Herzen's expressive phrase, is merely a midwife. It assists at the birth, but is not to be held responsible for what is born.[4] Wyclif may or may not have evolved his heresies because of high blood pressure, as Mr. McFarlane recently suggested;[5] but Wyclif's blood pressure does

---

1 Ed. H. Harington, *Nugae Antiquae* (1769), I, pp. 84–5.
2 Tawney, *Harrington's Interpretation of his Age*, pp. 20–1. A recent writer even makes it ground for complaint against Harrington that he took it for granted that there had been large-scale transfers of land 'as a truth everybody knows' – as though this was a reason for regarding it as untrue (Pocock, *The Ancient Constitution and the Feudal Law*, pp. 130–1, 142–3). I also disagree with Mr. Pocock's view that Harrington was 'confused' in seeing feudalism in the Elizabethan system of clientage and retainers (pp. 140–2). But apart from these points at which he has been misled, Mr. Pocock's book is valuable. See p. 57, n. 4 above.
3 Hobbes, *The Elements of Law*, p. 21.
4 A. Herzen, *Selected Philosophical Works*, p. 50.
5 K. B. McFarlane, *John Wycliffe and English Nonconformity*, p. 85.

not explain why Lollardy won mass support. The history of thought is not the medical history of the thinkers.

Harrington systematized what many men had been vaguely feeling: his new contribution was his emphasis on the decisive significance of the economic foundation. If, he said, civil laws 'stand one way and the balance another, it is the case of a Government which of necessity must be new model'd; wherefore your Lawyers advising you upon the like occasions to fit your Government to their Laws, are no more to be regarded, than your Taylor if he should desire you to fit your body to his doublet'.[1] The old monarchy ('a Throne which had no foundation') had gone for good. Even if Oliver Cromwell accepted the Crown, or if the Stuarts were restored, they could never rule in the old way. Permanent stability and peace would be more likely under a republic, since it would best fit the balance. *Oceana* was a commonwealth.

III

Because the crisis which had been solved by civil war in England was a European crisis, England had the opportunity to bring liberty to other countries in which 'the Gothic balance' was tottering. Harrington advocated a revolutionary war, like that waged by Napoleon 140 years later: and indeed in the early sixteen-fifties it had seemed on the cards that the English republic, in alliance with the French Huguenots and perhaps the Dutch Republic, might have waged such a war.[2] Certainly the French government was desperately afraid of it. But Harrington was no Jacobin: he approved the subjugation of Ireland, and recommended an imperial expansion in which liberty should not be given to countries which he judged incapable of it. Ruling them would provide jobs for the English landed class – an early appreciation of the possibilities of Empire as a source of outdoor relief for the English aristocracy.

The downfall of 'the Gothic balance' in England had been due to the transfer of land from aristocracy to gentlemen, yeomen, and townsmen. Therefore it was essential, if a stable republic was to be preserved, to prevent any future concentration of property in the hands of a narrow group. Hence Harrington's most revolutionary proposal, his agrarian law. No landowner should be allowed to own land worth

1 *Works*, p. 59.
2 See above, pp. 118–30.

more than £2,000 a year: dowries were to be limited to £1,500. Primogeniture would be ended, estates being divided among all the children. By these devices, Harrington believed, the restoration of aristocracy and monarchy would be made impossible. 'An Agrarian is a Law fixing the Balance of a Government in such a manner that it cannot alter'.[1] Together with the agrarian law was to go secret ballot, to prevent landlords influencing Parliamentary elections. His complicated devices for voting by dropping balls into urns, which aroused much contemporary mirth, were perfectly serious arrangements to enable an illiterate population to vote secretly.

Harrington estimated that there were 300 landowners worth £2,000 a year and upwards when he wrote: under his agrarian law the number could never fall below 5,000, and would probably be considerably larger. This was no democracy. The supremacy of a class of rich landowners was assumed. Indeed Harrington's object was not only to protect his commonwealth from a restoration of the old monarchy and to show that a republic need not be 'that foul Beast, the Oligarchy',[2] such as had existed between 1649 and 1653, or a military dictatorship as in the years after 1653; his object was also to protect his commonwealth against what he regarded as the excesses of democracy. It is here that I believe his own social position is important. He was a member of the ruling class who was shrewd enough to see that the old basis of feudal society had gone for ever. But he retained a high opinion of the gentry, and a low one of the mass of ordinary men. He approved of the Revolution in which he had not participated, in so far as it had set the gentry free from the exactions of the monarchy: he did not wish to see gentlemen subordinated to their social inferiors. Such a possibility seemed to him mere anarchy, the overthrow of all political order. 'A People . . . reduc'd to misery and despair', he wrote, 'are beneath the Beasts'.[3] 'An Army may as well consist of Soldiers without Officers, or of Officers without Soldiers, as a Commonwealth . . . of a People without a Gentry, or of a Gentry without a People'. The making and governing of a Commonwealth 'seems to be peculiar only to the genius of a Gentleman'.[4] 'A Nobility or Gentry, in a popular Government not overbalancing it, is the very life and soul of it.'[5] One of Harrington's

1 *Works*, p. 291.
2 *Ibid.*, p. 479.
3 *Ibid.*, p. 151.
4 *Ibid.*, p. 56.
5 *Ibid.*, p. 42.

objects was to reconcile the people to the gentry, and even to the Royalists.[1] Just as the people, when 'under Lords, dar'd not to elect otherwise than as pleas'd those Lords', so Harrington believed that 'the People, not under Lords, will yet be most addicted to the better sort'.[2]

Let us consider more closely Harrington's use of the word 'people'. He described the sixteenth century as the period in which land passed from aristocracy to 'people'. But he must have known that this was the age in which countless poor tenants were evicted to walk the roads as vagabonds. 'The people' to whom Harrington referred, and to whom the land was in fact passing, had servants.[3] They were the gentry, merchants, and yeomanry. In *Oceana* 'servants' were not citizens. Now 'servants' in seventeenth-century parlance include wage labourers, all of whom were excluded from Harrington's franchise and from the army.[4] Full citizens were heads of households aged 30 and over. The point was made startlingly clear in a debate in the House of Commons in 1659. Then Captain Baynes (land speculator and Harringtonian) said 'Property, generally, is now with the people. . . . All government is built upon propriety, else the poor must rule it'. The poor were not people.[5] The division between freemen and servants in *Oceana* 'is not properly constitutive, but as it were natural'.[6] This attitude, of course, was not peculiar to the Harringtonians. Very few in the seventeenth century thought of the poor as having any rights at all. Locke certainly excluded them from 'the people'.

So though one object of *Oceana* was to establish a constitution which would protect the gentry from an absolute monarchy or military dictatorship, another was to protect 'the people' from the poor, from 'Robbers or Levellers'.[7] The fundamental laws are those which guarantee property.[8] Not only were the poor disfranchised in Oceana; citizens were divided into those with less than £100 a year and those with more: the latter (the richest yeomen and upwards) were over-represented in Oceana's Parliament. No one was to become an

1 *Ibid.*, pp. 56, 74.
2 *Ibid.*, p. 479.
3 *Ibid.*, p. 265.
4 Cf. the attitude adopted to servants in the Putney Debates by Harrington's friend Ireton.
5 Burton's *Parliamentary Diary*, III, pp. 147–8.
6 *Works*, pp. 436–7, 496–7.
7 *Ibid.*, p. 166; cf. pp. 264–5, 502.
8 *Ibid.*, p. 101.

alderman of London unless he was worth £10,000.[1] Elections to Parliament were indirect, and there was no single sovereign legislature; laws were proposed by a senate, representing an aristocracy of intellect, which Harrington made clear would also be a social aristocracy. The representative body voted on these laws without debate. So the 'better sort' had an absolute veto.

It may well be argued that Harrington's scheme was not so undemocratic as it seems. The Leveller plan for manhood suffrage, unchecked by secret ballot and indirect election, might have led to a return of the old régime if there had not been severe restrictions on the right to vote of Cavaliers and Presbyterians.[2] Richard Baxter criticized Harrington on precisely this point. 'Our common people', he wrote sternly in 1659, 'ordinarily choose such as their landlords do desire them to choose. . . . Let Mr. H[arrington] and his party get down the Army, and take off all the late restraints, and let parliaments be chosen by unrestrained Votes, and that party that hath most tenants, and that is most against Puritanes, will carry it'.[3] 'A free Parliament' was the Royalist slogan in 1660. Baxter had his own theological reasons for believing that it is 'next to an impossibility' that 'the Major Vote of the people should ordinarily be just and good'.[4] But Sir William Petty, who did not share Baxter's doctrinal prepossessions, agreed that 'the Elections in 52 shires and 211 Corporations are governed by lesse than 2,000 active men'.[5] Yet, when all this has been said, one still feels that Harrington really wanted safeguards against too much democracy.

IV

Harrington, like Hobbes, had a coldly secular attitude towards religion. He regarded the clergy (like lawyers) as bulwarks of reaction. The historian of toleration in England says that 'religious toleration enjoyed during the revolutionary period few stouter, more logical or more systematic defenders than James Harrington'.[6] He regarded religious toleration as essential to civil liberty:[7] but he disagreed with the radicals

1 *Ibid.*, p. 170.
2 *Ibid.*, pp. 432, 605, 609.
3 R. Baxter, *A Holy Commonwealth* (1659), pp. 236–7.
4 *Ibid.*, p. 94.
5 Ed. Lansdowne, *The Petty Papers*, I, p. 7.
6 W. K. Jordan, *The Development of Religious Toleration in England*, III, p. 288.
7 *Works*, p. 489.

of the period in that he wished to retain a state church and an endowed clergy. This was specifically because Harrington believed them essential to civil government.[1] His ministers were to be elected, by two-thirds or three-quarters of the parishioners, and paid at least £100 a year; but the democratic implications of this were modified by the requirement that they should have had a university education.[2] At the same time Harrington's rational approach to religion – he treated the Old Testament as a historical document to be examined and used like any other, and he described the rule of the saints as a mere oligarchy[3] – also made its contribution to the growth of a sceptical and tolerant spirit in the later seventeenth century.

Oceana was a nine day's wonder, especially towards the end of 1659, when almost any political experiment seemed possible. The famous Rota Club was visited by Pepys, Aubrey, Wildman. Royalists, Levellers, and Monck all expressed Harringtonian views. The Club collapsed at the Restoration, but as a purely secular political organization it may have been remembered by those who later used the Green Ribbon Club. The Rota's practice of voting by ballot was adopted by the Royal Society. In the short run Harrington was proved wrong in many respects. Charles II was restored – largely by the gentry, who thought monarchy a better protection against the lower orders than paper constitutions. The Restoration government clapped Harrington in jail, on an almost certainly false charge of conspiracy. He was never brought to trial, and went mad, some thought not without assistance from the prison doctor. He died in 1677. But in the long run his theories had greater success than he did. In 1660 he had prophesied that 'a Parliament of the greatest Cavaliers in England, so they be men of estates', would turn republican within seven years.[4] Seven years was too optimistic. But 1688 showed that there was sound sense in Harrington's prediction. James II tried to set the clock back behind 1640; and he was run out of the country and replaced by a Venetian Doge. England after 1689 was in Harrington's sense a republic. The gentry secured themselves very satisfactorily against King and people.

The theory that political power follows the balance of property was widely accepted in England in the late seventeenth and eighteenth centuries. In addition to Harrington's disciple or collaborator, Henry

---

1 *Ibid.*, pp. 516–17, 613.
2 *Ibid.*, pp. 87–8, 127, 450.
3 *Ibid.*, p. 488.
4 Aubrey, *Brief Lives*, I, p. 291, quoted above, pp. 182–3.

Nevill, whose *Plato Redivivus* was published in 1681, a long list of names could be quoted to show this – Dryden, Marvell, Mrs. Hutchinson, Algernon Sydney, Shaftesbury, Penn, Temple, Halifax, Locke, Defoe, Bolingbroke, Hume, Catharine Macaulay, Burke, John Millar. In 1700 Toland dedicated his edition of Harrington's *Works* to the City of London. *Oceana* did not have the honour of being burnt by the University of Oxford in 1683, with the political writings of Hobbes, Milton, and Baxter.

But after 1688 the emphasis shifted. Locke showed theoretically that property *ought* to rule, and enabled Defoe to state as a truism

> *'No man can claim a Power of Government,*
> *Where they that own the Land will not consent.'*[1]

But Harrington had also wanted to establish a balance between landowners and people. So far from an agrarian law limiting the concentration of landed property in few hands, the evolution of the strict settlement led to what he had wished to prevent – the consolidation of that landed Whig oligarchy which ruled England for the 150 years after 1688. Only in the nineteenth century was the perceptiveness of Harrington's analysis shown – that the propertied class could continue to rule even if the franchise was relatively democratic. Harrington also proposed some of the reforms realized even later – compulsory education to the age of 15, free for the poor; secret ballot, perpetual parliaments and payment of M.P.s, tax allowances for wives and children. His proposed limitation on dowries, Harrington believed, would end 'this wretched custom of marrying for Mony' and make possible marriage for love.[2]

v

Historians have often pointed out the influence of Harrington in the American and French revolutions of the eighteenth century. He had prophesied the American Revolution in a famous phrase about the colonies being 'yet Babes that cannot live without sucking the Breasts of their Mother Citys', but which would 'wean themselves' 'when they com of age':[3] and the men of 1776 remembered him. In 1779 it was

1 Daniel Defoe, *Jure Divino* (1706), Book V, p. 3.
2 *Ibid.*, p. 109; cf. pp. 332–56 below.
3 *Ibid.*, p. 44.

proposed to change the name of Massachusetts to Oceana. Harrington had also prophesied that if England failed to liberate Europe from the Gothic balance, France would do so:[1] and again Harrington was remembered. In 1792 a draft French constitution was modelled on his book. *Oceana* was translated into French in 1795. The division of France into departments, in order to obliterate the memory of the old feudal territorial provinces, may have sprung directly from one of Harrington's proposals. But it is worth noting the nature of his influence. John Adams, Harrington's American disciple, insisted that 'the great art of lawgiving consists in balancing the poor against the rich'. In France it was after Thermidor that interest in Harrington became widespread. The translation of 1795 was intended as an anti-Robespierrist document. The constitution of 1800 was probably Harrington-influenced; and Napoleon proclaimed that 'property is the fundamental basis of all political power'.[2] As in the English Revolution, Harrington's ideas took on when the Revolution was turning conservative; they protected the rich against the poor as well as against a restoration of the ancien régime. In England too, although one edition of the People's Charter had as frontispiece a Harringtonian device for dropping balls into urns,[3] Harrington's influence was in fact greater on early aristocratic republicans like Mrs. Macaulay than on later more plebeian democrats.

So Harrington helps to demonstrate not only the essential unity of the three great revolutions, but also the similarity of the problems set for the propertied classes in those revolutions when the overthrow of the old order had led to the emergence of democratic movements. Harrington has been called a precursor of Marx, but he never even approached that conception of class struggle as the motive force in history which Marx held to be his chief contribution: one object of Harrington's theory, on the contrary, was to explain the English Revolution as a natural phenomenon, and so to *exclude* the political activity of the masses of the population. Harrington was what Marxists call an economic determinist: he conceived of economic change as a blind impersonal force which somehow produced political change of its own accord, without the lever of mass political action. Law proceeds from will, either the will of one or few or many; and 'the Mover of the

1 *Ibid.*, p. 203.

2 H. F. Russell Smith, *James Harrington and his Oceana*, pp. 194–210.

3 I am indebted to Mr. John Saville for drawing my attention to this edition. A writer in *The Northern Star* of 2nd January 1847 referred to Harrington in terms of eulogy.

Will is Interest'.[1] Yet even here he was muddled, for he explained the economic transformation in England by arbitrary actions of Henry VII. And Harrington's own agrarian law was an attempt to control the movement of history not by human actions but by 'skill in . . . Political Architecture . . . wherof the Many are incapable'.[2] But until Marx it is difficult to think of anyone except Vico who had Harrington's breadth of historical vision.

I follow a recent historian in stating Harrington's achievement in three propositions: (1) 'History has a law, which may be comprehended.' (2) The causes of historical change are to be sought 'not in man's nature, but in his situation'. (Harrington wrote history 'in terms, not of man's character, but of the social structure'.) (3) So human actions can counteract the degeneration to which all constitutions are liable: once the laws of history are known, revolutions can be prevented by adjusting the balance.[3]

His weakness, his fear of democracy, is that of his class and time. For his class the Revolution had been directed not only against the Stuart monarchy, but also against the peasantry whom that monarchy (to maintain the Gothic balance) had tried to protect against eviction. The victorious gentry in the Revolution abolished feudal tenures for themselves, whilst preserving copyhold for their tenants.[4] In 1660 they replaced Charles II's revenue from feudal tenures by an excise – Harrington's favourite tax, which fell most heavily on his 'servants'. Primogeniture was strengthened, not weakened. Sovereignty of Parliament was used, in the eighteenth century, to facilitate enclosure and expropriation, which increased the numbers of that working class which Harrington had wished to exclude from citizenship. So the gentry, in their turn, as Harrington dimly foresaw, ultimately upset the balance which he had hoped to maintain. The 'servants' fought for and won the franchise, and founded the Labour Party.

1 *Works*, pp. 240–1.
2 *Ibid.*, p. 391.
3 Pocock, *op. cit.*, pp. 144–6.
4 See pp. 173–4 above.

ELEVEN

The Mad Hatter

The finer thou art in cloathes, Silver and Gold, fine Houses and
Lands more than thy fellows or thy neighbors, so much the more
hath the Curse of God power over thee.

> Roger Crab, *Dagons-Downfall; or The great Idol*
> *digged up Root and Branch* (1657), p. 13.

I

SOBER as a judge, drunk as a lord, black as a sweep: all these proverbial
expressions are self-explanatory, since they describe a condition which
is naturally incident to the occupation in question. But why mad as a
hatter? No obvious reason suggests itself why this trade should render
men especially liable to insanity. The answer appears to be that the
proverbial madness of hatters derives from one particularly notorious
example, Roger Crab, hatter at Chesham in the mid-seventeenth
century. Crab studied his New Testament carefully, and came across
the words 'If thou wilt be perfect, go and sell that thou hast, and give to
the poor'. Crab was not a rich young man, but he wanted to be perfect.
So he sold all he had, and gave it to the poor. Naturally all good
Christians thought him mad. If the text extended to us, Crab pictured
the rich saying, 'we should make the Poor richer than ourselves'. They
would rather deny Scripture than part from their riches.[1]

Roger Crab was an interesting character in many ways. He was born
somewhere in Buckinghamshire in 1621. He tells us that his mother
had £20 a year, or his father would never have married her:[2] they were

---

1 R. Crab, *The English Hermit, or Wonder of this Age*, in *Harleian Miscellany* (1745),
IV, p. 461. All quotations are from this source unless otherwise indicated. I have taken
some biographical details from *D.N.B.* and from F. Roberts, 'One of Cromwell's
Soldiers', *The Treasury*, I (1903).
2 *Dagons-Downfall*, p. 2.

not the poorest of the poor. About 1641 the young Crab, already seeking perfection, vowed to restrict himself to a diet of vegetables and water, avoiding butter, cheese, eggs and milk. 'Eating of Flesh is an absolute Enemy to pure Nature', he declared. He also decided to remain celibate, perhaps in despair of finding a lady who would accept his vegetarian régime. Next year war broke out between King and Parliament, and Crab joined the Parliamentary army. He served in it for seven years. On one occasion he was 'cloven through the skull to the brain', and once he was condemned to death by his Commander-in-Chief, Oliver Cromwell, and imprisoned for two years by Parliament. Punishments of such severity can only have been for political offences, and it may be suspected that Crab was involved in the Leveller agitation of 1647–9.

On demobilization he set up as a 'haberdasher of hats' at Chesham, where he lived from about 1649 to 1652. He can never have been very successful during the three years he carried on the business, since he held it a sin to make a profit even before he finally demonstrated his madness by giving away all his property to his poorest neighbours. He retained only enough to lease a rood of land at Ickenham, near Uxbridge, for 50s. a year. Here he built himself a house, and settled down to lead the life of a hermit. He quickly won a reputation as a herbal doctor, probably because he gave his patients the sensible advice to abstain from flesh and strong beer. He had often over a hundred patients at a time, he tells us, and was much sought after by women. He also indulged in prophecy, and was denounced as a witch by a local clergyman. He made his own clothes, of sackcloth, and wore no band, the seventeenth-century equivalent of a neck-tie. He thought it wrong to have a suit of Sunday best, since that was to observe times and seasons. As time passed he dropped luxuries like potatoes and carrots from his diet: he subsisted on bran broth and a pudding of turnip leaves and bran boiled together. Finally he got down to dock leaves and grass. On this diet he claimed to be able to live at a cost of ¾d. a week. In his old age he allowed himself the delicacy of parsnips. In 1657 he moved to Bethnal Green. He died in 1680, at the age of 59, and was buried in Stepney parish.

In the early sixteen-fifties John Robins, the Ranter, who believed he was God Almighty, prescribed a diet of vegetables and water for his disciples, many of whom died of it.[1] The same fate overtook Crab's one

1 L. Muggleton, *The Acts of the Witnesses* (1699), pp. 21, 46. See p. 128 above.

convert, a Captain Norwood of his regiment. This was probably the officer of that name who had Leveller connections. Norwood was associated with Theaureaujohn, who 'laid about him with a drawn sword at the Parliament House' a week after Augustine Garland and Sir Anthony Ashley-Cooper had moved that Oliver Cromwell be offered the title of King. Theaureaujohn was also a disciple of Robins.[1] In Bethnal Green, Crab joined the Philadelphians, a religious sect founded by John Pordage. Pordage was also a man with a radical political past. He had Theaureaujohn to stay with him in his house at Bradfield, near Reading, as well as 'one Everard', whom the *Dictionary of National Biography* identifies with Robert Everard, but who was more probably William Everard the Digger.[2] Pordage was accused of saying that he cared no more for the higher powers than for the dust beneath his feet. There would soon, he thought, be no Parliament, magistrate or government in England: the Saints would take over the estates of the wicked for themselves, and the wicked should be their slaves.[3] Pordage held 'visible and sensible communion with angels', one of whom commanded him to take no more tithes; 'but, since, he conceives he hath a dispensation', and was 'scandalously covetous' in exacting fees, although another story said he was 'much against Propriety'. He was alleged to have defended polygamy and said that marriage was a very wicked thing.[4] We should discount these hostile accounts, many of which Pordage himself denied; but it is clear that Crab's chosen minister was one who had moved on the extreme radical fringe, among Ranters and perhaps Diggers.

II

Crab wrote several pamphlets, including an autobiography, *The English Hermit, or The Wonder of the Age*, published in 1655. He had an interesting theology. Soul and body, he thought, are separate entities,

1 Ed. Lomas, Carlyle's *Letters and Speeches of Oliver Cromwell*, II, p. 394. Norwood is probably the Robert Norwood quoted on p. 71 above. He wrote an introductory epistle for one of Theaureaujohn's pamphlets, and is mentioned in others. See pp. 76, 128 above for Theaureaujohn (Thomas Tany).

2 J. Pordage, *Innocence appearing Through the dark Mists of Pretended Guilt* (1655), p. 9 and *passim*.

3 Christopher Fowler, *Daemonium Meridianum* (1656), pp. 172–7, quoted in G. P. Gooch, *English Democratic Ideas in the 17th century*, p. 266.

4 Pordage, *op. cit.*, pp. 16–19, 34, 91; *Reliquiae Baxterianae*, I, pp. 77–8.

which can be divided in life as they will be after death. The soul in natural (i.e. sinful) man is subject to the body, is indeed enslaved to the flesh. The only way to win true happiness is to make the body subject to the soul. This was the object of Crab's ascetic practices, his vegetarianism and celibacy. Here is his description of how he reduced his body to obedience: 'The old Man (meaning my Body), being moved, would know what he had done, that I used him so hardly. Then I showed him his Transgression. . . : so the Wars began. The Law of the Old Man, in my fleshly members, rebelled against the Law of my Mind, and had a shrewd Skirmish; but the Mind, being well enlightened, held it, so that the old Man grew sick and weak with the Flux, like to fall to the Dust. But the wonderful Love of God, well pleased with the Battle, raised him up again, and filled him full of Love, Peace, and Content in Mind. And [he] is now become more humble; for now he will eat Dock-leaves, Mallows or grass, and yields that he ought to give God more thanks for it than, formerly, for roast Flesh and Wines.' We are reminded of St. Francis of Assisi by this combination of extreme asceticism with a friendly attitude towards the body, seen as an alien entity.

Crab continued to hold many traditional Leveller views. Here is his account of the Civil War and its aftermath.[1] God 'hath tried almost every Sort of Men, and every Sort of Sects' in the government. First 'the King and Bishops were exalted'. Then 'the Parliament, who found Fault with them, not pulling the Beam of Covetousness out of their own Eyes, and their Sects depending, were all exalted instead of the other'. Thirdly, 'the Army, with their Trades and Sects depending upon the same Account, became exalted. So the Gentlemen and Farmers have had their Turn in Offices, . . . and now they will try inferior Trades, as Journeymen and Day-labourers . . . even to the Orphan and Almesman. . . . It will be a hard Matter for a low Capacity to judge which of all these Parties hath been most just. But I, being of the lowest Sort, and unlearned, being amongst Day-labourers and Journey-men, have judged myself with them the worst of all these Parties.' Bad as all the others had been, Crab thought, there was not much to be said for 'labouring poor Men, which in Times of Scarcity pine and murmur for Want of Bread, cursing the Rich behind his Back; and before his Face, Cap and Knee and a whining countenance'.

---

1 It may be derived from Joseph Salmon's *A Rout, A Rout: or, some part of the Armies Quarters Beaten up* (1649), p. 3.

So he concluded that all the social groups which had tried their hands at government during the Interregnum were equally unfitted for the task. The moral he drew was that fighting solved nothing. Like many an ex-Leveller Quaker, he became a pacifist, and washed his hands of responsibility for civil government. For all our fighting 'in pretence of Liberty and Peace', for all 'our fighting to regulate Government in the old Man, we see it still as bad [as], if not worse than it was before'. But – again like the early Quakers – Crab retained much of the fierce radical criticism of the existing social order, government and Church. 'All our proprieties', he wrote, 'are but the fruits of Gods curse'. Property causes 'the Murderer to kill, and the Thief to steal'. Hence Crab disapproved of the death penalty. How, he asked, can a man love his neighbour as himself 'whilest he encroacheth more Land, a finer House, or better Cloathing or dyet then his neighbor?'[1]

The Church for Crab was 'the old jade', 'that House of the Whores merchandise', a 'Bawdy-house'. To keep Sunday was 'to observe her Market-Day'. The Sabbath was 'an abominable idol' he told some J.P.s who objected to his habit of working on Sunday just like any other day. At Ickenham he was put in the stocks for this. He had no mercy for those enemies of Milton, the Levellers and Quakers – 'hireling priests', 'tithe-mongers', all ministers who did not depend on the voluntary offerings of their congregations. 'Pimps and Pandors' was Crab's elegant phrase for the clergy. Oxford and Cambridge, he thought were 'the Whores great eyes'. He made many offers to meet any minister in public disputation of the king beloved by the early Quakers; but these offers, he tells us, were never accepted. The sort of subject he wished to debate was: If the elect are chosen from all eternity, can priests convert a man not predestined to salvation? If not, how do they earn their money? One can see why there was a certain reluctance to debate with him.[2] Crab was also interesting on marriage, in regard to which he took an unusually feminist view. The husband, he complained, says he endows his wife with all his worldly goods; but in fact she has no legal right to dispose of them. Marriage is a purely economic transaction. The priest 'administers the Ordinance of Marriage, which he calleth of God, although they bargain and swop like Horse-Coursers'.[3]

Crab's vegetarianism and teetotalism were part of a political and

1 *Dagons-Downfall*, pp. 5–7, 13.
2 *Ibid.*, pp. 3–5, 24–8, 2, 12.
3 *Ibid.*, pp. 4, 15; cf. p. 2.

social programme. Drink and gluttony, he thought, raised the price of corn, and so led to high prices, high rents and oppression of the poor. Teetotalism was by no means typical of the early Puritans: we remember Oliver Cromwell telling the Governor of Edinburgh Castle that 'Your pretended fear lest error should slip in is like the man that would keep all wine out [of] the country lest men should be drunk'.[1] Crab was one of the earliest preachers of the sort of teetotalism that was to have a long history in English Nonconformity. It is interesting to find that for him it was already associated with political radicalism, just as it was to be for such advocates of total abstention as some of the Chartists, Keir Hardie, and Tom Mann. At one time Crab had accepted the conventional view that 'if we should not wear superfluous Things, Thousands of People would starve for Want of Trading, and so by Consequence bring greater Evil upon us'. But, by considering the birds and coming 'to know God in Nature', he learnt better. (Gerrard Winstanley the Digger also found God in nature.) The problem of poverty, Crab felt, could be solved by the poor for themselves if they freed themselves from that dependence on the things of the flesh by which the rich enslaved them.

Crab was very scathing about rich 'Christians'. 'If John the Baptist should come forth again, and call himself Leveller, and take such Food as the Wilderness yielded, and such Cloathing, and preach up his former Doctrine, "He that hath two Coats should give away one of them, and he that hath Food should do likewise", how scornfully would our proud Gentlemen and Gallants look on him, that hath gotten three or four Coats with great Gold and Silver Buttons, and Half a Score dainty Dishes at his Table, besides his gallant House and his Furniture therein. Therefore this Scripture must be interpreted some other Way, or else denied'. That is what men do 'if the Scripture will not serve our own Ends to fulfil selfish Desires, to uphold the old Man in his fleshy Honour'. 'Thus we see for the love of this world people are destroyed'. (With John the Baptist calling himself Leveller we may compare Winstanley's statement in 1650 that 'Jesus Christ ... is the head Leveller'.[2]) Crab ended, as Winstanley did in some of his pamphlets, with some lines of verse:

> 'Such are our Lusts and Covetousness,
>   The Belly and Back to please,

---

1 Abbott, *Writings and Speeches of Oliver Cromwell*, II, p. 339.
2 Sabine, *op. cit.*, p. 390.

With selling and buying, dissembling and lying,
      Yet we cannot live at Ease;
But still in Discontent abide,
      Desiring after more. . . .
If Pride should banish'd be away,
      Then Tradesmen out would cry:
"Come let us kill, eat, and slay,
      Or else for Want we die."
Then would the Gentry mourn,
      Without Pride they cannot live,
And Slaves to get them Corn,
      Whilst they themselves deceive.
Thus Pride becomes our God,
      And dear to us as Life;
Whose Absence makes us sad,
      And cannot please our Wife.
If the poor labouring Man
      Lives of his own increase,
Where are your Gentry then
      But gone among the Beasts?'

But, with the resignation common in the sixteen-fifties among former members of the defeated radical groups, Crab had no hope of immediate and rapid improvement. The conservative forces in society were too strong. The Fifth Monarchists hoped for the direct political intervention of Christ to bring about a change: Crab dreamed of a scarcely less miraculous inner revolution, without which political reform would not achieve its purpose. 'Let not the rich Men mistake me, and think that I would have them sell their Goods, before God hath enlightened their Understandings, and let them see the Danger of keeping it, for them they would play the Hypocrites, and do as Bad to themselves, as if they had kept it, although Good to others.' There was not much danger of social revolution here. And Crab's conclusion was

      'If Men and Angels do prove silent, then
      Why should not I, an inferior Man?
      Now am I silent, and indite no more:
      Pray use no Violence then against the Poor.'

Crab thus marks a curious transition. He looks back to St. Francis of Assisi and those mediaeval ascetics who strove to overcome the world by contracting out of it. But he also looks forward to those Nonconformist radicals who believed that man's life here on earth could be made better, and that the way to control the blind forces which rule our competitive society was through individual self-mastery.

We may conclude by quoting Crab's epitaph, since it not unfairly states his claim to the sympathetic remembrance of posterity:

> 'Tread gently, reader, near the dust
> Committed to this tombstone's trust;
> For while 'twas flesh it held a guest
> With universal love possesst –
> A soul that stemmed opinion's tide,
> Did over sects in triumph ride.
> Yet, separate from the giddy crowd,
> And paths tradition had allowed,
> Through good and ill report he passed,
> Oft censured, yet approved at last.
> Wouldst thou his religion know?
> In brief, 'twas this, to all to do
> Just as he would be done unto.
> So in kind Nature's laws he stood,
> A temple undefiled with blood,
> A friend to everything that's good.
>
> The rest angels alone can fitly tell.
> Haste thee to them and him. And so farewell.'[1]

1 Roberts, *op. cit.*, p. 1086.

TWELVE

John Mason and the End of the World

Methought I heard the Midnight Cry,
  Behold the Bridegroom comes:
Methought I was call'd to the Bar,
  Where Souls receive their Dooms.
The World was at an End to me,
  As if it all did burn:
But lo! There came a Voice from Heav'n,
  Which order'd my Return.

Lord, I return'd at thy Command,
  What wilt thou have me do?

John Mason, 'A Song of Praise for Deliverance from
  imminent Dangers of Death', *Songs of Praise*, 1683.

Man would be God, and down he fell,
  To teach him better Skill;
Yet he lifts up his bruised Bones
  Against his Maker still.

'A Song of Praise for the Patience of God', *ibid.*

I

THE doctrine that the end of the world is approaching, that Christ is
coming to rule with his saints in the millennium, is as old as
Christianity. It can be a harmless hope for a kingdom that is not of this
world. But in moments of acute social crisis some of the devoutest
believers may see signs that the kingdom is at hand, and may decide
that it is their duty to expedite its coming. At such moments millenarian
doctrines become equivalent to social revolution.[1] In the sixteenth and

---

1 Peter Worsley's *The Trumpet Shall Sound*, and N. Cohn's *The Pursuit of the
Millennium*, give fascinating accounts of revolutionary millenarianism, the first in

seventeenth centuries the prevalent form of this revolutionary doctrine was Fifth Monarchism. The four monarchies of Babylon, Persia, Greece, and Rome had passed away: the monarchy of Christ was imminent. Earnest men studied *Daniel* and *Revelation*, and identified the Little Horn of the Beast with whoever was their enemy of the moment. Since God's kingdom was about to be established, all earthly power which might compete with it must be rejected, nay overthrown. So Fifth Monarchism had the effect of a theory of anarchism. The state was evil.

In 1534–5, under John of Leyden, an attempt was made at Münster to realize the kingdom of God upon earth. Attacked by all the conservative forces of Germany, the Anabaptist leaders of the commune introduced a régime of 'war communism' – private property was requisitioned, buying and selling were prohibited, communal meals were established; ultimately polygamy was introduced. The commune of Münster was bloodily suppressed: henceforth its memory and that of John of Leyden remained as a horror story to make the flesh of heretics creep, or to justify suppression of the lower orders if they chanced to get out of hand. The thirty-eighth article of faith of the Church of England is directed against Anabaptist communism: 'The riches and goods of Christians are not common as touching the right, title and possession of the same, as certain Anabaptists do falsely boast'. The forty-first article of 1552, omitted in the Elizabethan prayer-book, was aimed specifically against the millenarian doctrine. In 1594 Thomas Nashe, in *The Unfortunate Traveller*, expressed a typical ruling-class attitude when he spoke of John of Leyden and his fellows as 'such as thought they knew as much of Gods minde as richer men'.[1] It was not for the poor to give themselves such airs. In the sixteen-forties Oliver Cromwell, Sir Arthur Hesilrige, and John Lilburne were all referred to as 'John of Leyden' by political enemies wanting to discredit them. But for the more radical groups Münster was not a horror story at all. The Leveller William Walwyn spoke of 'that lying story of that injured people . . . the Anabaptists of Münster'. Another Leveller, Richard Overton, asked 'Who writ the Histories of the Anabaptists but their Enemies?'[2] John Bunyan is said to have

---

Melanesia during the past century, the second in parts of Europe during the Middle Ages.

   1 Ed. Philip Henderson, *Shorter Novels, Elizabethan and Jacobean* (Everyman ed.), p. 285.

   2 Haller and Davies, *The Leveller Tracts, 1647–53*, p. 374; Haller, *Tracts on Liberty in the Puritan Revolution*, III, p. 230.

reflected the ideal of Münster in his picture of the town of Mansoul in *The Holy War*. In 1658 he had announced 'The judgment-day is at hand'.[1]

Many in the seventeenth century believed the end of the world was imminent. King James I himself considered that the contempt for the clergy shown by all classes of Englishmen was a 'signe of the latter dayes drawing on'.[2] Joseph Meade's *Clavis Apocalyptica* (1627), John Archer's *The Personall Raigne of Christ upon the Earth* (1641), and Hanserd Knollys's *A Glimpse of Sions Glory* (1641), were only three of many tracts published in the foreboding years which preceded the Civil War. Grotius was told that 80 such treatises had appeared in England by 1649. A respectable academic, later Fellow of the Royal Society, devoted much ingenuity to elucidating the mathematical problems which he believed were set by the book of *Revelation*. In September 1645 the Scot Robert Baillie wrote home from London: 'The most of the chief divines here, not only Independents but others, are express Chiliasts' (i.e. Millenarians).[3] 'Doomsday' Sedgwick was peculiar only by his imprudence in predicting the end of the world for next week. Milton was thus in good company when he wrote of Christ as 'shortly expected King'.

Indeed in the sixteen-fifties the doctrine had become almost a commonplace. In 1651 Brian Duppa advised a learned friend to take a year to think over his treatise on Antichrist before inflicting it on the world. The friend replied, in all seriousness, 'But what if the world shall not last so long? . . . I am confident it will not.' The near approach of the millennium was accepted by many who drew from it conclusions very different from those of the theologians or the social revolutionaries. Thus a speaker in the Barebones Parliament thought it important that 'the seas should be secured . . . in order to prepare for the coming of Christ'; and the author of *The Coming of Christs Appearing in Glory* knew 'of nothing more important than matters of trade, as tending to strengthen the position against all eventualities'.[4]

1 E. Troeltsch, *The Social Teaching of the Christian Churches*, II, p. 709; J. Bunyan, *Works* (1860), III, p. 722.

2 Ed. C. H. McIlwain, *The Political Works of James I*, p. 330.

3 Hugonis Grotii, *Epistolae* (Amsterdam, 1687), p. 895, quoted in G. F. Nuttall, *Visible Saints*, p. 157; Francis Potter, *An Interpretation of the Number 666* (1642); Baillie, *Letters and Journals*, II, p. 156. Cf. Hobbes, *The Elements of Law*, p. 40.

4 Ed. Sir Gyles Isham, *The Correspondence of Bishop Brian Duppa and Sir Justinian Isham, 1650–60* (Northants. Record Society, 1955), p. 37; C. Wilson, *Profit and Power*,

In 1643 soldiers in the Parliamentary army had repeated rumours that Christ would return to destroy King Charles: the Earl of Essex was rather surprisingly cast for the role of John the Baptist.[1] Revolutionary Fifth Monarchist doctrines spread among the middle and lower classes especially after the military suppression of the Levellers and Diggers in 1649–50 and the dissolution of the Barebones Parliament in 1653. Some former radicals took their defeat to mean that Christ's kingdom was not of this world: they drifted into the Quakers and similar sects in which pacifism and abstention from politics were ultimately to prevail. Others hoped to obtain through divine intervention what they had failed to win by political action. The sceptical John Pell wrote to Thurloe in March 1655, not unsympathetically: 'Men variously impoverished by the long troubles, full of discontents, and tired by long expectation of amendment, must needs have great propensions to hearken to those that proclaim times of refreshing – a golden age – at hand, etc. Nor is it a wonder that some should willingly listen to those that publish such glad tidings, under the name of the kingdom of Christ and of the saints; especially when so many prophecies are cited and applied to these times.'[2]

When in 1653 Oliver Cromwell was accused of personal ambition, the Fifth Monarchist Colonel Harrison said that Cromwell 'sought not himself, but that King Jesus might take the sceptre'. A Major Streater replied 'Christ must come before Christmas, or else He would come too late.' Streater was right. In December of that year, after the Barebones assembly had been dissolved, Vavasor Powell told his congregation to go home and pray, 'Lord, wilt thou have Oliver Cromwell or Jesus Christ to reign over us?'[3] In 1659–60 even a sober and intelligent politician like Sir Henry Vane supported the millenarians in opposing an oath against government by a single person; the Fifth Monarchists were expecting the Second Coming in the near future, and it would never do for King Jesus to be excluded in advance by act of Parliament.[4] In 1657, and again in 1661, Fifth Monarchist

---

p. 76; Glass, *The Barbone Parliament*, p. 52.

1 *Journal of Sir Samuel Luke* (Oxfordshire Record Society, 1947), p. 76.

2 Vaughan, *The Protectorate of Oliver Cromwell*, I, p. 156. Pell proposed emigration as a remedy. Cf. Fuller, *Mixt Comtemplations on These Times* (1660), in *Good Thoughts in Bad Times* (1830), pp. 270–3.

3 Abbott, *Writings and Speeches of Oliver Cromwell*, II, p. 634; Gardiner, *History of the Commonwealth and Protectorate*, III, p. 5.

4 F. P. G. Guizot, *History of Richard Cromwell and the Restoration of Charles II* (1856), II, p. 474; *C.S.P., Dom., 1659–60*, p. 207.

plots headed by the wine cooper Thomas Venner aimed to overthrow the government. They proposed to confiscate the estates of their enemies and to put them into a common treasury. In 1661, under the slogan 'For King Jesus!' a few Fifth Monarchist rebels held the City of London terrorized for days.

So throughout the period 1535–1661, certain characteristics are associated with Fifth Monarchism. First, Fifth Monarchists preach anarchist revolt against the state. In 1591 William Hacket proclaimed in London that Christ Jesus was come, and incited the lower classes to rise against the government. Secondly, this lower-class emphasis recurs. 'The voice that will come of Christ's reigning', Hanserd Knollys declared, 'is like to begin from those that are . . . the vulgar multitude, the common people'. It was a Fifth Monarchist ironmonger who in 1655 tried to organize a strike among nailers around Birmingham.[1] Thirdly, the accusation of communism (and of sexual promiscuity) is regularly made against Fifth Monarchists, often unjustly; though of course there were communist groups which were not Fifth Monarchist, like the Diggers. Finally, Fifth Monarchism had come to the surface in England during the Interregnum, and so was associated in the public mind with the Parliamentary cause, and especially with the left wing of the revolutionaries.

All these points should be borne in mind when we turn to the case of the Rev. John Mason.

II

Mason was born about 1646 in the neighbourhood of Wellingborough, Northants, where the Leveller rebel Thomson was finally captured in 1649, and where a collective farm was set up in 1650. After taking his M.A. at Clare Hall, Cambridge, Mason became vicar of Stantonbury, Bucks. Stantonbury was practically a deserted village, with no vicarage house: Mason was probably in fact chaplain to Sir John Wittewronge, who had been a Parliamentary officer in the Civil War. In 1674 Mason was presented to the rectory of Water Stratford, just west of Buckingham, by the widow of Sir Peter Temple, formerly a member of the Rump.[2]

1 H. Knollys, *A Glimpse of Sions Glory*, quoted in Woodhouse, *Puritanism and Liberty*, p. 234; W. H. B. Court, *The Rise of the Midland Industries*, pp. 62–3.
2 For Mason's career, in addition to *D.N.B.* and the sources cited below, I have

Until about 1690 Mason's career was orthodox. In 1683 he published his *Spiritual Songs*, which have their place in the early history of English hymnology and were very popular; by 1761 the book was in its sixteenth edition. Isaac Watts borrowed freely from Mason's hymns, and they are believed to have influenced John and Samuel Wesley. But at this stage Mason was by no means unorthodox. He adopted the covenant theology, and one of his disciples quoted John Preston: 'The making men new Creatures, is all the Miracles we have now left'.[1] Mason praised the Sabbath as 'England's Glory', in the best Puritan manner, and with the rather quaint metaphor 'This Market-Day doth Saints enrich'.[2] Richard Baxter, who died in 1691, is reported to have called Mason 'the glory of the Church of England'.[3] He certainly would not have said that if he had lived three years longer.

In 1671 Mason published a sermon which he had preached at the funeral of Mrs. Clare Wittewronge two years earlier. In this he dwelt lovingly on the Day of Judgment: 'It's wonderful to think, what infinite honours and privileges shall be conferred upon us (poor dust and ashes) in that day.' We shall be made Christ's 'Assessors whiles he is judging the world. . . . The very thought of Christs last Appearance, how sweet it is to a believing soul'.[4] The expression was perhaps odd; but there was no implication here that the Judgment Day was imminent. Twenty years later, however, Mason published another sermon, which he had already preached many times, under the title of *The Midnight Cry*. In this he argued that all the signs suggested that the Second Coming was at hand. 'We cannot say, Christ comes this Night, or next . . . but it is near'.[5]

Mason ultimately came to believe that Christ's reign of a thousand years on earth would begin in 1694. This date had been fixed on by a German professor Alsted, writing from the safe distance of 1627. Alsted's writings had been translated into English in 1642 and 1643, and were known to Mason. But other authorities favoured a date in the

---

used J. L. Myres, 'John Mason: Poet and Enthusiast', *Records of Bucks.*, VII (1897), pp. 9–42.

1 Ed. the Rev. John Mason (grandson of our John Mason), *Select Remains of John Mason* (1745), p. 34; Thomas Ward and Valentine Evans, *Two Witnesses to the Midnight Cry* (1691), p. 13. Preston is disguised as 'Dr. Prestian', but his identity can hardly be in doubt. See pp. 221–5 above.

2 John Mason, *Songs of Praise*, pp. 32–3.

3 *Select Remains*, p. xii; Ward and Evans, *op. cit.*, p. 22.

4 John Mason, *The Waters of Marah Sweetened* (1671), p. 19.

5 John Mason, *The Midnight Cry* (2nd ed., 1691), p. 21.

sixteen-nineties – John Archer, for instance, and Hanserd Knollys, who both wrote in 1641. Rather later, Thomas Beverley, rector of Lilley, Herts., predicted the end of the world for 1697. He was still alive in 1698, and wrote a book to prove that the world *had* come to an end without anybody noticing it. It appears to have been about 1693 that Sir Isaac Newton began an intensive study of the books of *Daniel* and *Revelation* in order to find out when the end of the world was due. There was a considerable consensus of opinion that it was imminent.[1]

> *'The Bride saith, Come; O come, O come!*
> *Thy Saints in France say, Come;*
> *So say the British, Irish, Dutch,*
> *And spacious Christendom.'*[2]

John Mason also believed that Water Stratford was 'the very Spot of Ground where his Standard was to be set up'. (*His Standard Set Up* had been the title of a manifesto issued by Venner in 1657.) Only on this Holy Ground – a plot south of the village, round the rectory – was safety to be found. The rest of the kingdom would be destroyed.[3] Mason held the rigid Calvinist view that most men are so bad that they cannot be redeemed: they will only corrupt the rest of God's subjects, and so are to be destroyed. 'His Preaching did commonly border upon the Predestinarian Points, and did often make his Hearers Melancholy, and now and then in danger of Despair'. We are hardly surprised. Nevertheless his preaching was very popular with 'the common People, and especially the Women'.[4]

Mason thought he was a messenger or harbinger of Christ, who would soon appear visibly in Water Stratford. He ceased to administer the sacrament, and preached on no other subject than the coming millennium. On Easter Monday, 1694, he saw Christ 'sitting in a chair' in his room. The Saviour told him that he would 'appear in the Air over Water-Stratford and judge the World on Whitsunday following'. Mason described this vision through his window to the crowd outside

1 Perry Miller, 'The End of the World', in *Errand into the Wilderness*, p. 228. See *The Trial and Condemnation of the Two Witnesses unto the Late Midnight Cry* (Anon., 1694), p. 5, for other prophecies of the end of the world at about the same date.

2 Hymns printed at the end of *The Midnight Cry*, p. 3.

3 H. Maurice, *An Impartial Account of Mr. John Mason of Water-Stratford* (1695), p. 4.

4 *Ibid.*, pp. 27, 39; *Select Remains*, pp. 76–7; Browne Willis, *The History and Antiquities of . . . Buckingham* (1755), p. 344.

the rectory, and repeated it to the Duke of Richmond and other 'noble Persons', who had forced their company upon him despite his refusal to receive them. Henceforwards Mason used no prayer but 'Thy kingdom come'. The reign on earth had already begun, and Christ was here with his disciples, though not visibly.[1] As one of Mason's followers put it, 'King William reigns properly in Scotland, ruling and governing, not being personally there'; so Christ would not dwell personally on earth, but would rule and govern from a distance.[2]

This was not the first vision Mason had experienced. Years previously he had upset a Mrs. Pashler by telling her that she had walked and talked with him for some distance at a time when she had been miles away. On that occasion Mrs. Mason persuaded Mrs. Pashler to take no notice of what her husband said, 'for it was nothing else but one of Mr. Mason's melancholy Fancies, and he was often subject to 'em'.[3] But Mrs. Mason died in 1687 and, like most of us, Mr. Mason obviously needed a good woman to keep him in order. It may be added that some attributed his delusions to excessive smoking. 'I seldom visited him', said a contemporary, 'but he was envelop'd in clouds of Smoke. . . . Generally while he smok'd he was in a kind of Ecstacy, and all his People flock'd about him to receive his Communications'.[4]

He attracted disciples to the Holy Ground of Water Stratford. Its normal population was about 100. A number variously estimated at from 100 to 400 began to squat there continuously; and many hundreds more of well-wishers came and went. Alarmingly enough, they practised communism. 'They had all things common among them at their first coming together, which was Thursday in Easter Week. They had £50 worth of cheese; And they have now (the Tuesday seven-night before Whitsuntide) 6 Fat Cattle, 60 Fat Sheep, 6 Milch Cows, 30 quarters of Wheat, besides other Provisions. Their Beds are in the House, several in a Room, and in the Barn'.[5] So many people living so huddled together naturally gave rise to dark rumours. And indeed some at least of those who came to Water Stratford did so

1 Maurice, *op. cit.*, p. 14; *Some Remarkable Passages in the Life and Death of Mr. John Mason* (Anon., 1694), p. 3; *A Letter from A Gentleman in Bucks., near Water-Stratford, to his Brother, Mr. Thomas Pickfat* (Anon., 1694), p. 5.

2 Ward and Evans, *op. cit.*, p. 21.

3 Maurice, *op. cit.*, pp. 35–6.

4 *Ibid.*, p. 52.

5 *Ibid.*, p. 5; *Some Remarkable Passages*, p. 4; *A Letter from A Gentleman*, pp. 4–5.

because they got free board and lodging. Those who were 'Poor, and having nothing to put into the Stock' were ultimately 'turned off'. One lady broke open a drawer and robbed her husband of money to contribute to Mason's funds.

There were more women and children than men among the settlers, and their behaviour at times verged upon the eccentric. There was continual praying, dancing, and singing. Their dancing was 'in no order, but after an Antick manner, sometimes Three taking hands and jumping round, other while leaping from one end of the Room to the other', with much clapping of hands and chanting of 'Appear, Appear, Appear'. This made 'a prodigious Noise', and the dancers were 'all in a sweat'. 'They usually entertained all sorts of Vagabond-Fiddlers, Singing-Boys, or Wenches, and hir'd them to stay with them, because they thought our Saviour would have all sorts of Musick to attend Him'. They sang Mason's hymns set to ballad tunes (this was a habit of the sect of the Muggletonians), accompanied by the music of violin, tabor, and pipe. This addition of vagabond singing wenches to the already rather heterogeneous population of the godly may have brought some complications with it.

Here is an example of one of their hymns:

> 'Our Jesus this Day is Proclaim'd in our Streets,
> He's visibly Crown'd and he's highly renown'd
> From the East to the West, from the North to the South:
> 'Tis the Language I hear in every one's Mouth,
> That Jesus is King; let us Joyfully sing
> Our Jesus is King, our Jesus is King.'[1]

('For King Jesus!' had been the slogan of Venner's revolt in 1661.)

'They are for the most part men of mean parts that pretend to this Revelation', admitted one of Mason's disciples, whereat 'some are offended'. Why did Mason, a learned man, turn to the ignorant, he asked; and replied 'You may as well wonder why the Noble and Learned, and Wise of this World, do not chiefly experience the Mysteries of the Gospel'.[2]

In the spring of 1694 Mason's behaviour became increasingly odd. He retired into an inner room and refused to communicate with the

---

1 *A Letter from A Gentleman*, pp. 6, 9; Maurice, *op. cit.*, pp. 32–3; Browne Willis, *loc. cit.*

2 Ward and Evans, *op. cit.*, pp. 14, 21–2.

outside world except through two lay disciples. His illness – quinsy – developed rapidly, and in May he died, leaving behind him 'A Short Paraphrase and Comment upon the whole Book of Revelation', and another unfinished essay on the same subject.[1] God had assured Mason that he should not die, his sister-in-law informs us; and his disciples expected him to rise again on the third day. Some of them thought they had seen him and spoken to him. They refused to believe that he was dead, and went on expecting his reappearance even after his successor in the living had had the corpse exhumed. Many had to be ejected from the Holy Ground. Thomas Ward, one of the favoured disciples, wrote of Mason's message, 'If I should grant this a Delusion, O! how it would break my Faith all in pieces!' Believers in the Second Coming of John Mason were still dancing and singing his hymns at a house in Water Stratford in 1710. The sect seems to have survived until about 1740.[2]

> 'It was a waking Dream they would conclude,
> A Juggle which our Senses did delude:
> Or did we something see? And something hear?
> Yet whence it came it doth not yet appear.'

So Mason, in the sober days of 1683, had warned those who asked for 'an Emissary from above', whose 'very Sight a future State would prove'.[3] But, in the words of his pious and Nonconformist grandson, 'It must be acknowledged . . . that towards the Close of Mr. Mason's Life, this fair and beautiful Scene was much discoloured. His fervid Zeal, and warm Affections for the Honour of Christ (attended with the Decays of Nature) betrayed him into some Excesses in the Millenarian Scheme, which no judicious Christian can approve. – A lasting Monument of this plain Truth, viz. That the greatest Piety doth not secure the best of Men from Mistakes'.[4]

III

Few would dissent from this conclusion. But perhaps we can derive

---

1 *Select Remains*, p. xv; Browne Willis, *op. cit.*, p. 345.
2 *Some Remarkable Passages*, pp. 5–8; Ward and Evans, *op. cit.*, p. 11; Browne Willis, *op. cit.*, p. 345.
3 *Songs of Praise*, pp. 177–9.
4 *Select Remains*, p. xiii.

other, no less profitable truths from Mason's career. For over a century millenarianism had been a socially terrifying doctrine, associated with violent revolution. As recently as 1661 Venner and his followers had set all London in a panic by proclaiming 'Jesus is King'. Mason collected far larger crowds together, under suspicious circumstances. Moreover, they were crowds of the lower orders – those to whom the revolutionary aspect of Fifth Monarchist teaching had traditionally appealed. And they thought that 'No Magistrate can meddle with them'.[1] Mason specifically taught that the poor were to be saved, not the rich: he did not even bother to discuss his opinions with learned men, regarding them as hopeless. (His early poem 'Dives and Lazarus' had contained some eloquent denunciations of the rich.) Even the traditional – and often incorrect – association of Fifth Monarchism with communism and sexual irregularities was recalled. Mason's followers on the Holy Ground of Water Stratford owned their property in common. Mason himself had written, even in his orthodox early days: 'We have nothing that we can properly call our own, but what we have reason to be ashamed of'.[2] Mason's unsympathetic biographer bracketed John of Water Stratford with John of Leyden, and referred specifically to Hacket and Venner. He addressed his book, as a horrible warning, to those 'who look upon all Government as Anti-christian'.[3]

If guilt could be proved by association, Mason's case looked bad. He was born near Wellingborough, which had Leveller and Digger associations. His patrons had been members of the Parliamentary party in the Civil War. One of the greatest influences on him was John Wrexham, formerly minister of Hampden's parish of Great Kimble.[4] In 'A Song of Praise for the Gospel', again one of his early productions, Mason seemed to go out of his way to identify himself with the Parliamentary cause. (We must recall that he was born about 1646):

> 'England at first an Egypt was;
>   Since that, proud Babel's Slave;
> At last a Canaan it became,
>   And then my Birth it gave.
> Blest be my God, that I have slept
>   The dismal Night away,

---

1 *A Letter from A Gentleman*, p. 4.
2 *Select Remains*, p. 2.
3 Maurice, *op. cit.*, pp. 55–6, 1.
4 *Ibid.*, pp. 41–2.

Being kept in Providence's Womb,
To England's brightest Day.'[1]

On the face of it, it all looked very suspicious.

Here then were all the traditional lower-class revolutionary doctrines preached, and even carried into action. Yet the government does not seem to have been bothered. The ecclesiastical authorities also appear to have taken no action at all against this Anglican clergyman. Consider what Laud would have done only sixty years earlier! The panic the restored Government of the early sixteen-sixties would have got into! What a transition! Religion had at last been divorced from politics. Within a generation since Venner's rising a new sceptical attitude had developed. Pamphlets were published about Mason not to denounce him with horror and detestation, but to make money out of him.

The new attitude is shown especially in the very cool biography of Mason written the year after his death by an Anglican clergyman who had known him well. This treats Mason as mentally ill. He suffered from 'excessive Vapours'. The author records a conversation between Mason and a Mr. Ives. Mason: 'I am sure ... that Christ is now entering upon his Reign here, as really and truly as ever King Charles, King James, or King William Reign'd; but mistake me not, for I do not mean that he will sit in the Parliament-House, etc.' This made Mr. Ives advise him 'to let Blood speedily'.[2]

That is what it had come to. The Royal Society had done its work. The age of reason had arrived.[3] The age of revolutionary Puritanism, with its heroes, its passions, its eccentricities, was over. For 150 years the proclamation of the millennium had roused the lower classes to revolt, had shaken the established foundations of society. Now, like John Mason, it was dead. Monmouth's rising in 1685 had seen the final defeat of the Good Old Cause, of the heirs of the radical revolutionaries of the Interregnum; and already in Monmouth's revolt, though his support came mainly from Nonconformists, the slogans and aims were political rather than religious. When, a century later, the lower classes raised their heads again, it was with the secular ideologies of Jacobinism, Radicalism, Chartism, Socialism: only a few village Messiahs proclaimed the Second Coming in the bad years after 1815.[4]

1 *Songs of Praise*, p. 25.
2 Maurice, *op. cit.*, pp. 40–1.
3 P. Miller, *Errand into the Wilderness*, esp. p. 232.
4 G. D. H. Cole and R. Postgate, *The Common People, 1746–1938*, p. 233.

Henceforth millenarianism became a harmless hobby for cranky country parsons. The Little Horn, the Scarlet Woman, and the precise significance of 'a time, times, and half a time' were relegated to that dim twilight in which the Lost Tribes of Israel wander around the Great Pyramid.

So the end of the world ended with John Mason – not with a bang, not even with a whimper, but with a sympathetic clinical analysis.[1]

1 I wrote more about the end of the world in my *Antichrist in 17th Century England* (1971).

THIRTEEN

Society and Andrew Marvell[1]

A gentleman whose name is Mr. Marvile; a man whom, both by report and the converse I have had with him, of singular desert for the State to make use of; who alsoe offers himselfe if there be any imployment for him.

John Milton to President Bradshaw, 21 February 1653.

Amongst these lewd revilers the lewdest was one whose name was Marvell. . . . He . . . daily spewed infamous libels out of his filthy mouth against the King himself. If at any times the Fanatics had occasion for this libeller's help, he presently issued out of his cave like a gladiator or wild beast.

Samuel Parker, Bishop of Oxford, *History of his own Time*, quoted in Masson's *Life of Milton*, VI, p. 708.

I

AT first sight the poetry of Andrew Marvell seems to bear little relation to the age in which he lived. Marvell wrote a good deal of political satire, which is of considerable interest to the historian, but of less poetic value; his greatest poems (except the 'Horatian Ode upon Cromwel's return from Ireland') have no direct reference to the political and social revolution of the seventeenth century. Yet this revolution transformed the lives of Englishmen; it faced them with intellectual and moral decisions which it was difficult to evade. I believe that if we study Marvell with a knowledge of the political background of his life we can discover in the great lyrics new complexities which will increase our appreciation of those very sensitive and civilized poems.

Marvell was born near Hull in 1621, his father being a clergyman whom Andrew described as 'a conformist to the established rites of the

1 See F. W. Bateson, *English Poetry*, pp. 96–101, for criticisms of this essay.

Church of England, though none of the most over-running or eager in them'.[1] Marvell went to Cambridge, then much the more Puritan of the two universities, and remained there until 1640. He then travelled on the Continent for four or five years, during which period the Civil War between Charles I and his Parliament broke out. Most of Marvell's friends at this time seem to have been aristocratic young cavaliers of the type he was likely to meet in continental salons; and when he returned to England his own sympathies were apparently Royalist. But we have no real evidence for his activities, and little for his views, until 1650, the year after the execution of Charles I. Then he wrote the 'Horatian Ode upon Cromwel's return from Ireland', from which it is clear that he was prepared to accept the triumphant revolution. In the following year he became tutor to Mary Fairfax, daughter of the famous general who had led the Parliamentary armies to victory.[2] This suggests that he was already accepted as a sound Parliamentarian. The period in Yorkshire with the Fairfaxes and the years immediately following seem to have been those in which his greatest poetry was written.

In his early thirties Marvell emerged as a more active supporter of the new government. In 1653 he was personally recommended by no less a person than Milton as his assistant in the secretaryship for foreign tongues.[3] Marvell failed to get this post then, becoming tutor to a ward of Oliver Cromwell instead. But in 1657 Marvell became Milton's colleague in the Foreign or Latin secretaryship. Like Pepys, he was one of the new type of civilian middle-class official who came into their own after the Civil War, during the soberer years of the Protectorate. In 1659 Marvell was elected M.P. for Hull, for which he continued to serve in successive parliaments until his death in 1678. His correspondence shows him to have been an indefatigable defender of the interests of his constituency. But his main activity was as a pamphleteer for the Parliamentary opposition to Charles II's govern-

1 *The Works of Andrew Marvell*, ed. Grosart, III, p. 322.
2 Alas! the girl whom Marvell used as a symbol of ideal virtue in 'Upon Appleton House' (see below) came to no good end. She was married to the second Duke of Buckingham (Dryden's Zimri) in 1657. The marriage caused something of a sensation at the time. For Buckingham, son of Charles I's hated minister and himself a notorious Cavalier, used the Fairfax marriage as a means for recovering his confiscated estates, the General giving Parliament his personal security for his son-in-law's good behaviour. It was hoped that other Royalists would follow Buckingham's example in thus making terms with the Protectorate. But Oliver Cromwell died in 1658, and after the Restoration Buckingham in his turn was able to protect Fairfax.
3 See epigraph.

ments and as a defender of religious liberty and freedom of thought, the struggle for which had originally attracted Milton and no doubt Marvell to the Parliamentary side.

Despite his early Royalist phase, then, Marvell became decidedly a partisan of the cause of Parliament: he was intimate with its noblest figures. He was not only the protégé of Milton, but also the friend of Harrington, shrewdest of the Parliamentarian political thinkers, and of Baxter, most resolute of Nonconformist divines. Marvell accepted the Revolution only in his late twenties; he was no juvenile or light-hearted enthusiast. But unlike Dryden, who took service under the Protectorate at the same time as Marvell, and who wrote eulogies of Oliver Cromwell which afterwards proved embarrassing, Marvell did not leave the ship when it began to sink. In the dark days after 1660 he retained his dangerous friendship with Milton, and his partisanship became increasingly open. He invented the nickname Cabal, which has stuck to the government of Clifford, Arlington, Buckingham, Ashley, and Lauderdale. Marvell dealt roughly with the sycophantic Samuel Parker; see epigraph to this chapter. He ran great risks by the outspokenness of his attacks on the cynical extravagance of the court, the brutalities of the advocates of religious persecution and the treacherous activities of the pro-French party at court.

Marvell's oft-quoted remark about the Civil War, 'The Cause was too good to have been fought for', does not mean what those who cite it out of its context appear to think – that Marvell was disavowing 'the Good Old Cause'. He meant, on the contrary, that the war *should* not have been fought because it *need* not have been fought, because the victory of Parliament was inevitable, war or no war. Here Marvell was following the historical and political theory of his friend James Harrington,[1] in just the same way as Halifax did later in his *Letter to a Dissenter*: 'You Act very unskilfully against your visible Interest, if you throw away the Advantages, of which you can hardly fail in the next probable Revolution. Things tend naturally to what you would have, if you would let them alone, and not by an unseasonable Activity lose the Influences of your good star, which promiseth you every thing that is prosperous.'[2] For Marvell, after saying the cause was too good to have been fought for, continued – with an exaggeration pardonable if we

---

1 See pp. 271–4 above. Marvell was a member of Harrington's Rota Club in 1659–60.
2 The Marquess of Halifax, *Complete Works* (1912), pp. 139–40.

recollect that he was writing under Charles II's censorship – 'The King himself, being of so accurate and piercing a judgement, would soon have felt where it stuck. For men may spare their pains where Nature is at work, and the world will not go the faster for our driving. Even as his present Majesty's happy restoration did itself, all things else happen in their best and proper time, without any need of our officiousness.'[1]

II

'The Warre was begun in our streets before the King or Parliament had any armies', wrote Baxter,[2] another of Marvell's friends, in whose defence some of his greatest pamphlets were later to be written. As the tension within society became more acute, so a new type of lyric arose, charged with the most intense feeling of the age. These lyrics, unlike the Elizabethan, were no longer intended to be sung: they had lost their social function, and existed only to resolve the conflict within the poet's mind. The poet has become an isolated individual in a divided society, and his own mind is divided too: we find this internal conflict in poets so dissimilar as Marvell's early friend Lovelace, Crashaw, and Vaughan.

A characteristic of the conceit, indeed, from Donne to Traherne (precisely the revolutionary period) is that it lays incompatibles side by side, that it unites the apparently unrelated and indeed the logically contradictory, that it obtains its effects by forcing things different in kind on to the same plane of reference. In this broad sense we may speak of the lyric of conflict, whose characteristics are an awareness in the poet's mind of the new and troubling (especially the new scientific discoveries) as well as the old and familiar, and an effort to fit them into a common scheme – first by the violent and forced juxtaposition of Donne, then by the unresolved conflict of the later metaphysicals; until finally, after the victory of the new political and intellectual forces, we get a new type of poetry drawing on new philosophical assumptions, and disturbed by none of the doubts which have tormented the sensitive since the days of Shakespeare.[3] The tortured conceit gives

1 *Works*, III, p. 212. Marvell's view of history is further analysed in Sections VI and VII below.

2 *A Holy Commonwealth* (written by Richard Baxter at the invitation of James Harrington, Esq., 1659), p. 457.

3 Swift, of course, is an exception to this general acceptance of the new synthesis;

way to the neatly balanced rhymed couplet. This new equilibrium satisfied poets less and less in the second half of the eighteenth century but was not finally upset until the fresh social and political crisis of the French Revolution – and Wordsworth.

The existence of a conflict of some sort in Marvell is apparent from the most careless reading of his poems. At the risk of alienating readers by an excessively crude and over-simplified statement, I wish to say briefly and dogmatically what I think may have underlain this conflict, and then to try to prove and illustrate this thesis. The suggestion is that Marvell's poetry is shot through with consciousness of a conflict between subjective and objective, between the idea and the reality, which it is perhaps not too far-fetched to link up (very indirectly, of course) with the social and political problems of his time. This conflict takes many forms, but we can trace a repeated pattern, a related series of symbols, which suggests that fundamentally all the conflicts are interrelated, and that this 'double heart' (Marvell's phrase) is as much the product of a sensitive mind in a divided society as is Day Lewis's 'divided heart'.[1] That of course is one reason why Marvell and the other 'metaphysical' poets have so attracted our generation.

One of Marvell's qualities which is most sympathetic to us is his humour, his refusal to take his agonies too seriously. This is in itself one of the aspects of the 'double heart', Marvell's ability to see both sides; but it also shows his attempt to come to terms with and to control the contradictions between his desires and the world he has to live in, his ideals and the brutal realities of the Civil War. Humour is for Marvell one way of bearing the unbearable: it is a sign of his enviable maturity, besides which Waller, Cowley, Dryden, and the other ex-Royalist and future Royalist panegyrists of Cromwell look so shabby. The opening lines of the 'Horatian Ode' perfectly illustrate this aspect of Marvell's manner:

> *'The forward Youth that would appear*
> *Must now forsake his* Muses *dear,*
> *Nor in the Shadows sing*
> *His Numbers languishing.'*

---

but I think his personal and political abnormalities could be explained in terms which would confirm rather than weaken the generalization.

1 Cf. Richard Sibbes: 'A kind of doublenesse of heart, whereby wee would bring two things together that cannot suit' (*The Soules Conflict*, 1635, p. 469). The phrase no doubt derives from *James*, i. 8.

Less than three years after writing these lines Marvell offered his services to the Parliamentary cause, which he was never to desert in the remaining twenty-five years of his life. The light touch, the self-mockery, the hatred of the portentous which are obvious in these lines should not obscure for us the genuine doubts and struggles, conflicts and despairs, which had preceded Marvell's acceptance of the position which he here states with an irony made possible only by deep conviction. Marvell has come through when he has gained this tone.

III

But I propose to defer consideration of the 'Horatian Ode' until after we have looked at some of the lyrics, in which the political approach is less obvious. Let us begin with 'The Definition of Love', for here the points can be made merely by quotation:[1]

> 'My Love is of a birth as rare
> As 'tis for object strange and high:
> It was begotten by despair
> Upon Impossibility.
>
> 'Magnanimous Despair alone
> Could show me so divine a thing,
> Where feeble Hope could ne'r have flown
> But vainly flapt its Tinsel Wing.
>
> 'And yet I quickly might arrive
> Where my extended Soul is fixt,
> But Fate does Iron wedges drive,
> And alwaies crouds it self betwixt. . . .
>
> 'And therefore her Decrees of Steel
> Us as the distant Poles have plac'd,
> (Though Loves whole World on us doth wheel)
> Not by themselves to be embrac'd. . . .
>
> 'As Lines so Loves oblique may well
> Themselves in every Angle greet:
> But ours so truly Paralel,
> Though infinite can never meet.

1 All my quotations of Marvell's poems are taken from H. M. Margoliouth's edition.

'*Therefore the Love which us doth bind,*
But Fate so enviously debarrs,
Is the Conjunction of the Mind,
And Opposition of the Stars.'

   This is a very sophisticated poem, playing about with newly fashionable geometrical theories. The main point, obviously, is the one that I have already suggested as typical of Marvell – the conflict between Love and Fate, desire and possibility. Fate 'defines' Love in both senses of the word – it both limits it and expresses its full significance. But the poem is far more than a clever conceit. The image in lines 11 and 12 is perfect for the age of Civil War. Fate is symbolized by the products of one of the industries which were transforming rural Britain, by the conventional symbol for warlike arms; and it 'crowds itself betwixt' with irresistible force: here Fate is thought of as a tumultuous multitude of human individuals, as well as abstract military and industrial processes. Nor is Fate merely an external force. As Miss Bradbrook and Miss Lloyd Thomas said, 'Material Fate and spiritual Love, though apparently in complete opposition, are in reality two aspects of the same situation:

"*Magnanimous Despair alone*
Could show me so divine a thing."

If "the Stars" were not so completely opposed, the love could not reach such heroic stature.'[1]
   The individual exposed to and triumphing over and through the buffetings of Fate is the theme of the bombastic rhodomontade of 'The unfortunate Lover':

'*See how he nak'd and fierce does stand,*
Cuffing the Thunder with one hand;
While with the other he does lock,
And grapple, with the stubborn Rock: ...

        . . . . .

'*This is the only* Banneret
That ever Love created yet:
Who though, by the Malignant Starrs,
Forced to live in Storms and Warrs:

1 M. C. Bradbrook and M. G. Lloyd Thomas, *Andrew Marvell*, p. 45. Their whole analysis of the dialectics of this intricate poem is most interesting.

> *Yet dying leaves a Perfume here,*
> *And Musick within every Ear:*
> *And he in Story only rules,*
> *In a Field Sable a Lover Gules.'*

Marvell too had been forced 'by the Malignant Starrs' 'to live in Storms and Warrs'; his finest music was wrung out of him in the grapple with a stubborn world.

Let us examine some of the other poems with these symbols and our main thesis in mind.

The titles of many speak for themselves: 'A Dialogue Between the Resolved Soul, and Created Pleasure', 'A Dialogue between the Soul and Body', In the first of these the conflict is between a militantly Puritan soul, conscious of its mission, its calling, its arduous pilgrimage to heaven, on the one hand, and the distracting and illusory pleasures of the senses and of idleness on the other. In the second poem the conflict is more subtle:

> 'SOUL. – *O who shall, from this Dungeon, raise*
> *A Soul inslav'd so many wayes?*
> *With bolts of Bones, that fetter'd stands*
> *In Feet; and manacled in Hands.*
> *Here blinded with an Eye; and there*
> *Deaf with the drumming of an Ear.*
> *A Soul hung up, as t'were, in Chains*
> *Of Nerves, and Arteries, and Veins.*[1]
> *Tortur'd, besides each other part,*
> *In a vain Head, and double Heart. . . .*

> 'BODY – *But Physick yet could never reach*
> *The Maladies Thou me dost teach;*
> *Whom first the Cramp of Hope does Tear:*
> *And then the Palsie Shakes of Fear.*
> *The Pestilence of Love does heat:*
> *Or Hatred's hidden Ulcer eat.*
> *Joy's chearful Madness does perplex:*
> *Or Sorrow's other Madness vex.*
> *Which Knowledge forces me to know;*
> *And Memory will not foregoe.*

---

1 In one of Quarles's *Emblemes* (Book V, No. 7) the soul is shown literally imprisoned within a skeleton, crying out 'who shall deliver me from the body of this death?' Cf. Rosemary Freeman, *English Emblem Books*, p. 119.

> *What but a Soul could have the wit*
> *To build me up for Sin so fit?*
> *So Architects do square and hew,*
> *Green Trees that in the Forest grew.'*

Here the antithesis is not just between soul and body, for the soul may betray the body as well as the body the soul; it is a complex, four-handed conflict, which blends the familiar themes of puritan asceticism against sensual pleasure with action against rest. (The symbolism of the last two lines is a favourite of Marvell's: the loss of certain natural qualities that the civilizing process makes inevitable. There seems, as will be shown later, to be a direct connection between this symbolism and the more obvious conflict of the Civil War.) Marvell's sympathies are here less decisively on one side than they were in the 'Dialogue Between the Resolved Soul, and Created Pleasure', where the moral issue was clear: here opposite concepts are jostling in Marvell's mind. (He is indeed one of the few Parliamentarian writers – if we except Winstanley on the extreme left – who frankly enjoys and praises the pleasures of the body.)[1]

The same complexity occurs in 'Upon Appleton House':

> *'As first our* Flesh *corrupt within*
> *Tempts impotent and bashful* Sin.'*

This is not just good against evil, but evil that is also good against good that is also evil. In these complicated problems and relationships there are no easy solutions or evasions:

> *'To what cool Cave shall I descend,*
> *Or to what gelid Fountain bend?*
> *Alas! I look for Ease in vain,*
> *When Remedies themselves complain,'*

cried Damon the Mower. The Soul Lamented to the Body that it was

> *'Constrain'd not only to indure*
> *Diseases, but, whats worse, the Cure.'*

1 Aubrey tells us of Marvell that 'he kept bottles of wine at his lodging, and many times he would drink liberally by himself to refresh his spirits and exalt his muse' (*Letters from the Bodleian*, II, p. 437).

Again, in complex form, though with a different solution, conflict pervades 'To his Coy Mistress'. It is no longer soul against body, but the sensual pleasures up against the hard facts of an uncongenial world in which effort is demanded. The moral is not 'Gather ye rosebuds while ye may.' It is –

> 'Let us roll all our Strength, and all
> Our sweetness, up into one Ball:
> And tear our Pleasures with rough strife,
> Thorough the Iron gates of Life.
> Thus, though we cannot make our Sun
> Stand still, yet we will make him run.'

That, as has been well said, is a Puritan rather than a libertine conclusion:[1] the sensual pleasures are put into a subordinate place:

> 'Had we but World enough, and Time,
> This coyness Lady were no crime.'

But as we have neither world nor time enough, coyness *is* a crime. The gates of life are iron, time's winged chariot is hurrying near:

> 'And yonder all before us lye
> Desarts of vast Eternity.'

We may compare Marvell's own lines on 'The First Anniversary of the Government under O. C.': ·

> ''Tis he the force of scattered Time contracts,
> And in one Year the work of Ages acts:
> While heavy Monarchs make a wide Return,
> Longer, and more Malignant then Saturn:
> And though they all Platonique years should raign,
> In the same Posture would be found again.'

It should not surprise us by now to find Marvell censuring 'heavy

1 Cf. Bishop Joseph Hall: 'A good man must not be like Ezechias Sunne, that went backward, nor like Joshuahs Sunne, that stood still, but Davids Sunne, that (like a Bridegroome) comes out of his Chamber, and as a Champion rejoyceth to runne his Race' (*Meditations and Vows*, 1901, p. 7). Cf. also the *Enchiridion* of Francis Quarles, first published in 1641: 'He only (if any) hath the art to lengthen out his taper, that puts it to the best advantage' (fourth century, No. LV).

Monarchs' in the same vein as a coy mistress, or praising Cromwell's political activity in the same terms as those in which he had invited the lady to 'sport us while we may'.

'To his Coy Mistress' strikes a note we shall find repeated. The individual and his desires come up against the outer world, life and time. The mock-serious moral of that flippant and very un-Puritan poem, 'Daphnis and Chloe', is the obverse of that of 'To his Coy Mistress'; it is better to forgo a pleasure than to be casual or half-hearted about it.

> *'Gentler times for Love are ment*
> *Who for parting pleasure strain*
> *Gather Roses in the rain,*
> *Wet themselves and spoil their Sent.'*

In the 'Coy Mistress' mere epicureanism is *rejected* for a more rigorous coming to terms with reality.[1] The laxity and ease of the *rentier* ruling class are contrasted with the effort, asceticism, concentration typical of Puritanism and commercialism. And again iron symbolizes the harshness and impersonality of this world which we *must* accept.

IV

The Mower, whose iron scythe cuts down himself as well as the grass, the innocent as well as the guilty, is a favourite symbol with Marvell. He appears in 'The Mower against Gardens', 'Damon the Mower', 'The Mower to the Glo-Worms', 'The Mower's Song', and 'Upon Appleton House'. The theme of 'The Mower against Gardens' is one which frequently recurs: it contrasts natural and artificial cultivation; the coarse toil and sweat of the mowers is set against the leisured sophistication, the luxury products of the garden. 'Luxurious Man', the Mower says

> *'First enclos'd within the Gardens square*
> *A dead and standing pool of Air:*
> *And a more luscious Earth for them did knead,*

---

1 Cf. Bradbrook and Lloyd Thomas, *op. cit.*, pp. 43–4, 73, on the structure of 'To his Coy Mistress' and of the 'Horatian Ode': the authors find in each 'a triple movement, the Hegelian thesis, antithesis, and synthesis'. See also T. S. Eliot, *Selected Essays*, p. 254.

>   *Which stupifi'd them while it fed.*
>   *The Pink grew then as double as his Mind. . . .*
>   *'Tis all enforc'd; the Fountain and the Grot;*
>   *While the sweet Fields do lye forgot.'*

And over all this ostentatious opulence the Mower stands brooding like Fate, confident in his power:

>   *'The* Gods *themselves with us do dwell.'*

But the nostalgia for a simpler pre-commercial age is qualified by an irony of humorous over-statement which shows that Marvell was arguing a case in which he did not wholly believe:

>   *'And* Fauns *and* Faryes *do the Meadows till,*
>   *More by their presence then their skill.'*

There is the same semi-serious regret in 'The Nymph complaining for the death of her Faun'.

The formal garden, as something essential to any gentleman's mansion, was relatively new in seventeenth-century England. There was still something exotically luxurious about it. 'God Almighty first planted a garden', but they began to become common in England as a result of the Tudor peace, of the internal order and security which allowed manor houses to replace baronial castles and created the conditions in which lesser gentry, yeomen, and merchants were able to prosper. In *The Faerie Queene* the garden is a symbol of the sheltered and opulent life of courtly society: Spenser follows in this the tradition of the mediaeval allegory of love.[1] Bacon wrote his essay to tell the very wealthy how a garden should be laid out. Stuart gardens, as the Mower has already told us, were still very formal: they were 'the greatest refreshment to the spirit of man', as Bacon put it, *because* of their contrast with rude Nature in the unenclosed waste outside. It is thus easy to see how the garden became a symbol of security, property, ease, repose, and escape:[2] it was shut off from the commons, the open fields,

---

1 C. S. Lewis, *The Allegory of Love*, p. 119.

2 'I . . . write . . . to those only, that are weather-beaten in the sea of this world, such as having lost the sight of their gardens and groves study to sail on a right course among rocks and quicksands' (Sir Fulke Greville, *Life of Sir Philip Sidney*, 1907, p. 224). Cf. also Shakespeare's *Richard II*, Act III, Scene 4. George Puttenham, *The Art of English Poesie* (1589), compared the poet to a gardener who improved on nature. The garden as

the sweaty vulgar outside, from the Mower. For other seventeenth-century poets as well as Marvell and Milton the garden is normally Eden rather than Gethsemane.[1]

If we take the garden as Marvell's equivalent of the ivory tower, the mere title of 'The Mower against Gardens' is a political tract in itself. The Mower symbolizes Fate, the historic process which lowers over these artificial and walled-off paradises, as Milton's Satan broods over the Garden of Eden.

> *'Sharp like his Sythe his Sorrow was,*
> *And wither'd like his Hopes the Grass.*'[2]

When he is lost he is guided by glow-worms:

> *' – Country Comets, that portend*
> *No War, nor Princes funeral,*
> *Shining unto no higher end*
> *Then to presage the Grasses fall.*'[3]

War and the death of kings are never very far away, even if they only point a contrast. In this poem and in 'The Mower's Song' the Mower is overcome by the power of love: Juliana –

> *'What I do to the Grass, does to my Thoughts and Me.'*

---

an image of order and harmony was a favourite of Bunyan's (J. Brown, *John Bunyan*, pp. 50–1; H. Talon, *John Bunyan*, pp. 302–3). Cf. also Gerrard Winstanley, *Fire in the Bush* (1650), *passim*. John Evelyn's *Elysium Britannicum*, begun about 1653, compared England to the Garden of Eden.

1 Maren-Sofie Røstvig, in *The Happy Man* (Oslo, 1954), studies the evolution of the cult of rural retirement in seventeenth-century England. She dates its beginning from the political crisis of the late sixteen-twenties and -thirties, rising to its peak in the 'forties and 'fifties with Mildmay Fane, Edward Benlowes and Henry Vaughan. She quotes a wide range of poets who deal with garden themes in the second quarter of the century. I would add to her list only Nathaniel Whiting, 'Upon Bellama's Walking in the Garden' (*Albino and Bellama*, 1638), George Wither, Hymn 30 (*Hallelujah*, 1641), Shirley, 'The Garden' (*Poems*, 1646), Nicholas Hookes, 'To Amanda walking in the garden' (*Amanda*, 1653). I should not myself altogether agree with Miss Røstvig's absolute opposition of the Royalist 'Hortulan Saint' to 'the grim figure of the Puritan pilgrim' (*The Happy Man*, p. 441). The case of Marvell suggests that it was more complicated than that.

2 'Damon the Mower'.

3 'The Mower to the Glo-Worms'.

(cf. the Fate and Love motive in 'The Definition of Love' and 'The Unfortunate Lover'). But in 'Upon Appleton House', as we shall shortly see, the Mower is directly related to the blind forces of the Civil War.[1]

The garden had its deep attractions for Marvell in the years before he plunged into public life. For he had his escapism, of which the opening of 'The Garden' is typical:

> 'How vainly men themselves amaze
> To win the Palm, the Oke, or Bayes;
> And their uncessant Labours see
> Crown'd from some single Herb or Tree.
> Whose short and narrow verged Shade
> Does prudently their Toyles upbraid;
> While all Flow'rs and all Trees do close
> To weave the Garlands of repose.'

But even here the poet is tripped up: 'Insnar'd with flow'rs, I fall on Grass.' The calm and peace are transient, an interlude: '*Temporis O suaves lapsus!*' says the Latin version. The garden is a place of temporary repose and refreshment, not a permanent haven. The mind seeks an intenser satisfaction than the merely physical pleasures of the garden: it

> 'Creates, transcending these,
> Far other Worlds, and other Seas.'

The soul looks forward to further activity even while the body is at rest:

> 'Casting the Bodies Vest aside,
> My Soul into the boughs does glide:
> There like a Bird it sits, and sings,
> Then whets, and combs its silver Wings;
> And, till prepar'd for longer flight,
> Waves in its Plumes the various Light.'

1 All Marvell's symbols, of course, are used partly unconsciously, and so their significance varies: the Mower is now the power of Love, now the scythe of Death or Fate; now the armies of the Civil War; at other times he stands for a pre-commercial simplicity which acquires an elemental force in contrast to the sophistication of the garden. So too the garden itself stands for different things in different poems: but I do not think this makes analysis impossible, provided we are careful to apply no rule-of-thumb symbol-equivalents. All Marvell's writing is packed with alternative meanings.

Whilst the soul thus anticipates eternity, the garden itself recalls Paradise before the Fall. But the ambiguous phrase 'Garden-state' hints at England, and the terms of the comparison remind us that Marvell's garden is in and of this world:

> '– 'Twas beyond a Mortal's share
> To wander solitary there.'

'Society is all but rude'; yet its needs impinge remorselessly upon the ideal world of escape, prevent it being final. Already in the second verse Marvell had doubted whether quiet and innocence were to be found at all on earth. The poem began by mocking at the vanity of human effort; in the last verse 'th' industrious Bee' is introduced, who – lest we should have missed the significance of the adjective – 'computes its time as well as we'. The garden clock, for all its fragrance, reminds us of 'Times winged Chariot'. We cannot think ourselves out of time any more than we can escape from fallen humanity.

'The Nymph complaining for the death of her Faun' pictures a garden-Eden shattered by violence from without: the violence of soldiers:

> 'The wanton Troopers riding by
> Have shot my Faun and it will dye.'

Marvell plays with the idea later to be elaborated in the 'Horatian Ode', of the innocent victim sacrifically redeeming the users of violence, but here rejects it:

> 'Though they should wash their guilty hands
> In this warm life-blood, which doth part
> From thine, and wound me to the Heart,
> Yet could they not be clean: their Stain
> Is dy'd in such a Purple Grain.
> There is not such another in
> The World, to offer for their Sin.'

There is no easy redemption. But the tone of the complaint is curious: 'Ev'n Beasts must be with justice slain.' The Faun symbolizes an escape, and is not uncritically regarded:

> 'Thenceforth I set my self to play
> My solitary time away,

> *With this: and very well content,*
> *Could so mine idle Life have spent. . . .*
> *Had it liv'd long, I do not know*
> *Whether it too might have done so*
> *As* Sylvio *did: his Gifts might be*
> *Perhaps as false or more than he.'*

As always in Marvell, the conflict is far from simple: he cannot wholly praise 'a fugitive and cloistered virtue'.

In 'The Coronet', the poet seeks 'through every Garden, every Mead' for flowers to crown his Saviour (flowers 'that once adorn'd my Shepherdesses head'). But –

> *'Alas I find the Serpent old*
> *That, twining in his speckled breast,*
> *About the flow'rs disguis'd does fold,*
> *With wreaths of Fame and Interest.'*

And the conclusion is

> *' – Let these wither, so that he may die,*
> *Though set with Skill and chosen out with Care.'*

The garden is not enough.

v

In 'Upon Appleton House', Marvell's longest poem, all this symbolism becomes specific. The house had been a nunnery, which had come to the Fairfax family at the Reformation. In the poem the retirement, the cultured and indeed opulent ease of the nunnery is frankly opposed to the claims of a Protestant and commercial civilization. The words which Marvell writes of the earlier Fairfax who acquired the Church lands clearly presage the dilemma of the Fairfaxes, father and son, when they had to take sides in the Civil War:

> *'What should he do? He would respect*
> *Religion, but not Right neglect.'*

The elder Fairfax build his family mansion and his fortune on the site of the nunnery; the younger Fairfaxes took up arms in the name of liberty against the Lord's Anointed.

In the poem England before the Civil War is depicted as a garden, in which Fairfax

> '– *did with his utmost Skill*,
> Ambition *weed, but* Conscience *till.*'

(That other great Parliamentary general, Oliver Cromwell, left 'his private Gardens, where He liv'd reserved and austere', at the call of duty in the Civil War.)

Fairfax's garden (or England) is clearly linked up with the Garden of Eden (stanzas XLI–XLIII), concluding:

> '*What luckless Apple did we tast,*
> *To make us Mortal, and The Wast?*'

The symbolism of the Mower, who blindly massacres all that he meets in 'the Abbyss . . . of that unfathomable Grass', is repeated in stanzas XLVI–LIII, and the reference to the Civil War is again explicit:

> '*The Mower now commands the Field;* . . .
> *A Camp of Battail newly fought:*
> *Where, as the Meads with Hay, the Plain*
> *Lyes quilted ore with Bodies slain:*
> *The Women that with forks it fling*
> *Do represent the Pillaging.*'[1]

War is no respecter of persons, cuts down the innocent and un-concerned together with the guilty:

> '*Unhappy Birds! what does it boot*
> *To build below the Grasses Root;*
> *Where Lowness is unsafe as Hight,*
> *And Chance o'retakes what scapeth spight?* . . .'

> '*Or sooner hatch or higher build.* . . .'

1 At Edgehill, Royalist Welsh infantry, very badly equipped 'with scythes, pitchforks and even sickles, . . . cheerfully took the field, and literally like reapers descend[ed] to that harvest of death' (quoted in J. R. Phillips, *Memoirs of the Civil War in Wales and the Marches*, I, p. 128). In 1649 scythes were a part of the equipment sent over to the English army in Ireland, for the rather different purpose of cutting down corn in order to starve the Irish into submission (J. P. Prendergast, *The Cromwellian Settlement of Ireland*, p. 14).

320PURITANISM AND REVOLUTION

The Levellers 'take Pattern at' 'this naked equal Flat', – 'A new and empty Face of things'.

> 'The Villagers in common chase
> Their Cattle, which it closer rase;
> And what below the Sith increast
> Is pincht yet nearer by the Beast.'

This direct reference to the Levellers, and hint at the destructive communism of 'the many-headed monster', is symbolically followed by a sudden inundation. Marvell 'takes Sanctuary in the Wood'. But escapism brings no neutrality: the forces shaping our lives can neither be controlled nor evaded. This reintroduces Marvell's other theme of the need for equalizing desire and opportunity, the conflict brought to a crisis by the brutal external force of the Mower. Thus Marvell's key ideas are linked in one symbol, suggesting the possibility that all his poems really deal with a single complex of problems.

In 'Upon Appleton House' there is humorously ironical escapism again (stanzas LXXI–LXXXI). The whole passage is of the greatest interest as evidence of Marvell's 'double heart'. On a careless reading the picture is one of ideal happiness, a Garden-of-Eden life, an escape, particularly, from war:

> 'How safe, methinks, and strong, behind
> These Trees have I incamp'd my Mind;
> Where Beauty, aiming at the Heart,
> Bends in some Tree its useless Dart;
> And where the World no certain Shot
> Can make, or me it toucheth not.
> But I on it securely play,
> And gaul its Horsemen all the Day.'

But Marvell makes continual digs at his dream-world:

> 'Strange Prophecies my Phancy weaves. . . .'

> 'I in this light Mosaick read.
> Thrice happy he who, not mistook,
> Hath read in Natures mystick Book.'

(The heavy emphasis their position gives to 'methinks' and 'not mistook' can hardly be entirely without significance.)

> '*Thus I*, easie Philosopher,
> *Among the* Birds *and* Trees *confer. . . .*'

> '*The Oak-Leaves me embroyder all,*
> *Between which Caterpillars crawl:*
> *And Ivy, with familiar trails,*
> *Me licks, and clasps, and curles, and hales.*
> *Under this* antick Cope *I move*
> *Like some great* Prelate of the Grove.'

'Easie' prepares us for incomplete acceptance, and the political note would strike for contemporaries the requisite undertone of disapproval in the last lines quoted, even without the hint of 'Caterpillars'. In the Old Testament 'groves' were traditionally the scene of pagan worship. A bishop and his vestments could not but call up reactions of hostility in a good Parliamentarian (cf. 'Safe from the Storms, and Prelat's rage' in 'Bermudas').

There is a snare hinted in the very placidity of this garden-world, in the attractions of its philosophy:

> '*And where I Language want, my Signs*
> *The Bird upon the Bough divines;*
> *And more attentive there doth sit*
> *Than if She were with Lime-twigs knit.*'

(Cf. 'The Garden' and the passage about the falconer in the 'Horatian Ode'.) For all its fair seeming, this Eden does not really satisfy the poet:

> '*– Languishing with ease, I toss*
> *On Pallets swoln of Velvet Moss;*
> *While the Wind, cooling through the Boughs,*
> *Flatters with Air my panting Brows.*'

('In this time', Hobbes wrote in 1651, 'that men call not onely for Peace, but also for Truth',[1] flattery was not enough.) Chains are not less chains because men cling to them, nor are half-truths truths because sincerely held:

> '*Bind me ye* Woodbines *in your 'twines,*
> *Curle me about ye gadding* Vines,

---

1 *Leviathan*, p. 390.

> *And Oh so close your Circles lace,*
> *That I may never leave this Place:*
> *But, lest your Fetters prove too weak,*
> *Ere I your Silken Bondage break,*
> *Do you,* O Brambles, *chain me too,*
> *And courteous* Briars *nail me through.'*

The idyllic scene suddenly suggests the Crucifixion.[1] And the succeeding stanzas show that escapism is not in fact Marvell's ultimate ideal. It is not the highest wisdom to discover 'I was but an inverted Tree'. For now Mary Fairfax enters. Whatever she symbolizes (and it is clear from stanza LXXXXI that she is associated with Puritan 'Goodness' as well as Fairfaxian 'Discipline'), there can be no doubt of the condemnation of 'loose Nature' (cf. 'easie Philosopher') in the lines describing her advent:

> *'See how loose Nature, in respect*
> *To her, it self doth recollect;*
> *And every thing so whisht and fine,*
> *Starts forth with to its* Bonne Mine.'. . .

> *'But by her* Flames, *in Heaven try'd,*
> Nature *is wholly* vitrifi'd.
> *'Tis* She *that to these Gardens gave*
> *That wondrous Beauty which they have;*
> She *streightness on the Woods bestows;* . . .
> She *yet more Pure, Sweet, Streight, and Fair,*
> *Then Gardens, Woods, Meads, Rivers are.'.* . .

> *'For* She, *to higher Beauties rais'd,*
> *Disdains to be for lesser prais'd.*
> She *counts her Beauty to converse*
> *In all the Languages as* hers.'

Her wisdom subsumes and includes the wisdom of the garden, just as her discipline and morals reduce its luxuriance to order.[2]

---

1 Cf. Lewis Bayley, 'A Divine Colloquy between the Soul and her Saviour': 'Soul – Lord, wherefore wouldest thou begin thy Passion in a Garden? Christ – Because that in a Garden thy Sin took first Beginning' (*The Practice of Piety*, 55th ed., 1723, p. 451).

2 Similarly, 'little T. C.' had been adjured to 'reform the errours of the Spring'; and the mind in 'The Garden' created worlds and seas which transcended reality. Cf. Lancelot Andrewes: 'Christ rising was indeed a Gardiner. . . . He it is that . . . shal turne all our grass into garden-plots' (*XCVI Sermons*, 2nd ed., 1631, p. 538).

> '*Go now fond Sex that on your Face*
> *Do all your useless Study place,*
> *Nor once at Vice your Brows dare knit*
> *Lest the smooth Forehead wrinkled sit:*
> *Yet your own Face shall at you grin,*
> *Thorough the Black-bag of your Skin;*
> *When* knowledge *only could have fill'd*
> *And* Virtue *all those* Furrows *till'd.* '[1]

The new standards and discipline transmute the old cosmos by putting it into its place, and a new reality emerges, so different that we might be at the Antipodes:

> '*Tis not, what once it was, the* World;
> *But a rude heap together hurl'd;*
> *All negligently overthrown,*
> *Gulfes, Deserts, Precipices, Stone.*
> *Your lesser* World *contains the same,*
> *But in more decent Order tame;*
> You Heaven's Center, Nature's Lap,
> And Paradice's only Map.'

(Cf. 'Clorinda and Damon' –

> 'D_{AMON} –   *These once had been enticing things,*
>   Clorinda, *Pastures, Caves, and Springs.*
> '$C_{LORINDA}$ – *And what late change?*
> 'D_{AMON} –   *The other day*
>   Pan *met me. . . .*')

In many of the poems Marvell is concerned to show the mutual indispensability of apparent opposites. He says of Fairfax in 'The Hill and Grove at Bill-borow' –

> '*Therefore to your obscurer Seats*
> *From his own Brightness he retreats:*
> *Nor he the Hills without the Groves,*
> *Nor Height but with Retirement loves.*'

In 'Bermudas' the garden-island (which is also an idealized England) is

---

1 Black-bag = mask. Death, the final external reality, equally reinforces the moral whether the invitation – as here – is to virtue, or – as in the 'Coy Mistress' – to pleasure.

not an escape from struggle, but its reward. It is 'far kinder' than the prelates' England but the emigrants have had to pass through storms to reach it, and the song is sung by men at work. The picture of the perfect haven is set between two quatrains which remind us unobtrusively of the difficulty of getting there.[1]

VI

The conflict in the poet's own mind between the attractions of evading reality in communion with Nature, and the necessity of coming to terms with the world, is shown in its most interesting form in the 'Horatian Ode upon Cromwel's Return from Ireland'. This poem was probably written before the great lyrics, before Marvell entered the Fairfax household, but it is convenient to consider it here since to some extent it sums up the argument by its direct political reference.

> *'The forward Youth that would appear*
> *Must now forsake his* Muses *dear,*
> *Nor in the Shadows sing*
> *His Numbers languishing . . .*
> *'Tis Madness to resist or blame*
> *The force of angry Heavens flame:*
> *And, if we would speak true,*
> *Much to the Man is due,*
> *Who, from his private Gardens, where*
> *He liv'd reserved and austere,*
> *As if his highest plot*
> *To plant the Bergamot,*
> *Could by industrious Valour climbe*
> *To ruine the great Work of Time,*
> *And cast the Kingdome old*
> *Into another Mold.*
> *Though Justice against Fate complain,*
> *And plead the antient Rights in vain;*
> *But those do hold or break*
> *As Men are strong or weak.'*

The poet is clearly arguing with himself rather than with Cromwell; note the garden symbol again. Then there comes the famous passage in which the Parliamentarian Marvell shows his sympathy for the old-

---

1 I owe some of these points to Mr. C. H. Hobday.

world virtues of the executed Charles I,[1] consoling himself with the vision of new life through sacrificial death:

> '*A bleeding Head where they begun,*
> *Did fright the Architects to run;*
> *And yet in that the* State
> *Foresaw it's happy Fate.*'

Again Marvell takes up the struggle with himself, and hints back at the lost ideals of the Garden in a passage where the needs of the state are again shown as triumphing over the private interests of the individual:

> '*So when the Falcon high*
> *Falls heavy from the Sky,*
> *She, having kill'd, no more does search,*
> *But on the next green Bow to pearch;*
> *Where, when he first does lure,*
> *The Falckner has her sure.*'

(The falconer is England, the state; but he is also Fate, the reality which has to be accepted, the historical process: he recalls the Mower). Marvell concludes reasonably on the side of action, the impossibility of neutrality:

> '*But thou the Wars and Fortunes Son*
> *March indefatigably on;*

1 Did Marvell see the execution? The lines –

> '*Nor call'd the* Gods *with vulgar spight*
> *To vindicate his helpless Right,*
> *But bow'd his comely Head,*
> *Down as upon a Bed*'

read like an eyewitnesses's recollection of a fact recorded by the Venetian Ambassador which Marvell's editors seem to have missed: 'As they doubted that His Majesty might resist the execution of the sentence, refusing to lay his neck upon the block, they fixed into the block at his feet two iron rings through which they passed a cord which, placed on His Majesty's neck, would necessarily make him bend by force, and offer his head to the axe, if he did not voluntarily resign himself to the humiliation of the fatal blow. But the King, warned of this, without coming to such extremes, said that they should use no violence; he would readily submit to the laws of necessity and the rigour of force' (E. Momigliano, *Cromwell*, English translation, p. 282; cf. also Sir P. Warwick, *Memoirs of the Reign of Charles I*, p. 385, and E. Warburton, *Memoirs of Prince Rupert and the Cavaliers*, III, p. 400).

> *And for the last effect*
> *Still keep thy Sword erect:*
> *Besides the force it has to fright*
> *The Spirits of the shady Night,*
> *The same* Arts *that did* gain
> *A* Pow'r *must it* maintain.'

('Shady', it will be observed, continues the symbolism; cf. 'Shadows' in line 3.)

Critics have frequently commented on the rather left-handed compliment to Cromwell in this poem: his use of force and fraud is indeed a little openly praised. I suggest that this is part of Marvell's own internal struggle, and is evidence of his desire to be honest with himself. The artist in him dislikes the unpleasant actions which alone can 'cast the Kingdome old into another Mold'; but like his master, Milton, Marvell has come to realize that the immortal garland is to be run for not without dust and heat. He has come down from the ivory tower into the arena.

In so far as Marvell is thinking of Cromwell at all, he is not treating him as an individual: the general is for the poet the personification of the Revolution, of victory over the King.

> *'Nature that hateth emptiness,*
> *Allows of penetration less:*
> *And therefore must make room*
> *Where greater Spirits come.'*

Cromwell draws his greatness from the events of which he has been the instrument – a view of history with which the Protector would have agreed and which Milton assumes in *Samson Agonistes*. For Marvell the Revolution is 'the force of angry Heavens flame', ruining 'the great Work of Time', something real which must inevitably be accepted, which cannot be wished away nor even excluded from the garden. ''Tis Madness to resist or blame' an elemental power of this kind. 'The world will not go the faster for our driving', but it will also not go the slower for our regrets. Wisdom is 'To make their Destiny their *Choice*'.[1] In the 'Horatian Ode' Marvell is clearly aware of a fusion of opposites: the life of the community demands the death of the individual, rest is obtainable only through and by means of effort, eternal vigilance is the

---

1 'Upon Appleton House', line 744.

price of liberty, freedom is the knowledge of necessity.[1]

But this paradox, this dialectical thought, recurs throughout Marvell's poems. The soul, in 'On a drop of Dew',

> *'Does, in its pure and circling thoughts, express*
> *The greater Heaven in an Heaven less. . . .*
> *Moving but on a point below,*
> *It all about does upwards bend. . . .*
> *Congeal'd on Earth: but does, dissolving, run*
> *Into the glories of th'Almighty Sun.'*

We find it in 'Ametas and Thestylis making Hay-Ropes', ironically, as in the 'Coy Mistress' seriously. The solution of the conflict may not be the victory of either side, but a fusion of aspects of both from which something new emerges. We find the synthesis again in 'Eyes and Tears':

> *'How wisely Nature did decree,*
> *With the same Eyes to weep and see!*
> *That, having view'd the object vain,*
> *They might be ready to complain. . . .*
>
> *'I have through every Garden been,*
> *Amongst the Red, the White, the Green;*
> *And yet, from all the flow'rs I saw,*
> *No Hony, but these tears could draw. . . .*[2]
>
> *'Thus let your Streams o'reflow your Springs,*
> *Till Eyes and Tears be the same things:*
> *And each the other's difference bears;*
> *These weeping Eyes, those seeing Tears.'*

VII

The suggestion then is that all Marvell's problems are inter-

---

1 'The thesis is the impersonal power of Cromwell. . . . The antithesis is the personal dignity and comeliness of Charles, which may offset Cromwell's achievement: and the synthesis is the acceptance of Cromwell, both his "forc'd Pow'r" and his personal unattractiveness. . . . The poem may well represent the steps of reasoning by which the friend of Lovelace threw in his lot with the Roundheads' (Bradbrook and Lloyd Thomas, *op. cit.*, p. 73).

2 Here again the garden fails to meet the poet's needs.

connected. They are the problems of an individual in an age of revolutionary change. I do not think the following lines from 'The Fair Singer' were intended to be taken at more than their surface value (though one never knows with Marvell); but they could be interpreted as a perfect allegory of the influence of society on the individual:

> *'I could have fled from One but singly fair:*
> *My dis-intangled Soul it self might save,*
> *Breaking the curled trammels of her hair.*
> *But how should I avoid to be her Slave,*
> *Whose subtile Art invisibly can wreath*
> *My Fetters of the very Air I breath?'*[1]

Soul and body, Love and Fate, illusion and reality, escape or action – all the poems in the last analysis deal with the adjustment of individual conduct to external conditions and forces. Marvell's life and his poetry form a single whole. I would also suggest that the resolution of the personal conflict revealed in the lyrics is almost exactly parallel to the resolution of the political conflict revealed in the political poems: the individual soul never can disentangle itself from society, never can save itself in isolation; 'the very Air I breath' even in the remotest garden comes from outside. Since we cannot escape we must submit.

The significance of this solution of his own crisis for Marvell is shown by the number of times he recurs to it. The moral of 'The First Anniversary of the Government under O.C.' is exactly the same as that of the 'Horatian Ode':

> *'For all delight of Life thou then didst lose,*
> *When to Command, thou didst thyself Depose;*
> *Resigning up thy Privacy so dear,*
> *To turn the headstrong Peoples Charioteer;*
> *For to be* Cromwell *was a greater thing,*
> *Then ought below, or yet above a King:*
> *Therefore thou rather didst thy Self depress,*
> *Yielding to Rule, because it made thee Less.'*[2]

---

1 Marvell may have noticed 'curld Trammels of thy hayre' in Drayton's *Second Nimphall.*

2 Lines 221–8. Cf. 'A letter to Doctor Ingelo', where Cromwell is described as '*Ducere sive sequi nobile laetus iter*'; on a noble course his joy was equal whether leading or following.

The subordination of self to political purposes which he believed to be right: that is the lesson Marvell had taught himself once he found that he could not escape from the disagreeable realities of the world. It was not only Cromwell

> *' Whom Nature all for Peace had made,*
> *But angry Heaven unto War had sway'd.'*[1]

Like so many other Parliamentarians, Marvell had been pushed reluctantly to approve of revolution and regicide since otherwise 'religion and liberty' could not be secured. Here again the wise and virtuous man 'makes his destiny his choice'.

> *'Far different Motives yet, engag'd them thus,*
> *Necessity did them, but Choice did us.'*[2]

Marvell was a true Cromwellian, truer perhaps than Milton, who could not accept the new tactics of the Restoration. For Marvell, as we have seen, the Restoration illustrated the point that 'things . . . happen without any need of . . . our officiousness'. He had Cromwell's carelessness of forms of government, provided the root of the matter were secure. Yet Marvell had Milton's sense – a conception surely born of the agonies and triumphs and sufferings of the Revolution? – of good through evil, of the impossibility of good without evil, of the meaninglessness of rejecting good because of concomitant evil. It was from the rind of one apple tasted in a garden that the knowledge of good and evil came into the world. Tearing our pleasures 'with rough strife Thorough the Iron gates of Life' makes them greater, not less.

> *'Thus, though we cannot make our Sun*
> *Stand still, yet we will make him run.'*

That is the final triumph over circumstance. The highest praise of Cromwell was that he

> *'As the* Angel *of our Commonweal,*
> *Troubling the Waters, yearly mak'st them Heal.'*[3]

1 'A poem upon the Death of O. C.', lines 15, 16.
2 'On Blake's Victory over the Spaniards', lines 141–2.
3 'The First Anniversary', lines 401–2.

Or as Endymion, who wanted the moon, said to Cynthia:

'Though I so high may not pretend,
It is the same so you descend.'[1]

By the time of 'The First Anniversary' and 'On Blake's Victory over the Spaniards', all Marvell's problems are solved: and the great poetry ceases.[2] Marvell became a public servant, and his experience in writing compact business prose helped him, with Pepys and Dryden, to contribute a fresh element of conciseness and clarity to English prose style. Though the Restoration was to bring new complications, the inward assurance Marvell had so hardly won in the 'fifties was never lost. The poet became a pamphleteer as soon as he saw some of the returned Cavaliers trying to set the clock back to before 1640, trying to interfere with liberty of thought. With a purity of style reminiscent of Pascal, Marvell laughed down the enemies of religious toleration. The irreligious fashionable world enjoyed his polished and sophisticated wit no less than Paris had enjoyed the *Lettres Provinciales* in which Pascal had exposed the Jesuits. It is no part of my purpose to discuss Marvell's admirable prose, but it is perhaps worth recording the judgment of Miss Bradbrook and Miss Lloyd Thomas that its wit and ridicule are based on 'a security of unquestioned and untroubled belief which gives him a standard by which he can relate the different levels of feeling, with their intensity'.[3] That is what we should have expected from our study of the poems.

This security, this stability in his political principles, this poised maturity and urbanity, are Marvell's peculiar strength: and they were won in the conflicts of the early 'fifties to which the great lyrics testify. In a lengthy simile in 'The First Anniversary', primitive man, terrified by the setting of the sun and the shadows, continues to look for light in the west, and is beginning to despair –

1 'Marriage of Lord Fauconberg and Lady Mary Cromwell'.

2 We do not *know* this. Miss Bradbrook and Miss Lloyd Thomas point out that some of the religious and philosophical poems might be dated after Marvell's state service began (*op. cit.*, p. 9). But I think the indirect internal evidence is strong enough to justify allotting all the great poems to the same period, roughly 1650–5.

I should like to think that the order of the lyrical poems in the 1681 edition (which Margoliouth uses) is chronological. Then we could trace the chronological as well as the logical sequence of Marvell's inner struggles. But the point is not material.

3 *Op. cit.*, p. 116. They contrast Swift – but that is another story. Swift, incidentally, was a great admirer of Marvell's prose.

'*When streight the Sun behind him he descry'd,*
Smiling serenely from the further side.'

That is the dialectic of life and change as Marvell came to know it.

FOURTEEN

Clarissa Harlowe and Her Times

If a man cuts my Purse, I may have him by the heels or by the neck for it; whereas a man may cut a woman's purse, and have her for his pains in fetters. How brutish, and much more than brutish, is that Common-wealth, which prefers the Earth before the Fruits of her Womb? . . . We see the Gifts of God, and the Bountys of Heaven in fruitful Familys, thro this wretched custom of marrying for Mony, becom their insupportable grief and poverty. Nor falls this so heavy upon the lower sort, being better able to shift for themselves, as upon the Nobility or Gentry. . . . We are wonderful severe in Laws, that they [our children] shall not marry without our consent; as if it were care and tenderness over them: But is it not, lest we should not have the other thousand Pounds with this Son, or the other hundred Pounds a year more in Jointure with that Daughter?

James Harrington, *Oceana*, in *Works*, pp. 109–10.

I

CLARISSA HARLOWE seems to me one of the greatest of the unread novels. Its greatness derives in part from what it says, by implication, about society and about the relations of individuals with social institutions. But it is a paradoxical book, whose achievement is more profound than the author himself seems to have been aware. It is difficult to come to grips with the moral problems which Richardson presents unless we approach them historically, from the seventeenth century: unless we know something about Puritan attitudes towards society, marriage, and the individual conscience. But our starting point, in considering the structure of the novel, must be economic.

In a recent article, Professor Habakkuk argued that the early eighteenth century saw 'an increasing subordination of marriage to the increase of landed wealth, at the expense of other motives for marriage'. 'Political power was becoming more dependent on the possession of landed wealth' than it had been in the sixteenth and early seventeenth centuries, when it owed more to royal favour; and so among the upper classes marriage was bent 'more systematically to the accumulation of landed wealth'.[1] Professor Habakkuk sees this as a cumulative tendency dating from the mid-seventeenth century, the result of technical legal changes by which the father became in effect life tenant of the estate. The eldest son came to occupy a unique position of authority; and the estate, the family property, acquired greater importance than the individual owner.

The new legal devices themselves sprang from 'profound changes ... in the attitude to the family and to land'. These changes were related to the necessity of adapting landownership to a society in which standards of expenditure were set by those whose wealth derived from sources other than land, and in which taxation fell heavily on landowners.[2] They were the consequence of the political compromises of 1660 and 1688, by which the landed class had been left in possession of its property but deprived of power to check the development of capitalism. Professor Habakkuk draws especial attention to the staying power of the greater gentry, to the importance of the concentration of estates for their survival, and to marriage as a means of increasing the size of estates.[3] Pamela's Mr. B. noted that 'We have so many of our first titled families who have allied themselves to trade (whose inducements were money only) that it ceases to be either a wonder as to the fact, or a disgrace to the honour'.[4]

The relevance of this to *Clarissa Harlowe* will become clear if we recall its elaborately described point of departure. The Harlowe family, Clarissa told Miss Howe, was 'no inconsiderable or upstart one, on either side'. Its wealth had already been increased by judicious marriages. But some families 'having great substance, cannot be satisfied without rank and title'. Among the Harlowes 'some of us' held 'the darling view ... of *raising a family*'. The whole family strategy was planned with this end in mind. The uncles, one enriched by the

---

1 H. J. Habakkuk, 'Marriage Settlements in the 18th century', *Trans. R.H.S.*, 1950, pp. 24–5.

2 Habakkuk, 'English Landownership, 1680–1740', *Econ. H.R.*, X, pp. 6–10.

3 *Ibid.*, pp. 3–5; 'Marriage Settlements', pp. 18, 27, 29.

4 *The Works of Samuel Richardson*, (ed. E. Mangin, 1811), III, p. 175; cf. Defoe, *The Complete English Tradesman* (1841), I, pp. 227–40; *The Complete English Gentleman* (1890), pp. 250–4.

discovery of minerals on his property, the other by the East India trade, intended not to marry. The eldest child, and only son, James, the real power in the family, thought that his two sisters might be provided for with £10–15,000 apiece; and then all the real estate – their grandfather's, father's, uncles' – and the remainder of their personal estates would descend on him. This, together with James's expectations of a great estate from his godmother, 'would make such a noble fortune, and give him such an interest, as might entitle him to hope for a peerage. Nothing less would satisfy his ambition'. He regarded his grandfather and uncles as his stewards, and daughters as encumbrances on a family: 'to induce people to take them off their hands, the family stock must be impaired'.[1] 'In order to give his daughter a dowry', wrote Professor Habakkuk, 'a landowner raised money by a mortgage on his lands'.[2]

But the grandfather's will 'lopped off one branch of my brother's expectations'. To the indignation of the whole family the old man passed over his sons and elder grandchildren in favour of Clarissa. The other members of the family, he thought, were adequately provided for; and he had been very fond of Clarissa. But this seemed to the rest of the family insufficient reason for disregarding the interests and ambitions of the family unit. To obviate jealousy, Clarissa gave up to her father's management everything she had inherited from her grandfather, contenting herself with what her father allowed her.[3] After she had left home, he still retained possession of her property.

The family had been in favour of Lovelace's proposals to the elder sister, because they hoped that this connection might help to gain a peerage. But when he switched his attentions to Clarissa, the design to concentrate the estates and aggrandize the family was seriously endangered. There was always the possibility that the uncles might follow their father's example and their own inclinations. Lovelace had a good clear estate, and prospects of a peerage; if he married Clarissa, why should not the family property be concentrated on them, since James could no longer have it all? 'This little syren is in a fair way to out-uncle, as she has already out-grandfather'd us both!' said James anxiously to Arabella. He and Arabella both had good reason to wish to

---

1 *Works*, V, pp. 80–1, 30–1.
2 'English Landownership', p. 7; cf. 'Marriage Settlements', pp. 15, 23–7.
3 *Works*, V, pp. 81, 90–2.

'disgrace and keep down' Clarissa quite apart from Arabella's jealousy of her sister, arising from Lovelace's transfer of his addresses.[1]

So it was proposed to marry Clarissa to the deplorable Mr. Solmes, and to tie the marriage up with conditions whose object was to keep her estates in the family if possible. Clarissa describes Solmes as an upstart, 'not born to the immense riches he is possessed of: riches left by one niggard to another, in injury to the next heir, because that other is a niggard'. Solmes was 'very illiterate: knows nothing but the value of estates, and how to improve them, and what belongs to land-jobbing and husbandry'. 'His courtship indeed is *to them*' – to James and Arabella. Mr. Solmes was ideal for their purposes. He had no relations whom he valued, and so was prepared to bid high for the honour of union with the Harlowes. He was 'mean enough', Clarissa said, '. . . and wicked enough to propose to *rob* of their just expectations his own family . . . in order to settle all he is worth on me; and if I die without children and he has none by any other marriage, upon a family which already abounds'. 'Now a *possibility* is discovered (which such a grasping mind as my brother's can easily turn into a *probability*) that my grandfather's estate will revert to it [the Harlowe family] with a much more considerable one of the man's own.' So Clarissa's marriage to Solmes would positively contribute to 'family aggrandizement'. Mr. Solmes, Clarissa's mother assured her, 'has even given hopes to your brother that he will make exchanges of estates, or at least that he will purchase the northern one: for you know it must be entirely consistent with the family-views, that we increase our interest in this county. . . . A family so rich in all its branches, and that has its views to honour, must be pleased to see a very great probability of taking rank among the principal of the kingdom.' To this Clarissa replied: 'for the sake of this plan of my brother's am I, Madam, to be given in marriage to a man I never can endure?'[2]

The grandfather's will from the start sets personal affection in conflict with family ambition. Richardson originally intended to call the novel *The Lady's Legacy*, as though to emphasize this setting. He stressed it again in his Postscript, when defending the slow start of the novel. The altercations in the Harlowe family, he said, are 'the foundation of the whole'. It was because she would 'rather be buried than marry Mr. Solmes' that Clarissa first contemplated throwing

1 *Ibid.*, V, pp. 79, 85–7.
2 *Ibid.*, V, pp. 48–9, 87–90, 130.

herself on Lovelace's protection, and later became a half-willing accomplice in his abduction of her.[1] Then her family utterly cast her off, and she was left in the complete isolation which was so important for the development of Richardson's plot.

Critics have sometimes suggested that Richardson's picture of the Harlowes was overdrawn. Harrington's words quoted at the head of this essay, and Professor Habakkuk's conclusions, suggest that Richardson was depicting, even if in a heightened form, a typical attitude among the bigger landowners. Lady Bradshaigh, who at one time 'thought it scarcely possible that there could be such a father as old Harlowe', came across a similar real-life story in March 1751.[2] So, although the alternatives of love or money in marriage were old ones, they were especially topical in Richardson's day; and with them the related problems of parental authority, of the daughter's right of choice.

It was Miss Howe who drew the moral, and it is not clear whether Richardson intended us to agree, or to regard it as an example of her warm-hearted impetuosity: 'You are all too rich to be happy, child. For must not each of you, by the constitutions of your family, marry to be *still* richer? . . . Is true happiness any part of your family view? So far from it, that none of your family but yourself could be happy were they *not* rich.' But Clarissa came very near to the same moral in a moment of bitterness about the family schemes. 'And yet, in my opinion, the world is but one great family. Originally it was so. What then is this narrow selfishness that reigns in us, but relationship remembered against relationship forgot?' Soon afterwards Clarissa, in her isolation and loneliness, now longing for death, cried out with tragic intensity: 'What a world is this! – What is there in it desirable? The good we hope for, so strangely mixed, that one does not know what to wish for! And one half of mankind tormenting the other, and being tormented themselves in tormenting'.[3]

II

Where did Richardson obtain these insights, in his apparently uneventful rise from industrious apprentice to successful printer

1 *Ibid.*, XII, p. 432; II, pp. 359–66.
2 *The Correspondence of Samuel Richardson* (ed. A. L. Barbauld, 1804), VI, p. 100.
3 *Works*, V, pp. 61, 50; VI, p. 39.

holding court to middle-class ladies in his Hammersmith grotto? He can only, I think, have learnt them from his society, the society which produced *The Fable of the Bees*, *Gulliver's Travels*, *The Beggar's Opera*, and *Jonathan Wild*; the society in which another great artist pre-occupied with the relation of the sexes was advancing from 'The Harlot's Progress' *via* 'The Rake's Progress' to 'Marriage à la Mode'.

The novel as a literary form arose with the bourgeoisie: and it was Richardson's bourgeois characteristics that were his main appeal. Polite circles were offended by his style and his morality. It was especially in sexual behaviour that the standards of the bourgeoisie differed from those of the aristocracy. In the years just before Richardson wrote, the word 'prude' made its first appearance as 'a courtly word for a female Hypocrite': it was a word of the anti-Puritans. 'Indelicate' and 'indelicacy', which arose at the same time, represent the middle-class contribution to the vocabulary of feeling.[1] It was Pamela's bashfulness that revealed that she was 'not of quality'.[2]

Nor should we ignore Clarissa's bourgeois characteristics, which are part of her no less than of Richardson, however unattractive we may find them. The diary which she kept in order to avoid waste of time is very much in the Puritan and bourgeois tradition. Her charity at 10 per cent, with its prim restriction to 'the lame, the blind, the sick, and the industrious poor, and those whom accident has made so, or sudden distress reduced' is in the same tradition. 'The common or bred beggars I leave to others, and to the public provision'. This programme of philanthropy reads rather like the prospectus of a Quaker firm which has discovered that charity pays.[3] Richardson's own habit of hiding half-crowns among the types in his printing-office to reward the earliest riser is illuminating in its condescending kindness towards those workmen with whom their employer did not care to communicate except in writing.

The social background to *Clarissa*, then, is this developing bourgeois society, of which Richardson was part and parcel, and which was the main novel-reading public. The aristocracy owed its continuing predominance in part to its concentration of family property by entail and marriages for money. Political compromise between aristocracy and bourgeoisie had been arrived at in the seventeenth century; but

1 See R. P. Utter and G. B. Needham, *Pamela's Daughters*, pp. 63, 44. The quotation is from *The Tatler*, No. 199 (1710).

2 *Works*, III, pp. 171–2.

3 *Ibid.*, XII, pp. 344–7; VIII, p. 238; III, p. 151.

compromise in the realm of ideas was still being worked out. Richardson's novels, Mrs. Leavis tells us, are 'bourgeois art'.[1]

III

Dr. Arnold Kettle, in the most illuminating pages on Richardson known to me, remarked on 'the solidity of his scene', and suggested that it is the social situation that gives *Clarissa* its strength, even despite Richardson. 'Though Richardson is sentimental, *Clarissa*, by and large, is not.' Richardson 'stumbled on a situation fully tragic'.[2] Most other critics have been misled by the way in which Richardson defended his novel against contemporary attacks. His object, he then alleged, was the defence of Christianity against scepticism; and he claimed that poetic justice triumphed in *Clarissa*, even if only in the next world. But we should take more seriously what the novel says than what its author thought it necessary to say in rebuttal of criticism on the moral plane. Richardson resolutely refused to let poetic justice triumph on earth by allowing a penitent Lovelace to be happily married to Clarissa. 'The man who has been the villain to me that you have been shall never make me his wife'.[3] Clarissa had advanced beyond the conventional 'marriage-covers-all' morality which makes Pamela so nauseating.

What the novel does is to examine the effect on men and women of property marriage and all that goes with it. How do individuals react to this monstrous perversion, which we must take as given? How does it affect their relationships with other human beings? These are the questions Richardson seems to ask: and the novel is his answer. It is difficult to tell how far his criticisms are conscious: it all seems as natural and unpremeditated as Shakespeare. Richardson wished his public to believe that he worked without a plan. But a synopsis of *Clarissa*, substantially as we know it, had been written before mid-1744, over two and a half years before the book was completed.[4] The structure at least was carefully thought out.

There is also evidence within the novel itself that the economics of marriage was a conscious target. Indeed the attitude of the Harlowes

---

1 Q. D. Leavis, *Fiction and the Reading Public*, p. 122.
2 A. Kettle, *An Introduction to the English Novel*, I, pp. 68–71.
3 *Works*, XII, pp. 410–35; IX, p. 357.
4 *Correspondence*, V, p. 258; VI, pp. 117–18; A. D. McKillop, *Samuel Richardson*, p. 120.

seems at times to be used to explain, if not to justify, Lovelace's conduct. One of the stories told to his discredit was of his seduction of Miss Betterton. Here is Lovelace's version: 'Miss Betterton was but a tradesman's daughter. The family, indeed, were grown rich, and aimed at a new line of gentry; and were unreasonable enough to expect a man of my family would marry her. I was honest. I gave the young lady no hope of that; for she put it to me . . . Indeed, when I got her to the issue, I asked her no question. It is cruel to ask a modest woman for her consent. It is creating difficulties for both. Had not her friends been officious, I had been constant and faithful to her to this day, as far as I know.'[1] An element in the high comedy of that passage is the parallel between the Harlowes and this family, slightly lower down the social ladder, which 'aimed at a new line of gentry'. The subimplication that all is fair when such schemes are afoot might extend to the original Harlowe plan to marry Lovelace to Arabella. He often speaks of his hatred for the whole Harlowe family, Clarissa excepted, and of his desire to be avenged on them. Schemes for property marriage lead to breakdown of respect for the institution; that is the conclusion. Marriage by purchase stimulates sex-war, as in Restoration comedy.

'Are we not devils to each other? – They tempt us – we tempt them. Because we *men* cannot resist temptation, is that a reason that *women* ought not, when the whole of their education is caution and warning against our attempts? Do not their grandmothers give them one easy rule – Men are to ask – Women are to deny?' It is good social comment, even though it is unplausibly introduced in a rebuke from Lovelace to Belford for invalidating 'the force which a virtuous education ought to have in the sex, by endeavouring to find excuses for *their* frailty from the frailty of ours'.[2] 'Do not the mothers, the aunts, the grandmothers, the governesses of the pretty innocents, always, from their very cradles to riper years, preach their oaths, vows, promises? – What a parcel of fibbers would all these reverend matrons be, if there were not now and then a pretty credulous rogue taken in for a justification of their preachments, and to serve as a beacon lighted up for the benefit of the rest? Do we not then see, that an honest prowling fellow is a necessary evil on many accounts? . . . At worst, I am entirely within my worthy friend Mandeville's assertion, that *private vices are public benefits*.'[3]

1 *Works*, VII, p. 256.
2 *Ibid.*, VII, p. 313.
3 *Ibid.*, IX, pp. 242–3.

Lovelace's own offer to Clarissa, the only time he came near to making one, was sordidly financial. 'All will be my own', he wrote shortly afterwards, 'by deed of purchase and settlement'. It was because she was holding out for favourable terms, he supposed, that Clarissa, 'makes every inch of her person . . . sacred'. '*MARRIAGE, with these women . . .*' wrote Lovelace with heavy emphasis, 'is an atonement for all we can do to them. A true dramatic recompense'.[1] Lovelace might have learnt the sentiment from *Pamela, or Virtue Rewarded*. His sneer was justified, but it was aimed not at Clarissa but at his own female relatives, who were still trying to arrange a marriage.

Lovelace's own morality was 'to marry off a former mistress, if possible, before I took to a new one: to maintain a lady handsomely in her lying-in; to provide for the little one, if he lived, according to the degree of the mother, if she died. And the promise of this was a great comfort to the pretty dears, as they grew near their times'. His more constructive proposal was for marriage on an annual lease, terminable at will by either party. He made it flippantly, yet also produced some rational arguments: such an arrangement would work in certain respects to woman's advantage: all 'married tyrants' must be 'upon good behaviour from year to year'. Some might prefer Lovelace's attitude to Richardson's own platonic leanings towards polygamy.[2]

Lovelace, then, is clear enough. As the name suggests, he descends from the heroes of Restoration comedy, who were also much obsessed by the relation of the sexes in a world of property marriages and post-Puritan hypocrisy. Lovelace came of an aristocratic family with long traditions. He looked down on the Harlowes as a family 'not known to the county a century ago'. Clarissa's uncle approved of Lovelace's feudal attitude to his tenants. 'It was a maxim with his family, from which he would by no means depart, never to rack-rent old tenants, or their descendants.' He liked to see all his tenants look fat, sleek and contented, even if his rent-roll was £300 or even £400 the worse for it.[3] That was a very old-fashioned attitude in 1748.

Lovelace is intelligent, witty, unscrupulous. We are meant to think his attitude towards women deplorable; but Richardson seems almost to suggest (e.g. in the Miss Betterton affair) that society is partly to blame for it. Faced by the fact that marriage is a matter of money, not

1 *Ibid.*, VIII, pp. 106–7, 360; X, p. 252.
2 *Ibid.*, VII, p. 256; IX, pp. 296–300; *Correspondence*, VI, pp. 179–218. See p. 352 below.
3 *Ibid.*, VIII, p. 49; V, p. 83.

affection; that society trains women to trap men into matrimony, Lovelace hits back at the sex indiscriminately and without mercy. He is in the tradition which leads from Restoration comedy through Mandeville (whom we have just seen him quoting) on to Jack Wilkes, with whom we are in the world of modern politics.

For Lovelace is more than a stock stage profligate. Richardson gives him another dimension.. He sets him firmly in the social context by putting some curiously radical political views into his mouth. It is difficult to be sure how Richardson meant us to take them. Are we to disapprove, as is suggested by his condemnation of 'Revellers as well as Levellers' in a letter to one of his young lady friends?[1] Or did he use Lovelace as a mouthpiece for ideas for which he wished to take no responsibility? Or was he merely building up a complex, witty and intelligent character? I suspect Dr. Kettle is right in suggesting that Richardson was more attracted to Lovelace than he himself realized.[2] We recall his friendship for the disreputable Colley Cibber; his kindness to Mrs. Laetitia Pilkington, who truthfully said of herself and Cibber 'neither of us set up for immaculate chastity'.[3]

Richardson's political flirtation in the seventeen-twenties with the 'witty and wicked' Duke of Wharton, 'a kind of Lovelace', is also relevant. Wharton may indeed have been the former patron from whom Lovelace is believed to have been drawn, and who also served as model for Mr. B. in *Pamela*.[4] Richardson's naïve surprise that ladies found Lovelace attractive, and his anxiety to blacken his character in his correspondence, suggest an uneasiness about his creation. The standard comparison with Satan in *Paradise Lost* is just.

Whatever the explanation, there Lovelace's views are. He was in favour of annual Parliaments, as well as of annual marriages. He attacked lawyers, though far less vigorously than did Fielding.[5] He pilloried war and military glory, not once but many times. Moreover, on almost every occasion Lovelace went out of his way to attribute the responsibility for wars to 'royal butchers'. 'I have not the art of the least artful of any of our Christian princes, who every day are guilty of ten times worse breaches of faith; and yet, issuing out a manifesto, they

1 *Notes and Queries*, 4th series, iii, p. 376.
2 Kettle, *op. cit.*, I, pp. 69–70.
3 *Correspondence*, II, p. 130. Mrs. Pilkington was trying to persuade Richardson to spare Clarissa. Cf. J. Nichols, *Literary Anecdotes of the 18th century* (1812), IV, p. 583.
4 Nichols, *op. cit.*, IV, p. 580; McKillop, *op. cit.*, pp. 11, 108–20, 133–4.
5 *Works*, IX, p. 300; X, p. 7.

wipe their mouths, and go on from infraction to infraction, from robbery to robbery; commit devastation upon devastation; and destroy – for their glory! And are rewarded with the names of *conquerors*, and are dubbed *Le Grand*; praised, and even deified, by orators and poets, for their butcheries and depredations. While I, a poor, single, harmless prowler; at least *comparatively* harmless; in order to satisfy my hunger, steal but one poor lamb; and every mouth is opened, every hand is lifted up, against me'.[1] The tone is almost that of *Jonathan Wild the Great*. And again it is society that is at fault. Lovelace, if not justified, at least felt his guilt extenuated by the crimes committed in society's name.

Nor, it seems, were princes for Lovelace simply personifications of the state. More specifically, they stood for the money power, the power that bedevilled the relation of the sexes, that drove Clarissa to her doom. 'The pretty simpleton knows nothing in the world; nor that people who have money never want assistants in their views, be they what they will. How else could the princes of the earth be so implicitly served as they are, *change they hands ever so often*, and be their purposes *ever so wicked?*' In the last resort, indeed, as the platitudinous Lord M. reminds us, the King of England was subordinate to the money power represented in the House of Commons. 'That house has the giving of money: and *money makes the mare to go*; ay, and queens and kings, too, sometimes; to go in a manner very different from what they might otherwise choose to go.'[2]

There are in fact two moralities in Lovelace's world: the morality of the rich and of the poor. The two nations are quite distinct. 'Poverty is generally susceptible', Lovelace noted: Clarissa was less likely to believe she was being taken to a brothel if the madame was well dressed and proposed handsome marriage arrangements for her 'nieces'.[3] Here is 'family aggrandizement' again in a bitterly ironical context.

The poor have morality thrust upon them. Lovelace observed that Miss Howe's messenger 'seems to be one *used to poverty*, one who can sit down satisfied with it, and enjoy it; contented with hand-to-mouth conveniences, and not aiming to live better tomorrow than he does today, and than he did yesterday. Such a one is above temptation, unless it should come clothed in the guise of *truth* and *trust*. What likelihood of corrupting a man who has no hope, no ambition? Yet the

1 *Ibid.*, VIII, pp. 141, 281; X, p. 7; XII, p. 261.
2 *Ibid.*, X, p. 14; VIII, p. 263.
3 *Ibid.*, VII, p. 358.

rascal has but *half* life, and groans under that', Lovelace added, dispelling the illusion of poverty as an idyllic state. He was trying to screw himself up to get rid of the 'half-alive' man by killing him, but decided against it. 'Were I a king, or a minister of state . . . it were another thing.'[1]

Lovelace is too often shown conscious of the contrast between his light-hearted wickedness and the honesty of the poor for it not to be intentional. 'Were it not for the poor and middling, the world would probably, long ago, have been destroyed by fire from Heaven. Ungrateful wretches the rest, thou wilt be apt to say, to make such sorry returns, as they generally do make, to the poor and middling!' Even Clarissa thought that 'the low and the illiterate are the most useful people in the common-wealth', and therefore it would be a pity to educate them unless they wish it very much or are exceptionally talented, 'as a lettered education but too generally sets people above those servile offices by which the business of the world is carried on', and certainly makes them no happier.[2]

The lower classes have hard work and morality thrust upon them. In contradistinction to this theme of morality shaped by society, Richardson introduces the counterpoint of 'free' individuals shaping their own morality. Clarissa, criticized for being too considerate to servants, replied 'I have my choice, *who* can wish for more? Why should I oppress others to gratify myself? You see what free-will enables one to do; while imposition would make a light burden heaven'.[3] Wealth and connections make Clarissa free, and Lovelace too. But, unlike Lovelace, Clarissa is virtuous because she freely (under the guidance of divine grace) chooses what is right. The contrast between bourgeois morality and that of their betters was put even more clearly by Pamela, who told Mr. B. that he should above all boast that 'brought up to an affluent fortune, uncontrolled in your will, your passions uncurbed; you have, nevertheless, permitted the divine grace to operate upon your truly noble heart, and have seen your error', and married Pamela. Richardson's attitude is much less robustly attractive than Fielding's sneers at the nobility from whom he descended;[4] but it is also a social criticism.

1 *Ibid.*, VII, p. 181. Cf. Pamela's cry: 'For, O! what can the abject poor do against the mighty rich, when they are determined to oppress?' – I, p. 127.
2 *Ibid.*, VII, p. 361; VIII, pp. 160–1; cf. VIII, p. 298; III, p. 363.
3 *Ibid.*, XII, pp. 343–4.
4 E.g. *Joseph Andrews* (Everyman ed.), pp. 19, 117–19, 145–6.

Lovelace, like Clarissa and Mr. B., is 'free' by his wealth and connections. Others, including Pamela herself, have conventional morality ground into them by social pressures, have no freedom of choice. The truly virtuous are those of the 'free' who 'permit' divine grace to operate upon their hearts: and so voluntarily, not of social necessity, take virtue upon them. (Historically, predestination was usually a middle- and lower-class theology; the conception of free-will was then possible only above a certain income level.)

One of the morals of Clarissa, then, was that expressed, in large type, in her dying words 'God Almighty would not let me depend for comfort on any but Himself.'[1] Clarissa was one of the 'free'; yet by divine grace she managed, even in the totally isolated state in which she found herself, to be as virtuous as Pamela, even if not so rewarded. Her isolation is important. The family's insane desire to raise itself leads to her being cut off from it, and she is left entirely alone, with no one she can trust. The isolated individual, and a woman at that, has to fight single-handed – not, like Robinson Crusoe, against nature, but against all the resources of 'free' man, she who had believed that all humanity was one family.

Yet this 'freedom' is an illusion, as Richardson involuntarily shows. The individual cannot escape from his society. Lovelace sawed off the branch on which he sat. His 'freedom' was the result of his inherited wealth, of the property marriage system: so his refusal to play the property-marriage game meant the end, so far as his family was concerned – unless he abandoned that part of his freedom on which he most prided himself, his sexual irresponsibility. Clarissa, by refusing to marry Solmes, separated herself from her family. Though she won a greater freedom of moral choice by her isolation, yet nevertheless this did not save her from finally being cut off from all possibility of living in her society. Freedom, in each case, turned out to be merely ignorance of necessity. Therefore Richardson was reduced, in defending the only conscious positive morality he depicts, to call in the next world to redress the balance of this.

IV

Richardson very carefully created the Robinson Crusoe situation: one suspects he had some difficulty in stopping Miss Howe from rushing to

1 *Works*, XII, p. 92.

Clarissa's side. This abstraction of the individual from society is, of course, not peculiar to Richardson. It was an essential part of the Puritan tradition. The Puritan heroes wrestled alone with their God. In *Paradise Lost* the drama which decided the fate of humanity, but which also prefigured the struggle within every man and woman, was enacted in a garden, in the pre-social state. Adam and Eve's unity in isolation before the rest of creation was emphasized in the closing lines of the poem:

> '*They hand in hand with wandring steps and slow,*
> *Through* Eden *took their solitarie way.*'

The same tradition set Samson alone to work out his reconciliation with God, led Christian to desert wife and children in the quest for salvation. *Robinson Crusoe* was preceded by Henry Nevill's *The Isle of Pines*, published the year after *Paradise Lost*; and Gulliver was no less isolated from the societies in which he found himself. The Hobbist and the Lockean individuals both existed before society: society is artificial, not natural. At the same time the Noble Savage was coming into fashion, beginning with *Oroonoko* (1698, but probably written 25 years earlier).

This is a complex subject on which it is easy to over-simplify, but at least one common factor in these various examples of a literary and philosophical fashion is a desire to cut the individual free from the inherited traditions, customs, and laws of society, to set him alone to work out his personal salvation in the sight of God only, in a state of 'freedom'. It is of a piece with that individualism which the new bourgeois society created, in reaction against the corporate loyalties and customs of subordination which had united feudal society. The individual must decide for himself how to behave: the Puritan conduct books had tried to help individuals to solve their own moral problems which had previously been dealt with by the priest at the confessional.

We can, I think, see the same trend in the contemporary popularity of literature about criminals and social outcasts (*The Beggar's Opera*, *Jonathan Wild*, later *The Newgate Calendar*). Again we contemplate the actions of men and women, if not in a state of nature, at least in a social state which is not bound by the traditional inherited conventions: and this criminal society is regularly used to satirize the conventions of existing society, just as Rousseau was to use the state of nature to criticize the laws and institutions of states in his day. Society would keep breaking in, and the desire to create a Robinson Crusoe situation is no more than a tendency. But I believe it helps us to see the links connecting the Puritan individualism of Milton, Bunyan, and their successors with the romanticism of the French revolutionary epoch, which posed the individual *against* society, no longer merely separated him from it.

V

The property family confronted Clarissa in the form of parental authority, which had its economic basis in the father's ability to grant or withhold marriage portions.[1] Many passages in the novel discuss this necessary accompaniment of 'family aggrandizement' – necessary even where, as with the Harlowes, the father's authority was only a fiction, the reality usurped by the son.[2]

In putting the problem of marriage and property relations in the centre of his novel, Richardson was following a well-worn track. Dialogue III of Defoe's *Religious Courtship* has a plot similar to that of *Clarissa*, turning on the alternatives of marrying for money or for religion. *Moll Flanders* and *Roxana* explore the position of women in the society of Defoe's day. Passages like Mr. Badman's courtship of a rich young lady are perhaps more direct antecedents of the eighteenth-century novel than *Pilgrim's Progress*. Such works show the Puritan conduct books and sermons leading straight on to the novel, and cast a retrospective light on the social importance of the former in forming and expressing public opinion, as well as on the moral functions which early novels had to perform or pretend to perform. When we recall Richardson's own *Letters written for Particular Friends*, which immediately preceded *Pamela*, the links become clear and direct. What is remarkable is the extent to which in *Clarissa* Richardson has thrown off the bonds of the religious treatise.

Clarissa represents the supreme criticism of property marriage. But in this it is a culmination of the Puritan tradition. In mediaeval society, aristocratic marriage had been a property transaction pure and simple: courtly love was sought (in literature at all events) outside marriage. But matrimonial fidelity was less highly valued, in either sex, before or

1 Richardson made this point in his *Letters written for Particular Friends*, 7th edition, p. 98.
2 *Works*, V, p. 298; VI, pp. 152–4; VII, pp. 215–16, 220–3, 234; VIII, pp. 76, 85–6.

after marriage, than later. It was a common form for the noble dame of the Middle Ages to have a lover; and the father who announced that the lady was his wife when he heard that she had borne him a son was not unique.

The rise of capitalism and Protestantism brought a new conception of marriage, of which Harrington's and Milton's is the highest: a companionship based on mutual affection. The social basis for this view of marriage was the small workshop or farm in which the wife was in fact a helpmeet to her husband:[1] there was no such practical co-operation between the rentier landlord and his lady. In the Puritan conception fidelity in the wife, and pre-marital chastity, begin to be insisted on with a new vehemence. Since love was ideally the basis of marriage, then the marriage must be inviolate. In practice in most marriages property was still the main consideration: and in the world of capitalist production expensive goods must not be shop-soiled or tarnished. The first lesson Shamela's mother taught her was that 'a Married Woman injures only her Husband, but a Single Woman herself'.[2] Insistence on absolute pre-marital chastity goes hand-in-hand with the bourgeois conception of absolute property, immune alike from the king's right to arbitrary taxation and the Church's divine right to tithes. Dr. Johnson noted that the chastity of women was 'of the utmost importance, as all property depends upon it'; and, in contra-distinction to the elder Mrs. Andrews, he thought a wife who broke her marriage vows more criminal than a husband who did the same – because of the doubts that would be cast on the succession of property.[3]

Richardson's challenge to conventional assumptions seems almost to have been deliberate. He rejected the appeals of his friends to save Clarissa. He refused to allow a happy ending in which, in Lovelace's words, 'marriage covers all'.[4] Having put Clarissa to the supreme test, in isolation, and she having come through with her virginity triumphantly preserved, Richardson pressed the logic of the situation (and of the Puritan conception of virtue) a stage further than most of his contemporaries would have dared. Apparently determined to establish the principle that chastity of the mind is more important than chastity of the body, he allowed Lovelace to rape Clarissa under the

1 Cf. Defoe, *The Complete English Tradesman*, I, pp. 219–20.
2 *An Apology for the Life of Mrs. Shamela Andrews* (1741), p. 35.
3 Boswell, *Life of Johnson* (Everyman ed.), I, pp. 347–8, 623–4; II, pp. 287–8.
4 *Works*, X, p. 252.

influence of drugs. The goods, from the point of view of the market, were irreparably damaged.

Clarissa's standards, however, are those of the Puritan ideal, not those of conventional market morality.[1] From the beginning she had consoled herself in her desperate situation by the purity of her motives. 'Let me wrap myself about in the mantle of my own integrity, and take comfort in my unfaulty intention!' – 'As to my reputation, if I leave him – that is already too much wounded for me, now, to be careful about any thing, but how to act so that my own heart shall not reproach me. As to the world's censure, I must be content to suffer that'.[2]

Clarissa's attitude is a logical application of the Protestant theory of justification by faith, with its emphasis on the inner intention of the believer rather than on his external actions. Purity of motive, chastity of mind, is more important than formal rectitude of behaviour.[3] That is why Clarissa's fate appealed so desperately to eighteenth-century English men and women brought up in the Protestant tradition. Her dishonour was outward, formal only: internally she remained spotless. So Miss Howe: 'Comfort yourself . . . in the triumphs of a virtue unsullied; a will wholly faultless.'[4] Virtue has its own aristocrats, superior to the aristocracy of birth: that was an old Puritan theme.

Milton's Lady had told Comus

> *'Thou canst not touch the freedom of my minde*
> *With all thy charms, although this corporal rinde*
> *Thou hast immanacl'd while Heaven sees good.'*

The last four words beg the question which Richardson dared to ask. He put to the extreme test Milton's proposition:

> *'Vertue may be assail'd, but never hurt,*
> *Surpriz'd by unjust force, but not enthrall'd,*
> *Yea even that which mischief meant most harm*
> *Shall in the happy trial prove most glory.'*

But society was too strong, as Clarissa had already realized. She had no sense of guilt: her conscience was clear. But she knew what society's

1 Cf. L. L. Schücking, *Die Familie in Puritanismus* (Leipzig, 1929), p. 184.

2 *Works*, VII, p. 287; VIII, pp. 212–13.

3 Contrast, as so often, Fielding's resolute defence of justification by works in the dispute between Parson Adams and Parson Tulliber (*Joseph Andrews*, pp. 126–7).

4 *Works*, X, p. 213.

verdict would be. Its standards are those of the market: justification by faith was for Sundays only. Society judges by events, not by motives. Clarissa knew it, and it was this that made her death inevitable. How could she have lived? There was no room in a commercial society for flawed goods. She regarded death, in fact, as a release, for 'she has no *wilful* errors to look back upon with self-reproach'. So Belford explained to Lovelace, adding that 'the reason is evident' why Lovelace could not view death with equal fortitude.[1] Clarissa's standards, high Puritan standards, were not of this world: they could only be realized in the after-life. They are a *criticism* of this world's standards. That, surely, is the damning indictment of his society that Richardson drew up, even if he was not fully aware of all its implications.

VI

There had, we can now see, been a fundamental flaw in Puritan morality, upon which Richardson, however unconsciously, laid his finger. Historically Calvinism made for equality against feudal privilege or arbitrary royal rule: but in Calvinist theory some men were more equal than others. The Calvinist conception of the Church was a dual one: in one sense the Church was the whole community, in another sense it was the elect only. So a minority had special rights in the government of the Church, the election of ministers, the administration of discipline. And in practice the minority of the godly was all too easily equated with the minority of the propertied. Locke transferred this dualism to political theory, as Professor Macpherson has brilliantly shown: his society in one sense includes every inhabitant, but in another excludes those who have no property.[2] At an earlier stage Calvinist political theory had obtained the same consequences more crudely by saying that revolt was justified when led by the lesser magistrate – J.P.s, House of Commons – but not when it was a spontaneous outburst of the many-headed monster.

Now if some men were more equal than others, *a fortiori* men were more equal than women. From the earliest days of Protestantism the position of women had presented difficulties. On the one hand the wife's status was elevated: she became her husband's helpmeet. If all

---

1 *Ibid.*, XI, p. 388.
2 C. B. Macpherson, 'The Social Bearings of Locke's Political Theory', *The Western Political Quarterly*, 1954, pp. 1–22.

believers are priests, do not women have the same direct relation to God as men? In some sects they were admitted to full church membership. In the most radical congregations women were even allowed to preach.

Yet the Protestant sects attributed divine inspiration to the letter of the Bible, newly translated into the vernacular for all to read; and the Bible is explicit on the subordination of women. Woman is made for man, not man for woman, said St. Paul. The economic environment of early capitalism helped to prevent women rising to full equality with men. It was a patriarchal society. In the family farm or small business, although there was partnership between man and wife, the husband was still the senior partner. He for the market only, she for the market through him. And even this precarious economic balance of the heroic age of Puritanism was breaking down in the late seventeenth and eighteenth centuries, as the domestic stage of industry began to be superseded. The workshop was separated from the home. In factories, however atrociously female labour was sweated, women began to enjoy an equality in exploitation with men. But the wife in the lower middle-class family became less a helpmeet in the business and more tied to domestic duties: among the new upper middle class she became a sentimentalized angel of the home excluded from all other interests, a lady of leisure – and a novel-reader.[1] Economic, legal, and religious developments combined to depress the status of these women. Nunneries no longer offered fathers of families 'convenient stowage for their withered daughters';[2] the Virgin was no longer at the right hand of her Son to intercede for her sex. In her place stood St. Paul and the Patriarchs.

The difficulties are apparent in the greatest Puritan and post-Puritan literature. Milton's noble hymn to wedded love nearly burst through the theological bonds of 'he for God only, she for God in him' when Adam decided that Paradise would be well lost for Eve. Defoe in many of his novels was concerned with the conditions on which women might attain freedom, and concluded, coolly enough, that money was the necessary basis. Women who did not inherit wealth had been left with no marketable commodity but their sex, which they could trade either in the open marriage market, as Pamela taught them, or on the

1 Utter and Needham, *op. cit.*, Chapter 2; Alice Clark, *Working Life of Women in the 17th century, passim.*
2 Milton, *Prose Works*, III, p. 80.

black market like Roxana and Moll Flanders. Marriage remained the more desirable state: Moll Flanders 'kept true to this notion, that a woman should never be kept for a mistress that had the money to make herself a wife'.[1] For the freedom even of a Roxana was limited by the ultimate sanctions of a society in which the laws are made by men, as Clarissa and Lady Bradshaigh both pointed out.

Yet in this world of male economic dominance, the small Puritan voice still whispered that women have souls, that salvation is a matter of direct personal relationship to God. Women should by co-operation with the divine purpose be as capable as men of receiving the grace that makes free; even if their attainment of this freedom would shatter the standards taken over by patriarchal bourgeois society from an earlier age.

It is Richardson's greatness, it seems to me, that his respect for Clarissa's integrity led him to push the Puritan code forward to the point at which its flaw was completely revealed, at which it broke down as a standard of conduct for this world. His *conscious* desire in writing the novel was to assert the bourgeois and Puritan conception of marriage against the feudal-cavalier standards of Lovelace and the Harlowe emphasis on concentration of property. But the contradictions of subordination in equality which were inherent in the Puritan view of women were too strong for him. Hence the inadequacy of his own later explanations of the moral of *Clarissa*, his uneasy reassertion of defences whose weakness he must have suspected. He appealed to other-worldly sanctions. He insisted, ludicrously, that after all Lovelace was no atheist. He quoted all the best authorities, from Aristotle to Addison, to buttress his claim that poetic justice triumphed. 'In all reciprocal Duties the Non-Performance of the Duty on one Part is not an excuse for the Failure of the Other.' That, he told Miss G. in January 1750, was the 'Great Rule, inculcated throughout the History of Clarissa'. The Harlowes would be punished, and Clarissa rewarded, in the next world.[2] It is the morality of *Familiar Letters written for Particular Friends*, and of *Pamela*, which *Clarissa* had in fact left behind.

Most revealing was Richardson's long discussion with Lady Bradshaigh. That sensible woman used the logic of *Clarissa* against its author. This fact, and the vogue of *Clarissa*, suggests that the problems with which Richardson fumbled were set by society, were problems of

1 Defoe, *Moll Flanders* (Shakespeare Head ed.), I, p. 60.
2 *Notes and Queries*, 4th Series, III, p. 376.

which others were conscious once Richardson had formulated them. We may compare Mrs. Knowles's discussion with Boswell, who thought that she was too ambitious in hoping that women could ever be the equals of men, even in heaven.[1] Lady Bradshaigh (without acknowledgment) used Clarissa's point that the laws of society were made by men, adding provocatively that men had made them 'to justify their tyranny'.[2] Lady Bradshaigh argued for equality in sex relationships, since 'perfect love casteth out fear'. Richardson was reduced to differentiating between divine and human love, to quoting the authority of St. Paul and of Milton on Divorce. But he also launched into a theoretical defence of polygamy, citing the patriarchs of the Old Testament. ('What do I care for the patriarchs!' Lady Bradshaigh retorted boldly. 'If they took it into their heads to be tyrants, why should we allow them to be worthy examples to imitate?')

The possibility of polygamy seems always to have lurked behind the Protestant conception of equality-inequality of the sexes. Luther was prepared to authorize it in certain circumstances. Milton defended the lawfulness of polygamy in his treatise *Of Christian Doctrine*; and in his divorce pamphlets he had cited an impressively long list of Protestant theologians in defence of the analogous right of the husband to put away his wife. We may also recall the Harringtonian Henry Nevill's *The Isle of Pines*, that early example of the Robinson Crusoe situation, which showed a reversion to the state of nature that included a happy polygamy. Richardson too thought that 'the law of nature does more than allow of polygamy'. It was to be eschewed only because forbidden by the law of England. 'I am extremely well satisfied with the laws of my country. Were polygamy to be allowed by them, I know not my own heart, if I would give in to the allowance'.[3] Parson Williams's defence of polyandry in *Shamela* (one husband for money, another for sexual satisfaction) was a shrewder thrust at Richardson than its author knew.[4]

So, though Richardson came near to breaking through the dualism of bourgeois and Puritan modes of thought in *Clarissa*, he could not escape from it in his own convictions. Emotionally, the author of *Clarissa* was of Lady Bradshaigh's party without knowing it. Intellectually, the husband of a lady who had 'high and Harlowean ideals of parental authority' succumbed in part to her outlook. He was as

1 Boswell, *op. cit.*, II, p. 207.
2 *Correspondence*, VI, pp. 193–4, 205–6.
3 *Correspondence*, VI, pp. 190–4, 205–9, 218, and *passim*.
4 *Shamela*, p. 49.

unsuccessful in establishing a human relationship with his own daughters as Milton had been, and had to defend himself on this score from those who thought he was not living up to his own ideals.[1] The pace was going rather fast: one wonders how the master printer would have reacted if his daughters *had* behaved like Clarissa.

Yet the novel remains. Clarissa did break through the social conventions of her time by pressing to its ultimate implications the religious orthodoxy of her society. Dr. Kettle again puts it well:

'Tragedy occurs when a situation arises which men, at the particular point in development that they have reached, are unable to solve. Such a situation in the eighteenth and nineteenth centuries – and the problem is not yet answered – was the growing consciousness of women of the necessity of their emancipation (by which is not meant mere formal emancipation, Parliamentary votes, etc.) and the inability of class society to admit such freedom without destroying something essential to itself. Clarissa *has* to fight her family and Lovelace; they for their part *cannot* let her win without undermining all that is to them necessary and even sacred.'[2]

I am not sure that, in practice, women before Mary Wollstonecraft were *conscious* of the need for emancipation. Some may have resisted the pressures that degraded and humiliated them, but resistance was as yet hardly more than passive in face of an irreversible trend. This, then, was the tragic situation that forced itself upon the attention of the artist and writer. It is Richardson's achievement that he encompassed this situation and depicted it in such a way as to bring it to general consciousness. So he helped, more, certainly, than he would have wished, and in spite of the limitations of his creed and outlook, to prepare women for an awareness of 'the necessity of their emancipation'.

VII

Seen in this perspective, the moral issues raised by *Clarissa* have their place in the evolution of ideas from Luther's doctrine of the priesthood of all believers, through the Puritan conception of the infallible conscience, on to the romantic individualistic revolt. Clarissa's behaviour, she explained to Miss Howe, arose 'principally from what

1 *Correspondence*, I, p. clxxxix; VI, p. 282.
2 Kettle, *op. cit.*, I, pp. 70–1.

offers to my own heart; respecting, as I may say, its own rectitude, its own judgment of the *fit* and the *unfit*; as I would, without study, answer *for* myself *to* myself, in the *first* place; to *him* [Lovelace] and to the *world*, in the *second* only. Principles that *are* in my mind; that I *found* there; implanted, no doubt, by the first gracious Planter: which therefore *impel* me, as I may say, to act up to them . . . let others act as they will by *me*.'[1] The philosophical implications of that heavily emphasized explanation are worth pondering. It contains the spirit that had enabled the seventeenth-century Puritans to withstand persecutions and to win revolutionary wars; but it also looks forward to the not very Puritan Mary Wollstonecraft and Shelley.

'For myself,' Clarissa told Lovelace, 'if I shall be enabled, on due reflection, to look back upon my own conduct, without the great reproach of having wilfully, and against the light of my own judgment, erred, I shall be more happy than if I had all the world accounts desirable'.[2] So the regicides had spoken in 1660, knowing that they would be condemned in earthly courts. Clarissa was not yet a romantic rebel; and the heroic age of Puritan individualism was over when its doctrines were applied to the matrimonial problems of a middle-class young lady. Clarissa's age was no longer revolutionary: 'everybody' knew what was right; the light of nature told them. The tyranny of the static society was too powerful. And yet Clarissa knew that society could not refute her, even if it would not forgive her. The fact that she could be justified only in heaven witnesses to the breakdown of the noblest aspirations of Puritanism in face of the realities of bourgeois society. In seventeenth-century England the Puritan revolution had failed: the bourgeois revolution had succeeded. The religious revolutionaries had been forced to conclude that Christ's kingdom was not of this world, whilst their emasculated doctrines continued to be proclaimed once a week in Vanity Fair. Professor Perry Miller has traced a similar decline and fall in New England from a City on a Hill of the Pilgrim Fathers to the eighteenth-century acceptance of religion as good for business and social subordination.[3]

It is instructive to compare *The Atheist's Tragedy* (1611) with *Clarissa Harlowe*. The plot of Tourneur's play turns on D'Amville's scheme to

1 *Works*, VIII, p. 105; cf. p. 213, quoted on p. 348 above.
2 *Ibid.*, IX, p. 254.
3 Perry Miller, *The New England Mind: from Colony to Province, passim.* The contradiction between what I say here and what I wrote about pre-revolutionary Puritanism on pp. 218–19 above, is, I believe, only apparent.

arrange marriages and set aside rival heirs in order to focus the descent of wealth on his sons. In Tourneur's day such schemes were absolutely evil: worship of the money power was specifically related to atheism. But D'Amville thought his mere murders insignificant when compared with economic oppression by landlords in decaying feudal society, in just the same way as Lovelace set his theft of 'but one poor lamb' against the robberies and devastations of 'royal butchers'. Either passage might have inspired Chaplin's M. Verdoux.

Tourneur's Atheist anticipates Hobbist man in desiring power after power infinitely, in fearing death above all. His cowardice enables the God-fearing Charlemont to get the better of him. Puritanism tamed this absolute Marlovian individualism, adapted it to existence in a competitive society. By setting men free from the fear of death it gave them the courage which the atheist lacked. By Richardson's day, thanks to the courage of the religious revolutionaries, a society had been established in which the money power ruled. Accumulation for heirs was socially accepted and blessed by the Church. And Lovelace regarded jests on sacred subjects as a mark of ill-breeding.[1]

Diderot's and Rousseau's enthusiasm for *Clarissa*, then, was not fortuitous; though Richardson, who was 'disgusted' by the *Nouvelle Héloïse*,[2] would have appreciated it as little as Luther did the German peasants' appeal to his authority. For under a new revolutionary impulse in the later eighteenth century, the same inner voice to which Clarissa listened led more flamboyant spirits on to a *deliberate* flouting of the conventions which the old-maidish Richardson could not have conceived without horror. The advice which inner voices give tends to change as society changes, and to change more quickly than the official philosophies of society.

Anna Howe felt no pity for Mrs. Harlowe because she had deprived herself of the power to show maternal love and *humanity*. The stress on the duty to mankind is a good Puritan sentiment;[3] but the word *humanity* again links Richardson with the ideologues of the French Revolution. Belford, in his supreme appeal to Lovelace, urged him 'to be prevailed upon – to be – to be *humane*, that's all – only that thou wouldst not disgrace our common humanity'.[4] Only! it was a very large only. For it was not merely the individual wickedness of Lovelace that

1 *Works*, XII, pp. 426–7.
2 Nichols, *op. cit.*, IV, p. 598.
3 Cf. John Preston, p. 246 above.
4 *Works*, VII, pp. 76, 375.

disgraced 'our common humanity'. It was also the greed of the Harlowes, it was property marriage, it was society and its institutions. I quote again, because I think they have an added significance if my analysis is at all correct, Clarissa's bewildered words at the beginning of the novel: 'And yet, in my opinion, the world is but one great family. Originally it was so. What then is this narrow selfishness that reigns in us, but relationship remembered against relationship forgot?'[1] 'Owing to Richardson', wrote Diderot, '. . . I feel more love for my fellow creatures'.[2]

Clarissa travelled, if this is not fanciful, through the whole history of humanity. She looked back to days when mankind was all one family – legendary days which had been vividly imagined realities to the seventeenth-century democrats whom Richardson's Monmouthite father must have known; she passed through and revolted against the feudal-patriarchal family and the tyranny of money; she looked forward to a society in which women shall have attained full equality of status. She died with words on her lips which were a verbal expression of the purest Protestant and bourgeois individualism, and yet which in the context ('one half of mankind tormenting the other and being tormented themselves in tormenting') had their fullest meaning only for the outcasts and the 'unfree' of eighteenth-century society, and transcended that society's possibilities: 'God Almighty would not let me depend for comfort upon any but Himself.'[3]

1 *Ibid.*, V, p. 250.
2 Quoted in *ibid.*, I, p. xv.
3 *Ibid.*, VI, p. 39; XII, p. 92.

Index